Radicals

Radicals

Politics and Republicanism in the French Revolution

LEIGH WHALEY

SUTTON PUBLISHING

First published in 2000 by
Sutton Publishing Limited · Phoenix Mill
Thrupp · Stroud · Gloucestershire · GL5 2BU

British Library Cataloguing in Publication Data
A catalogue record for this book is available from the British Library

ISBN 0 7509 22389

Typeset in 10/13pt Photina.
Typesetting and origination by
Sutton Publishing Limited.
Printed in Great Britain by
Bookcraft, Midsomer Norton, Somerset.

CONTENTS

PREFACE

The subject of this book is a political history of the French Revolution told from the perspective of a group of leading radical politicians. In the context of this book, a radical is defined as a politician with advanced liberal views and desiring major changes to the existing political system. All of the men under consideration in this book fit this description, although their degree of radicalism varied before and during the French Revolution. The nature of their radicalism will be considered below, as will be the inconsistency of their political views.

At the present time, historians have taken a renewed interest in the political history of the French Revolution. Some recent books on this subject include Norman Hampson, *Prelude to Terror: The Constituent Assembly and the failure of consensus* (Blackwell, 1988), Michael Fitzsimmons, *The Remaking of France: The National Assembly and the Constitution of 1791* (Cambridge, 1994) and most recently, Timothy Tackett's *Becoming a Revolutionary: The Deputies of the French National Assembly and the Emergence of a Revolutionary Culture (1789–1790)* (Princeton, 1996). All of these books are concerned with the politics of and political alignments during the Constituent Assembly. C.J. Mitchell's work, *The French Legislative Assembly* (E.J. Brill, 1991), has shed much light on the workings and political factions of that revolutionary assembly. This study is an attempt to uncover the activities and political behaviour of a group of revolutionaries during the years from 1789 to 1793. The work, although by no means comprehensive, in the sense that it does not deal with every revolutionary, should fit neatly into this trend of a renewed interest in the political history of the French Revolution without duplicating the new works by the historians named above.

Keith Baker, François Furet and Norman Hampson have all stressed the importance of Jean-Jacques Rousseau's ideology, particularly his concept of the 'general will', on revolutionary behaviour. The general will, according to this view, made dissenting views difficult, if not impossible for revolutionaries.[1] The writings of these scholars have been particularly enlightening and influential and have provided many useful insights for the present author in her interpretation of the revolutionary behaviour of the men under consideration here.

The problem of political allegiances and factions during the early years of the first French republic has been an interest of mine since I undertook research for my D.Phil. thesis, 'The Emergence of the Brissotins' (University of York, 1989). That study was principally concerned with the evolution of one political faction, centred around the revolutionary politician, Jacques-Pierre Brissot. My conclusion was that there was indeed a group of politicians called 'Brissotins', but that as a political faction, they emerged much later than had previously been believed. The term 'Brissotins', a contemporary term, was defined as the handful of men associated with Jacques-Pierre Brissot. Most were personal friends of Brissot many years before the French Revolution began and the focus of their activity was Paris rather than the provinces. This work led me to the present one, which is much broader in scope.

To my knowledge, no one has written a full length study of political allegiances and the fragmentation of the republican movement into two warring camps in the French National Convention of 1792–1793 since the days of the French historians Albert Mathiez and Albert Soboul, who both wrote in the mid-twentieth century.[2] Their histories were written from a Marxist perspective, which most historians today no longer accept. This does not mean, however, that their contributions to this field of study were not extensive. The present author is greatly indebted to their numerous books and articles.

The most important studies on political factions in the Convention in English are those by M.J. Sydenham and Alison Patrick. Sydenham's work focuses on one faction, the so-called 'Girondins'. His purpose was not to produce a comprehensive history of this group of politicians, but to refute a number of myths about them which had been fostered by French historians. His goal was to scrutinize what he denoted an historical myth, the Girondin party, created by French historians sympathetic to the 'Mountain' deputies and especially to Robespierre. He concluded that a 'Girondin' party did not exist. Sydenham's work begins rather late in the revolution, with the opening of the Legislative Assembly in October 1791.[3]

Patrick's study of the French National Convention is concerned with analysing political alignments in this assembly. Her goal was 'to establish comparable information about all deputies rather than detailed information about some of them'. Patrick opposed Sydenham's argument, and claimed that there was a decidedly right-wing element in the Convention which she equated with the 'Gironde' and also attested to a distinct 'Mountain' or 'Jacobin' element. This does not address the question of how politicians came to hold those particular political views.[4]

The approach taken here is rather different. Instead of considering all of the deputies elected to the Convention, numbering over 700, and primarily examining them in the context of this representative assembly, a handful have been chosen for scrutiny. This study deals with the important extra-parliamentary activities of these revolutionaries in addition to their behaviour in the three revolutionary assemblies, rather than just the Convention. Examining every revolutionary politician who has been considered by historians either a future 'Girondin' or 'Montagnard', would necessitate considering several hundred people. This would mean treating people as statistics rather than as individuals. An essential part of the argument of this book is that people made their final choices for reasons that were, in part, personal. Therefore, restricting the number of actors is essential. The political figures under discussion below, have been selected because of their prominence in national French revolutionary politics between the years 1789 and 1793. They include well-known revolutionaries who would later become members of the Committee of Public Safety such as Robespierre, Saint-Just, Danton and Couthon in addition to their colleagues and later rivals, Brissot, Pétion, Buzot and others.[5] All of these politicians were elected deputies to the French National Convention in 1792; some had sat in previous legislatures, the Constituent and Legislative Assemblies. A few had served as officials in Parisian politics. By 1792, all were household names throughout France. In addition to their significance in the various legislative assemblies, these men were important for their contributions to extra-parliamentary political activities. All of them had been leading members of revolutionary clubs and societies, including the Jacobins, Cordeliers, and Cercle Social, and a good number were prominent journalists whose newspapers were read in Jacobin clubs and popular societies throughout the nation.

Traditionally, these politicians have been divided into two conflicting factions which dominated the National Convention, known to historians as 'Girondins' and 'Montagnards'. These categories have long seemed inaccurate and unhelpful in reaching an understanding of the political behaviour of French revolutionary politicians. This is due mainly to the characteristics attributed to the two groups. Most of the so-called 'Girondins' did not originate from the département of this name and thus did not represent the shipping and commercial interests of the wealthy maritime city of Bordeaux. Nor were they moderates who recoiled in the face of violence. The 'Montagnards' (a more accurate term) meaning 'Mountain', referred to those deputies who sat on the highest benches in the Convention. Their reputation has often been associated with more extreme Jacobins and Cordeliers (not always deputies) during the most radical phase of the revolution, the High Terror of the year II. The 'Mountain' deputies were just as middle class as their so-called opponents, who, in the early years of the revolution, were their allies. In reality, the division between these politicians occurred very late, it did not necessarily take place because of the war debates, and it does not make sense to describe them in terms of two warring factions until at least December 1792.

My book presents a new look at a central aspect of the development of the French Revolution: it investigates the reasons why the republican movement which successfully overthrew the monarchy on 10 August 1792 immediately fragmented into two bitterly hostile groups, whose rivalry diverted the revolution into populist extremism. I propose to demonstrate that they emerged from within a previously homogeneous movement, which dated from the late 1780s in Paris, and that the initial motives for the cleavage were essentially tactical and personal. As the two groups began to coagulate, their search for support forced them into the kind of positions which have been wrongly assumed to have been there in the beginning.

The historical context of *Radicals: The Politics of Republicanism* is the political and cultural environment of late eighteenth-century France. The work begins with an examination of the pre-revolutionary careers of the future revolutionaries, which were divided between those in Paris and those in the provinces. The formative years of many future Parisian revolutionaries were spent in the French provinces where these late eighteenth-century figures sought to advance themselves in the world of the old regime as lawyers, men of letters, teachers, and scientists. My study therefore starts with an introductory chapter set in both the Paris literary world of the late 1780s, and in the French provinces, which was home to many of the men who would later dominate national politics. Chapter 2 covers the early years of the French Revolution, from 1789 to 1791. During these years, many prospective politicians came to Paris and involved themselves in journalism, revolutionary clubs and local politics. Others remained in their provinces where they gained similar political experience. The chapter seeks to explore the nature of the reaction of both Parisian and provincial revolutionaries to the new circumstances which presented themselves in 1789. The political culture of the French Revolution changed substantially during the year of the Legislative Assembly, from October 1791 to September 1792. The radicals gained political education and experience regardless of whether or not they were elected to this Assembly which prepared them for the National Convention, to which all were elected deputies the next year. Chapter 3 investigates the political behaviour and activities of these men through an examination of their responses to the growing problems which faced France during 1791–2, the most significant being the arguments for and against a decision to launch a foreign war. It will examine the various factions and provide reasons why they developed. The threat of foreign invasion dominated politics in Paris during the summer of 1792. Chapters 4 and 5 will study the way in which the radicals responded to the growing problems which determined the crucial events of the summer of 1792. These include the overthrow of the monarchy and the conflict between the illegally established Paris Commune and the Legislative Assembly after 10 August 1792. Chapter 5 also covers the important elections to the Convention and how they affected the radicals. The domination of the Paris elections by Robespierre and Danton eliminated many Parisian radicals who, interpreting this as a personal attack, turned to the provinces. Chapters 6 to 9 cover the period of the French National Convention, chronicling the emergence of two warring political factions, and the reaction of these often fluid factions to external crises such as the impact of foreign war, civil war and pressure from the working people of Paris, or the sans-culottes. The final chapter covers the period of the insurrection of 31 May to June 1793 and the Convention after 2 June until the end of the summer. It endeavours to demonstrate that the uprising of 2 June was not the decisive event in the downfall of the 'Brissotins', and the reason for their subsequent execution in the autumn of 1793. Rather, it was a combination of the illegal activities carried out by a majority of those expelled – twenty-one out of twenty-nine successfully fled and rebelled – and other events, including the murder of Marat, which determined their sorry fate. The Convention immediately after 2 June has tended to be ignored by historians of the revolution.

This book is intended for historians of Europe, particularly those studying the eighteenth century, specialists of the French Revolution, graduate students in history and senior undergraduates. It should also be of interest to a multi-disciplinary audience including students of politics, military studies and French studies. The book deals with the effects of war on domestic revolutionary politics. Finally, this book should appeal to anyone seeking to understand the nature of revolutionary behaviour.

ACKNOWLEDGEMENTS

This book could not have been written without the assistance and encouragement of Professor Norman Hampson who not only read drafts of the entire manuscript, but also provided much constructive criticism. Professor Hampson has been a source of inspiration to the author for many years. I am also indebted to the Calgary Institute for the Humanities, which provided me with a Visiting Research Fellowship (1996–7). This fellowship gave me time off my teaching at the Queen's University, Belfast to write most of this book. I am grateful to Professor Jeremy Black for recommending my manuscript to Sutton Publishing. I would like to thank Christopher Feeney, editor at Sutton for his wonderful help and support throughout the preparation of the final manuscript. Finally, I would like to thank my parents for their enduring support.

ABBREVIATIONS

AHR	American Historical Review		JRF	Journal de la République Française
AHRF	Annales Historiques de la Révolution Française		LM	Réimpression de l'ancien Moniteur
			MN	Mercure National
AmP	Ami du Peuple		MU	Mercure Universel
APL	Annales Patriotiques et Littéraires		NR	La Nouvelle Revue
AP	Archives Parlementaires		PD	Père Duchesne
AR	Annales Révolutionnaires		PF	Patriote Français
AJFS	Australian Journal of French Studies		PRF	Publiciste de la République Française
BdeF	Bouche de Fer		RFB	Révolutions de France et de Brabant
CG	Courrier de Gorsas		RF	Révolution Française
CP	Chronique de Paris		RH	Revue Historique
DHS	Dix-Huitième Siècle		RP	Révolutions de Paris
FH	French History		RHB	Revue Historique de Bordeaux
FHS	French Historical Studies		RHMC	Revue d'histoire moderne et contemporaine
FP	Feuille de Paris			
Hist Parl	Histoire Parlementaire		RQH	Revue des questions historiques
HS	Historical Studies		SR	Sewanee Review
JF	Journal Français		TJ	Thermomètre du Jour
JMH	Journal of Modern History		UNS	University of Nebraska Studies

FUTURE RADICALS: AN INTRODUCTION TO THE MEN OF 1792

The purpose of this chapter is to introduce the men who would later emerge as important radical politicians during the French Revolution. In addition to informing the reader of their pre-revolutionary activities, an attempt will be made to ascertain the extent of their pre-revolutionary radicalism. In other words, I shall seek to discover how many of these future radicals were deeply dissatisfied with the existing order, and had already anticipated reforms not unlike those which were to take place during the Constituent Assembly and beyond, in their writings. The question as to how far the political culture of these men made the revolution inevitable will be examined. Finally, the connections, between these people, if any, will be considered.

   The following deputies are the principal political actors who together form the subject of this book: Robespierre, Danton, Marat, Saint-Just, Couthon, Fouché, Condorcet, Brissot, Garran Coulon, Billaud-Varenne, Fabre d'Eglantine, Collot d'Herbois, Barère, Vergniaud, Guadet, Gensonné, Desmoulins, Mercier, Manuel, Robert, Pétion, Buzot, Carra, Gorsas, Louvet de Couvray, and Barbaroux. In terms of age, these men divide into three decades (see Appendix 1). During the years which immediately preceded the French Revolution, they could be classified in terms of geography – Paris or province based; by profession or occupation, and the degree of success achieved; and finally, by the extent of their radicalism. Here I am referring to evidence of radical ideas and their future revolutionary colours. The majority of them lived in the provinces and pursued similar careers. Of the twenty-six men, seventeen had some legal training and of this seventeen, fourteen were practising lawyers. The other three had abandoned the law to try their luck in the world of letters. Two were in the theatre, and one was a mathematics and science teacher. The remainder included a successful *philosophe*, aspiring scientists, booksellers, and pamphleteers, and sometime police informers.

THE MEN FROM THE PROVINCES

It is clear that among those who chose to stay in their native town or region, the legal profession was by far the most popular. Robespierre, Barbaroux, Vergniaud, Guadet, Gensonné, Couthon, Robert, Barère, Pétion and Buzot all practised the law with the majority having a good deal of success before the revolution. In addition, with the exception of Pétion and Robespierre, and Robespierre came later to it than Pétion, none of these men showed much inclination towards radicalism. In other words, the majority of them demonstrated little if any desire to make changes to the system of the old regime. They were settled in their careers and were making the best way forward in their chosen profession of the law.

Robespierre

Robespierre was the son of a lawyer, and after completing his studies as a scholarship boy at the prestigious Collège Louis-le-Grand in Paris, began a law practice in his home town of Arras in 1781. Through the memory of his father, Maximilien was made secretary to M. de Madre of the Conseil d'Artois, and after only one year of practising, he was made a judge at the bishop's court.[1] Although he did not have many cases, he was successful with most of them. What all this added up to was the young Robespierre was in no need of a revolution to make a successful career for himself.

Not only was Robespierre doing reasonably well in professional terms, he was also making a name for himself in provincial academic circles. He had been a member of the Arras Academy since 1783, and he spent his spare time competing for various academic essay prizes dealing with local poets and such subjects as the extension of shame from the criminal to the family. There is very little, if anything, in these essays to foreshadow the future revolutionary.[2] All of this stimulated his interest in literature – it was a chance for him to make a name for himself as a local intellectual – and it enhanced his social standing in the community. In 1786, he was made president of the Arras Academy, and in the same year he joined a local literary society, the Rosati, a group of young men who met once a year, toasted the rose and wrote poetry.[3] Thus, not only was he a successful barrister, but he was also a man of letters and intellectual in his leisure time.

One of the few traces of the future Incorruptible appeared in the case of the former soldier Dupond at the end of 1788. In his defence of Dupond, whose family had imprisoned him by a *lettre de cachet* to strip him of his inheritance, Robespierre condemned that arbitrary system, ministerial despotism, and he demanded a revolution, although a moral rather than a political one. Instead of criticizing the king, Robespierre saw Louis XVI's role as that of leader of a moral crusade which would make men happy and restore their rights 'through virtue'.[4] Robespierre did not begin writing really radical pamphlets until his bid for election to the Estates-General early in 1789.

Barbaroux

Barbaroux, also a lawyer, practising in Marseilles, had been conducting a pre-revolutionary career remarkably similar to that of Robespierre. The major difference between them was that Barbaroux had money behind him. He came from a wealthy commercial Marseilles family. After receiving a good education from the Oratorians of Marseilles, he was received as a barrister at the age of twenty. He won the great majority of his cases.[5]

Not long after qualifying as a barrister, Barbaroux went to Paris, insisting that 'a stay in Paris was a necessity in a young man's education'. It appears from his correspondence that he spent the latter half of 1788

Robespierre, by anonymous artist. (Musée Carnavalet)

in Paris, studying at the Ecole des Mines.[6] Fascinated by physics, Barbaroux took Marat's optic courses in Paris in 1788, although he never referred to Marat in his correspondence at this time.[7]

Rather than dabbling in *belles-lettres* like Robespierre, Barbaroux chose the equally fashionable world of science as his hobby. Ironically, unlike Marat and Carra, who tried unsuccessfully to make a career out of it, Barbaroux did attain some recognition. His articles were published in the prestigious *Journal de Physique*, and at the age of eighteen, he was corresponding with Franklin. Barbaroux's main interests at this time were money, science and fame.[8]

Barbaroux frequented a literary society run by the future president of the Marseilles Jacobin club. It sounds very similar to Robespierre's Rosati group, except that Barbaroux's society not only read poems and essays, they also discussed scientific problems.[9]

Couthon

Couthon shared many of the characteristics of his contemporaries in terms of background, profession and outlook. The son of a notary born in the parish of Orcet in the Auvergne, Couthon studied law at Rheims like Saint-Just, Brissot and Danton. One did not so much 'study law' at this time as buy a degree. These four men all received their legal qualifications from this shady source. By 1783, Couthon had qualified for the law and was practising in Clermont, where he gained a reputation as a poor man's lawyer.

Like Robespierre, Barbaroux and many other provincial lawyers, Couthon was a member of the local literary society. Very little is known about his activities in the group, except that he delivered a speech about patience. There is no evidence that he wrote literature or entered academic contests. He did join the masonic lodge of Clermont, 'Saint-Maurice', in 1778.[10]

Georges Couthon. (Musée Carnavalet)

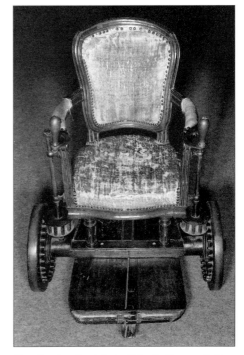

Couthon's wheelchair. (Musée Carnavalet)

Couthon gained his first political experience in 1787. On 13 November, the provincial assembly of Auvergne met and Couthon was appointed to the 'Judicial Consultative Committee', composed of two other celebrated lawyers: Bergier and Gaultier de Biauzat. As a member of this committee, Couthon was at the receiving end of denunciations of the feudal system.[11] His career appeared to be progressing well; he was a member of the right societies and had gained a respected reputation as a lawyer among his local contemporaries.

Vergniaud as president of the Legislative Assembly and Convention, by Calbatz. (Musée Carnavalet)

Marguerite-Elie Guadet, elected president of the Legislative Assembly on 22 January 1792. (Bibliothèque nationale de France)

Vergniaud, Guadet and Gensonné

The careers of the three future Bordelais deputies were faring equally well. After studying law in Bordeaux, Vergniaud, the son of a purveyor to the Limoges garrison, was received at the bar in the same year as Robespierre. He became one of the leading lawyers of the Bordeaux bar. Guadet, the son of the mayor of Saint-Emilion, received his bachelor of law in 1778 after he studied at Guyenne and the University of Bordeaux. He, too, registered as a lawyer for the Parlement of Bordeaux in 1781. Like Guadet, Gensonné, who was the son of an army surgeon, was educated at the college of Guyenne where he was taught philosophy by Garat's brother, Dominique. He was chosen by Leberthon, the first president of the Parlement of Bordeaux, from twenty-five of the best students at the age of sixteen to train as a barrister. He was called to the bar in 1779.[12] Thus, Vergniaud, Guadet and Gensonné were all members of the Bordeaux bar before 1789.

Vergniaud's interest in literature – he wrote light verse – was shared by his future colleague, Gensonné. He, Vergniaud, Ducos, Boyer-Fonfrède (and perhaps Guadet) were members of a Bordeaux literary society, the *Musée*, which Vergniaud described as a 'sort of academy'.[13] The *Musée* had been founded in 1783 by a freemason, the abbé Dupont des Jumeaux, as a more democratic competitor to the Bordeaux Academy. It was under the patronage of Queen Marie-Antoinette and the direction of the Intendant of Guyenne. Although the *Musée* had as its motto '*Liberté et Egalité*', there was nothing revolutionary about this very respectable old regime club of letters. Its members were drawn from the elite of this prosperous city: they included wealthy businessmen, barristers and judicial officers. Roche argues that it was modelled on a Paris society of the same name, and that it was Bordeaux's attempt to get itself on the literary and philosophical map. It was typical of the growing number of Enlightenment-style groups

An engraving of Arnaud Gensonné, deputy from the Department of the Gironde to the National Convention, year one of the Republic, by Bonneville. (Bibliothèque nationale de France)

Bertrand Barère, deputy from the Department of Hautes-Pyrenées to the National Convention and a member of the Committee of Public Safety. (Bibliothèque nationale de France)

throughout France, and in the spirit of enlightened toleration, both Jews and Protestants were admitted.[14] As eminent Bordeaux barristers and members of an elite literary and cultural institution, it is clear that these men were in no need of a French Revolution to rescue them from failure.

Barère

Nor was Barère a discontented loser before 1789. His background was slightly more upper class than most of the others, with the exception of the Marquis de Condorcet; Barère and Buzot had aristocratic mothers. Barère's father was a middle-class lawyer who possessed a small fief. After he had studied in Toulouse, his father purchased for him the post of councillor at the seneschal's court at Bigorre. He did not perform the duties of this post, but worked as a successful barrister for the Toulouse Parlement starting in 1775. Like Barbaroux, Robespierre, Couthon and the Bordelais, Barère led an extremely conventional life before 1789. When not practising law, he was writing essays in competition for academic prizes. His first essay, an *Eloge de Louis XII*, got him elected to the Academy of Floral Games at Toulouse, one of the oldest literary academies of this city. As well as Toulouse, Barère was also elected to the Montauban Academy. For someone who made a career at being on the winning side, the evidence shows that Barère was doing very well at it before 1789. He was also a freemason, belonging to the '*Encyclopédique*' lodge, where he presided over the Science Committee.[15] He wrote eulogies of both Montesquieu and Rousseau. What emerges is a portrait of someone who was doing his best to get ahead by making all the right moves in the world of the old regime.

François-Nicolas-Léonard Buzot contemplating the portrait of Madame Roland, by Charles Etienne Leguay. (Musée Carnavalet)

Pétion de Villeneuve, mayor of Paris, by an anonymous artist. (Musée Carnavalet)

Pétion and Buzot

Like Barère, Pétion and Buzot were the sons of attorneys at the local *bailliages* of Chartres and Evreux respectively. Pétion's father was the local presiding judge. Both fathers took great care in providing their sons with a good classical education from the local colleges. Following in their fathers' footsteps, they became lawyers. Pétion had qualified by the age of twenty-five, and by 1789, had risen to the position of sub-delegate to the Intendant of Chartres.[16] Buzot had qualified for the bar by 1786 and was practising at the local *bailliage*. The next year he was elected a notable to the electoral body of Evreux. Where he differed from many of the others was that he did not appear to have any literary or scientific ambitions. He showed no interest in a side-line of literature; nor was he a freemason. Danton shared this feature with Buzot and Robert.[17]

Robert

Robert was the only revolutionary to originate from outside France – he was from Gimnée, Belgium – but in common with many of the others, he was the son of good bourgeois stock. His father, an innkeeper, and a local municipal official, owned four farms. Before he qualified for the law, Robert studied at an Oratorian school. After obtaining his qualification from the University of Douai, he went on to practise law in the city of Givet, near Gimnée. In common with the provincial lawyers in France, he led a very conventional and settled life before 1789.[18]

Collot

Pursuing an entirely different career from law was Collot d'Herbois. Although born in Paris, he left the capital at an early age to seek fame and fortune in the provinces and abroad. Collot tried to make a career in the theatre, acting, writing plays and managing theatres throughout Europe. By the age of twenty in 1769, he was acting in plays in Toulouse and Bordeaux. His first authored play, *Lucie ou les Parents imprudents*, met with success. It was performed in several provincial theatres: Nancy, Toulouse, Brussels, and a second edition appeared in 1774. Collot continued to write a series of plays, which did well. His *Bon Angevin, ou l'Hommage du coeur* (1775), was praised by the town officials of Angers and the town paid for the printing of 500 copies of the play.[19] He was thus able to make a reasonable living from writing plays.

In addition, Collot's acting career had taken off. In one year alone, 1786, he performed in Avignon, Bordeaux, Nantes, Caen, Douai, Lille, Rouen and the Hague. In 1787, he became a theatre director in Lyon and he took the stage name of d'Herbois. Here he received praise from both the public and the Intendant de Flesselles, who defended the theatre and dined with Collot.[20] Two years later, he moved to Geneva where he prospered by managing a theatre company. His play, *Bonne justice ou le Paysan magistrat* was performed with him in the leading role.[21] Darnton's designation of Collot as a 'frustrated actor-playwright' does not seem to fit the evidence of Collot's pre-revolutionary successes both materially and in terms of self-respect.[22] Rather than challenging the existing authorities, he not only received their encouragement, but was their invited dinner guest. This is hardly an indication of someone who had become an embittered individual discontented with the existing order.

Fouché

Fouché, in common with Billaud before he went into law, pursued a teaching career before the revolution. Like Billaud and several others, Fouché was educated by the Oratorians. It is quite possible that Fouché knew Billaud, for they were colleagues at the Collège de Juilly around the same time. Billaud was the Latin and French verse teacher, while Fouché taught physics and mathematics. In contrast to Billaud, however, Fouché enjoyed a good deal of success with the Oratorians. Around 1788, Fouché was promoted and moved from Juilly to be the head of sciences at the Collège d'Arras.

Fouché was well-acquainted with Robespierre. The future colleagues met at the Rosati society. Fouché's interests, apart from attending Rosati meetings, not surprisingly included those connected to science: conducting experiments related to hot air ballooning, which had recently come into fashion with the Montgolfier brothers, and those concerned with the mechanism of lightning conductors.[23]

Saint-Just

Saint-Just was born in 1767, the same year as Barbaroux, but accomplished much less before 1789. In common with many of the others, he received an education at an Oratorian college and some legal training. He registered at the Rheims law school in 1787. It is not clear whether or not he received his degree, but even if he did, as Bruun asserts, he most likely purchased it.[24] What is clear is that he never practised law.

Like Louvet, Garran Coulon, Vergniaud and Manuel, Saint-Just fancied himself as an author, which, rather than the law, was his youthful passion. An extremely ambitious young man, he left

Saint-Just, by an anonymous artist. (Musée Carnavalet)

for Paris with the family's silver, which would be his means of support. Unfortunately, when his mother found out, she had him put under house arrest, and he was imprisoned there for six months. Afterwards, he returned home. By this time, it was 1789.

Before the revolution, Saint-Just produced a one-act verse play, *Arlequin-Diogène*, and while he was in prison, a satirical epic, *Organt*. According to his biographers, he had counted on this work to launch his career in literature, which it failed to do.[25] By 1789, although there was no indication of discontent with the current regime in his works, it did look as though Saint-Just was in as much need of a revolution as many of the other would-be *philosophes*.

THE MEN FROM PARIS

Pre-revolutionary Parisians can be divided into two groups: firstly, those who were born in Paris, and second, those who were from the provinces but tried to make a career for themselves in the city. A minority of the men under consideration were born in Paris. These include Louvet de Couvray, Mercier and Collot d'Herbois. With the exception of Collot, who, as has been explained, left Paris to pursue his theatrical career in the French provinces and abroad, Louvet and Mercier tried their luck at *belles-lettres* in Paris during the pre-revolutionary period. The most successful of the three was unquestionably Mercier. He was also the oldest, born in 1740, the son of a skilled artisan.[26]

Mercier

Mercier studied at the Collège des Quatre Nations, and during his youth he frequented the literary world of the Café Procope. He was a professor of Rhetoric at Collège de Madeleine in Bordeaux at the time of the suppression of the Jesuits. It was at this time that he began his career as a writer with an *Eloge de Descartes* and the *Bonheur des Gens de lettres* (1763). Like Fabre and Collot, he was also a playwright. By the 1770s and early 1780s, Mercier was one of the most successful writers in France. His *L'an 2440* ranked at the top of the list of illegal works sold by booksellers who were supplied by the Société Typographique de Neuchâtel, while his *Tableau de Paris* was placed fourth, according to the number of books ordered, behind such Enlightenment luminaries as Voltaire, d'Holbach and the lesser known Pidansat de Mairobert.[27]

Mercier showed some discontent with the old regime in his writings, although his works lacked consistency. His *L'an 2440* was a Rousseauist Utopian vision of a future Paris without inequality and injustice. Mercier was not anti-monarchical for he advocated a kind of philosopher-king ruler. His most successful work, the *Tableau de Paris*, was not political. It was a celebration of all aspects of Parisian life, including its manners and customs. A political treatise, *Notions claires sur les gouvernements* (1786), contained a number of critical allusions to Rousseau, without mentioning his name. In addition, it embodied numerous references to Montesquieu's *L'Esprit des Lois*. Mercier was much more a man of *belles-lettres* than a radical pamphleteer advocating revolutionary change. He was very much a man of his times, imitating Voltaire, Montesquieu and Rousseau in his writings.[28]

Louvet

Louvet was trying to achieve similar successes to Mercier in the old regime world of letters. He was the son of a paper merchant, according to Aulard, while Michaud wrote that Louvet's father was a haberdasher. At any rate, he appears to have been from lower bourgeois stock, with his father intending him for a career in small business. Nothing is known about his education and youth, other than that he was an enthusiastic reader of literature. At the age of seventeen, he dressed up like a woman and worked as a secretary to the mineralogist P.F. de Dietrich. Soon he began working in Pruault's bookshop, peddling pornography, and began writing his celebrated novel, *Les Amours du Chevalier Faublas*, of which the first part appeared in 1787.[29] The book was commercially successful, but it was licentious enough to cause a scandal which forced Louvet to move out of Paris to Nemours. It was a combination of pornography and praise for Rousseau. His lover, a woman married to a wealthy Parisian jeweller, fled with him. He called her Lodoiska and she served as a model for the heroine of his novel.

An engraving of Jean-Baptiste Louvet, deputy to the Council of 500 from the Department of the Haute Vienne by Bonneville. (Newberry Library, Chicago, Illinois)

The second group of Parisians was composed of the men who were born in the provinces, but who came to Paris in the 1780s to carve out a career for themselves. This group included the lawyers, Danton, Desmoulins, Billaud, and Garran Coulon, and the would-be *philosophes* and scientists, Brissot, Carra, Marat, Gorsas, and Manuel. Condorcet was the only one of the aspiring *philosophes* and scientists who was successful.

Billaud

Unlike Robespierre, who did not take the risk of attempting a career in Paris, preferring the much safer environment of his hometown of Arras, Desmoulins, Danton, and Billaud took the Parisian gamble with varying degrees of success. Billaud was yet another lawyer and lawyer's son. His father had high ambitions for his son, who was educated at the Collège d'Harcourt in Paris and in Poitiers. At this stage in his career, Billaud's interests were more literary than legal. While employed as a prefect of studies at the Oratorian Collège de Juilly, during the years 1783 and 1784, he wrote comedies such as *Morgan*, which was too libertine for the fathers. He left the college to a start a sensible legal career. Unable to find a practice in his native La Rochelle, he went to Paris on his father's money when he was twenty-eight. He soon found a job working on a part-time basis for Danton, but other than that, he seems to have been unemployed most of the time.[30] Palmer characterized him as an 'ineffectual drifter' during the pre-revolutionary Parisian years presumably because he never had a full-time post like many of his future colleagues who had done quite well for themselves.[31]

An engraving of Billaud-Varenne, deputy from the Department of Paris to the National Convention and condemned to deportation in year four of the Republic, by Bonneville. (Bibliothèque nationale de France)

Georges Danton on his way to the guillotine, 5 April 1794, by Jan Georg Wille. (Musée Carnavalet)

Although Billaud was not writing essays for academic prizes, in addition to his plays, he did produce two serious works, one radical, but in terms of religion; the other, about politics, and very conventional. Both were written on the eve of the revolution. The first, *Le Dernier Coup porté aux préjugés et à la superstition*, was completed in 1787, and published anonymously in London during the same year, and in France in 1789. It is a critique of the current state of the Roman Catholic religion, which foreshadowed some of the revolution's attacks on the established church. Billaud criticized the laziness of the regular clergy, and he advocated several reforms including a simplification of ritual, the prohibition of clerical vows, the marriage of priests, and a limitation on their numbers. This does sound similar to proposals made by various deputies during the Constituent Assembly in 1789. He did not, however, go nearly as far as the Constituents. The nationalization of church lands and the clerical oath were not present in Billaud's pamphlet. This was very much an Enlightenment critique of the church, similar in many respects to Voltaire's attacks. What Billaud was advocating was a cleaning up of abuses within the church and a return to a simpler and purer form of Catholicism. It was the work of a keen deist.

Billaud's second pamphlet, *Despotisme des Ministres de France*, was completed in 1788, and published anonymously in Amsterdam in 1789. This work was far less radical. Its major theme was that the natural alliance between king and people had been destroyed by the rise of ministerial despotism, threatening a 'terrible revolution'. Billaud approved of the proposed reforms of Turgot and Necker whom the Paris Parlement attacked and he advocated the abolition of monastic vows, free trade and the abandonment of seigniorial dues in return for compensation. The goal of reform, according to Billaud, was to avert revolution. Unlike Pétion, Billaud saw no need for the drafting of a new constitution.[32]

Danton

Billaud's employer Danton was one of the few men who made a success out of the Parisian gamble, but he went heavily into debt achieving it. Born in the village of Arcis-sur-Aube in Champagne, Danton came from peasant stock, although his father had risen to become a lawyer. Like Saint-Just, Billaud, Couthon and Brissot, Danton received his law degree, after his studies at a local Oratorian college, from the University of Rheims, notorious for its trade in law degrees. At the age of twenty-one, he was in Paris working as a lawyer's clerk. With the financial assistance of his father-in-law, Charpentier, owner of the Procope, Danton was able to purchase his office as advocate to the royal councils in Versailles in 1787. What followed was a very respectable career working for the king's councils.[33] Danton was exceptional in the sense that he did not write plays or poetry and showed no interest in either academic prizes, literary salon conversation, or fashionable science before the revolution. Nor was he writing radical propaganda like Pétion. In fact, Danton had done precisely what Pétion had condemned: he had purchased his office; Pétion was almost unique in that he had not done so.

Desmoulins

Things did not work out quite so well for Danton's future colleague Desmoulins. In common with so many of these future radicals, he was the son a country lawyer, who was the lieutenant-general of the *bailliage* of Guise. Desmoulins was a scholarship boy at the Collège Louis-le-Grand where he was an acquaintance of a fellow future colleague Robespierre. Desmoulins' biographers vary widely in terms of what they have to say about his pre-revolutionary activities. All agree that by the age of twenty-four, he was in Paris and had qualified as a barrister, and that, although he was very bright, a speech impediment prevented him from having a successful legal career. From here the stories vary from his leading a bohemian existence, living in cheap rooming houses, and spending his days at the Café Procope (perhaps trying to imitate the young Mercier) to supporting himself as a copier for a lawyer called M. Hardouin. Apparently he also earned a living by drafting petitions for the *procureurs*, but he was frequently out of money, requiring subsidies from home to keep going. He was associated with the freemason lodge of Neuf Soeurs.[34]

Bust of Camille Desmoulins, by Martin. (Musée Carnavalet)

Two literary works have been attributed to Desmoulins by one of his biographers. Both are written in verse form, are satires, and date from 1786–7. One is anti-Calonne and complains about paying more taxes: 'In order to pay my taxes, I must sell saucepans'; while the other is anti-Marie-Antoinette and calls Louis a 'fat and stupid king'.[35] There is really nothing very radical here. Perhaps this was Desmoulins' attempt to make it as a writer, since his legal career had been such a failure. Complaining about taxes is understandable since he was always short of cash.

Garran Coulon

Garran Coulon had studied law and medicine in Poitiers and Orléans. He arrived in Paris in 1783. Accounts about him vary: some say he worked as secretary to the *jurisconsulte* Henrion de Pansey, while others insist that he was frequently unemployed and welcomed the revolution as an

An engraving of Jean-Philippe Garran Coulon, the great '*procurateur*' of the nation and deputy from Paris to the National Assembly, 1791, by Bonneville. (Newberry Library, Chicago, Illinois)

opportunity to get out of that state. In common with several others, he was an aspiring man of letters, apparently having authored at least forty-three works of a philosophical and literary nature. There is no evidence, however, that any of his poems and essays were published.[36]

What this adds up to is anything but fulfilment in comparison with the careers of Robespierre, Couthon, Danton, Barbaroux, Barère and the Bordelais, who were clearly making the most out of the dying years of the old regime, both in terms of the success they achieved as provincial lawyers, and in some cases, in their literary and scientific pursuits. Collot was also making a name for himself in theatrical circles, and Fouché in the Oratorian colleges as a brilliant young mathematics and science teacher. It would appear that Desmoulins and Garran Coulon had more in common with the disgruntled failures like Marat, Brissot, Carra, Fabre and Gorsas, than the successful barristers. It is not unreasonable to conclude that for the most part, those who stayed in the provinces and played it safe, rather than taking the Paris gamble, were much more successful in their given careers.

Fabre

Darnton's classification of a group of embittered grub street hacks, who were in desperate need of a revolution to make a career for themselves, could apply to Fabre, Carra, Manuel, Marat, Brissot, and Gorsas. Fabre, born in Carcassone, the son of a cloth merchant, was an aspiring actor and playwright. He adopted the name of 'd'Eglantine' after allegedly winning a medal, an '*églantine d'or*', a wild golden rose, in a literary contest in the Floral games of Toulouse in 1771. By the time he moved to Paris in 1787, he was penniless, and had left behind him a succession of debts and scandals. In 1777, Fabre was condemned to death for seducing a girl aged fifteen whom he had met while acting in the theatre of Namur. He received an amnesty from Charles of Lorraine.[37]

Philippe-François-Nazaire Fabre d'Eglantine, 1794. (Bibliothèque nationale de France)

Like Collot, whom he met in Lyon, Fabre lived an itinerant existence moving from country to country with his travelling theatre company. Unlike Collot, he achieved very little success before 1789. He acted in his first play in Strasbourg in 1778, from which remain the famous lines, '*Il pleut, il pleut bergère.*' (It's raining, it's raining shepherd). Although this was a success, most of his plays were not. By the 1780s, he was trying his luck in Paris. His first tragedy, a failure, *Les Gens de Lettres, ou le provincial à Paris,* was performed for the first time in Paris on 21 September 1787.[38] Fabre's police file depicts him as 'a poor poet, who drags about in shame and destitution; he is despised everywhere; among men of letters he is considered an execrable subject.'[39]

Carra

Carra was frequently in trouble with the law and his employers. The son of a commissioner of seigniorial rights, Carra was born in the market town of Pont-de-Veyle, in south-east Burgundy. He was accused of theft in his youth, and perhaps in later life as well. In common with Brissot, Manuel, Saint-Just, Fabre and Gorsas, he was imprisoned before the revolution. This incident left a lasting mark on him and undoubtedly helped to contribute to his negative attitude towards the old regime. It is impossible to determine whether or not he committed the offence as the proceedings of the trial have disappeared. Carra later denied any participation in the theft and insisted that on the night in question he was at Pont-de-Veyle with his brothers and sisters.[40]

He subsequently led an itinerant existence, writing pieces on natural law and geography for the *Encyclopédie ou Dictionnaire universel raisonné des connaissances humaines*. In 1771, he accused his employer Fortune-Barthélmy de Félice, a defrocked Franciscan monk turned Protestant, of incompetence and theft. His next employer, Robinet, a former Jesuit turned writer, accused him of plagiarism while Carra thought he was paid less than the sum to which they had agreed.[41]

Like Marat, he made an ill-fated attempt at becoming an accepted member of the scientific establishment. In 1785, Carra obtained the position of second keeper in the manuscripts department of the *Bibliothèque du Roi*. There he quarrelled with the former police lieutenant, Lenoir, the same Lenoir who had apparently engaged Brissot in spying activities. The origins of Carra's problems with Lenoir are no clearer than conflicts with his previous employers, but mutual accusations of theft and mismanagement were involved. Apparently Carra never carried out his duties properly at the library as he was too occupied with his scientific writing.[42]

Gorsas

Gorsas was born into a comfortable family of artisans at Limoges. His father was employed as a cobbler, and his family, in common with those of Desmoulins and Robespierre, had local connections.[43] A clerical friend of the family, Renaud, acquired a place for Gorsas at the Collége du Plessis in Versailles where, like Vergniaud, he was destined for the ecclesiastical life. Gorsas, however, did not feel a religious vocation, and after completing his studies, he founded a school there. The establishment flourished and Gorsas even received a certificate from the War Ministry, and the institution was named a '*maison militaire d'éducation*'. All this success came to an end in 1788 when, according to Guibert, Gorsas' enemies, who remain unidentified, accused him of corrupting the morals of his students. The result was a term of imprisonment in Bîcetre.[44]

Manuel

Manuel's background is strikingly similar to that of Louvet. Both came from the class of lower middle-class shopkeepers or artisans. A contemporary anonymous pamphlet claims Manuel's father had a haberdashery and clothing business, while other sources state his father was a potter.[45] He attended the seminary at Sens to please his parents and ended up in Paris in 1785 employed at a bookshop. He wrote many pamphlets, such as the *Essais historiques, critiques, littéraires et philosophiques* (1783), which landed him a three-month detention in the Bastille. Like Brissot, he was allegedly a police spy and peddler of pornography.[46]

Brissot

Although not born in Paris, Brissot, the son of a comfortable restaurateur, arrived there at the age of nineteen in 1774 after being educated at the local college where he received the standard classical training of the day. Brissot left the Collège de Chartres with the decision of his parents to enter the legal profession, but after a short stint of working in a law firm in Paris, Brissot abandoned the law for a literary career.[47]

From the start of his literary career up to the outbreak of revolution, Brissot wrote numerous volumes of works on a wide variety of subjects, ranging from reforms in the penal and canon laws to attacks on various ministers. He began his career as a rather innocent, but extremely ambitious young man, forsaking a safe legal career, in contrast to so many of his contemporaries, for the gamble as a man of letters. Unfortunately for Brissot, this gamble did not pay off. Although he did win the odd academic competition, in the majority of cases his works were largely ignored by those he wanted to impress, and in 1784 he was charged with producing libels and thrown into the Bastille.[48] By 1789, Brissot, now a family man, for reasons of poverty was doing and writing almost anything, including spying for the police, to survive. Like Fabre, he was clearly in need of a revolution to rescue him from a rather disappointing pre-revolutionary career.

In common with many of the provincial lawyers, Brissot submitted a number of essays to academic contests. Brissot's essays tended to be politically radical, containing seeds of the future revolutionary in them, especially the *Théorie des Lois Criminelles*. It went beyond a critique of the penal system to an attack against tyrannical governments, the abuses made by those responsible for the levying and collecting of taxes, the *fermiers-généraux*, and the faulty social system which was responsible for crime. Like Pétion and Billaud, Brissot was fiercely anti-clerical, denouncing the idleness of celibates, particularly the regular clergy, whom he regarded as parasites. Unlike Billaud, who was writing a few years later and who tended to be radical only when attacking religion, Brissot found fault with both the existing political system and the religious system.[49] However, Brissot, unlike Pétion, never proposed concrete solutions to the old regime's problems.

Marat

For several years, Jean-Paul Marat, originally from a Calvinist family in Boudry, Neuchâtel, had been unsuccessfully attempting to become accepted in the established world of science in eighteenth-century Paris. Like Carra, Marat had lived a peripatetic life in Europe. He studied medicine in Toulouse, Bordeaux, and Paris, and lived in various Dutch cities, London and Edinburgh. His medical degree came from St Andrews, a university notorious for selling its degrees. He finally settled in Paris in 1776 and became the physician to the comte d'Artois' bodyguard, a post which he held until 1786.[50] Dr Marat spent most of his time conducting experiments on electricity and combustion, and in order to finance them, he charged exorbitant medical fees. Between 1779 and 1787, Marat published a number of scientific treatises, none of which were taken seriously by the French Academy of Sciences. Condorcet was a member of the Academy of Sciences' panel, which dismissed Marat's experiments and also denied his admission to the academy. The common feature among his pamphlets was his allegation to have disproved all previous theories.[51]

While Brissot was working on one of his many pre-revolutionary works, *De la Vérité*, in the early 1780s, he came into contact with Marat, a man strikingly similar in mentality and outlook. Eleven years his senior, Marat became an idol for Brissot. He praised Marat's scientific efforts and referred to him as a 'celebrated physician'. According to Brissot, Marat had courageously corrected Newton's scientific errors. Not surprisingly, the only support Brissot received was from Marat.[52]

Brissot had just as much trouble breaking into the literary establishment of Paris as Marat had in the accepted world of science. Rejection was the main feature that they shared. Before the revolution, Brissot waged a campaign for Marat, denouncing scientific academies which continually turned him away.[53] Marat later said Brissot knew many of his persecutors personally and that he strove to expose them in his *De la Vérité*.[54]

A further characteristic which Marat had in common with Brissot was his ability to write anything for anyone as long as it ensured a reward at the end. Marat was in

Jean-Paul Marat, by Joseph Boze. (Musée Carnavalet)

many ways an ambitious chameleon who wrote what he thought would attain success for him, whether it was an academic prize – both Brissot and Marat entered pamphlets in the Economic Society of Berne contest – or a job. Marat wrote a very conservative *Eloge de Montesquieu* (1785), in which he conveniently ignored Montesquieu's critique of various aspects of the old regime, in the hope of getting the Bordeaux Academy's prize. When hoping to get the post of secretary to the new Madrid Academy, he presented himself as a pillar of religious orthodoxy, as someone who was scandalized by anti-clericalism in France.

His political works were in no way radical: he wrote whatever he thought would please his readers. In 1774, he published, in English, his *Chains of Slavery* in support of the Wilkites during the British elections in the hope of getting a job afterwards. This was radical in the Wilkite sense whereby John Wilkes and his followers were instrumental in focusing public opinion on ideas of liberty and for involving the ordinary people in politics.[55] The only evidence of consistency in Marat's character was his huge ambition. He praised Frederick the Great of Prussia as 'the greatest of kings', when begging Frederick for some token of appreciation for his experiments.[56] It may well be true that by 1789 Marat did not trust constituted authority, as one of his biographers claims, but there is little evidence that before that year he was ready for revolution.[57]

Marat, Carra and Brissot all three criticized Newton, while Carra and Marat, in their campaign against the academies, insisted that they had outdone him. The two of them directed their attack against a particular individual, Joseph-Jérôme Lalande, who was a member of sixteen academies, and held the chair of Astronomy at the Collège de France. Carra not only ridiculed Lalande, but accused him of plagiarizing his scientific discoveries, particularly the *'noyau de soleil'*. Carra did not give up with the failure of his *Nouveaux Principes*. He submitted a treatise on the physical phenomena of fire and heat, *Dissertation*, in an unsuccessful attempt at the prize offered by the

Academy of Dijon. Failure to win the prize reinforced his disenchantment with the scientific community and heated up his campaign against Lalande. Carra now accused Lalande of organizing a conspiracy to close all the academies which deviated from Newtonian principles.[58]

Condorcet

The complete opposite in terms of success *vis-à-vis* the French Academy was the Marquis de Condorcet, who came from an old noble family. Although born in Ribemont in Picardy, he had been in Paris since his student days at the Jesuit College of Navarre. Unlike Marat and Carra, whose scientific works were not recognized, Condorcet's mathematical investigations gained him election to the French Academy of Sciences in 1769. He had published his first mathematical treatise, *Essai sur le calcul intégral*, at the age of twenty-two. Several others followed, and he was soon considered the Descartes of his day, attracting the admiration of mathematicians like d'Alembert. In recognition of his works, he was made the Academy of Sciences' permanent secretary in 1776, a position which he held until its abolition in 1793. In 1782, he was admitted to the French Academy. Thus, by the early 1780s, Condorcet had become a leading mathematician and thinker.[59]

Given his social standing and academic success, Condorcet did not move in the same circles as Brissot, Carra and Marat. This does not mean that Brissot did not try to attract the interest and patronage of the great *philosophe*; indeed he attempted to interest Condorcet in his *lycée* project – an institution intended to be a world centre of learning – through the auspices of a cleric named Villar. Apparently Condorcet had doubts about Brissot's character – perhaps he had heard about his activities as a police informer – and the company Brissot kept.[60]

In addition, Brissot wrote to Condorcet begging for a job. Condorcet, taking pity on him,

An engraving of Marie Jean Antoine-Nicolas de Caritat Condorcet, deputy from the Department of Aisne to the Convention in 1792, by Bonneville. (Newberry Library, Chicago, Illinois)

proposed his services as a tutor to a Prussian baron. As Condorcet's biographer points out, this did not prevent Brissot from addressing a very insulting pamphlet, *Un Mot à l'oreille des académiciens de Paris*, to the French Academy.[61]

Brissot's final pre-revolutionary connection with Condorcet was through an anti-slavery society, which Brissot had established in 1788. Lafayette brought Condorcet to a meeting of the *Société des Amis des Noirs*, which counted among its members, Pétion, Carra, and Mercier. All of these men had known each other for a number of years. Mercier had first met Brissot in Paris in 1780.[62] Pétion, Brissot's childhood friend, was a regional associate. Once a member, Condorcet dominated the group. He drew up the society's regulations and became its president.[63]

During the later 1780s, Brissot, Carra and Gorsas were all writing pamphlets for a faction called the Kornmann group, which had grown out of a mesmerist society, the *Société de l'Harmonie Universelle*.[64] Its members included Bergasse, Brissot, Clavière, Carra, Marat, Gorsas, Pétion, l'abbé Sabatier, Lafayette, and Duval d'Eprémesnil. Brissot claimed his attraction to the group was its political radicalism and that it was more interested in revolution than animal magnetism. Apparently Brissot and his long-time supporter and current employer, the Genevan banker Clavière, were the only two members in favour of a republic. Brissot had first met the wealthy banker and financier Etienne Clavière on a journey to Switzerland in search of collaborators for his *lycée* in 1782.[65] Brissot more likely joined the group in order to re-launch his attack against the academies.[66] Interest in science brought these men together, and attacks on the men of the academies and salons were a unifying factor.

Rather than promoting revolution, the Kornmann group appeared to have been organized firstly, for the writing and publishing of financial pamphlets, which had the goal of boosting Clavière's financial investments; second, to attack Calonne the Controller General of Finance for his financial policies; and third, for producing propaganda in support of Kornmann for his adultery case against his wife. The group was composed of a strange mixture of discontented individuals: Brissot and his friends, who by this time had been unsuccessful in their careers; and men like Lafayette, who were not at all disgruntled radicals, but establishment figures. What they had in common was their lack of faith in Calonne. Brissot met Carra and Gorsas in the group. All three were hack writers employed by Bergasse, Clavière, Mirabeau and Kornmann to write their pamphlets.[67]

Brissot's attack on ministerial despotism was furthered in his *Point de Banqueroute*, a pamphlet produced when he was employed by the Marquis Ducrest, himself employed by the Duc d'Orléans as his secretary. It demanded the development of provincial assemblies and the calling of the Estates-General as a means of decreasing what Brissot called '*l'aristocratie ministérielle*'. He continued his denunciation of Calonne, and like Billaud, he supported the Parlements, which by this time were recommending the meeting of the Estates-General and its right to levy taxes. Once again, Brissot was writing whatever his employer required, with the hope that there would be a reward at the end of it.[68]

Pétion, Brissot's school friend from Chartres,[69] followed the activities of the group very closely as is revealed in the letters he wrote to Brissot. He took a great interest in the Kornmann affair and he urged Brissot to send him the latest pamphlets. In another letter, Pétion wrote that he had 'put all of my imaginable energy into the Kornmann affair'.[70]

Pétion had been involved in the writing of radical propaganda since the early 1780s.[71] His ideas deserve some elaboration given the fact that he was unique in the extent of his radicalism. His first work, *Les lois civiles* (1782), was an attack not only on the current state of the law in France, but on an entire society. In it, he demanded a transformation of the French legal system, including the election of judges and the abolition of the venality of offices. Moreover, the *Lois civiles* contains much more than a discussion of law reform. Much of it is a blueprint for future revolutionary legislation. Society, he explained, needed moral regeneration because it was 'rife with corruption'. He attacked many of the major institutions of the old regime in France. One such institution was that of the Intendant. Pétion, as one of the sub-delegates or assistants to the Intendant of Orléans, would have experienced firsthand knowledge of the working of this office. He disapproved of the unrepresentative nature of the Intendant whom he described as an official who 'often has neither the time, the energy nor the will to carry out his duties competently. Therefore, he delegates his duties to subalterns who abuse their authority.' He argued that provinces which still retained their assemblies, composed of representatives from each of the three orders, known as *pays d'état*, were far more beneficial to the people than those controlled by the Intendant, known as *pays d'élection*.

In contrast to the *pays d'état*, the tax burden in the *pays d'élection* was not so onerous to the ordinary people. The distribution of the tax burden in provinces controlled by the Intendant, as in Pétion's home province of Orléans, was arbitrary. In provinces administered by the Intendant, the representatives of the people had no voice in voting on taxation.[72]

Pétion's treatise, *Avis au Français*, published in 1788, was a virulent condemnation of every institution of the old regime. It was so radical that the editor of the 1793 edition wrote, 'the more you read this work, the more you believe it was written after the revolution. The constitution is found there in complete form and there are some articles which seemed to have been copied. It is difficult to cite six constitutional decrees which are neither mentioned nor developed.'[73] Like his earlier works, the *Avis* fiercely denounced the institutions of the old regime, but went much further in that it set out a plan for a regenerated society.[74]

Foreshadowing the work of the Constituent Assembly, which was responsible for drafting France's first written constitution, Pétion insisted on such a document. In 1788 he was arguing in favour of the three most celebrated maxims of the French revolutionary constitution: liberty, equality and fraternity. Liberty was the goal towards which all should work; equality was the soul of liberty, and fraternity was the nation as represented by a truly national assembly. Pétion did not treat these founding revolutionary principles as abstract concepts, but envisaged them as goals which could be realized through a representative body elected by all citizens of the realm.[75]

Pétion demanded the union of the three orders of society and that the elimination of all privileges of the first two orders be the first piece of business in the Estates-General. Once privileges had been prohibited, the 'national assembly would form nothing more than a large family, linked by the same interests, animated by the same feeling and spirit; there would only be one order and the third estate would be able to surrender itself confidently.' If privileges were not eradicated, 'the revolution would not have been brought about'.[76]

Much ink was spilt over the ills of the old regime on the eve of the French Revolution. Pétion was not simply another dissatisfied hack, he was unique in his prescriptive remedies. In contrast to Brissot, Marat, Fabre, Carra and Gorsas, Pétion had not been unsuccessful in his pre-revolutionary career. As noted above, in addition to his legal practice, he served as a subdelegate to the Intendant of Orléans. In other words, he was a respectable citizen who saw many faults and injustices in the old regime.

What emerges from this examination of the pre-revolutionary careers up to 1788 is a group of men who divide into three categories. The first group is composed of the successful provincial professionals. All were lawyers, with the exception of Fouché, who did very well for himself as a lay teacher in several Oratorian schools. The provincials who became lawyers had attained their goals of established legal careers, and would have continued to be solid respectable country lawyers had there not been a revolution. They were a fairly ambitious group, with active interests beyond their professions. They seemed to see themselves as minor *philosophes* pursuing scientific and literary interests. This made them men who were critical of the status quo, or ambitious to create a name for themselves, but not in the revolutionary sense. Very few of this group had radical ideas before the political crisis of 1788. With the exception of Pétion, who was among the success stories, and writing radical treatises about specific political reform as early as the early 1780s, the political culture of these men reflected the attitudes of the previous generation. They were clearly deeply influenced in their thinking by important thinkers of the age, such as Montesquieu and Rousseau. It was the quite unexpected political crisis of 1789 that suddenly made people raised in this tradition responsible for governing and reorganizing the country. The revolution forced them to change their previous ways of thinking to cope with new problems raised by events, which no one, in the dying years of the old regime, could have foreseen.

The second category, composed of provincials who took the Parisian gamble, were a different kettle of fish. Generally speaking, they had far less success in their chosen careers, whether they were lawyers or aspiring men of letters, or of science. However, lack of success did not necessarily make them politically radical.

Of these born in the provinces who went into law in Paris – there were four of them – only Danton was doing well. Of the potential *philosophes*, whether they were men of science or of *belles-lettres*, with the exception of Condorcet, who possessed many advantages: birth, intelligence, wealth and connections the others did not have, the remainder failed to become leaders in their field. Some had a legal background, such as Brissot and Gorsas, which they had forsaken to become professional *philosophes*, but they had to concentrate on making a living. Many of those who failed in Paris were poor, had spent some time in prison, or had been in trouble with the law, and as a result, they were embittered by the time of the outbreak of revolution. Generally speaking, the group in Paris during the 1780s were a far less respectable lot than their provincial counterparts. This does not necessarily mean they had radical ideas. However, the fact that they were poor and in need of an income turned them to pamphleteering, and sometimes they wrote political pamphlets. They hired out their pens to men like Mirabeau and Clavière, and in Brissot's case, the Marquis Ducrest, who were trying to operate within the existing system. This group were embittered not because they were unsuccessful in their endeavour to change the system of the old regime – men like Brissot had advocated reform rather than revolution – but because, for one reason or another, they had not been able to achieve any degree of success in it. In common with the established lawyers in the provinces, with the exception of Pétion, it took an unexpected political crisis to convert them to radicalism.

The final category comprised the three who were Parisian born. Of these, one, Collot, was unique in that he left Paris to pursue a successful theatrical career in provincial France rather than the other way round. Mercier and Louvet, two Parisians who remained in Paris, were prospering. Perhaps they knew something about Parisian survival the others did not. Mercier did have more time than the others in that he was older, having been born in 1740.

There were some connections between those in the provinces. Billaud and Fouché were colleagues at the same Oratorian college for a time, and Fouché became friendly with Robespierre at the Rosati society when he was promoted to the college at Arras. Desmoulins met Robespierre at school in Paris, but there is no evidence they were very close during their school years, or that they communicated between the end of their school days and the start of the revolution. In contrast to them, Pétion and Brissot, who had been at school together in Chartres, had kept up their friendship. The three future deputies from the Gironde, Vergniaud, Guadet and Gensonné, were legal colleagues in Bordeaux, and Gensonné and Vergniaud knew each other through their shared interest in literature and culture at the *Musée*. Fabre and Collot had met in Lyon working in the theatre in 1782.

Of the Parisian group, Marat, Carra, Gorsas, Manuel, Condorcet and Mercier all knew Brissot, but it is not clear if they all knew each other. Carra knew Gorsas from the Kornmann group and Mercier from the *Amis des Noirs*. Marat and Carra's shared animosity toward the academies brought them together. Danton and Billaud, it seems, did not know any of these people, but knew each other. There is no evidence that Desmoulins was in contact with any of these men. In the main, it took a revolution to bring the majority together, although it can be argued that Brissot had made the most contacts with future revolutionaries during the late 1780s in Paris.

What these men had in common was their ambition and their determination to make a name for themselves within the parameters of the established world of the old regime, either through the law, or by acquiring a reputation in the arts or sciences. Even those who had never possessed a 'real job', or had renounced it for literature or science, were more involved in Enlightened theorizing like their more established counterparts in their provincial literary societies, than suggesting specific policies. They were as much taken by surprise by the real revolution of 1789 as the part-time literati in the provinces.

2

REVOLUTIONARY NETWORKING, 1789–91

During the first two years of the French Revolution, the years of the National Constituent Assembly, between 1789 and 1791, a group of radicals emerged in Paris. It was composed of a majority of the individuals introduced in the previous chapter. Of this group only Buzot, Robespierre, Pétion and Barère had been successfully elected as deputies to the Estates-General. They came to Paris where they met other radicals and immersed themselves in the revolutionary fervour of 1789. Those who had not been elected deputies took part in revolutionary networks ranging from journalism to clubs. Saint-Just, Barbaroux, Couthon, Fouché and the Bordelais, who remained in the provinces during these years, greeted the revolution with an equal amount of enthusiasm. They involved themselves in revolutionary politics at the municipal level and earned reputations as local Jacobin leaders. This chapter seeks to explore the nature of the reaction of both Parisian and provincial revolutionaries to the new circumstances which presented themselves in 1789.

PARISIAN REVOLUTIONARIES

Almost all of the non-deputies who were in Paris had been in the capital before 1789. Many of those who had not, were soon attracted there by the revolutionary fervour. Robert was chosen commander of the National Guard of Givet. He was delegated to Paris in August 1789, and seeing the excitement in the capital, he decided to remain there. Collot, from the first days of the revolution, left the theatre in Geneva for Paris. He joined others, such as Desmoulins, Garran Coulon, Billaud, Fabre, Brissot, Danton, Marat, Carra, Mercier, and Gorsas, who were already resident in Paris. They welcomed the revolution with open arms. The revolutionary changes, which included the end of censorship, opened up the possibilities of new careers for these men who had not fared so well under the old regime, and stirred an interest in politics for those who had been successful. Given the ambitious nature of these men, it is not surprising that they were enthusiastic about the changes which 1789 brought about. Many threw themselves actively into new careers of journalism, pamphleteering, and popular activism.

Those who turned to journalism recognized themselves as a band of writers. Carra, when he felt that Desmoulins' newspaper and some others were under attack, proposed a 'Federative Pact of writers and patriot journalists', to protect themselves from their enemies. He proclaimed that they all wrote useful articles on the 'progress of reason and enlightenment and the maintenance of the rights of man'. In addition, they uncovered aristocratic plots. Therefore, they should unite to protect their interests.[1]

These men not only agreed on specific issues, but cooperated in a Parisian network of newspapers, societies, and clubs. This was true in terms of their attitudes towards political issues, whom they supported in the Constituent Assembly and the causes which they espoused. In an attempt to further their aspirations, they formed societies such as the society for the abolition of primogeniture, the Cordeliers and the Cercle Social. Deputies were only marginally involved in the more popular societies. They concentrated on making their mark at the more prestigious and respectable Jacobin club. A number of the radicals participated in municipal politics for a short time. The consequences of this in terms of political allies will be investigated.

ISSUES AND POWER BASES

Before examining the specific attitudes of the radicals towards constitutional issues such as the veto and the new judicial system, it seems appropriate to describe the general revolutionary context in which they were operating. Firstly, in terms of political principles, the Constituent Assembly may be roughly divided into royalists, *monarchiens*, a revolutionary centre and a small group of democrats and advocates of popular sovereignty. The essential aim of the royalists was to preserve as much power as possible for the king. Following the lead of Montesquieu, the *monarchiens* advocated a genuine balance between the executive and legislative branches of government. They were constitutional monarchists, who favoured the monarch having an absolute veto. The centre left supported a constitutional monarchy, weighted in favour of the legislative power. For them, the victory of the revolutionaries had not yet been assured and therefore they tended to pressure the king in order to make him accept their terms for a compromise that would leave him with similar powers to the king of England. This group, composed of men like Barnave, Duport and the Lameth brothers, opted for a suspensive, or temporary, veto, and their proposal carried the day. Finally, the extreme left preferred a nominal monarchy, which left the king with very little power. He would have no veto and all power would rest with the legislature. The group of men, both deputies and non-deputies, under consideration in this book formed the extreme left.

Second, there is the matter of power bases, with each group stressing the importance of its own political organization. Closely linked to that was each one's attitude towards popular sovereignty. Deputies of the centre left (who held a majority in the Assembly), tended to argue that, while sovereignty was located in the people, elections transferred its exercise to the Assembly. A majority in the Assembly must therefore be regarded as an expression of the 'general will', meaning that their will was morally binding on those who opposed it. The extreme left, always a tiny minority, composed of Pétion, Robespierre and Buzot, insisted on the right of the sovereign people to assert its authority, even against the will of the Assembly. At a lower level, the Paris Commune, for a time composed of men like Brissot, Garran Coulon and Condorcet, while professing its devotion to the Assembly, claimed to be the sole representative of the people of Paris. Their authority was challenged by some of the sixty districts (these units of local government replaced the sections after 1790), particularly the Cordeliers, who insisted that their approval was necessary for the arrest of anyone who lived in their area.

The position held by the radicals concerning a number of political or constitutional issues, and their reaction to revolutionary events, is illustrative of their principles. In the case of the veto, for example, all agreed that the absolute veto was unacceptable, and thus were in agreement with Barère, Pétion, Buzot and Robespierre, who argued against the *monarchien* deputy Mounier's suggestion for it. Pétion specifically insisted that it was the 'nation from whom all power emanates', while Buzot, putting it a different way, stated that 'sovereignty resides in the nation'.[2] Although

The king's speech at the signing of the 1791 constitution at the National Assembly, 14 September 1791. (Bibliothèque nationale de France)

Barère counted among his friends during the early days of the Constituent Assembly men like Mirabeau and Bailly, at times he took a more radical stance on the issues. He argued that 'the idea of an absolute veto is absurd', and he had reservations about the suspensive veto.[3] At one point during the debate, Pétion came up with the idea of holding a referendum on the suspensive veto, illustrating his preference for popular sovereignty over representative democracy. This proposition was never acted upon by the Assembly.[4]

Concerning the attitude of the non-deputies, with the exception of Brissot, who, influenced by the American constitution, suggested an American-style veto, the remainder advocated no veto at all.[5] Carra, at this time a regular contributor both to Kéralio's and Desmoulins' newspapers, simply commented, 'no veto'.[6] Carra had written quite extensively about the veto in his pamphlet, *L'Orateur des Etats-Généraux pour 1789*. He attacked the proposals made by the more conservative deputies. This opinion was repeated by Robert in June 1790, and later in April 1791 when he wrote, 'Any sort of veto is contrary to reason.'[7] Desmoulins was also opposed to the king having a veto in any form and expressed this in his newspaper. Marat, in his analysis of the veto question, sided with Lanjuinais who opposed the absolute veto on the grounds that it was 'a criminal attempt on the liberty of the citizens'. He considered it to be a 'threat treasonable against the sovereignty of the people and public freedom. It should therefore be annulled by the Nation . . .'[8] Finally, Condorcet rejected both forms of veto.[9]

Related to the question of the king's veto was the matter of his general role. Again there was virtually no difference in attitude: all were in favour of a very limited role for the executive branch and an extended one for the legislature. Carra was so intent on limiting the king's role that he advised it was not necessary for him to attend meetings of the National Assembly. If he desired to attend, he could do so merely as 'first citizen'. The nation was 'sovereign'.[10] Brissot and Robert had been specifically criticized by the Jacobin Laclos in his newspaper for preaching republicanism. Brissot responded by denying this assertion and affirming his faith in a constitutional monarchy, but in 'a popular monarchy, where the scales are balanced in favour of the people. The best form of government', he maintained, 'was representative and elected and one in which the power of the king was derived from the people or the nation which was superior to the executive power.'[11]

Robert and Carra insisted that the king's power ought to be very restricted. In an article written on the subject of the 'legitimate authority of the king', Carra spoke the same language as Brissot: 'But the power of kings should come from the people to be legitimate; this authority is only legitimate when it is totally distinct and separate from the legislative and judicial powers; it is in the legislative power that this authority must be concentrated.' Robert thought that the king was the 'first officer of the nation, having no rights, only duties'. Finally Carra quoted Pétion and Lameth to illustrate that the nation, rather than the king, was the sovereign power: 'The nation is sovereign and it delegates royalty; it is nothing, this royalty, but a landlord.'[12]

The women's march to Versailles, and the support for it provided by the Cordeliers district and its newspapers along with radical journalists from elsewhere, demonstrate the unity amongst the non-deputies. Newspapers published by future members of the Cordelier club, such as the *Révolutions de Paris*, and Desmoulins' journal, not surprisingly praised the event and the role of the people: 'Go and march brave citizens, you carry with you the destiny of France; our hearts follow you.'[13] Gorsas likewise honoured the role of the Cordeliers district in the uprising and quoted one of its decrees: 'Finally, this fortunate suspicion held many citizens under arms and certainly prevented the counter-revolution that was under preparation.'[14] Danton, at the time president of the Cordeliers district, undoubtedly drafted the insurrectionary petition and sounded the tocsin in the district, although he did not take part in the march himself.[15] Brissot, who did not march either, defended the people who did march to Versailles when he wrote that 'their only object is to bring to the King the vehement concerns of the city of Paris, and to obtain from him a resolution to calm its inhabitants'. Marat depicted the royal arrival in Paris as 'a festival' and claimed that the royal presence in the capital would mean that people would no longer die of hunger.[16] Carra's first signed article in the *Annales Patriotiques et Littéraires*, edited with Mercier, was written on 6 October, and concerned a proposal to provision the people of Paris. The next day, his entry was a lengthy description of the women's march demanding bread, a march of which he approved given the lack of food in the city.[17]

The events of 14 July had already converted Louvet to radicalism and convinced him to move to Paris. Louvet was in Versailles at the time of the march to the king's palace. Although there is no evidence that he participated in the events of that day, he wrote a pamphlet in response to Mounier's accusations that the invasion had been brought about by a Parisian mob. In *Paris Justifié contre M. Mounier*, he defended the actions of the day. This pamphlet gained him admission to the Jacobin club. Meanwhile, he continued to write during this period, producing three plays in which he criticized titled royalists, the pope and the *émigré* 'armies'.[18]

The deputies were more circumspect in their comments about the happenings of 5–6 October. Pétion did not remark at all on the events, although he disapproved of the banquet which had been held at Versailles in honour of the newly arrived Flanders regiment and which had sparked the

A page from Camille Desmoulins's journal, *Révolutions de France et de Brabant*, no. 15, 8 March 1790. This illustration accompanied the previous article and is captioned, 'General Alton chased by patriotic street lamps or lights'. (Thomas Fisher Rare Book Library, University of Toronto)

Motion made by Camille Desmoulins at the Palais Royal, 12 July 1789, by Berthaut. (Musée Carnavalet)

march. Robespierre offered his support to Maillard who headed the deputation of women when they entered the Assembly. Barère equated the October days with the mob violence of 14 July of which he disapproved. In notes he made for his newspaper which remain unpublished, he described 14 July as 'the work of the people in their cruel fury'.[19] There is no evidence that even the most advanced of the deputies praised the march, which perhaps reflects their more cautious attitude towards the 'sovereign people', or the crowd.

The position taken by the radicals towards the nature of the new judicial system further establishes their harmony. Pétion had attacked the judicial system of the old regime extensively in his pre-revolutionary works, beginning in 1782 with the publication of his *Lois civiles*. This treatise was re-issued in 1790. Brissot spoke of it as a handbook for the revolutionaries in devising the new judicial system which would be rational and elected. Likewise Carra, in his review, wrote: 'Today the Assembly is concerned with the re-organization of the judiciary, the re-printing of the *Lois civiles* becomes of great utility . . . One finds here almost all of the reforms proposed today . . .'. Desmoulins' article entitled, 'Pétion, the friend of good sense', analysed a session of the Assembly where deputies were deliberating over the powers of judges in general and Article 1: 'Justice shall be rendered in the name of the king, in particular.' On this point, Pétion argued that 'it was not in the name of the king which justice ought to be rendered but in the name of the entire society'. Desmoulins remarked that Pétion's principles were 'clear and incontestable . . .'.[20]

Buzot and Robespierre concurred that there should be juries for both criminal and civil trials. Buzot argued that without 'the establishment of juries, there could be neither justice nor liberty'. In his argument in favour of juries, Robespierre stated that there was no difference between the civil and the criminal when it came to 'life, honour, and fortune'. In addition, he pleaded that all rights of citizens rested on the same guarantee, and it was the 'sacred duty of society to embrace all of them'. The Assembly did not vote the radical line. The final decree, passed on 30 April, established juries only in criminal trials.[21]

MUNICIPAL POLITICS

A number of politicians who had been unsuccessful in their attempt to be elected as deputies, participated in municipal Parisian politics. The Paris Commune provided them with a power base for a short period of time during the preliminary years of the revolution. Brissot, Carra, Condorcet, Garran Coulon, and Nicolas de Bonneville, one of the founders of the Cercle Social, sat on the left of the Parisian municipal assembly.

Brissot, for example, had to be content with municipal politics when he failed to get elected to the Estates-General despite a concerted effort on the part of himself and Pétion. Pétion, who was successfully elected to the Estates-General as a deputy for the Third Estate from Chartres, had put Brissot's name forward as a candidate there. Even though Brissot's name appeared third on an anonymous list of twenty-one 'Amis du Peuple', who merited the choice of the electors of Paris, he failed to be chosen even as an elector.[22]

Brissot was chosen president of his district, Filles-Saint-Thomas, on 23 April, and it was this position which enabled him to become elected to the Municipal Assembly of the Paris Commune, which met for the first time on 25 July. Collot d'Herbois was also a member of this section and perhaps met Brissot there. They lived in the same neighbourhood: Brissot on the rue Grétry, and Collot on the rue Favart.[23]

Many other radicals were active in the political life of the Paris Commune. Carra, also a member of the same district as Brissot, was named elector to the general Assembly of Paris electors. Carra, like Brissot, had published a pamphlet, *Projet du Cahier*, which, although inserted by Camus in the *Collection Officielle*,[24] had not won him election to the Estates-General. Both Carra and Marat had a grievance against the academies, which had rejected their works. Carra's persistent hostility to the academies formed a major part of his *Projet*. He believed the academies should be controlled by the Estates-General which would regulate the funds destined to them and to their personnel.[25]

Garran Coulon was an elector, a substitute deputy for the city of Paris in April 1789, and in July he was a member of the Insurrectionary Committee of the Palais Royal, which planned the storming of the Bastille. He was a leading member of the Paris Commune's Research Committee, formed on 22 October. The committee's purpose was 'to receive denunciations and depositions of plots, conspiracies, and in case of necessity, to keep under surveillance the persons denounced'.[26]

Condorcet had attempted to be elected in Mantes and Paris for the nobility. Although he had drafted a *cahier* in Mantes, and had written a *Déclaration des Droits* to assist the authors of *cahiers*, his liberal views prevented him from election in Mantes. In Paris, where birth and money counted for everything, Condorcet was not high enough in the noble pecking order to get elected. In addition, his hostility to the Parlements had not helped him. He threw himself into revolutionary activity, and joined the Parisian National Guard and not only got elected to the new Municipal Assembly, but also wrote its constitution.[27]

During these formative years of the revolution, there were often divisions of emphasis. One of these was Marat's conflict with the municipal government of Paris, and especially with the *Bureau de la Ville* in September 1789. Marat first appeared before the Communal Assembly on 28 September because of his denunciation on the 25th of that month for producing an issue of his journal in which he attacked the district of Filler-Saint-Thomas; Brissot was president of this district at the time. On 7 October, after he had been threatened with arrest by the Châtelet, Marat went into hiding.[28]

His radical friends came to his support. They defended Marat in their capacity as fellow journalists. In November, Marat appealed to the Cordeliers district for protection and received it from Danton, then president. His friends in the Cordeliers district such as Kéralio, considered Marat to be a good citizen, but even they thought he sometimes went too far for his own good. Kéralio expressed this opinion clearly in a letter to Brissot where she wrote: 'I do not know M. Marat, I have never seen him, I have only read one number of his paper; I see him as a good citizen whose excess of zeal takes him too far. I accord all right to those whom he has attacked . . . and he should make a public apology. But I want it to be legal and not arbitrary.'[29] What she meant was that Marat was on their side, but he should keep within the law. Desmoulins was not entirely sympathetic when he wrote: 'One day I said to Marat during the only conversation I've had with him, what I thought of his hastiness in judging, of his even larger facility to accuse, of the danger of some of his opinions'; nevertheless, he defended Marat's courage and great character.[30] Carra came to Marat's support in an article written in defence of the freedom of the press. He strongly defended the Cordeliers district's declaration that the 'liberty of the press follows naturally on that of the individual so that no one should be prevented from expressing one's thought . . . One hopes that this example will be followed throughout France.'[31] Gorsas, who wrote the strongest condemnation of Marat, could not understand how the Cordeliers district, of which he was an admirer, could defend such an 'impure serpent'.[32] There appears to have been two local foci, the Filles Saint-Thomas and Cordeliers districts, which may have been rivals.

Although Marat might not have been aware of it, Brissot had written to Desmoulins in an effort to help his old friend in January immediately before the Châtelet attempted to arrest him. In the letter, Brissot advised Desmoulins of an 'odious persecution exercised against a journalist by the *Bureau de la Ville*, and that it was necessary that all come to his assistance'. Moreover, it was 'necessary to denounce this atrocity in the only district where I know a certain vigour, the Cordeliers'. He concluded by saying M. Delapoype would provide him with the details. On the day that the Châtelet attempted to arrest Marat, Brissot simply wrote: 'Some authors of incendiary writings have been arrested.'[33] Perhaps out of fear of being arrested himself, he remained impartial in his newspaper.

Marat's conflict with the commune demonstrates that most radicals had some reservations about Marat, although, with the exception of Gorsas, all approved of the general position taken by the Cordeliers district. It illustrates the temporary divisions and squabbles among these men, for example, the disagreement between Desmoulins and Garran Coulon ended when the matter was resolved. Marat scolded Desmoulins for siding with Garran Coulon in the 'conflict' between the

Paris Commune's Research Committee and Marat. Garran Coulon presided over this committee. His mandate was to take measures to guarantee the tranquillity of Paris. An exchange of heated letters occurred between the two men, but everything ended amiably. Garran Coulon wrote a letter addressed to Marat which he had printed in Brissot's journal in which he denied any denunciation by the committee of Marat.[34]

A new conflict emerged in 1790 between the Cercle Social, the executive council of the Commune, which aspired to govern Paris, and the districts, primarily the Cordeliers. Fauchet, the unofficial leader of the Communal Assembly, was closely allied with Bonneville, Brissot, Condorcet, and Garran Coulon, all members of the Communal Assembly.[35] Each of these groups saw themselves as representative of the sovereign people. Each, therefore, was inclined to stress the extent of its own authority. Brissot, as a member of the Paris Commune's Assembly, was strongly opposed to district power in a plan which he designed for the municipal government. His plan thus called for authority to rest in the Communal Assembly rather than in the districts.[36] The Cordeliers district resented what they considered an abuse of political power by the representatives of the Paris Commune which they claimed led to the 'usurpation of power'. Excerpts from their deliberations in which they 'promised to oppose anything the Representatives of the Commune would do to prejudice the general rights of the constituent citizens', were printed by Prudhomme.[37]

Brissot's plan was rejected and this conflict dissipated when the two groups found a common enemy in the mayor and decided to join forces to prevent Bailly's re-election. Desmoulins printed Brissot's attack on Bailly, 'What is a mayor of Paris?', in which he exclaimed: 'M. Bailly may be an elegant historian of sciences, an excellent academician, but he understands nothing when it comes to administration and contentious matters.' Desmoulins, in his commentary, applauded Brissot's reflections, and he proposed Danton, Fauchet and Garran Coulon as candidates for mayor.[38] Desmoulins' recommendations indicated that at this stage, the radicals were an undifferentiated mass. The fact that Danton had become a member of the Communal Assembly in January 1790 is presumably a further factor accounting for the rapprochement. Despite the joint efforts of the two groups, Bailly was re-elected as mayor with an overwhelming majority of the votes, 12,500 out of a possible 14,000. As Desmoulins reported, the radicals in the Communal Assembly, Brissot, Danton, Carra and Fauchet, had been forgotten by ungrateful Parisians. Less than a year later when Danton had been elected to the Department of Paris, he added: 'how could the electors of Paris have forgotten MM Manuel and Brissot'.[39]

SOCIETIES AND THE PRESS

Between 1789 and 1791, a number of extra-parliamentary power bases emerged. These included the Jacobins, and the more popular societies, such as the Cordeliers and Cercle Social. Each of these organizations stressed its own self-importance.

The Jacobins, dominated until the spring of 1791 by the mainstream left, was a rather exclusive club, originally for deputies only, the membership of which was expensive. Members saw themselves as the most important club – for example, they refused to participate in the central committee of the popular societies – and they had contacts with local Jacobin clubs all over France.

Although the radicals tended to be supportive of the Jacobin club – Brissot referred to Jacobin members as 'our brothers the Jacobins' – they focused their attention on other organizations dominated by non-deputies, such as the popular societies. In a letter to Desmoulins, Robespierre praised the 'illustrious Jacobins', naming exclusively centre-left deputies: Barnave, Lameth, Duport, and d'Aiguillon. Brissot, however, criticized the exclusiveness of the Jacobins in the sense that the club kept out passive citizens.[40]

Marat, who had plenty of praise for individual Jacobin members, was less laudatory about the club in general. He was particularly critical of the club's leniency towards the more conservative members, and its tendency to be all talk and no action.[41] Marat conceived his own plan for a popular society, which would be called 'Club of Avengers of the Law'. It was intended to be composed of twenty-five people and 'associates' consisting of 'honest citizens'. Members would be very carefully chosen. Not only would they need to show 'proof of their authentic public virtue'; they would also be required to be 'wise and eloquent'. They would be defenders of public and individual liberties. No one except the king would escape their surveillance. Although the 'society of avengers' never saw the light of day, all patriot writers were associated with Marat's crusade.[42]

Desmoulins, in response to a speech by the club member Laclos at the Jacobins, in which the latter accused the Cercle Social of attempting 'to divide France into two sects', wrote that the Cercle Social 'preached the same doctrine as the Jacobins'. He pointed out that the only difference between the two clubs was that the Jacobins had a higher admission fee.[43] Up until the period preceding the king's flight to Varennes in June 1791 (see p. 39), the debates in the Jacobin club tended to be dominated by moderate deputies, with the radical non-deputies following the club's debates, but not always participating in them. Although a good number of them were members – the names of Carra, Gorsas, Fabre, Collot, Louvet, Billaud, Mercier, Robert, Manuel, Desmoulins, and Garran Coulon appear on the incomplete membership list of 21 December 1790 – most were not actively engaged in the debates and committees until the king's flight which resulted in the Feuillant-Jacobin schism, or the division of the Jacobin Club into two parts. As Lucile Desmoulins recounted, 'During this time [meaning Varennes], Camille, with all the other patriots, was always at the Jacobins.'[44] The radicals meanwhile seemed to be preoccupied with the more popular societies.

This does not mean the radicals did not take a stance on issues confronting the Jacobins. The mutiny at Nancy in August 1790 of three regiments of the French army was an issue of major concern to them and it caused an important rift in the Jacobin club between the more moderate deputies led by Lameth and his followers, Barnave, Duport etc., who at this time dominated the club, and the radical non-deputies led by Collot, Carra and Desmoulins. This mutiny, caused by low wages and poor treatment of the soldiers by their aristocratic officers, resulted in severe penalties inflicted on many soldiers by General Bouillé; Lafayette supported his actions. The Lameths and Barnave urged obedience to the officers in the club's circular of 10 September.[45] The radicals, in most cases, took the side of the mutinous soldiers. Desmoulins denounced Lafayette as 'liberty's most dangerous enemy'. Marat wrote of a counter-revolution begun by Bouillé.[46] Collot wrote two reports in defence of the imprisoned soldiers, demanding their rehabilitation, while Billaud wrote against both Bouillé and Lafayette.[47] Carra, one of the most enthusiastic partisans of the mutinous soldiers, was shouted down by the Jacobin right wing. Danton also defended the soldiers at the Jacobins. Brissot and Gorsas were less hostile to Lafayette: Brissot for personal reasons, as he thought that Lafayette would provide him with funds to keep his newspaper going. Gorsas was more impartial, arguing that the incident served as a pretext for new attacks against General Bouillé, but he admitted that the general did look very bad. He felt that Prudhomme and Desmoulins had gone overboard in their newspaper attacks.[48] The reaction to Lafayette and

Bouillé's demand for obedience had produced the first major division in the Jacobins, between those who would later form the Feuillants, and the more radical Jacobins. Although Brissot and Gorsas were more conciliatory towards Lafayette in their journals, neither actively participated in the club's debates and there was no hostility between the radicals at this stage.

Many of the Parisian radicals formed numerous societies to further their causes during the 1789 to 1791 period. Brissot's friend, Lanthenas, created a society whose purpose was to force the National Assembly to abolish primogeniture. Besides Lanthenas, the members of this society were Brissot, Mercier, Carra, Bosc, Bancal, Desmoulins, Sergent, Delacroix, and Bonneville. Pétion, if not a member, was heavily involved in bringing this matter to the attention of the Assembly. The society, formed in July 1790, was called the 'Society of Friends of Union and Equality in families'.[49] Lanthenas had already published a book on this topic, *Inconvéniens du droit d'aînesse*, which was advertised by Brissot and Desmoulins. A decree of 15 March 1790 had abolished primogeniture in the case of the nobility, assuming that goods included land. Lanthenas' speech in favour of equality of inheritance was read by 28 Parisian sections. In addition, he wrote to the Jacobins, urging them to support his motion.[50]

Desmoulins was an enthusiastic supporter of the cause. He praised Lanthenas' work and the address to the society in which he 'vigorously denounced all of the disadvantages in the inequality of distribution'.[51] The address to which Desmoulins was referring was read to the National Assembly by Pétion who was supplied by Lanthenas with the substance of his speech. Pétion was able to acquire more than 4,000 signatures to a petition which was sent to the Constitution Committee with the address for discussion.[52] Three months after he read this speech on behalf of the society, their goal was achieved and the society was subsequently dissolved.

Brissot and other radicals such as Lanthenas, Pétion, Buzot and Robespierre attended meetings at Madame Roland's, usually after sessions at the Constituent Assembly where they discussed matters of policy. She explained how Brissot was responsible for these meetings and she drew attention to the importance of living close at hand, as well as sharing similar views:

> Born in Chartres and a school friend of Pétion, Brissot became increasingly involved with him during the Constituent Assembly, where many times, his insight and work helped his friend . . . He even arranged that they would meet at my house four times a week during the evenings, as I was sedentary, well-lodged and my apartment was not out of the way for those who made up the little committee . . . There were only a few unshakeable men who dared fight for their beliefs, and to that end, it almost reduced itself to Buzot, Pétion and Robespierre.[53]

The members of this group in general, and Lanthenas, Roland and Robert in particular, were especially interested in the creation and propagation of popular

Madame Roland. (Bibliothèque nationale de France)

An engraving of Jean Marie Roland, by Bonneville. (Newberry Library, Chicago, Illinois)

societies. Lanthenas had conceived of a vast plan of popular societies to be established throughout France under the patronage of the Jacobins in Paris. He had written to them for assistance explaining the sort of society he was keen to establish. The activities of these societies were intended to parallel those of the Cordeliers of Paris. Robert was the head of the central committee of popular societies in Paris. It was composed of four members from each of the clubs, except for the Jacobins which refused to send members.

These societies, which were to meet in small groups, would constitute a focal point where commissioners would run 'correspondence and communication centres'. They would meet every two weeks where they were to 'diffuse instruction and brotherhood'. Roland shed further light on the nature of these planned societies, urging Lanthenas to form a society of 'instructors of the people'. Announcements of meetings would be publicized in the popular newspapers, and a suitable building would be found for meetings.[54]

Robespierre was also engaged in this plan for popular societies. He lost two manuscripts, most likely on his way home from one of the group's meetings at Madame Roland's. One contained Lanthenas' project for the fraternal societies, while the other concerned the freedom of the press.[55] Brissot considered the loss of the manuscript significant enough to put a notice about it in his newspaper which read: 'Lost manuscript. M. Robespierre left in a cab he had taken at 9.30 p.m. Thursday night on the quai des Augustins, a manuscript on the indefinite liberty of the press and on popular societies. He beseeches all good citizens who would have heard about this to help him find it.' The previous day, Robespierre had read a long speech supporting the freedom of the press at the Jacobins in which he declared that it should be 'indeterminate and complete or it does not exist at all'.[56] It is possible that Lanthenas was helping Robespierre with the writing of his speeches in supplying him with information on the subjects of the freedom of the press and popular societies. The evidence suggests that they were working in close cooperation.

The Cordeliers club, with very low membership fees, was both more working class and more militant than the Jacobins. The Cordeliers district, and later club, was one of the two centres of radicalism which emerged in Paris during this phase of the French Revolution, while the other was the Cercle Social. What developed were two separate and corporate identities whose only difference seemed to be geographical, with the Cercle Social centring its activities in the circus building located on the Palais Royal gardens on the right bank of the Seine, while the Cordeliers had its headquarters in the area between the Sorbonne and the Jardin du Luxembourg on the left bank. The Cordeliers district was controlled by Danton, who had created this political organization, complete with its own propaganda centre of radical journalists which included François and Louise de Kéralio, Robert, Desmoulins and Prudhomme. Many of the men introduced in the previous chapter formed the nucleus of the Cordeliers district, and later the club. These included Fabre, Collot, Manuel and Billaud. Fabre was chief editor of Prudhomme's *Révolutions de Paris* after

Loustallot's death in 1790. He was secretary of the Cordeliers district from 11 December 1789, and he lived in the neighbourhood. He was made president of the Cordelier club in February 1790. Fabre and Collot combined writing with revolutionary activism. It could be argued that they used the revolutionary stage to launch their political careers. By 1791, both had successes with their plays, Fabre with his *Philinte de Molière ou la suite du Misanthrope* and Collot with *Le Procès de Socrates: ou le régime des anciens temps* among others. Collot used revolutionary events and themes, such as the anniversary of the storming of the Bastille, *La Famille Patriote ou la Fête de la Fédération* (1790), and equality, *L'inconnu* (1789), as subject material for his plays.[57] When Fabre's *Philinte de Molière* was printed in 1791, he wrote in a preface that his purpose in changing Molière's play was to support 'the people', and to attack the aristocracy.[58] Billaud had known Danton before 1789 as his some-time secretary, but the others met after the revolution had begun. Billaud neglected his legal career from the spring of 1789 when he began writing pamphlets, such as *Le peintre politique ou Turif des opérations actuelles*, published anonymously in November. In it, he disapproved of the suspensive veto. This pamphlet gained him admission to the Jacobins, but he did not take an active part in the debates until Varennes. Instead, he focused his energy on the Cordeliers. Manuel was made an inspector of the book trade on Bastille Day. He was hailed as a defender of press freedom by Brissot when he published his *Bastille Dévoilée*.[59]

Similarly, the abbé Fauchet and his journalist friend, Bonneville, set up a similar establishment of their own, which they called the Cercle Social. During the summer of 1790 after the reorganization of the Paris Commune with the elimination of the districts and their replacement with the sections, and when the Cordeliers transformed themselves into a club, the Cercle Social also restructured itself into a much larger group than it had been previously, and now called itself the 'Confederation of the Friends of the Truth'. It viewed itself as a federation of all clubs with Paris acting as a 'weekly rendezvous of all clubs, societies and committees'.[60] The members of the Cercle Social, tended in the main to live on the right bank in the same quarter as the Palais Royal, while the vast majority of the Cordeliers lived close to the rue du Théâtre Français where the Cordeliers held their meetings. In common with the Cordeliers, the Cercle Social had lower membership dues than the Jacobins.

Radical Parisians were often associated with both clubs. Desmoulins was both a Cordelier and Cercle Social member and secretary. In a discussion of newspapers, Desmoulins defended Bonneville as editor of his newspaper from rumours circulating that it was an aristocratic publication. He supported the Cercle Social a second time when it was attacked by Laclos at the Jacobins early in December 1790. Laclos regarded the Cercle Social as a sort of rival club to the Jacobins and contended that it was the intention of the Cercle Social directory to break up the Jacobin club. Against this accusation, Desmoulins protested to the contrary.[61] During the spring of 1791, his newspaper was published by the Cercle Social's printing press. Collot also published with it; his *Almanach du Père Gérard* was published in English in London by the Cercle Social, which also had a press there, while the French version was sold at the office of the *Patriote Français*.

Although the names of Gorsas and Carra do not appear on the membership list complied by Gary Kates, their newspapers provide ample evidence to demonstrate that they were full of praise for Fauchet and his club. Carra praised both Fauchet's speech of 27 September 1789 at Notre Dame concerning the blessing of the flags of the Parisian National Guard, and his speech of 22 December demanding that Paris be made a department. He also gave Fauchet's book, *De la Religion Nationale* a favourable review. In a supplement to his newspaper, he printed a review of and an extract from the *Bouche de Fer*, the club's main organ.[62] Gorsas called Fauchet 'a worthy citizen',

ALMANACH
DU
PÈRE GERARD.

PREMIER ENTRETIEN.

DE LA CONSTITUTION.

LE PÈRE GERARD *ne cessoit de dire à ceux qui l'entouroient* : O la bonne constitution, que la constitution françoise ! elle assure notre bonheur et celui de nos enfans.

UN PAYSAN, *approchant en se grattant l'oreille, lui dit* : Père Gerard, je ne suis pas en gêne de savoir ce que c'est que la chose que vous nommez CONSTITUTION. Nous l'aimons bien la chose ; mais ce mot-là m'embarrasse. Pourquoi

B 3

Almanach du Père Gérard, by Jean-Marie Collot d'Herbois. (Thomas Fisher Rare Book Library, University of Toronto)

and praised the club's first meeting, commenting, 'The institution of the Cercle Social bases itself on complete liberty . . .'.[63] Carra frequently advertised the club's meetings, and like Gorsas, gave Fauchet a strong endorsement.[64]

The radical press served as both an informal political club and a mutual support network for radical politicians, most of whom were not deputies. Desmoulins' journal, begun in November 1789, identified who was and who was not a part of this club. There are frequent references to 'patriots' and to the 'glorious apostolate', composed of Brissot, Clavière, Carra, and Kersaint. Robespierre is described as 'incorruptible' and 'one cannot speak of Robespierre without Pétion . . . Carra is our tocsin for the exterior, Marat, for the interior. Gorsas maintains the correspondence between the 83 departments.'[65] Brissot, Pétion, Robespierre and Desmoulins were described as 'the Jacobins of the Jacobins'.[66] The names of the witnesses on the marriage register at Desmoulins' wedding on 29 September 1790 clearly indicate who were his closest companions: Pétion, Robespierre, Mercier and Brissot.[67]

Other journalists sought Brissot's advice when they were launching their newspapers. Kéralio wrote to Brissot requesting an announcement of her new journal, the *Mercure National*. She approached Brissot because she knew his paper was already established, and she thought a few supportive words from him would give her own paper a boost. Brissot did not disappoint her. On 21 August, Brissot, in reply to her request, wrote: 'Mlle Kéralio has just published the first number of her journal. It breathes pure patriotism and contains the most rigid and sound political principles.' He continued to support Kéralio's press throughout this period, by praising it with remarks such as the following: 'The best principles are developed in this democratic Journal', and by printing various extracts from it in the *Patriote Français*. Brissot went even further than providing collegial support for their journal: he lent the couple money a number of times.[68]

Further evidence for cooperation amongst this radical band of journalists may be found in the support Brissot lent to Marat. Marat received free advertisement for a newspaper he was about to launch. On 18 September, Brissot announced Marat's new journal, entitled *Le Publiciste Parisien, L'Ami du Peuple*. In his advertisement, Brissot praised his old friend and urged his readers to read the first five editions of Marat's newspaper.[69]

Brissot's newspaper was not unique in isolating certain individuals and groups, such as the Jacobins, for praise. Kéralio and Robert behaved in a similar manner. They singled out Pétion for special attention. Their journals were overflowing with praise for him. Everything he wrote from speeches to books was reviewed in glowing terms. When Pétion's *Avis au Français* was reissued in 1789, Robert proclaimed: 'M. Pétion de Villeneuve constructed in the most brilliant manner the rights of man.' This is almost the same language spoken by Carra: 'There are few writers who are so eloquent and who write with as much originality and precision as him.' Kéralio, reviewing Pétion's speech on the abolition of the slave trade, described Pétion as 'one of the supporters of French liberties, one of the unshakeable bulwarks of the constitution'.[70]

Jérôme Pétion, deputy from Chartres to the National Assembly in 1789 and elected president of the Criminal Tribunal of the Department of Paris in 1790, by Levanchez. (Musée Carnavalet)

(49)

RÉVOLUTIONS
DE FRANCE
ET DE BRABANT.
Nº. 15.

FRANCE.

Les journalistes peuvent dire aujourd'hui à l'Assemblée nationale, ce que Boileau disoit autrefois à Louis XIV :

Grand roi, cesse de vaincre, ou je cesse d'écrire.

En parcourant cette multitude de décrets qui ont signalé la présidence de l'évêque d'Autun, je sens que trop d'abondance appauvrit la matière. Qui n'a pas admiré la sagesse de l'Assemblée nationale, d'avoir établi des différences entre les religieux & les religieuses, entre la jeunesse & la caducité ; & sa justice, d'avoir supprimé la différence entre les religieux de la dernière réforme & ceux de l'ancienne, les ci-devant jésuites, licenciés avec une cartouche jaune, & sans avoir eu une retraite

Nº 15.   A

A page from Camille Desmoulins's journal, *Révolutions de France et de Brabant*, no. 15, 8 March 1790. This article details decrees passed by the National Assembly concerned with religion. (Thomas Fisher Rare Book Library, University of Toronto)

'Le Gourmand' – Louis dining while being arrested at Varennes, 21 June 1791. (Bibliothèque nationale de France)

THE VARENNES CRISIS

The political situation in Paris altered considerably in the spring of 1791. Inflation combined with the abolition of guilds resulted in a good deal of agitation by the workers over wages.[71] On this issue, the reaction of the left was to back the employers, in the name of public order. This time of economic crisis climaxed in the Varennes crisis and the Champ de Mars petitioning.

It was during this period, May 1791, that the Cercle Social joined forces with the Cordeliers to contest various pieces of legislation passed by the Assembly. The Constituent Assembly was nearing the end of its session and the leaders of the left seemed to think that the time had come to offer some concessions to the king, in the hope that he would agree to play a constructive part in making the new constitution work. The new conservative legislation included the decree of 10 May which banned collective petitioning and introduced the 'silver mark', or a fairly steep tax qualification to participate in politics. Both decrees were considered an attempt to exclude the people from the political process. In protest at the voting qualifications, petitions were drafted and presented to the Assembly and posted on the streets of Paris. The Cercle Social and Cordeliers dedicated several meetings to this matter.[72]

Partnership between the two clubs reached its height during the Varennes crisis. This was true equally in terms of the stance they took on the king's flight and the concerted activities they organized. As stressed above, prior to June 1791, not even the radicals desired a republic. All were content with a very limited role for the king. It was the king's aborted attempt to flee which changed attitudes towards the role of the monarchy.

The initial response of the radicals to Louis' flight was to proclaim him a traitor to the nation. A petition written by the Cordeliers demanding a republic was first printed by Bonneville. Gorsas and Desmoulins also published the petition in their journals. In addition, upon hearing the news of the king's flight, Bonneville published an article entitled, 'No More Kings'. Gorsas denounced the Assembly's decree which declared that Louis XVI should not be tried. Its decision, in his words, was an 'indecent conclusion' for not designating Louis' act as 'criminal'. Radical journalists including Brissot, Desmoulins and Carra echoed the statement of Gorsas.[73] When Billaud proposed a republican government at the Jacobin session on 1 July, he was expelled from the club. He went immediately to the Cordeliers where he was embraced by Danton. This speech was soon published as a pamphlet, *L'Acéphocratie*. Billaud was later readmitted to the club during the 'scrutin épuratoire', run by the radicals after the Varennes crisis.[74]

Buzot, Pétion and Robespierre were the only deputies to join the group of republicans which met at Pétion's immediately after the king's flight. Other participants were Clavière, Dumont, Madame Roland, Condorcet, Thomas Paine, Lanthenas, Bonneville and Duchâtelet (Condorcet's friend). They met to discuss starting up a republican newspaper, *Le Républicain*. The only deputies to advocate a king's trial were those on the extreme left, especially Pétion and Robespierre. Pétion's

The arrest of Louis at Varennes, 22 June 1791. (Bibliothèque nationale de France)

The massacre of petitioners by the National Guard at the Champs de Mars, July 1791, by Louis Laffitte. (Musée Carnavalet)

first speech to the Jacobins on 8 July was one of the most radical.[75] In short, in the period immediately following Varennes, the radicals responded in like fashion. They no longer recognized Louis as their king; they demanded his trial and replacement.

This attitude contrasted conspicuously with that of the deputies with the exception of those on the extreme left. When the king's flight was first reported to the Assembly, the president announced that he had been 'abducted' and Lafayette spoke of a 'criminal attempt' against the king; in other words, the 'official' line was adopted from the start. The first move made by the Assembly was to dispatch the National Guard to arrest those who had 'kidnapped' the king. Louis' flight was thus qualified as an abduction, and the Assembly refused to attribute responsibility for the flight of Louis, and made him look like an innocent victim. Unlike Brissot and other radicals, the deputies in the Assembly declared only those who were responsible for the king's abduction and not the king himself, to be traitors. Only those deputies of the extreme left, Buzot, Pétion, Robespierre and Grégoire stood out in their opposition to the Assembly's decree. Their response can be starkly contrasted with that of Barère, which was moderate in comparison. Although he voted for the king's suspension until he signed the constitution, unlike Pétion he did not demand his trial.[76]

On 15 July, the Cordeliers joined the members of the Cercle Social and other popular societies at a huge gathering, which numbered between 3,000 and 8,000 at the Palais Royal gardens. This was the last meeting of the Cercle Social, which was closed during the repression that followed the Champs de Mars massacre. Discussions at the meeting centred round the best means of deposing the king. After a few hours of turbulent rhetoric, a resolution was passed by the vast majority to reprimand the Assembly for deciding against debating the question of Louis' guilt. As soon as the meeting ended, many Cordelier and Cercle Social members went to the Jacobins. A spokesman informed the Jacobins that their plan was to go to the Champ de Mars the next day to sign a petition against the reinstatement of the king. He invited the Jacobins to join this group.

The Jacobin club, which had become increasingly democratic and radical with the influx of non-deputy radical members, many of whom were members of the Cordeliers and Cercle Social, was very divided over this issue. The radical deputies from the Assembly sympathized with the Cordelier–Cercle Social alliance, while the more conservative members such as Barnave and Barère favoured a reinstatement of the king as soon as the constitution had been completed. The Jacobins did agree to designate a committee to draft a petition for the intended demonstration the next day. A committee of Jacobin officers was appointed for this purpose: Brissot, Danton, Sergent, Lanthenas, Ducancel and perhaps Laclos. Controversy continues over whether or not Laclos was a member of the drafting committee. A problem arises from the final clause in the petition which stated that the king would be replaced by 'constitutional means', which meant that the duc d'Orléans would replace Louis XVI as a regent for Louis XVII. Since the original copy of the petition has been lost, historians have no means of ascertaining the truth concerning the author of the clause.[77] What is important is that the replacement of the king by a regent was only one of many possibilities which had been suggested by members of the Jacobin club. Danton advocated a council, while Carra openly proposed a regent, though not necessarily an Orléans regency. Even Robespierre was not entirely committed to the idea of a republic as he stated that 'a nation can be free with a monarch'. For this remark he was criticized in the *Révolutions de Paris* which, like the *Bouche de Fer*, had openly advocated a republic.[78]

The Cercle Social and Cordeliers opposed the petition because of the controversial phrase and refused to sign it. A new petition was drafted by Bonneville and Robert. Their petition replaced the words 'by constitutional means' with 'nor any other', meaning they did not want a monarch of any sort. It was this petition which was read at the gathering on 17 July at the Champ de Mars.[79] At this gathering, the unarmed crowd was fired upon by Lafayette and the National Guards. About fifty people were killed, and this incident became known as the Champ de Mars 'Massacre'.

While the Cercle Social–Cordelier alliance was preoccupied with petitioning, the Jacobin club had divided into two separate factions, with a minority of members remaining in the original club. The Feuillant secession took place on 16 July, when the moderate deputies heard about the petitioning going on in the Jacobin club. Apparently a radical petition falsely attributed to the Jacobins was intentionally circulated to mislead deputies. This led the triumvirate, Barnave, Duport and Lameth, and approximately 300 others, all deputies, to depart to a Feuillant monastery located close to the Assembly and to form, '*la société des amis de la constitution, séante aux Feuillants*'. There were three sorts of deputies who became Feuillants: those who believed the Jacobins had become too radical and did not like the club's growing affiliation with more democratic societies such as the Cercle Social and the Cordeliers; conservatives who wanted to reinstate the king and ensure the new regime; and finally, deputies who had been misled by rumours perpetrated by radicals that the club was planning to exert 'insurrectionary pressure' on the Assembly. The latter group consisted of less than 100 men.[80]

Robespierre and Pétion played the most significant roles in keeping the original club from disappearing. Pétion's part has been underestimated by historians. It was he who took the lead at this crucial moment in the club's history. He regretted the schism in the club on 17 July; however, he asserted that one of the reasons why many deputies had fled to a new club called the 'Feuillants' was that they had lost their influence in the Jacobins and the formation of a new club was their method of recovering lost power. The Feuillants, Pétion exclaimed, had complained about 'suspect men being introduced in the society' and that the society had lost its original goal which was to protect the laws made by the Assembly. Instead they declared 'it attacks and destroys them'.[81] The reflections in the *Journal de la Révolution* confirm Pétion's suppositions. It explained that before Varennes, some members of the Constituent Assembly had demanded the reform of the society and the expulsion of 'seditious elements'. They threatened to leave the society if they did not obtain their reform. Their intention was to replace the Jacobins as the most powerful club, and to this end they were preparing an address to be sent to all affiliated societies.[82] Pétion was infuriated at this attempt to take over the leadership of the society.

There is no evidence that even the most radical deputies such as Pétion and Robespierre, who were the heroes of the Parisian radicals, were members of either radical club, the Cercle Social or the Cordeliers, nor were they actively contributing articles to newspapers or editing them. Of the deputies, Barère showed himself to be the least radical, and the one who changed his allegiances the most often. Pétion, Buzot and Robespierre had never been members of the Cercle Social or the Feuillants, whereas Barère had been a member of both. He had deserted the Jacobins when it looked as though they were on the verge of collapse. Unlike Pétion and Robespierre, he was not prepared to put his principles on the line when things got difficult. Barère's desire to be a winner kept him from that.

PROVINCIAL REVOLUTIONARIES

The response to the new circumstances of 1789 by the minority of radical protagonists who remained in the provinces was very similar to those in Paris: most enrolled in the National Guard, they joined or even formed their local Jacobin societies, and became involved in municipal politics. In addition, like their Parisian counterparts, some edited journals. Barbaroux and Couthon fit this pattern to the letter. Barbaroux had enrolled in the National Guard of Marseilles, was a founder and secretary of the Jacobins of Marseilles in 1790, and was also one of the editors of the club's newspaper, *L'Observateur*, although he did not found it, as he claimed. He remained one of the club's leading members until he went to Paris in 1792. This club was among the first to seek close association with the Jacobins of Paris. It subscribed to the mother society's newspaper and, generally speaking, sided with the radicals on important issues. In addition, the Marseilles Jacobins were closely associated with the new municipality. Despite his youth, Barbaroux became the municipality's secretary on 2 September 1790, and in effect, one of its most important administrators. He was only twenty-three at the time. Saint-Just, the same age as Barbaroux, who had been successfully elected to the chairmanship of a local assembly to choose a justice of the peace, was forced to resign ostensibly on the grounds of his age. The real reason was that the local politicians wanted another man for the job.[83]

The Jacobins of Marseilles responded very much like the radicals to Louis' flight. News of it reached the city on 25 June. The club became openly republican, demanding the removal of the king from his throne. It staunchly defended the most radical politicians in Paris, and particularly Robespierre.

Although not a National Guardsman, Couthon took part in municipal and regional politics after he failed to be elected a deputy to the Estates-General. He had been an elector for his home parish of Orcet, and for reasons unknown he was not elected a deputy. He was a member of the permanent committee of Clermont after the municipal revolutions which took place during the summer of 1789. On 24 January 1790, he was elected to the municipal assembly of Clermont. While a member of the assembly's general council, Couthon voted in favour of selling off the great religious chapter of Clermont. The final local office he held was president of the District Tribunal of Clermont.[84]

Like the radicals in Paris and Barbaroux of Marseilles, Couthon was converted to republicanism by the Varennes crisis. He had been a member of the Jacobins of Clermont since its foundation in March 1790. He helped draft a petition demanding the dethronement of the king. It was read at the Paris club on 24 June and published by Brissot in his newspaper.[85]

Saint-Just embraced the revolution with zeal, rising to the position of a commanding officer in the National Guard and becoming active in municipal politics. He was too young and lacked a property qualification to hold a local office. In 1789, he made a visit to Paris in search of a publisher for his epic poem, *Organt*. While there, he sat in on National Assembly and Jacobin sessions and met Desmoulins. He managed to get his poem published, and Desmoulins gave it brief mention in his newspaper. He wrote a flattering letter to Robespierre on 19 August 1790, in which he praised Robespierre, saying that he knew him 'as one knows God, by miracles'.[86]

Guadet helped draft the *cahiers* of the Third Estate of Saint-Emilion. He had tried to get elected as a deputy, but failed because of his youth. He therefore became involved in local politics and was nominated an administrator of the department in 1790.

Vergniaud and Gensonné greeted the revolution with equal enthusiasm. Both were captains of local National Guard regiments. Vergniaud became president of the electoral assembly of the district of Bordeaux, and was later elected to the general council of the department, while Gensonné was an administrator of the Commune of Bordeaux.

The Jacobin club of Bordeaux was founded on 16 April 1790 by former *Musée* members Vergniaud, Ducos and Fonfrède, all future Bordeaux deputies. They had resigned from the *Musée* once the revolution began because of the society's conservatism. Several other former *Musée* members soon joined the club, such as Guadet, who was voted vice-president on 19 May, and president a month later. Gensonné, while president, wrote the society's statutes and Guadet prepared an address informing the National Assembly of the club's formation, and its goals. Its stated purpose was 'the popularization of the decrees passed by the National Assembly'. Vergniaud, who was a secretary, prepared a similar letter for the municipalities.[87]

Fouché was in Arras until the end of 1790 when he was transferred to Nantes where he took up the post of college principal. He remained at the Collège de Nantes until the Oratorians' closure in 1792. While still at Arras, he had recommended that a delegation from the college be sent to Paris to support the deputies of the Third Estate. He remained a close friend of Robespierre while he was in Arras, lending him money for his trip to Versailles upon election to the Estates-General. He was also a founding member of the Arras Jacobin club and the journal, *Bulletin des Patriots de l'Oratoire*. Once settled in Nantes, he became a member and early president, 17 February 1791, of the local Jacobins.[88]

It is clear that 1789, and all the changes which came with that year, offered new opportunities for these men, and they were anxious to seize them. There was little difference between those who had been successful before 1789 and those who had not, in terms of their attitude towards the revolution. Several of the men who were not already in Paris were attracted there by the revolutionary fervour. They immediately immersed themselves in revolutionary activity beside those who had been there since the late 1780s. Many collaborated on newspapers and joined revolutionary societies and clubs. A good number lived in the same neighbourhood, that of the Cordeliers district, and later became members of the club. Although most were Jacobins, their main interests were focused on more radical clubs until Varennes, when they took over the leadership of the society.

The major divide at this stage appears to be between those who were deputies and those who were not. Between 1789 and the spring of 1791, conflicts did arise. They often depended upon an individual's power base, whether it was the Paris Commune, the Cordeliers district and later club, the Jacobins, or the Constituent Assembly. What is crucial here is that these conflicts were resolved when the problem was no longer relevant, as in the case of the districts and the municipal assembly, which clashed over political influence. When the districts were abolished and the Communal Assembly was renewed, the conflict disappeared.

The greatest degree of cooperation among the radicals occurred during the Varennes crisis. It also produced the first major division within the Jacobin club, resulting in the formation of a new club, the Feuillants, composed of conservative members, all of whom were deputies. The result was a new Jacobin club, now dominated by radicals.

The men who remained in the provinces were no less enthusiastic about the changes in circumstances which occurred in 1789. Although they did not renounce previous careers – the majority were still practising law – they involved themselves in revolutionary activities such as the local Jacobin clubs, newspapers, the National Guard and local politics. They shared many of the same goals and ideas held by the Parisian radicals even if they only knew them by reputation. Some had already made contacts with Parisian radicals either through flattering letters, or by visits to the capital. The provincial politicians made reputations for themselves at the local level which they hoped would enhance their chances of being elected to the Legislative Assembly of 1791.

RADICALS DURING THE LEGISLATIVE ASSEMBLY

The political culture of the French Revolution changed substantially during the Legislative Assembly term which ran from 1 October 1791 to 20 September 1792. The radicals gained political education and experience, regardless of whether or not they were elected to this Assembly, which prepared them for the National Convention, to which all were elected deputies the following year. The character and composition of the Legislative Assembly were entirely different from its predecessor. Gone were the clerics and nobles who had composed about one-half of the deputies elected in 1789. The self-denying ordinance of 1789 passed by the Constituents made Pétion, Robespierre, Buzot and Barère ineligible for election to its successor. All 745 deputies to the Legislative Assembly were financially comfortable, having been elected while the *marc d'argent* requirement was still in force. Few, however, owed their wealth to trade or industry. Most were lawyers. Over two-thirds came from local government or were magistrates or judges in the new courts.

How did the radicals fare in the elections to this Assembly? For many of the men from the provinces who had been active in municipal politics, this Assembly offered these unknown provincials the national stage for the first time. This was true for the three deputies from the Gironde, Vergniaud, Guadet and Gensonné, and for Couthon, representing the department of the Puy-de-Dôme. Brissot, Condorcet and Garran Coulon, all of whom had been active in Parisian municipal politics, were successfully elected deputies from Paris. Danton was an elector for Paris, chosen by the section of Théâtre-Français, but he never received more than forty votes in the numerous ballots. Those who were not deputies during the months between October 1791 and September 1792, but were in Paris, played even more significant political roles in their extra-parliamentary activities in clubs and journalism than they had during the first two years of the revolution. Indeed, the most passionate debates of this period, over whether or not France should launch a limited war, took place not in the Assembly, but at the Jacobin club and in the various radical newspapers. During this year, the Parisian radicals became prominent Jacobins, and their names became recognizable throughout France. Some, such as Pétion, Danton and Manuel, were active in municipal politics. Saint-Just, Fouché and Barbaroux remained in the provinces, although Barbaroux came to the capital in February 1792 on behalf of the municipality of Marseilles. Both Barère and Buzot returned to their native cities of Tarbes and Evreux at the end of the Constituent Assembly.

This chapter will explore the political behaviour and activities of these men through an examination of their responses to the growing problems which faced France during this year, the most significant being the arguments for and against a decision to launch a foreign war. It will seek to investigate the various factions which developed and provide reasons why they did.

PARIS: ISSUES AND RADICAL RESPONSES

Refractory Clergy and Emigrés

Two major issues confronted the revolutionaries at the opening of the Legislative Assembly. These were the problems posed by the refractory clergy and the *émigrés*. The refractory clergy were those priests who had refused to take the oath to the Civil Constitution of the Clergy. In areas of widespread oath refusal, such as Brittany, the departments often introduced their own policy of exiling or imprisoning notorious refractories. Revolutionaries were not confronted merely with a handful of malcontents, but with dangerous popular movements. Before his election to the Legislative Assembly, Gensonné had been commissioned to report on these movements in the departments of the Vendée and Deux-Sèvres. His research in these areas found widespread oath refusal by priests, an overwhelming lack of support for the constitutional priests – only ten to twelve people out of parishes of five to six hundred were taking mass from a constitutional priest – and a real scission between refractories and non-refractories. Clearly, measures needed to be taken to end this religious and political division.[1] The second problem, that of the *émigrés*, who the revolutionaries believed were conspiring with foreign powers, had intensified after the king's flight to Varennes. On 15 October, Louis issued a formal appeal to those who had left to return to help make the constitution work.

In the Assembly, the offensive against refractory priests was dominated by the radicals, or those who sat on the left: Guadet, Gensonné, Vergniaud, Condorcet and Couthon advocated vigorous measures against the refractory priests. Couthon complained of replaced priests who were remaining in their posts. Gensonné blamed the troubles in the provinces entirely on the existence of 'religious quarrels'.[2] Garran Coulon wanted to prevent Lecoz, a non-juring bishop from the department of Ille-et-Vilaine, from speaking in his capacity as a priest.[3] Condorcet demanded 'terrible punishments' for those who would not take the oath.[4] On 29 November, the Assembly decreed that all non-juring priests should take a new civic oath and those who refused should lose their pensions. These 'double refractories' were to be regarded as 'suspects'.

The *émigrés* were believed to be supported by German princes in planning counter-revolutionary activities. Brissot made his first speech on the topic in the Assembly on 20 October. Princes and public functionaries would be distinguished from ordinary citizens, with the former receiving harsher penalties for conspiring with foreign princes if they failed to return.[5] Brissot's emphasis on the leaders, such as the king's brothers, was his tactic to force the king to take a stand for or against the revolution. His speech met with great acclaim, both inside and outside the Assembly. Inside the Assembly, the deputy Chabot demanded that the speech be printed and distributed. Outside the Assembly, the Parisian radicals approved of it. Desmoulins spoke of it as 'superb' and described Brissot's draft of a decree as 'cutting the evil at the root'.[6] Marat, who reproduced parts of Brissot's speech in his newspaper and supported his programme, commented that it was about time his old friend had discovered the problem of the *émigrés*.[7] Collot, speaking at the Jacobins, also approved, proclaiming that 'the resolutions taken by the National Assembly concerning the *émigrés* are those of the entire nation'.[8]

A modified version of Brissot's more radical proposal was passed on 9 November: the decree did not make mention of ordinary citizens, but only referred to princes and public officials. Those *émigrés* who had not returned by 1 January 1792 would be sentenced to death, and their property would be sequestered. Condorcet had opposed the death penalty in his proposed decree.[9]

During the autumn of 1791, the Jacobins were as preoccupied with the political problems of the *émigrés* and refractory clergy as the deputies, and there was undeniable support for the radical line. This is hardly surprising since the debates in the Jacobins were dominated by many of the radicals, some of whom formed the left of the Assembly. Buzot, Bourdon, Robespierre, Lanthenas, Clavière, Brissot, Pétion and Carra were on the Correspondence Committee from 16 July until 7 October when it changed to include Collot, Robespierre, Billaud, and Pétion. Brissot became president on 3 October, Fauchet on 14 October, Condorcet on 2 November and Couthon on 16 November.[10] Brissot was given a vote of thanks for the courage with which he spoke in the Assembly on 21 October.[11] The circular sent from Paris on 16 November clearly reveals the unity between the left of the Assembly and the Jacobins both in terms of principle and personnel: 'The society of Paris, who, by the advantage of its position, by its intimate union with the patriot members of the Assembly which it gathers in its midst, presented the greatest impediment to the perverse plans of the false friends of the constitution.' It demanded that affiliated societies should send, as soon as possible, information about 'seditious priests' and 'troops in garrisons' in the departments. This bulletin was drafted by the Correspondence Committee, at the time composed of a majority of radicals who had been in Paris since at least 1789 and who had fought battles together over previous issues.[12] The circular of 9 December focused on the Jacobins' concern about the king's intentions to veto the Assembly's decree on the non-juring priests.[13]

War or Peace

The problems of *émigrés* and refractory priests soon led to the more pressing issue of whether or not to launch a limited war. Before the war debates took place, there were no serious divisions between the radicals. This was true even in the case of the two men who dominated the debates, Brissot and Robespierre, who did part company over the war. As late as the middle of November, Robespierre was writing friendly letters to Brissot, requesting that he insert one of his articles in Brissot's paper.[14] Brissot, for his part, on 12 December, wrote a complimentary review of Robespierre's address to the Jacobin club's affiliated societies in which he praised Robespierre for 'eloquently refuting dangerous principles'.[15]

The war debates between Robespierre and Brissot thus began on friendly terms with both men conducting themselves in a gentlemanly fashion. Brissot, for example, stated that Robespierre 'likes to render homage to the right and patriotic intentions of those who support a contrary system'. Robespierre, for his part, referred to Brissot as a 'patriotic legislator'.[16] The nature of these arguments also deserves attention. The war issue involved political tactics rather than political principles. There were no hard ideological differences between the pro- and anti-war forces. Moreover, the question was not argued in terms of class. Brissot did not advocate a war because he was concerned about the threat to commercial interests posed by the *émigrés* and foreign powers, as some historians have contended. He did however argue that the war, by defeating the *émigrés*' hopes of counter-revolution, would strengthen the *assignat* (revolutionary currency), that is, he did have an economic argument for war, but this was not a question of defending the interests of a particular class.[17]

Brissot criticized the war minister for spreading rumours against the 'patriots' who were not pro-war. In defending the war, he claimed that France's honour, safety and public credit all rested on it;

war was crucial for the consolidation of the revolution. He thought that France could annihilate her internal enemies by destroying her neighbours. Even more importantly, Brissot argued that war was the only means by which one could know whether or not Louis was on the side of the revolution; war would finally force him to take a stand. If the king was 'of bad faith, he would not delay in betraying [the revolution].' Only war would reveal the true friends and enemies of the constitution.[18]

Robespierre was not initially opposed to war. On 28 November, he recommended threatening not merely the minor German princes, but Léopold of Austria. This would mean involving France in a major war.[19] Nowhere did he explain the reasons for his change in opinion, but it may have been due to the appointment of a new war minister Narbonne, as it was almost immediately after Narbonne's appointment on 7 November that Robespierre spoke out in opposition to the war. Narbonne was friendly with Lafayette and the Feuillants, who were considered to be traitors by Robespierre. His first speech opposing the war, delivered on 12 December, in all probability was inspired by an earlier speech by Billaud, who directed his attack against Narbonne, whom he believed to be responsible for inspiring the war campaign.[20] In his speech of 18 December, a reply to Brissot's, Robespierre did not oppose the idea of going to war, but he did condemn the sort of war which was propagated by the executive.[21]

In essence, Brissot and Robespierre were trying to achieve the same objective: a consolidated revolution with the implementation of the constitution. Where they disagreed was in tactics rather than in policy or principle. Robespierre feared that a war controlled by the king, his ministers and untrustworthy generals like Lafayette, would reverse the accomplishments of the revolution and return France to a state of despotism. Brissot, on the other hand, thought of war as a means to strengthen the revolution; he was also eager to force the king into making a definite decision concerning the revolution. Robespierre felt that since the French were unprepared militarily, it would be politically inexpedient for them to launch a war which they could never hope to win.

When Louis XVI appointed Narbonne as Minister of War, who instigated a vigorous pro-war campaign, Brissot's arguments in favour of war became suspect. Since the ministry desired war, how could the patriots endorse it? Robespierre stated many times that the war policy was in the hands of the executive power and that could only spell disaster for the revolution. With Narbonne conducting war policy and Lafayette in charge of one of the three armies, the revolution was certain to be lost.[22] He became even more suspicious of Brissot when the *Patriote Français* published a eulogy of Lafayette; Brissot defended himself by denying he knew anything about the letter. He claimed it had been inserted by his assistant editor, Girey-Dupré, who had been overseeing daily operations since Brissot had become a deputy. Brissot had not, however, enclosed a note informing readers that this letter did not reflect editorial policy.[23]

The question of whether or not France should go to war did eventually separate the radicals into two opposing factions, with Brissot and Robespierre as their unofficial leaders, but this division did not follow what were to become 'Girondin'/'Mountain' lines, meaning that the 'Girondins' represented the party of war, while the 'Mountain' was the party of peace. The majority of the radicals, presumably swayed by the powerful rhetoric of the pro-war faction, supported Brissot.[24] The only men who came out strongly against the war, and who agreed with Robespierre, were Desmoulins, Marat and Billaud. Some never publicly committed themselves. Although Gorsas was particularly partial to Robespierre, he never attacked the pro-war side. Gorsas described Robespierre's speech to the Jacobins on 11 December as 'full of wisdom and proof that we have

N°. 987.

LE PATRIOTE FRANÇOIS.

Une gazette libre est une sentinelle qui veille sans cesse pour le peuple.

DU LUNDI 23 AVRIL 1792, L'AN 4me DE LA LIBERTÉ.

ASSEMBLÉE NATIONALE.

(PRÉSIDENCE DE M. BIGOT.)

SÉANCE du samedi 21 avril 1792, au soir.

La guerre que nous entreprenons est la guerre du genre humain, contre ses oppresseurs; il appartenoit donc à l'orateur du genre humain de venir le premier féliciter l'assemblée nationale de cette grande démarche. Anacharsis Cloots lui a apporté 12 mille francs pour contribuer aux frais de cette sublime et philosophique croisade, et son livre de la *République universelle*. Ce don étoit assez éloquent; le discours du pétitionnaire ne l'a pas moins été.

Un citoyen présente à l'assemblée une épée d'argent, dont il destine le produit aux frais de la guerre.

Un artisan dépose sur le bureau quatre louis en or, fruits de son industrie.

Ces différens dons, inégaux en valeur, égaux par les sentimens de patriotisme qui les offroient, ont été également applaudis. Ils ont fournis à M. Hérault une idée grande et révolutionnaire, c'est d'en employer le montant à récompenser les soldats qui abandonneront les drapeaux de la tyrannie, pour se ranger sous les enseignes de la liberté. L'assemblée s'empressera sans doute d'accueillir cette proposition, qu'elle a renvoyé à l'examen des comités.

L'humanité a décidé en gémissant la guerre que nous venons de déclarer, l'humanité doit s'occuper à adoucir et à réparer les maux inséparables de toute guerre, mais qui seront plus rares dans celle-ci. L'assemblée a décrété l'établissement et l'organisation d'hôpitaux ambulans à la suite des rassemblemens de troupes.

Une députation du directoire de Seine et Oise, présidée par M. Lebrun, ex-député, a fait l'inconstitutionnelle demande d'un tribunal particulier, pour juger les auteurs des troubles qui ont éclaté dans ce département.

Le comité militaire a présenté un projet de décret pour la formation de six légions, dans lesquelles seroient incorporés les satellites du despotisme qui voudroient devenir les soldats de la liberté. — Ajourné.

M. Garan a proposé de former une légion de volontaires nationaux à cheval. — Renvoyé au comité.

Second trimestre, année 1792.

SÉANCE du dimanche 22 avril 1792.

On a répondu par des argumens sans replique, à ceux qui ont combattu par des sophismes la nécessité de la guerre; aux esprits égoïstes et resserrés qui ne sont pas dignes de croire à la vertu, et qui ne comptent pas sur les effets de l'enthousiasme d'un peuple libre, nous répondrons par des faits. Nous leur présentons le relevé des dons patriotiques qui ont été offerts dans cette séance, et qui ont été accueillis au milieu des plus vifs applaudissemens.

Une citoyenne, mère de sept enfans, et éloignée du lieu de sa résidence de cent cinquante lieues, offre 12 livres en argent, seul numéraire qu'elle ait à sa disposition.

Un citoyen fait à la nation la remise du remboursement de sa lettre de maître; il fait aussi la remise d'indemnités qu'il est en droit de reclamer.

Un ancien fabriquant de chapeaux, envoie dix louis en or, qu'il réservoit pour subvenir à des besoins pressans; il donne la préférence à la patrie.

Un étranger demande à participer aux frais de la guerre. Il donne 13 liv. en argent, et promet 6 liv. par mois.

Des secrétaires commis de plusieurs comités, offrent différentes sommes.

Un négociant de Paris, qui veut être inconnu, envoie 300 liv. en argent, avec promesse de fournir la même somme tous les mois.

Les commis de l'administration de la vente des biens nationaux, établie au Saint-Esprit, prient l'assemblée d'accepter 200 liv. pour les frais de la guerre; ils renouvelleront la même demande tous les ans.

Touchée de cet empressement généreux du riche à sacrifier son superflu, de l'artisan à se priver du fruit de longues épargnes, de la veuve à porter son denier, du pauvre à partager sa subsistance, l'assemblée a voulu aussi faire son don patriotique; elle a adopté, par acclamation, la motion d'un de ses membres, qui a demandé que tous les députés fissent, pendant trois mois, le sacrifice du tiers de leurs indemnités. Espérons que tous les fonctionnaires public se hâteront de suivre cet exemple; espérons que le premier, que le plus riche des fonctionnaires publics, en sera aussi le premier imitateur.

A page from Jacques-Pierre Brissot's journal, *Le Patriote Français*, issue of 23 April 1792 – Legislative Assembly Proceedings, Praise of War declared 20 April 1792. (Thomas Fisher Rare Book Library, University of Toronto) everything to fear in preventing the hostile projects of our enemies'. He continued by agreeing with Robespierre's caution in an attack where 'the dangers for us would be incalculable'. As with Robespierre, he believed the court was behind the war but that its success was doubtful.[25] When the majority of the members of the Jacobin club were pro-war, Gorsas remained steadfast in his position. As far as Brissot was concerned, Gorsas did not oppose him personally: he presented his arguments in an impartial manner and invited the reader to judge for himself.[26] What Gorsas opposed were personal attacks and he admonished the pro-war member Louvet to adhere to the issue when Louvet began personal attacks against Robespierre. This was not, in Gorsas' opinion, the way in which good citizens ought to behave. It was especially damaging for the patriots, as the ministers and aristocrats would use this discord to their advantage. He wrote that while that group were united, the radicals were becoming divided.[27]

While Gorsas presented a very accurate and unbiased account of the arguments on both sides of the war issue, and if he leaned in one direction, it was towards Robespierre, Carra ardently promoted war. In fact, he was making speeches at the Jacobins supporting the war even before Brissot, the so-called leader of the war party. It was Louis' veto of the Assembly's first decree which provoked Carra into his radical stance. On 9 December at the Jacobins, Carra announced that the emperor had written in a letter to Louis XVI that the foreign powers were planning to come to Louis' support. Before Carra heard this news, he proclaimed that Louis had intended to support the National Assembly's decrees against the *émigrés*, but this move by the emperor had caused him to change his mind. He ended the speech by announcing that it would be necessary to begin the attack by way of Liège. Robespierre, in his reply to Carra, felt that it was good to be on the defensive, but that foreign powers intended only to frighten rather than attack them.[28] A debate between Carra and Robespierre continued over the next few sessions, with Robespierre concluding that it would be absurd trying to resolve such a question except in the National Assembly.

In his speeches and articles concerning the war, Carra examined all possible facets of the question. Although he advocated war, he continued to respect Robespierre's opinion. He declared in a speech of 4 January that he agreed with Robespierre about defensive warfare if France could 'do everything at once: correct the vices of our constitution and vanquish our enemies', but the revolutionaries would also have to deal with 'external enemies who were insulting and threatening'. In other words, Carra did not feel France could conquer both internal and external enemies simply by defensive warfare.[29]

Louvet's political career was launched with a pro-war speech. Previously, he had devoted himself to his writings, such as his most recent novel, *Emile de Varmont* (1791), which advocated divorce and the marriage of priests. He presented his speech to the Assembly on behalf of the Lombards section on 25 December 1791. In it, he insulted the nobility, calling them 'vagabonds', and demanded that the princes and other *émigrés* be arrested. Like Brissot, he also demanded an offensive war. This speech was warmly welcomed by the Assembly.[30]

The fears of Robespierre that a war engineered by the court might undo the revolution did not deter Couthon from supporting it. His viewpoint is disclosed in his letters to his constituents. Because the gatherings of the *émigrés* had not disappeared, war was the only route to follow. As with Brissot, he thought that the revolution required a war to consolidate it.[31] His letters were full of praise for the speeches delivered by the pro-war partisans Brissot and Condorcet to the Legislative Assembly. On 3 January, he announced that he was sending copies of Brissot's speech and Condorcet's manifesto to the municipality of Clermont. In this letter, he designated them as 'distinguished patriots'.[32] According to one source, Couthon's reasons for supporting the pro-war faction were at least partly due to ambition. Couthon believed he would rise to power by backing Brissot's popular aggressive policies. Whatever his motivation may have been, Couthon was unwavering in championing the war.[33] Other radicals who supported war included Collot and Manuel. Collot, who was more preoccupied with the freedom of the Château-Vieux regiment which had been condemned to the galleys during the Nancy revolt than with the war debates, supported Dumouriez when he spoke in favour of the war at the Jacobins on 19 March. Manuel, not a frequent speaker at the club, did deliver one speech on the war.[34]

Along with Robespierre, it was Billaud, Desmoulins and Marat who formed the basis of the anti-war faction. As noted above, it may well have been Billaud who convinced Robespierre to adopt this position. Although Billaud rarely spoke at the Jacobins during these months, he never missed a session and it was during the sitting of the Legislative Assembly that he became known throughout the country. He spoke of the war of which he was a partisan, but only in principle on 19 December. He was convinced that France should go to war, but only after the revolutionaries had taken precautions against the court. Desmoulins came to share Robespierre's hesitations about war: his solution was to defend first, and then, if necessary, attack. He contended that attacking was 'playing the game of our adversaries'.[35] Marat, who had originally endorsed war, soon echoed Desmoulins' sentiments in opposing it, arguing that 'our means of defence should be calculated on theirs of attack'.[36] However, a number of Jacobins were non-committal about the war.

Danton, whose unsuccessful attempt to be elected to the Legislative Assembly was supported by Brissot, did not want to commit himself to either side. Although preoccupied with his position as Manuel's assistant in the Paris Commune – Manuel was elected *procureur* when Pétion was elected mayor – he did speak occasionally on the war. He outlined specific conditions which had to be present for the country to go to war: a change in French tactics and a formal charge against the rebel princes and their adherents of the outer Rhine. Danton did want war, but more importantly he thought that keeping watch over the agents of the king, in order not to be fooled by them, was more important.[37] Moreover, unlike Brissot, he considered war to be a last resort rather than a means to save the revolution. Desmoulins later claimed that Danton had ulterior motives in not opposing the war outright. This was a tactic to keep in with Brissot in the hope that he would be appointed to the 'patriot' ministry. A parallel could be drawn here with Couthon and his motives for being pro-war, which may not have been entirely disinterested.[38] Likewise, Fabre did not take sides during the war debates.

Pétion never once voiced his opinion on the war. He was elected to the criminal court on 15 June, with Robespierre's support, and resigned from this post when, on 16 November, he was elected mayor of Paris with 6,728 votes to Lafayette's 3,126.[39] Presumably, the duties of his office kept him too busy to be making speeches at the Jacobins. Always concerned with maintaining personal popularity, Pétion may not have wanted to antagonize either Brissot and the pro-war group and Robespierre's anti-war faction. When he finally did speak there, his concern was first and foremost to keep the Jacobins from splitting apart as they had done only a few months previously with the Feuillant schism during the Varennes crisis. The club had only recently returned to its pre-schism strength.

The influence of the radicals increased steadily in the Paris Jacobins during the winter of 1791–2. This could be partially explained by the revival of the Feuillant club, the breakaway club dating from the time of Varennes, to which about 300 deputies and up to 800 former deputies and men of letters belonged.[40] The Feuillants attracted the more moderate deputies and former deputies, who were still committed to making the constitution of 1791 work and a policy of peace. This can be contrasted with the Jacobins' policy of war. Control of the Correspondence Committee meant virtual monopoly over the club's propaganda and the pro-war group exploited their positions as members of the committee to proselytize the war in writing to provincial societies. They began with a circular dated 17 January 1792, which stated that war was the question occupying the minds of all Jacobins. Arguments on both sides were presented, but the general conclusion was that the necessity of an attack was the result of the opinion of most orators. Although aggressive war 'had been combated by many', wrote the committee, there was no doubt that the message it was attempting to convey was that war was a necessity. It would be 'entirely beneficial to the regime'. The circular listed the 'patriot' newspapers, which included those of Gorsas, Carra and Mercier, and Brissot, as well as the *Chronique de Paris* edited by Condorcet, the *Journal Universel* edited by Audouin, Prudhomme's *Révolutions de Paris*, and the *Chronique du Mois*. The members of the Correspondence Committee who signed this document included Brissot, Chabot, Carra, Desmoulins, Couthon, and Louvet.[41] The fact that this circular was less hawkish than the next one, dated 15 February, was presumably because there were still a few opponents to the war on the committee. The circular of 15 February appears to have been written by those who desired war including Brissot, Carra and Couthon. The publication announced that there was only one solution to France's problem and that was war. The reasons for going to war were summarized as follows: 'We need it to consolidate the constitution and to affirm our national existence. The nation desires it passionately.'[42] At the session of 24 February, Robespierre vehemently denounced the Correspondence Committee. He accused the committee of interpreting the wishes of the society without bothering to consult it. This was made plain by its statement that the Jacobins were in favour of war. Robespierre had not renounced his point of view for a 'party which I regard as the most dangerous for liberty'.[43] The club would not print his version of the circular and he was accused of attempting to disseminate his personal opinion rather than that of the club.[44]

While the Jacobins were in the midst of their quarrel over the war, Barbaroux came to Paris. He arrived in mid-February and remained until the end of August. Barbaroux was there on a mission on behalf of the municipality of Marseilles as secretary of the commune. At the time, the Commune of Marseilles was engaged in a power struggle with the department of the Bouches-du-Rhône. Members of the commune claimed the department was betraying the constitution by not giving appointments to 'patriots'. Barbaroux with his colleague Loys came to Paris to seek the Assembly's support in their struggle against the more conservative department.

Upon his arrival in Paris, Barbaroux attended meetings of the Paris Jacobins where he met prominent Jacobins including Pétion, Guadet, Vergniaud and Robespierre. In fact, these Jacobins, both inside and outside the Assembly, were united in their support for Barbaroux's cause. At the Jacobin session of 4 March, Robespierre moved to support the efforts of the 'brave citizens of Marseilles'. Both Pétion and Robespierre wrote letters to the municipality expressing their support.[45] Guadet suggested that the petition presented by Barbaroux be sent to the Petition Committee and Pétion promised that this committee would defend the cause of Marseilles.[46]

The 'Patriot Ministry'

Combined with their belligerent war policy were the Jacobins' mounting attacks on the Feuillant ministers. Carra and Manuel were among the most ardent critics and they centred their attack on the Minister of Foreign Affairs, Delessart, and the Minister of the Marine, Bertrand de Moleville. Condorcet accused the entire ministry of treason, while Brissot had also long been a critic of the ministry which he held responsible for all of the country's woes.[47] Immediately following Louis XVI's dismissal of Narbonne on 9 March, Brissot registered a formal complaint before the National Assembly criticizing the Diplomatic Committee for letting the Delessart affair disappear. On 1 March Delessart had made a report to the Assembly of his correspondence with the emperor's ministers. The failure of the committee to make an immediate report infuriated Brissot, and he launched his attack the day after Narbonne's dismissal. On 10 March, Brissot delivered a violent speech against Delessart in which he exclaimed that Delessart had concealed the intentions of the foreign powers from the Assembly and what was worse, had carried on secret negotiations with them. He demanded the impeachment of Delessart on the grounds of high treason based on his charge of the minister's alleged betrayal of the interests of France as revealed in the dispatches between the Austrian Minister of Foreign Affairs and himself. Brissot's motion for impeachment in the Assembly was carried by a large majority.[48]

Brissot and his friends exploited the ministerial crisis that followed. According to a contemporary observer, Dumont, Brissot's actions were not entirely in the interests of his country, but aimed at obtaining ministerial positions for his friends. Brissot, in Dumont's account, believed that Delessart's ministry was out to destroy him. Brissot relied on his friend Garran Coulon, at the time chief of the High Court of Justice, to take care of the court proceedings. Garran Coulon, writing to Brissot, seemed doubtful of Brissot's tactics. When Dumont expressed shock at Brissot's machiavellian behaviour, Brissot replied: 'You do not know what is going on; the minister Lessart is getting rid of us, we must distance ourselves at any price; this is a temporary measure; I know Garran Coulon's integrity; it is necessary to save France and we can only destroy the Austrian cabinet by putting a dependable man in foreign affairs.'[49] Delessart was murdered along with other High Court prisoners in September 1792, so that makes Brissot indirectly responsible for his death. It had not been Brissot's goal to have him murdered, but simply removed from office. Since Dumont was writing in 1799, his report of the conversation might not have been entirely accurate. However, Brissot's friends replaced the Narbonne ministry shortly thereafter; Brissot's draft of the articles of impeachment against Delessart was accepted on 14 March and the new ministers, Clavière, Roland and Dumouriez, were appointed by the king, on the advice of Dumouriez, at the time connected with the Jacobins, about a week later. Desmoulins certainly thought Brissot was behind the ministry when he wrote: 'It was he who made the list of Dumouriez, Roland and Clavière. It was on his presentation that they were named to the embassy and all the jobs.'[50]

The appointment of the 'patriot' ministry by the king raised a number of questions for the Jacobins. Had the Jacobin ministers betrayed the revolution by accepting positions in the government? What were the implications for the Jacobin club now that some of its members were part of the government? Almost immediately after their appointment, Roland, Clavière and Dumouriez appeared at the club expressing the hope that members would support them. At the session of 21 March, the member Boisguyan presented the draft of a circular intended for the provincial societies. In it, he enthusiastically praised the new ministers. Robespierre refused to give it his sanction, and the club declined the printing of it. Clearly, not everyone approved.[51]

The Jacobin press was in the main favourable, but urged caution. The papers of Marat and Gorsas recommended that ministers be vigilant in resisting temptations offered by the court. Desmoulins categorically disapproved of the ministry.[52]

Among individual members, reactions to the appointment of the 'patriot' ministry were varied. Couthon approved, while the choice of new ministers clearly did not please Robert and Collot, who had been seeking posts themselves.[53] Robert, who had been experiencing financial difficulties for some time, was in desperate need of the income an official post would bring. Brissot had recommended Robert to Dumouriez as a possible candidate for the position of ambassador. Robert, writing almost immediately after his failure to obtain the appointment, claimed that Dumouriez had promised him a diplomatic post of some sort and that Brissot had told Robert he had, 'asked on my behalf, the embassy of Constantinople, Petersburg, or Warsaw, and that in eight days it would be done'. When he was invited to a dinner at Pétion's, he was convinced that he had the position. However, this was not the case: 'M. Brissot told me that the ministry was completely full; that was the case, but I would have what I had been craving. M. Dumouriez told him to ask if I had counted on the embassy appointments, and M. Dumouriez demonstrated some anxiety over what they called the exaggeration of my principles.'[54] According to Madame Roland, Robert's wife, who was as ambitious for her husband as Madame Roland was for Roland, had visited her several times in an attempt to obtain a post for Robert. The Rolands had sheltered the Roberts during the repression which followed the Champ de Mars massacre, and the couple were frequent visitors to the Roland home. When Roland was appointed Minister of the Interior, Madame Robert exclaimed: 'Oh, your husband has been employed; the patriots should serve each other reciprocally, I hope you have not forgotten mine.' Brissot tried to convince Dumouriez that Robert was 'honest, possessed an excellent heart, filled with true civic virtue and needed work'. However, Dumouriez refused to hire Robert, stating that he 'did not employ fools like him'.[55]

The case of Collot, who had been considered as a possible Minister of the Interior, apparently had similar consequences. Madame Roland alluded to this in a letter dated 23 March, the day the names of the new ministers were announced. She wrote: 'They were talking about Collot d'Herbois for internal affairs.'[56] In its speculations on the new ministers, the *Patriote Français* also cited the name of Collot as a possibility along with Clavière, Dietrich, and Roland.[57] Barbaroux, in Paris at the time of the appointment of the new ministry, wrote to his colleagues at the municipality that Collot had been nominated as a minister.[58] When Collot did not get the position, he became hostile towards Brissot, whom he openly denounced at the Jacobins on 23 April. The *Révolutions de Paris* explained the reasons for Collot's attack in the following terms: 'M. Brissot could only see in Collot d'Herbois' zeal the vigour of disappointed ambition; M. Collot d'Herbois had aspired to be minister of the interior, he had more recently aspired to a post of civil commissioner of the colonies and the ardour of his denunciation is the effect of failing at both attempts.'[59] In both of these situations, it was a matter of thwarted ambition rather than one of policy difference which made them turn against Brissot.

Conduct of War

Since the cause of the division among the radicals had been the war, one would logically conclude that once war had been declared, any disagreements would have disappeared and there would be total unity among the patriots. This was hardly the case and the debates over the war continued raging, culminating in the divisive session of 25 April. On the very day France declared war against Austria, Robespierre disagreed with Brissot's pleas for support of the generals. He continued his line on keeping close watch over domestic enemies, meaning the executive power.[60] Although there was no disagreement in that everyone wanted to win the war, differences emerged in tactics. Arguments

Robespierre guillotines the executioner having guillotined all Frenchmen, by an anonymous artist. (Musée Carnavalet)

urned from whether or not France should go to war to how the war should be conducted. Robespierre was almost obsessively suspicious of Brissot's association with Lafayette and with the king now that his friends were in the ministry. He believed Brissot had sold out to the court, and that Brissot's friends, now ministers, were false patriots who, with the help of Lafayette and Narbonne, intended to do a deal with the monarchy and establish themselves in power. The role of generals in the army emerged as an issue of utmost importance. It is interesting to take notice of Brissot's changing attitude towards the generals. He had declared not many months before war began that too much discipline in the army was undesirable and that under certain conditions, soldiers could even question their superiors. During the Nancy affair, for instance, when soldiers had revolted, Brissot had expressed sympathy for them and had criticized the Marquis de Bouillé who put the rebellion down. A year later, he stood firmly in favour of discipline: 'What is the first means by which liberty can be made to triumph over the coalition of slaves armed against it? It is discipline. What is the second means? It is discipline.'[61] This is exactly the opposite of what Robespierre wanted. Not only did he urge patriotic soldiers to disobey Lafayette, but he demanded the dismissal of the general.[62] Brissot defended himself by denying all accusations made against him by Robespierre without attacking the latter personally. He claimed not to have had any relations with Lafayette since 23 June 1791 and not to have had any influence on the king's choice of ministers. He began by defending Condorcet whom he called a 'respectable patriot', and he accused Robespierre of making false accusations and of wanting to become a popular idol. Although he attacked those members of the club who did not support the present ministry, Brissot did call for an end to the trivial quarrels and for a united stance behind the war effort.[63] Robespierre attacked Condorcet, but in his newspaper rather than at the club, on the premise that the latter had defended the 'intriguer Narbonne', who was allied with Lafayette. Condorcet was unmoved by these attacks and continued to shield Narbonne, who, he said, had done nothing to incriminate himself.[64]

In response to Brissot's speech, Robespierre replied that his most ardent adversaries were not Brissot and Guadet, but Lafayette. He presented Brissot with a peace offering resting on the condition that they would unite the fatherland in order to save and defend the principles of the revolution as deputies and as writers against Lafayette and Narbonne. Robespierre, whom Brissot had attacked in his newspaper for being, 'the author of the division which tears apart the society', was making an effort to unify the club.[65] Robespierre's speech was very moderate in tone and was more of a justification of his career to date than anything else. Surprisingly, he stated that Brissot and Condorcet had made irresponsible republican pronouncements just after the king's flight to Varennes, when he and his Constituent colleagues were defending the institutions, such as the constitution, created by them.[66] His speech was celebrated by members who were presumably becoming weary of the personal antagonisms. They urged its printing and distribution to provincial societies. On the other hand, there were no such demands for the printing of the speeches by Brissot and Guadet, who had them printed privately.

Divisions at the Jacobins

Gorsas exhorted the patriots to forget their quarrels and unite.[67] On 30 April, Robespierre had denounced an article from the *Courrier* reporting the Jacobin session of 27 April to which Gorsas replied that all he had done was provide advice to the 'apostle of equality' and he hoped Robespierre would give his approval. He was well disposed towards Robespierre. Barbaroux seemed to think that all had been settled on the 27th. At that session, he reported everyone had 'rendered justice to the virtue and public spirit of the inestimable Robespierre, and everyone also praised Brissot and Condorcet'.[68]

Pétion, who had not participated in the war debates, attempted to appease the Jacobins. He was deeply saddened by recent events and the session of 25 April particularly perturbed him. These developments brought him to the club on 29 April when he delivered an impassioned plea for unity and reconciliation. In his speech, he correctly stated that all Jacobins 'held the same principles, were animated by the same views and wanted to arrive at the same goal, but they did not employ the same means'. Although the 'most zealous defenders of the people were not always in agreement, they were of good faith and desired the best'. The society ordered the printing and distribution of his speech to its provincial affiliates. Privately, he conveyed his feelings to his friend and colleague from the Constituent Assembly, expressing dismay that the Jacobins were destroying each other with their own hands. He found the disturbances at the club so perturbing that he had lost a night's sleep over them. He attributed the discord mainly to 'hurt pride and thwarted ambition', no doubt referring to the disappointed ambition of Collot, Robert and perhaps Danton. He urged Robespierre to assist him in doing all possible to 'help us [the Jacobins] find a way out of this terrible situation'.[69]

Carra praised Pétion's efforts at unification and claimed his speech of 29 April 'reconciled everyone'. Carra, who had been an ardent war supporter, shared Robespierre's mistrust of Lafayette. Although they did not share the same opinion concerning the war, Carra was in no way an adversary of Robespierre. In addition, Carra supported Marat. In a reference to Beugnot's motion in the Assembly to prosecute Marat for provoking soldiers to massacre generals, Carra wrote: 'The senselessness continued and concluded with a motion of prosecution against the authors of periodicals entitled L'Ami du Peuple and Les Annales Patriotiques.'[70]

Danton, like Pétion, rarely had time for Jacobin meetings. He had not been caught up in the personal quarrels at the Jacobins, and he had taken a fairly ambiguous stand on the war issue, favouring Brissot, if anyone. Danton finally broke his silence on 10 May when he defended Robespierre: 'It is therefore not the love of one's country, but a base jealousy and all the most injurious of passions which incite against him the violence of his adversaries.' Although it is difficult to account for Danton's stand, it is presumably closely associated with the suspicion aroused by the 'patriot' ministry, and perhaps by his disappointment in not receiving a post in the ministry as Desmoulins had noted.[71]

It is hardly surprising that there was much anxiety among radical revolutionaries. The war, which had been intended to consolidate the revolution, was turning into a disaster. The French army was poorly organized and badly equipped. With the emigration of so many nobles, it was lacking in experienced officers. Entire regiments were deserting to the enemy. General Rochambeau had resigned and Lafayette started to think about deserting. The economy was in a shambles with the value of the *assignat* declining by about a third and economic unrest pervasive in the countryside. The club's letter of 4 June had stressed precisely these problems, in addition to Louis' veto of the Assembly's decree against the refractories, the threat posed by the supposed '*comité Autrichien*', and a concern over the future of the constitution.[72]

The king's dismissal of the 'patriot' ministry on 13 June as well as his vetoing of the Assembly's decrees, provided a basis for cooperation amongst the Jacobins. The removal of the ministers had been brought about by Madame Roland's insolent letter to the king. In the letter, signed by her husband, she demanded the royal sanction of the decrees, concerning refractory priests and an

rmed camp composed of 20,000 *fédérés* (National Guardsmen from the provinces) to be stationed
n the periphery of Paris. Although it is difficult to discern the reaction of individual members, the
emoval of the ministers from office did restore unity to the club. The Jacobins were delighted with
his demonstration of patriotism, which proved the former ministers had not deserted the forces of
iberty. Chabot, in his capacity as president, spoke on the club's behalf: 'MM. Servan, Roland,
Ilavière spoke to him [the king] in truthful language; they preferred a king's council with popular
pinions; that is to say, the principles of liberty.'[73] The club's circular to affiliated societies expressed
upport for Roland's action: 'We urge you, friends and brothers, to circulate and spread profusely,
he letter written to the king by the patriot Roland. It is one of most correct writings to make
nown.'[74] Although he had defended Robespierre just a few days before against his 'adversaries',
vhich presumably meant Brissot and the pro-ministry faction, Danton condemned the court for its
lismissal of the ministers.[75] Desmoulins, who had also been suspicious of the ministers, seemed
lelighted with Roland's letter and gave the credit to Lanthenas, who had been his secretary.[76]

Robespierre apparently took a line of his own apart from the other members of the club. He
ould not see the point of making a fuss about a few ministers while Chabot, Danton and Pétion
vere endeavouring to unite the radicals. He claimed that the dismissal of the patriot ministry was
iot the key issue. The more pressing problem was that of the safety of the nation and of the
\ssembly. Nevertheless, even Robespierre felt that now that the Jacobin ministers were no longer in
he service of the king, they could be reconciled and that all would rally to the 'principles and
orget personal insults'. He called upon members to forget their quarrels and unite before the threat
iosed by Dumouriez and the crown.[77] Brissot took a similar line and criticized Dumouriez who had
luped his fellow ministers.[78]

Lafayette's denunciation of the Jacobins on 18 June provided a further motivation for the
eunification of the club. In his letter to the Assembly, Lafayette reproached the three former
ninisters, demanded the closing of the Jacobin club, and urged deputies to rally around the king
ind restore order. Robespierre, Brissot, Collot, Danton, and Robert were united in denouncing the
general as a traitor. Robert viewed the occasion as an opportunity for Brissot, Guadet and some of
he other members of the pro-war faction to reconcile themselves to the club; it was the time for the
nembers to unite.[79]

Provincials

During the year's interval, 1791–2, between the Constituent Assembly and the Convention, Buzot,
Barère, Saint-Just and Fouché remained in the provinces, far away from the heated political
itmosphere of Paris. Saint-Just worked in a law practice for the year and wrote a book entitled,
L'Esprit de la Révolution et de la Constitution. It sketched his evaluation of the revolution up to the
ieriod immediately before the Varennes crisis. He published it just before the king's flight, in June
1791. The book reveals Saint-Just as a constitutional monarchist, which made it out of date by the
ime it was published. He supported the majority of the Assembly's decrees, including its decision
in war and peace. In the more theoretical sections, he showed himself as an admirer of both
Rousseau and Montesquieu, with Montesquieu as the favourite at this time.[80]

Buzot took a break from political life during the interval between the Legislative Assembly and the
Convention. He was elected vice president of the criminal court of Paris, a position for which he had
een warmly recommended by his colleague Robespierre.[81] However, he turned it down and returned
o Evreux where he was elected president of the criminal court for the department of the Eure.

Barère was elected a judge of the Court of Appeals in Paris in October 1791, a post which he held until January 1792. Afterwards, he returned to Tarbes where he was still very popular with the locals: the National Guardsmen turned out to greet him up upon his arrival and he was elected president of the local Jacobin club. During this interval, one of his correspondents was Dumouriez, who had been his neighbour in Paris during the sitting of the Constituent Assembly. Barère's letter of 30 March is full of praise for the general, who had just been appointed Minister of Foreign Affairs. It reads: 'My dear friend and distinguished patriot . . . What a brilliant career is opening before you!'[82] It is interesting that Barère, the consummate politician, does not reveal where he stood on the war issue. If the stance taken by the Jacobins of Tarbes, of which he remained president until the early spring of 1792, is any indication, then he was pro-war. In his study of provincial clubs, Kennedy indicates that out of the 154 clubs which articulated an opinion on the war, 141 were in favour and only 3 opposed and Tarbes was not among them.[83] Barère remained in Tarbes during most of the summer of 1792 until 8 August when he was summoned back to the capital in his official capacity as a judge.

Fouché was preoccupied with the duties of his post as principal of the Oratorian college at Nantes during the years 1791–2. He wrote new rules for the school that reflected the new revolutionary climate. All students were instructed in the 'catechism of the constitution'. He submitted the new curriculum to the district on 8 December 1791. Ambitious by nature, Fouché strongly desired to be a deputy. He was designated an elector by the section of Saint-Clément, but since Nantes had chosen too many electors, ninety instead of the fifty it was allocated, Fouché was one of those asked to withdraw. Following his failure at election, he was part of a delegation that went to Paris in late October, which expressed disapproval over irregularities in the recent elections to the Legislative Assembly.[84]

The conflict which emerged during the war debates lasted until the middle of June when the 'patriot' ministers lost their positions of power. The question of whether or not it was a good idea to launch a limited war did result in divisions among the radicals, but they were not permanent except in the case of Brissot and Robespierre who previously had been on excellent terms. Although their arguments began on a friendly basis, by the time war had been declared, they had degenerated into a bitter personal conflict. Even here, there were reconciliations in January and April. But Robespierre's suspicion of the court and of Lafayette, and his fear of the type of war which Brissot advocated, would produce a serious and lasting schism between the two men. At the start of the debates, Robespierre viewed Brissot as a misguided patriot, a friend who had been duped, and he did his best to convince Brissot to change his views. By the end of the debates, Robespierre had convinced himself that Brissot had only supported the revolution for selfish reasons. When Brissot's friends became part of the government, Robespierre became even more suspicious. Brissot's mistake was to equate ministerial office with power. After the dismissal of the 'patriot' ministry, Robespierre was perhaps ready to forgive Brissot if he provided proof of true repentance, but he was very much on his guard and even more suspicious than usual.

Although it was the issue of war that convinced Robespierre that Brissot was not merely wrong, but a counter-revolutionary, Robespierre was very much on his own. He was in a minority at the Jacobin club. Moreover, disagreements in the Jacobins, which had escalated to grave proportions by mid-April resolved themselves after the dismissal of Brissot's friends from the ministry. Much of the problem over the war was one of political tactics rather than political principle. Everyone desired to achieve a similar goal, that of the consolidation of the revolution and of the constitution, but there were differences over the best means by which this goal could be realized.

Personal antagonism between individuals counted for much in making people enemies, as in the case between Brissot and Robespierre. Disappointed ambition was another factor in turning friends into foes. What is vital to understand at this stage of the revolution is that the battles were fought among individuals. Although the suspicion between Robespierre and Brissot was permanent, it looked, in mid-June 1792, as though most of the Jacobins could reunite on a programme of opposing the king and Lafayette and denouncing the generals. As Danton had remarked, it was 'jealousy' and the most 'injurious passions' which were key in understanding conflicts between these men.

4

The Demise of the Monarchy

The threat of foreign invasion dominated politics in Paris during the summer of 1792. By mid-June, the revolutionaries found themselves in a critical position: France was losing the war, the 'patriot' ministry was out of power and the king appeared to be on the side of the counter-revolution, actually desiring to lose the war. Brissot's gamble in advocating an offensive war to consolidate the revolution and make the king decide once and for all about the revolution, was proving to be a costly mistake. The following chapter will examine the way in which the radicals responded to the growing problems which determined the crucial events of the summer of 1792.

Demonstration of 20 June

The causes and purposes of the demonstration which occurred in Paris on 20 June have never been precisely determined. Was it an attempt by Brissot and the deputies from the Gironde to press the king into returning the 'patriot ministers' to office, or was it a failed insurrection intended to overthrow the monarchy? Which radicals were involved? Was there an alliance similar to that formed in 1791, at the time of the Varennes crisis, between Cordeliers and the Cercle Social?

The conventional wisdom concerning the 20 June uprising is that it was an entirely 'Brissotin' inspired movement. French historians Mathiez and Soboul subscribe to this view.[1] This interpretation is totally understandable given the contemporary accounts of many of Brissot's future enemies who accused him of organizing the demonstration. However, their statements can be misleading as they were made some time after the uprising. Sergent, who was a police commissioner at the time, later wrote that the event had been organized in Madame Roland's salon mainly by Clavière and Roland. Also implicated were the deputies Brissot, Guadet and Gensonné. However, in the report he filed the day following the uprising, Brissot's name was not cited.[2] Chabot, in a lengthy statement at Brissot's trial, blamed the 'Brissotins', anxious to regain their positions, for the demonstration.[3] This is a striking contrast to what he said at the time. On 14 June at the Jacobins, he had reproached the king for his dismissal of the ministers. Moreover, on 19 June, he visited the 'headquarters' of the fermentation, the *faubourg* Saint-Antoine, to inform the leaders that the 'Marseillais had just sent an address to the National Assembly in which they offered . . . to come to Paris to defend and support the first conquerors of liberty.' He then instructed the group as to how they ought to behave during the march, 'with moderation, equality and peace during tomorrow morning's uprising'.[4] Barbaroux aided in getting the Marseillais to Paris. He wrote to the mayor of Marseilles, Mourraille, on 19 June asking him for 600 men.[5]

Journée des sans-culottes – the health of the nation. The citizens of the *faubourgs* Saint-Antoine and Saint-Marcel petition the king. Louis XVI wears the red cap of liberty and cries 'long live the nation' and drinks to the health of the sans-culottes. (Bibliothèque nationale de France)

Recently, historians have brought to bear evidence which suggests the movement was more broadly based than had been thought previously. R.B. Rose cites a contemporary account by the National Guardsman La Reyne who attributed inspiration to a group of prominent Cordeliers. La Reyne, who was hostile to the movement and thus possibly an unreliable source, claimed that a committee in the *faubourg* Saint-Antoine which met at Santerre's was composed of 'Pétion, the mayor, Alexandre commander of the Saint-Marcel battalion, Manuel, assistant to the mayor and Robespierre'.[6] The *faubourgs* were originally suburbs of Paris, but by the time of the French Revolution they were within the city walls. The two most well known were the *faubourgs* Saint-Antoine and Saint-Marcel, which were composed of working people. Bertaud thinks the movement was Jacobin inspired and he names Brissot, Robespierre and Danton as being behind it.[7] Rose suggests that the movement, 'reflected so closely the long established objectives and attitudes of the popular societies that it may be seen as almost a resumption of the post Varennes agitation of July 1791, but this time with the forces balanced very differently'.[8]

One of Billaud's biographers posits that many radicals were involved in the planning of 20 June. He thinks that there was an alliance between the Cordeliers, the Gironde, and the Jacobins, although Robespierre and Billaud were not involved.[9] His theory is supported by contemporary documents. According to one contemporary, the abbé Ratel, who was part of an espionage network conducted by d'Antraigues, the majority of Cordeliers and Jacobins including the Cordelier Merlin were in favour of an uprising. The exception was Robespierre, who thought an insurrection was premature. As far as responsibility is concerned, Ratel offered the following thesis: he blamed Lafayette and the Feuillants. Although he acknowledged the importance of the dismissal of the Jacobin ministers and the refusal of the king to sanction the two decrees, he believed these to be 'apparent causes' and asserted that 'the hidden and true causes lie in the struggle between the Monarchiens-Feuillants and the Jacobins. Lafayette's letter, read at the Assembly on 18 June, had been the combat signal between the two parties.' The importance of Lafayette's letter is evident in a letter written by Ratel to the comtesse de Montaynard, which although it acknowledged the importance of the veto and the dismissal of the ministers, stressed the impact of Lafayette's letter: 'The veto against the two decrees concerning the deportation of priests and the removal of the prepared camp near Paris, the reversal of the Jacobin ministers and their replacement by Feuillants and most of all, by the letter of general Lafayette to the Assembly, produced abominable scenes on Wednesday 20 June. The Jacobins pushed to the limit by the Feuillants went to the extreme.'[10] Ratel's thesis provides further evidence that the demonstration was the work of a coalition of revolutionaries not dissimilar to the coalition assembled during the Varennes crisis.

Mortimer-Ternaux and Braesch have attributed the rising to the people of the *faubourgs*. Mortimer-Ternaux cited the *faubourg* Saint-Antoine and its leader Santerre as the culpable parties. He referred to the petition this group presented to the Paris Commune on 2 June demanding permission to assemble. This, he contended, was simply the start of the fermentation which came to a head on 20 June.[11] Braesch merely cited the 'people of the *faubourgs*' as 'intervening brutally in the quarrel between the legislature and the king'.[12]

There is no doubt that both Santerre and Alexandre, leader of the *faubourg* Saint-Marcel, were both deeply involved in the day's preparations. Hébert, in his account of the events, claimed he united the two *faubourgs* to lead the forces 'to demand of the king, if he wants to do his job or not'.[13] Gorsas also named Santerre and Alexandre at the head of this popular movement. He began his explanation by placing his stamp of approval on insurrection during moments of great crises in which 'the rights of the people are attacked and laws are infringed'. The uprising of 20 June occurred under such conditions: the conduct of the king, who had continually insulted the people since the Varennes crisis through acts such as refusing to sanction the two decrees and the dismissal of the ministry, had aroused the passions of the people. In addition, he suggested Lafayette's letter as a pretext for the uprising.[14] Carra, for the most part, reiterated Gorsas' remarks. Neither Carra nor Gorsas indicated that the objective of 20 June was to overthrow the monarchy.[15] Their articles are supported by Alexandre's report of the meetings of his section on the eve of the uprising in which he recounted 'the stormy meetings on 17 and 18 June in which they spoke openly about marching to the chateau and of forcing the king to lift his veto'.[16]

According to Pétion then mayor of Paris, Santerre, Alexandre and their followers presented themselves to the Paris Commune on 16 June to inform him of their intention to petition the Assembly and the king, followed by the planting of a tree of liberty in memory of the Tennis Court Oath (the oath taken by the Constituent Assembly deputies never to break up until they had drafted a written constitution for France, so-called because they took the oath on the queen's tennis court). The subject of their petitions was the two decrees.[17] This concurs with Alexandre's testimony of his discussion with Pétion on the same day.[18] In response to the announcement by Santerre and Alexandre, the general council of the commune decreed that armed gatherings were illegal. Nevertheless, by 19 June, Pétion seemed resigned to the fact that the uprising would take place regardless of the commune's actions. Although uneasy about the march, the mayor authorized it.[19]

Unlike Pétion who neither prevented nor put down the demonstration, Roederer, the *procureur-général syndic* of the department of Paris, took a firm stand. He disagreed with Pétion's proposal to allow the armed march to take place, and he requested the directory of the department to order the mayor, the municipality and the commander of the National Guard to do everything in their capacity to avert the movement.[20] The left wing of the Assembly, composed of Brissot, Condorcet, Fauchet, Couthon, the deputies from the Gironde as well as Chabot and Basire, welcomed the entrance of the petitioners into the Assembly. Vergniaud, in his reply to Roederer's plea, stated that the gathering had been authorized by the organs of the law; however, some deputies were opposed to it. This did not prevent the petitioners from entering the Assembly.[21]

Jacobin meetings on the days immediately preceding 20 June were dominated by members' reactions to Lafayette's letter and the king's vetoes. Both events stirred strong emotions and brought about a general reconciliation. There was talk of a popular movement by Fabre, who advised the club to invite the sections to assemble to 'reinforce the patriots in the Legislative Assembly'. Danton demanded that Fabre's suggestion be printed and posted on the walls throughout Paris. He also urged the club to 'openly take the side of the national assembly . . .', and to 'inspire it with strength'. The motion was carried.[22] At the society's meeting on 19 June, Desmoulins called for an insurrection, or a popular movement that would 'defend the constitution', and even deprive the king of his veto. What he opposed was the 'return of the Jacobin ministers'.[23] Afterwards, he heaped glowing praise on Pétion for saving Paris and the king whom he depicted as the innocent victim of 'the fanaticism and hypocrisy of priests'.[24] Desmoulins seemed to imply that some Jacobins felt an insurrection would be too risky, even though most of them wanted it.

Not surprisingly, the club as a whole supported Pétion, who had been suspended from his position by the conservative department for not having done his duty in putting down the demonstration. At the session of 24 June, an address written by Pétion was read thanking the society for its sensitivity and interest. It was applauded and the society's president, Hérault, moved that the society should draft an address to the Paris Commune to illustrate its satisfaction with its conduct. Pétion and his assistant Manuel also had the support of a majority of the sections. Paris, at the time of the Revolution, was divided into forty-eight sections or units of local government. The sections replaced the districts, which had numbered sixty in 1790. The districts, created in 1789, were the original electoral units whose purpose had been to elect deputies to the Estates-General. Several sections wrote letters of congratulation to them and addressed petitions to the Assembly demanding their reinstatement. The section of the Tuileries claimed that Pétion's 'sage, prudent and firm conduct' had saved Paris from 'civil war'.[25] The *faubourg* Saint-Marcel, one of the organizers of the march, also wrote a petition in Pétion's defence, as did individual citizens, such as Bardin, who demanded the punishment of the Department of Paris for its persecution of the 'immortal patriots' Pétion and Manuel.[26] Concerning the actual demonstration, by the middle of July, twenty-seven out of forty-eight sections ratified it.[27] At this point, Pétion and Manuel were popular heroes with the people of Paris.

On 21 June, the club informed its affiliated societies that 'a great and salutary movement which has the promise of the happiest results has just taken place in the capital'. Could these 'happy results' mean the return of the 'patriot' ministers to office? This letter was signed by Hérault, president, Sillery, vice-president with Fabre, Réal, Mathieu, Garran Coulon, Maribon-Montaut, Auduoin and Chénier as secretaries. On 1 June, Chabot was made president, Manuel vice-president and Montaut, Garran Coulon, Fabre and Chénier remained as secretaries. The registers of the club proceedings do not provide the names of the new correspondence committee members.[28] Judging from this letter, the Jacobins were in complete agreement with the uprising. They attributed its origins to the inhabitants of the two *faubourgs*, rather than to Brissot.[29]

Rather than being opposed to the uprising of 20 June, it appears that the majority of the Jacobins, with the exception of perhaps Robespierre and Billaud, supported it, even though there is little evidence that the club organized it. Most Jacobins were still very reluctant to do anything outside the law. What the uprising did not do was terminate the general reconciliation in the club, which had resulted from the dismissal of the 'patriot' ministry, and Lafayette's insulting letter.

Lafayette's appearance at the Legislative Assembly on 28 June protesting against 20 June and demanding the arrest of its instigators as guilty of treason, reinforced the reconciliation of club members which had occurred at the time of the dismissal of the 'patriot' ministers. He implored deputies to rally round the crown and distance themselves from radical clubs.[30] Without actually naming it, he once again denounced the Jacobin club, calling it a 'sect which has invaded national sovereignty and tyrannized citizens'. Two days later, he stressed that measures should be taken to put down 'a sect which impedes all authorities, threatens their independence, and after having provoked the war, does its best to completely misrepresent our cause and take away its defenders'.[31] All joined in a common denunciation of the general. Carra reported this in glowing terms: 'The friends of the constitution are strengthened from union and zeal; their energy level has been raised to meet the circumstances; and, in the session of 28 June, Brissot and Robespierre proved themselves to be sincere friends of liberty who are always in agreement when it comes to the welfare of the people.'[32] Desmoulins, who had clashed with Brissot over the war, now spoke of him in favourable terms: 'But Brissot at the session of 28 June has finally made an apology to the Jacobins concerning his eulogies of Lafayette which had led patriots astray.' He particularly welcomed the reconciliation between Brissot and Robespierre. Desmoulins' line was very similar to Robespierre's on Brissot. He was a patriot, but one who had been misguided by his blind admiration for the generals, particularly Lafayette. Now, at last, he appeared to have woken up to the true colours of these traitors. Robespierre replied to Brissot's pleas to forget the past by stating that: 'This feeling is in all hearts.' He continued with the expression of feeling pleasure upon hearing Guadet's speech at the Assembly that morning as well as Brissot's at the Jacobins. Guadet had demanded that Lafayette be censured.[33] Billaud, in a major speech at the Jacobins, delivered on 29 June, repeated Brissot's calls for unity; he denounced Lafayette and the group surrounding Marie Antoinette. He echoed the general wish for unity in the club against a common enemy. This speech was printed by Brissot's press.[34] Collot delivered a powerful speech against the 'traitor' general on 1 July, demanding reasons for the Assembly's hesitation in impeaching him. According to Collot, Lafayette had deserted his post with the purpose of coming to Paris to declare war against the people.[35] In addition, he drafted a petition demanding revenge against the general which was presented to the Assembly on 8 July on behalf of the sections of Théâtre-Français, Mauconseil, Croix-Rouge and Fontaine-de-Grenelle.[36]

The themes of Vergniaud's speech at the Assembly on 3 July: the king's continual attempt to undermine the legislature's authority and his suspicion of Louis' connections with the counter-revolutionaries, were repeated by club members. In recognition of the seriousness which he considered the threats against the safety of the nation to be, he concluded his speech with the expression, 'the fatherland is in danger', and he demanded the Assembly officially proclaim it.[37]

Condorcet's approach remained consistent throughout this period of mounting crisis. He would not step outside the law. On 7 July, he delivered his first speech since the declaration of war. He proposed constitutional measures on how to reduce the king's powers: mainly by forcing his ministers to submit to the will of the Assembly and by censuring the Ministers of War and Interior. At the close of his speech, he issued an ultimatum to Louis: 'decide between the assembly and the seditious . . .'[38]

THE BORDELAIS AND LOUIS XVI

By the middle of July, Jacobin solidarity began to break down when the three Bordclais deputies entered into secret negotiations with the king in an attempt to restore the 'patriot' ministry. Initially, they communicated by letter through Boze, a court portrait painter. Boze, probably on behalf of the king, had asked Gensonné for his opinion on the current situation and what he thought could be done by the king to decrease the fears of the patriots. In a conversation with Guadet, Boze stated that he knew a movement was being planned on the part of the patriots on the one hand and the king on the other, and that it would be advantageous to all parties if such an event were prevented. In the reply, which was signed by the three deputies from the Gironde, they inquired as to why the king chose to surround himself, in these critical times, with a suspect group of men. Why did the king not choose those men who were most devoted to the revolution? The letter clearly indicated their perception of the importance of the king's choice of ministers: 'The choice of ministers has always been one of the most important functions of the king; it is the thermometer according to which the public can judge the dispositions of the court. A truly patriotic ministry would be one of the greatest means which the king could use to regain confidence.'[39]

Barbaroux, writing to his municipality on 18 July, the day the Feuillant ministers resigned, maintained that the former ministers were quite certain of their return to office. According to him, Roland, Servan and Clavière had agreed to take their positions back on the condition that Lafayette was dismissed. He concluded the letter by reporting the following ministers as appointed: Roland to Interior, Servan to War, Clavière to Foreign Affairs and Louvet to Justice.[40] The letter written by the three Bordeaux deputies to Boze was presumably their unsuccessful attempt to fill the places of the empty ministry.

It is difficult to determine whether or not Brissot was involved in the ministerial manoeuvring of the deputies. There is no evidence that Brissot aided with the letter writing, but there was a definite change in his attitude towards the monarchy during the month of July, and the importance that he placed on ministerial office suggests that it was a possibility. When Guadet proposed, in the name of the 'extraordinary commission of twelve', on 26 July, to send a message to the king to invite him one last time to rally round the nation and separate himself from the enemies of the constitution, Brissot supported his motion. From 25 July, the change in Brissot's attitude towards Louis XVI is striking. On 9 July, he had declared that since the king had retracted his oath a committee should be appointed to investigate his conduct.[41] In his speech of 25 July, Brissot shifted his position. He was now attempting to delay a decision on the dethronement of the king. Brissot also disagreed with proposals for the convocation of primary assemblies for the election of a national convention. He even went so far as to say that the condemnation of the king before the nation was convinced of his guilt would be most dangerous.[42]

Pierre-Victurnien Vergniaud in prison,
engraving by Raffet. (Musée Carnavalet)

The second letter addressed to the king by the Bordeaux deputies was written by Vergniaud and dated 29 July. In it, he warned Louis about the coming insurrection: 'A new revolutionary fermentation disturbs the foundation of a political system which has not yet had time to consolidate itself.' Vergniaud advised the king that in the light of the present circumstances, the only way to keep his throne would be to 'popularize the ministry'. He suggested that the king could appoint to his council four members of the Constituent Assembly.[43] Brissot, in his newspaper, was not in agreement with the idea of adding four former members of the Constituent Assembly to the ministry.[44] It appears that Vergniaud was not necessarily pressing for the return of Brissot's men, Roland, Clavière and Servan, to office, but rather seemed to prefer former members of the Constituent Assembly. He was therefore in disagreement with Brissot over the personnel of the ministry.

In addition, there is the abstract of an undated letter of Vergniaud to De Joly, the former Feuillant minister. This abstract provides a series of instructions to the king on how to preserve his throne. In essence, it stipulated similar conditions to those outlined in the letter of 29 July: the 'popularization' of the ministry and the appointment of the four Constituent deputies to the advisory council. These former deputies would be without title, but would offer free advice to the king. Pétion and Roederer were named as two former deputies who ought to be on this council.[45] The deputy Choudieu's statement that the tactic of the 'Girondins' (meaning the deputies from that department) was to intimidate rather than overthrow the court, and that their goal was to have their ministers returned to office, supports the theory that the Bordeaux deputies were negotiating with the king. He implied that their goal was to have the former ministers reinstated. Nowhere did he refer to Vergniaud's advisors from the Constituent Assembly. They were not opposed to the king as long as he would be their puppet. When Louis refused to cooperate, the 'Girondins' supported those who desired his dethronement.[46]

Other Jacobins would have no part in this deal with the king. By mid-July, most radicals who previously had been satisfied to work within a constitutional monarchy, had now completely lost faith in the crown. This frame of mind had arisen from the continuing failures of the French armies and the behaviour of the generals, particularly Lafayette. The Assembly seemed powerless. They were united in their general condemnation of the king, but less so on the way to proceed.

Vergniaud was reproached on 18 July for moderation in his comments on the monarchy and for pursuing a policy to put his friends back in office. Robespierre, during the session of 29 July, replying to Brissot's speech, stated that both the legislative and executive branches should be regenerated.[47] On 1 August, a member actually proposed that Brissot be struck off the list of members. Antoine, who had supported the motion, listed the charges against Brissot. He had promoted war when he knew France had not been prepared for it; he had failed to denounce

Lafayette at the Assembly when he had promised to do so; he had persecuted patriots at the Reunion club,[48] and finally, he had made the return of the three ministers to office, rather than the deposition of the king, the most important issue in the political debates.[49] The member, Desfieux, who demanded the expulsion of Brissot and Vergniaud from the club, referred to the session of the Reunion club of 30 July in which Isnard had suggested sending Robespierre and Antoine to Orleans, i.e., before the High Court, on a charge of treason. Apparently Brissot had not only supported this motion, but had improved on the threats against the two members of the Jacobins. Another member, whose name is not provided, complained about the 'partial measures of some members of the left side', whose goal was to name the ministers, choose the generals and exercise all the functions attributed to the executive power.[50] This suggests an extraordinary change at the club since 28 June.

On 29 July, the club learned of a letter written by Montesquiou, commander of the southern French army, to the Marseilles society. In it, he urged members to remove their support from the mother society in Paris, which he denounced as the cause of all France's problems. In addition, he wrote that the Jacobin club of Paris was doing the Assembly's job of making the country's laws. This letter merely reinforced the Jacobins' growing hostility to and suspicion of the generals.[51]

THE EXTRAORDINARY COMMISSION

Throughout the period leading up to 10 August, the Legislative Assembly's extraordinary commission, which Brissot thought should draft a report on the king's conduct, was devoted primarily to stalling the imminent insurrection.[52] The deputies who comprised this committee preceding the insurrection of 10 August were Bigot, Lacépède, Lacuée, Pastoret, Muaire, Tardiveau, Vaublanc, Guadet, Lemonty, Jean Debry, Guyton-Morveau and Ruhl. These members had been appointed on 18 June. On 18 July, the deputies Sers and Lecointe-Puraveau suggested that nine substitute members be added in order to give the left of the Assembly control over the committee. Condorcet and Vergniaud were supporting members. On 21 July, Condorcet became president of the Assembly.[53] A few days later, the deputy Duhem demanded that the question of dethronement be discussed. Vergniaud told him he would have to wait for the commission's report on the reasons why the country was in danger. Dethronement of the king was considered to be a last resort. The next day, Crestin demanded that the conduct of the king be examined.[54] According to Roederer, 'this proposition produced a scandalous scene'. The commission intervened and argued that the king ought to have the full power endowed on him by the constitution as long as he 'reported to responsible ministers'. At this time, the three deputies from the Gironde were in the midst of their negotiations with the king. At the session of 3 August, Vergniaud and Condorcet were chosen to present 'a report concerning measures to be taken before and after the dethronement of the king, under the conditions where the National Assembly is obligated to declare the king dethroned'. The next day, 4 August, the section of Mauconseil presented a decree which declared that it no longer recognized Louis as king. The Assembly, in the name of the commission, and on Vergniaud's proposition, annulled the decree. At the same time, Condorcet, in his newspaper, wrote that the Mauconseil section wanted the 'good of the country'. In short, Condorcet saw insurrection as 'the last recourse of an oppressed people', which was fine if the people did not have 'faithful representatives'.[55] In Condorcet's view, they did.

The commission also had the task of preparing a report on Lafayette. It decided that Condorcet should draft it. By this time, rumours had swept through the sections and popular societies that Lafayette was planning to dissolve them and then steal away with Louis. The commission recommended Lafayette's impeachment on 8 August, but the Assembly defeated this motion by 406 to 224 votes. Brissot, who had finally denounced Lafayette in the course of the debates, voted for impeachment, while Condorcet, on the basis of his long friendship with the general, abstained. He explained that he could not be the judge of a close friend. Garran Coulon was on leave from the Assembly. The Bordelais were divided, with Guadet and Vergniaud voting in favour and Gensonné abstaining.[56] Given their attitude towards Lafayette, the Jacobins reacted as to be expected with extreme anger and a feeling of betrayal by the Assembly, which they had previously supported.

UPRISING OF 10 AUGUST 1792

It seems probable that an alliance of Cordeliers, *fédérés*, and Jacobins prepared the insurrection of 10 August. The first two organizations played the more important role. The *fédérés* were a group of National Guardsmen from the provinces who had been sent to Paris to celebrate the anniversary of the storming of the Bastille, 14 July 1789, or the *Fête de la Fédération*. Marat, still not a member of the Jacobin club, once again criticized it for being all talk and no action. He had urged insurrection in July, arguing that only by 'popular insurrection could the ills of the country be rectified'.[57] And he was not alone in his reproach of the Jacobins. At the general meeting of the Luxembourg section on 24 July, a petition entitled '*Le Jugement Dernier*' was read. It attacked generals like Montesquiou, who led the armies of the Midi, and the Jacobins for their inaction. The petition even took on the 'Incorruptible' Robespierre, who was 'always preoccupied with himself and his glory . . . accusing anyone who did not share his opinions of being unpatriotic'.[58] Like Marat, the section considered the Jacobins to be orators rather than actors. At the club, a gradual consensus for the suspension of the king, and the convocation of a democratically elected convention gradually emerged – this was very similar to what occurred one year previously – but most Jacobins were still reluctant to take steps outside the law. In many ways, the Jacobins seemed as unwilling to risk insurrection as the deputies of the left. Billaud, for example, in a speech of 8 July insisted on primary assemblies, while on 15 July, he called for 'decisive measures', but never once mentioned insurrection. He focused on the king, who had diminished the power of the Assembly; however, rather than demanding his dethronement, 'a false and imperfect measure', Billaud thought a new Assembly was the answer as well as the arrest of generals Lafayette and Luckner.[59] Throughout July, the *fédérés* and Cordeliers continually petitioned the Jacobin club and the Assembly. The Bordeaux *fédérés* began petitioning the Jacobins on 8 July; they were followed by those of Côte-d'Or, Pas-de-Calais, Calvados and others at the session of 12 July. The demands of the Calvados *fédérés* were typical. They included the dethronement of the king, and the convocation of primary assemblies for the purpose of electing a national convention, which would draft a new constitution. At the same session, Robert proposed renaming the *fédérés*, 'insurgents'.[60]

A number of Jacobins who were also Cordeliers directed the activities of the *fédérés*. Cordelier members Robert, Chaumette, Antoine, Hébert, Lebois and Momoro were commissioned by the club on 15 July to draft a petition demanding the suspension of Louis XVI and the convocation of a national convention. This petition would be delivered to the Assembly.[61] The next day, the Cordeliers decided that the *fédérés* should present a petition to the Assembly on the same matter. The section Théâtre-

The 10 of August, or the fall of the monarchy, dedicated to the patriots. (Bibliothèque nationale de France)

Français, home of the Cordeliers club, drafted a petition on 30 July asserting their repugnance for privileges and demand for primary assemblies. It was signed by Danton, Chaumette and Momoro.[62] The *fédérés* appeared before the Assembly on 17 and 23 July demanding the suspension of the king and the convocation of primary assemblies. On 29 July, Manuel made threatening remarks to the Assembly, stating that if it did not propose solutions to the nation's problems within eight days, the people would remedy things on their own. On the same day, Robespierre and Antoine insisted that the *fédérés* remain in Paris and not leave for the front as some members of the Assembly, such as Lasource, had advocated. They argued that the role of the soldiers was in the capital.[63]

For Robespierre, who delivered a major speech at the club on this date, the root of the problem lay not only with the king, but also with the legislature which could be 'saved' by the constitution. In fact, the king was not even governing. The real leaders were the generals. Like Billaud, he argued that the dethronement and suspension of the king were simply partial measures. Elections to a national convention, composed of entirely new members, were indispensable. Nowhere did Robespierre demand an insurrection. He preferred to speak in philosophical terms saying that the representatives of the people, who had once recognized the sovereignty of the people, had now destroyed it.[64]

Gorsas printed the *fédérés'* petition of 23 July in his newspaper under the title, 'The last cry of the nation'.[65] This petition reiterated the belief that the source of the nation's problems lay with the king and called for his judgement. On 2 August, the Marseillais addressed the legislature demanding the dethronement of the king.[66] Throughout July, Hébert praised Carra and Gorsas, referring to Carra as a 'colleague' and to Gorsas as 'a friend'. Shortly following the uprising of 10 August, Hébert wrote that the king had wanted the blood of the Cordelier trio of Merlin, Chabot and Basire, 'friend Gorsas and his own'.[67]

Manuel, in a violent speech at the Jacobins on 18 July, demanded what appeared to be a second gathering at the Champ de Mars, not unlike the one which had taken place during the previous July, calling for 'the people of the 83 departments represented by the *fédérés* united with the citizens of Paris, to form a large and majestic assembly at the Champ de Mars to deliberate once and for all about our true interests'. His proposal was renewed by a *fédéré* from Dijon at the next session who invited the Jacobins to sign an address inviting the forty-eight sections to meet on 26 July at the Champ de Mars.[68]

Braesch stressed the importance of key sections such as Théâtre-Français, Gravilliers, Mauconseil and Lombards, who were also petitioning the Assembly. According to the Lombards section's proceedings, 'The commissioners of the section are authorized to vote for dethronement.' The commissioners were Louvet and Joly. The Lombards section of which Louvet was elected vice-president on 6 August,[69] supported the decree of the Mauconseil section, as Louvet explained in a letter to Brissot: 'I arrived at my section, the Lombards, where we had unanimously agreed to the decree passed by Mauconseil'. This decree stated that the section 'no longer recognizes Louis XVI . . . and that it will be faithful to the nation alone'. He continued by urging his friend to come to his senses: 'Wake up! Strike at the court and at the same time outwit the agitators. Today we have commissioners from 47 united sections; we demand dethronement.' In an emotional appeal, he begged Brissot to abandon his delaying tactics: 'Brissot, in the name of the endangered public good, stop delaying. Your eternal delay, the false prudence of your measures, aggravates the dangers of the fatherland; the enemy is preparing. The Court is playing with you. Brissot, I beg you in the name of the glory of the fatherland, do not lose a day. But vote, without delay, for suspension and then we will be saved.' However, Louvet appeared more cautious in his newspaper, *La Sentinelle*, telling Parisians that it was 'in the interest of the enemies of the people to invade the palace'. The people should support their mayor and the deputies.[70] How can this contradiction be explained? Perhaps the article in *La Sentinelle* was Roland's line as he was funding the newspaper, or Louvet might have changed his mind at the last minute, fearing the possible failure of the insurrection.

Roederer, in his statements concerning the developments of 9 August, also emphasized the coordinated efforts between the sections, the Jacobins and Cordeliers as well as other popular groups. The toscin was set 'to ring around 11.00 p.m. to assemble all those intending to head towards the palace'.[70] At the section of Quinze-Vingts, the decision was made to sound the tocsin at midnight on 9 August.[71]

A central committee composed of some Jacobins, all of whom were non-deputies, which worked in conjunction with a group of *fédérés*, illustrates the close union formed between Jacobins, Cordeliers and *fédérés*. The committee installed itself in the room of the Jacobin Correspondence Committee. Its first task was to address the *fédérés* to exhort them 'to assemble themselves en masse in Paris'. Fournier l'Américain, Carra and Alexandre referred to a secret committee formed at Antoine's which was composed of Carra, Gorsas, Vaugeois, Westermann, Santerre, Desmoulins, Alexandre, Antoine, Lajouski and Garran Coulon.[72] To these names, Choudieu added the Cordelier trio of Chabot, Merlin and Basire.[73] According to Fournier, the secret committee met on 26 July, 4 and 9 August. 26 July and 4 August were the days which preceded the aborted uprisings. A group of revolutionaries composed of *fédérés* and Cordeliers assembled on 9 August. Discussion centred round the presentation of a new petition to the Assembly. This idea was opposed by Fournier who pushed for immediate insurrection. The meeting closed with a decision to go to the Tuileries.[74] A copy of this petition, never presented to the Assembly, which was entitled, 'Petition from the men of 14 July', was printed by Gonchon of the *faubourg* Saint-Antoine in his newspaper on 8 August. It was signed by Parrain, 'orator' and Fournier, 'president of the Conquerors'. The paper also produced an article, 'More on the dethronement', which demanded the dethronement of Louis XVI who was no longer recognized as king.[75] Carra recounted three meetings of the secret directory. He boasted that during the second meeting, towards the end of July, he drafted, 'by his own hand the entire plan of insurrection, the march from the columns, and the attack of the chateau'.[76] Choudieu, commenting on Carra's account, argued that Carra had overestimated his own importance. However, he did confirm Carra's story about the role of the *fédérés* and the sections, and especially those of the *faubourgs* Saint-Marcel and Saint-Antoine, where the secret directory met.[77] Carra, in an article entitled 'On the just and indispensable necessity of removing Louis XVI', of 4 August, revealed his impatience with the deputies and the need to take more drastic measures to save the country from civil war. He wrote:

> Poor orators, poor politicians, poor legislators! You strangely separate yourselves from simple good sense and true principles in your desire to refine constitutional politics that you do not understand, and you become very unconstitutional in the sense that you separate the rights of man from national sovereignty and the supreme law, the law of the people. Remove the traitor Louis XVI, and the foreign war will soon be over, and all fears of a civil war will be dissipated because the combined germs will be entirely destroyed by that action. I defy anyone to reply to these arguments . . . We are on the extreme edge of the abyss, and the people . . . will be forced to find recourse in a universal insurrection for their salvation . . .[78]

Barbaroux, leading the Marseillais, advocated insurrection as the only means to retain liberty. He stressed the need for Parisians to join forces with the Marseillais to overthrow the monarchy and afterwards a 'Convention will be formed which will give a republic to all of France'.[79] His *Mémoires* support the accounts provided by Fournier, Carra and Alexandre. He wrote that there were several groups demanding the dethronement of the king: Marat and the Cordeliers, the Jacobins, the popular societies in Paris, and the forty-eight sections. According to Barbaroux: 'the fédérés assembled at Gorsas', at Carra's; there was a central committee of Jacobins presided over by Vaugeois.'[80] Although he mentioned Marat as one of the agitators calling for the dethronement of the king, Barbaroux also suggested that Marat became frightened as the insurrection approached. Marat first wrote to Barbaroux on 1 August asking him to take him to Marseilles; he repeated this request on the 3rd and again on the 7th. Finally on the 9th Marat was desperate, as Barbaroux suggested: 'On the night of the 9th, I was struck that nothing was more urgent and he proposed again that he disguised himself as a jockey. At that point, he was definitely no longer thinking about a revolution that took place the next day, and since then Marat has glorified himself as having been the driving force.'[81] Unfortunately, Barbaroux, in case the insurrection should be unsuccessful, destroyed Marat's letters. Even if we can believe Barbaroux, he only implied that Marat fled from Paris, disguised as a jockey. Carra pointed out that neither Marat nor Robespierre took part in the preparations.[82] Barbaroux was summoned to the mayor's office by the abbé Douré de Verteuil, a friend of Robespierre, where Fréron and Panis were also waiting for him to arrive. There they discussed strategy on uniting the Marseillais forces with those of the Cordeliers. The next day involved a meeting with Robespierre over the same subject.[83] Confirmation of this meeting may be found in a pamphlet written by the deputies of the Bouches-du-Rhône:

> Barbaroux held a conference with Panis on the movement of the Marseilles battalion to the Cordeliers' barracks at the mayor's office during the first days of August. Panis showed himself to be an excellent citizen and Barbaroux did not spare any fraternal embracements. One or two days later, the same person who had him taken to the mayor's office, besides Panis, came to propose a conference at Robespierre's; it lasted four hours. There, Panis found Rebecquy with Barbaroux. It was proposed to them after a conversation to unite behind a man who was very popular and who could save the fatherland by his courage. In leaving, Panis told them that this man was the virtuous Robespierre and that they needed him as a dictator.[84]

In his final speech before the insurrection, delivered at the Jacobins on 3 August, Billaud repeated Servan's proposition for an armed camp to surround Paris until the revolution had been completed. Barbaroux had supported this measure as a means of 'scaring' the king into 'changing his system' (referring to the vetoes) back on 21 June. Billaud concluded the speech not by exhorting the people to revolt, but by speaking in much more nebulous terms, telling the 'bourgeois of Paris' to become 'citizens'. If they were not 'patriots' for the sake of the revolution's success, then at least support it for their wives, children and themselves.[85] This seems to be very moderate in tone, in comparison to the petitions from the sections and *fédérés*.

On the evening of 9 August Danton apparently returned from Arcis-sur-Aube, where he had been since the 6th. Lucile Desmoulins wrote in her memoirs on 10 August that she had held a dinner for the Marseillais on the evening of the 9th. After the dinner, they went to Danton's. She recounted that he feared that the event might not come off. It is difficult to discern the actual role of Danton, Robert, Fabre, Collot and Desmoulins. In a statement made at his trial, Danton claimed for himself a major role: 'I prepared 10 August . . . I never went to sleep . . . I was at the Cordeliers.'[86] Lucile's account contradicts that of Danton. She wrote that 'he went to city hall and returned to go to bed'.[87] Although Collot had argued in favour of the king's dethronement at his section of the Bibliothèque in the days preceding 10 August, his name is not on any of the lists of organizers.[88] Nor is Fabre's, and he did not speak before 10 August as he had before 20 June. According to one study, he took his place at the Carousel among the assailants at the Tuileries, although there is no contemporary evidence that he did. Like Danton, he claimed responsibility for the insurrection's success at his trial.[89] Danton's biographers have pointed out that the minutes of the Cordeliers' session on the evening of 10 August make no reference to Danton.[90] Presumably, all of the big men kept out of the action, Robespierre and Danton, as much as the deputies.

While the secret directory was finalizing its strategy, members of the Reunion club were deciding what measures to take. The last meeting of this club occurred on the evening of the 8th at a house on the rue Saint Honoré. The members, composed solely of deputies, had been warned of the imminent insurrection. Choudieu demanded that a deputation of six members be sent to Pétion in order to discuss what to do if the Tuileries were attacked. 'The president Calon', recalled Choudieu, 'designated three members of the Gironde and three members of the Mountain: Gensonné, Isnard and Grangeneuve; Duhem, Albitte and Granet de Marseille.' Pétion replied categorically that he would go to the Tuileries and 'if he was attacked, he would drive back force with force'. Concerning the attitude of these deputies toward the king, Choudieu said that by this time, 'all they wanted was dethronement, and Pétion wanted nothing else'. Thus, Pétion was advocating dethronement, yet at the same time he was prepared to put the insurrection down. At this meeting, the deputies from the Gironde proposed the dethronement of the king and the convocation of a national convention to decide on the king's fate. Choudieu specifically mentioned his 'intimate relations' at the time with the two 'Girondin' deputies Ducos and Vergniaud. Presumably, the purpose of the Reunion club's meeting was not to conduct the insurrection, 'but to support it, and in order not to be betrayed, we expressed the desire without taking a resolution'.[91] If what Choudieu has recorded in his *Notes* is true, then it may be concluded that the only difference between the revolutionaries depended upon whether or not one was a deputy. The deputies assembled at the Reunion, if one can believe Choudieu, were not opposed to an insurrection, but were not involved in the actual organization and preparation. Choudieu's remarks are supported by those of Guadet, who, writing to a childhood friend, stated that he was not part of the secret directory, but was not opposed to it.[92]

Pétion, as mayor of Paris, was in an almost impossible position. He later wrote: 'I desired the insurrection, but I trembled that it would not succeed. My position was critical. I had to do my duty as a citizen without neglecting that of a magistrate . . . There was a deadly battle between the court and liberty and one of them had to succumb.'[93] Nevertheless, similar to his conduct during the Varennes crisis, Pétion showed himself to be more outspoken than many in the Jacobin club. He appeared at the head of a group of petitioners from the Commune of Paris on 3 August. Pétion delivered the petition, a violent diatribe against Louis XVI, alleging that the name of the king 'is the signal of discord between the people and magistrates, the soldiers and the generals. His conduct is a formal and perpetual act of disobedience to the constitution.' The speech demanded Louis' dethronement and temporary replacement with an executive council.[94] Presumably, this petition was a reaction to the heightening of tensions in the capital. Parisians had just learned of the Brunswick Manifesto, which threatened dreadful revenge on Paris if invading armies were repulsed and the royal family harmed.

When Pétion and Robespierre were no longer on friendly terms, Robespierre claimed that Pétion had pleaded with him to intervene at the Jacobins to prevent the insurrection. In the account, Robespierre seemed to imply that he himself did not participate in the preparations of the uprising. Rather, the day was planned by an alliance of *fédérés* and Jacobins: 'On 7 August, I went to the mayor's office . . . You talked to me for an hour about the dangers of the insurrection. I had no particular influence on the events, but since I often frequented the society of the friends of the constitution, where the members of the directory of the *fédérés* habitually met, you strongly pressed me to preach your doctrine in that society.' Robespierre went on the say that Pétion was not able to guarantee the court's abandonment of their alleged plan to murder the revolutionaries. He accused Brissot of postponing a decision on the dethronement of the king with the aim of intimidating Louis with the threat of insurrection as a way of returning his friends to office. However, Robespierre recalled that because of the confidence he had in Pétion, he spoke to the Jacobins on his behalf on the 8 August. By that time it was too late to prevent the movement from going ahead as 'the people and the *fédérés* no longer believed you; everything was prepared for the insurrection'.[95] Robespierre did speak at the Jacobins final meeting before the insurrection, on 8 August. Although his speech seems to be lost, the official journal of the club provides a summary: 'M. Robespierre demonstrated the difficulty in this plan of movement. He engaged patriots not to be fooled by this manoeuvre and to dismiss all discussion which could be insulting to deputies.'[96] Unfortunately, this summary of Robespierre's speech is too cryptic to make a valid interpretation. He appeared to be saying to Pétion that he had argued at the Jacobins on 8 August for the postponement of the insurrection.

On the same day, Barère returned to the capital when he was summoned there as a public official. He had no involvement in the organization of the insurrection, which in fact, he later denounced. Barère was no supporter of popular demonstrations: he had the same attitude towards 10 August as he had about previous revolutionary uprisings, including 14 July and 5–6 October 1789. Preferring to work within the confines of the law, he supported the Assembly's suspension and imprisonment of the king.[97]

The demonstration of 20 June 1792 was a wider based operation than historians have previously believed, involving members from popular societies and men from the *faubourgs*. Its objectives appeared to have been twofold: to return the 'patriot' ministers to office, and to force the king to sanction the two decrees he had vetoed. There does not appear to be any contemporary evidence to support the supposition that it may have been intended to overthrow the monarchy. Nor can it be proved that Brissot was behind it. The uprising enjoyed general support with some exceptions. Robespierre, for example, who had opposed the idea of an armed camp near Paris, seems to have thought that it was too risky. The 20 June demonstration did not disturb the unity among the radicals and the Jacobin club remained unified behind a common enemy, Lafayette. What did rock the boat were the clandestine negotiations which the Bordelais carried out after the king refused to reappoint the Jacobin ministers to office. Although Brissot's name did not appear on the letters, the change in his attitude towards the monarchy indicates that he, too, was a party to the manipulation of the king. Brissot's obsession with the ministry was his fatal mistake: he incorrectly equated power with office. At this point there seemed to have been a two-way division among the radicals in Paris. There were those who were willing to do a deal with the king either to reappoint the 'patriot' ministers or to appoint ministers from the Constituent Assembly, such as the other deputies from the Gironde and perhaps Brissot and those who were in favour of a full-scale insurrection, such as Carra, Billaud, Collot, Manuel and Gorsas.

The organization of the insurrection of 10 August 1792 involved a broadly based group composed of Jacobins, Cordeliers, and *fédérés* from Marseilles led by Barbaroux. The important point is that all of the 'big' men kept out of the insurrection. It was organized by smaller fry such as Carra, Gorsas, Fournier l'Américain, Lanthenas and Barbaroux, among others. Even Marat balked at the last minute, and, according to Barbaroux, stole off into the night disguised as a jockey!

The only parallel with 1791 was the schism at the Jacobins. In both cases, the splinter group consisted of moderate deputies who disagreed with what was occurring at the mother society. The difference between 1791 and 1792 can be found in the players who were involved in the creation of the new clubs. In 1791 it had been Barnave, Lafayette, the Lameth brothers and others, while in 1792 it was deputies to the Legislative Assembly, including Brissot, Condorcet, the deputies from the Gironde and a good number of future 'Mountain' deputies. Thus the principal division in August 1792 was between deputies on the one hand, and the clubs and sections on the other. Deputies, for the most part, were stalling for more time, while non-deputies were ready to revolt. What separated the members of the Reunion or club of the deputies and those of the Jacobin/Fédéré/Cordelier alliance was strategy or political tactics, rather than ideology. As Guadet and Choudieu stressed, on the eve of 10 August no one was opposed to the suspension and dethronement of the king; however, the deputies who defected from the Jacobin to the Reunion club tended to favour less radical means, i.e. staying within constitutional and legal limits, in order to achieve the same end.

5

NEW CONFLICTS

The success of 10 August meant the end of the divisions between deputies and non-deputies, which had arisen from the question of whether or not to risk an insurrection. The political situation changed after 10 August. The result of the insurrection was a conflict between the revolutionary Commune of Paris illegally established during the insurrection and the Legislative Assembly. Both of these power bases considered themselves to be manifestations of the general will and to represent the people of France. It is important to stress that the friction which arose between these two bodies did not follow the same pattern of division as the one which would later come about in the Convention. Firstly, those who started the attack against the Paris Commune were not Brissot and his friends, and second, many of the deputies attacking the Paris Commune would end up on the other side in the Convention. The following chapter will examine the extent to which the power struggle between these two centres of influence, and the extraordinary circumstances which faced politicians during the months of August and September of 1792, were to play a vital role in contributing to the breakdown of relations between a number of radicals who had not previously aligned themselves unconditionally with Brissot or Robespierre. It will seek to determine whether or not the republican movement which had successfully overthrown the monarchy had begun to fragment into two warring factions.

POWER BASES: COMMUNE VERSUS ASSEMBLY

Both Commune and Assembly changed after 10 August. A significant number of radicals became members of the new revolutionary Commune. These included Robespierre, Collot, Billaud, Robert, Louvet, Fabre, Pétion and Manuel. Billaud and Robert were chosen by the Théâtre-Français section. Robert, Billaud and Robespierre were among its most influential members.[1] The members of this new insurrectionary Commune suspended the former council when they entered its chambers on the evening of 9–10 August. Pétion and Manuel were the only members of the former commune who remained in their posts. Immediately after 10 August, Louvet, an important member of the Lombards section, applauded the actions of the new council of the Paris Commune, which 'detained Pétion at home so that the respected mayor would not fall victim to some cowardly plot'. In addition, he congratulated Paris on the leading role it had taken in saving the country.[2]

Control of the Assembly lay in the hands of an extraordinary commission of twenty-five, which Brissot came to dominate after becoming a member on 12 August. Gensonné was also a member.[3] The conflict which emerged between these two centres of power may be explained in the following terms. Both the Assembly, the legitimate authority, and the revolutionary commune took credit for the victory of the insurrection, and each competed for the support of the rest of France after

10 August. The two bodies differed in terms of political principles. The Assembly, unlike the commune, would not deviate from the constitution. The suspension of the king by the Assembly did not go far enough for the Paris Commune, which wanted Louis XVI dethroned. Vergniaud's reply to this criticism was that the Assembly had done all that it could within its constituted powers. It had decided that a national convention would be elected to settle the question of dethronement.[4] Brissot, who supported Vergniaud, added that although the king was suspended and a convention was called, the governing of the country was still being carried out in accordance with the constitution.[5] On the other hand, the commune was ready to act outside the confines of the constitution, threatening to use force, if necessary, to achieve its objectives.

The Assembly attempted to garner support in the provinces by proposing an 'official' explanation of the uprising on 13 August. Presented by Condorcet, it stressed that the Assembly had done nothing illegal. It was within its constitutional power to suspend the king, a necessary measure carried out in a time of emergency when foreign armies were preparing to invade France. Moreover, the report emphasized the Assembly's attempt to work out some sort of constitutional compromise with the king before the insurrection in an effort to prevent violent action. To make the insurrection palatable to the French nation, the commission played down the violent and popular aspects of the uprising. The report made no mention of the commune's role. Brissot proposed that the Assembly adopt the motion that the speech be printed and distributed to all cities and departments throughout France.[6]

Curiously, the commune did not respond to the legislature's interpretation of the overthrowing of Louis XVI, at least in the form of petitioning the Assembly. During the days immediately following the unanimous passing of the 'official' view on 13 August, the addresses delivered by petitioners from the commune consistently opened with warm statements of praise for the Assembly. This was as true for the petitions presented by Collot, Manuel, and Léonard Bourdon as by the mayor, Pétion, immediately following 10 August.[7] The exception was Robespierre. On the evening of 10 August, he stated that it was the duty of the Jacobins to explain the meaning of 10 August to the rest of France. To accomplish this, he suggested sending commissioners to the eighty-three departments. The *fédérés* should begin by writing to their departments.[8]

Robespierre was convinced that the extraordinary commission was directing the attack against the commune. He declared that from 11 August the members of the commission, 'had prepared a decree whose object was to annul the influence of the commune, by restraining the limits of the powers of the general council which had preceded it'. He later claimed that his petition of 12 August was supported by many members of the Assembly. This seemed unlikely judging from the hostile statements made by members of the Assembly at the time, and even the man he named as his supporter, Delacroix, seemed doubtful.[9] Delacroix was elected vice-president of the Assembly on 11 August and president on 19 August and was one of the leading opponents of the commune at this time. His response to Robespierre's threat was to advise the department of Paris to supervise the operations of the commune.[10]

PATRONAGE POLITICS: PROPAGANDA

The success of 10 August also meant that Danton, one of the leading insurgents, had become a minister with the support of Brissot. Fabre suggested Danton to Brissot as Minister of Justice, and Brissot agreed this offer. Danton was elected with 222 out of a possible 284 votes. Lebrun was elected to foreign affairs, while Roland, Servan and Clavière reassumed their previous ministries without a vote. Brissot later said that Danton's appointment was the 'seal of their reconciliation'.[11] Writing to Brissot at the end of August, Danton revealed their friendly relations by giving a job to one of Brissot's friends, whom he left unnamed: 'The testimony, my dear Brissot, which you have rendered, has made me make up my mind in his favour. I announce to you with pleasure that the place has been conferred on him and he will present himself to you straight away.'[12] Condorcet also backed Danton's election, stressing his personal strengths, which would be of benefit to the country in this time of crisis.[13] Danton chose Barère to be his assistant and Robert his first secretary. Fabre and Desmoulins also worked for Danton as secretaries. After Danton's election as minister, Billaud took over his post as Manuel's substitute.

Those who attained power used it to reward their supporters. Roland utilized his financial authority to provide funds for publicists who were on the side of the Assembly. One week after Roland returned to the ministry, on the proposition of Lasource, the Assembly voted a sum of 12,000 *livres* which the minister was to use for the 'printing and distribution in the departments and the armies all writings designed to shed light on criminal plots of enemies of the state and on the true causes of the evils which have for so long divided the country'.[14] Roland continued to finance Louvet's *Sentinelle*, as well as various pamphlets on national education written by Lanthenas and Bancal. He subsidized Gorsas' newspaper, in addition to those of Lemaire and Dulaure. He used his influence to appoint Carra to the position of librarian at the National Library on 19 August, only one day after he had returned to the ministry.[15] Roland also spent ministerial money on personal friends. This issue of allocation of propaganda funds was to become an important source of hostility amongst deputies once the Convention began its debates. What is significant about the propaganda ministry is the ill will that it engendered by not allocating funds to certain individuals. Roland's reluctance to support Marat's pre-revolutionary works is illustrative of the animosity it caused between the Rolands and Marat. Danton and Fabre were also denied funds from Roland for a journal which they intended to publish.[16]

Danton behaved in a very similar fashion to Roland. He not only provided his personal followers with positions in the ministry, but, as with Roland, he had considerable funds at his disposal. It appears that Fabre, as secretary to the Minister of Justice, was allotted money to be used for certain official purposes. The evidence seems to indicate that Fabre, who, for the first time, had some money for himself, did not spend it the way he was supposed to. Servan wrote to Fabre demanding expenditure receipts for the 48,000 *livres* he had given to Louvet for 'diverse supplies'. A few months later, Fabre had still not complied with the minister's demands, for the new Minister of War, Pache, wrote that Fabre had not accounted for 30,000 *livres* which were meant for boots and shoes for the army.[17]

PATRONAGE POLITICS: 'PATRIOTIC' MISSIONS

About a fortnight after the victory of the insurrection of 10 August, both the Legislative Assembly and the Paris Commune sent agents into the countryside to justify the insurrection. These missions were a further manifestation of each power base striving to extend its influence throughout France. The Assembly began on 15 August by dispatching commissioners to the four armies to inform them of the revolution which had just been achieved. As soon as the commune heard about the Assembly's missions, it responded with its own. At its session of 17 August, a proposition made by a delegation from the section of Pont-Neuf was accepted: 'The general council has decreed that each section will nominate three commissioners who will go to Lafayette's army to inform it of the events which took place on 10 August. All expenses will be paid by the commune.'[18] These initial missions were to prove another cause of tension between commune and Assembly.

The next set of missions were an understandable response to the critical military situation in which Paris found itself with the news of the fall of Longwy on 23 August. The road to Paris lay open. In response to this serious setback, the Assembly ordered a reinforcement of 30,000 men for Luckner's army and also decided to send out representatives to the provinces to recruit as many volunteer soldiers for the army as possible and to rouse patriotic sentiment. The decision to send out commissioners resulted in yet a further decline in the relationship between the Paris Commune and the Assembly in general and, on a more personal level, between Roland and Danton. Their personal hostilities were to have ramifications well beyond these two men. The first problem concerned the choice of the commissioners. Roland, behaving as indecisively as he had with the allocation of funds from the *Bureau d'esprit public*, preferred some time to think about it, while Danton took the initiative and proposed members of the commune as he believed Paris had 'furnished us with excellent patriots'. Roland neither scrutinized nor disputed the names proposed by Danton, but merely signed the order. Madame Roland later commented negatively about the appointments: 'Here is a cluster of unknowns, schemers from the sections and rowdies from the clubs, very devoted to Danton their protector and easily captivated by his habits and licentiousness; here are the representatives of the executive council in the departments of France. Successfully executing that project has always seemed to me to be one of Danton's greatest coups and the most humiliating for the council.'[19]

Thirty commissioners were named on 29 August and 3 September. Caron has supplied the names of twenty-four of the commissioners, all of whom were members of the Paris Commune. Many included prominent Cordeliers, such as Chaumette, Momoro, Ronsin, Vincent, Billaud and Audouin.[20] This was Danton's method of rewarding those who had supported him in the Cordelier club. The commissioners were officially ministerial, but they ended up as being spokesmen for the commune. Their activities infuriated members of the Assembly. Upon arrival in provincial localities, they made themselves known to the local authorities and demanded meetings of the local councils where they endeavoured to indoctrinate those who were present. The commissioners were a propaganda agency for the Paris Commune, as wherever they went they instructed local authorities with the commune's version of the events of 10 August: Paris was now the legitimate authority for the whole of France because it had saved the country. Some of the missionaries went even further as Buzot noted, stating that they preached the agrarian law in the departments, which alarmed local inhabitants.[21] In other words, that particular group of Cordeliers was propagating very radical ideas not shared by the leaders of either side. Carra, who at this time was neither a deputy nor a member of the commune, denounced the doctrine of agrarian law which Momoro and Dufour were preaching. He reported that these commissioners had disobeyed their instructions from the executive council and were spreading false ideas which could lead to disastrous consequences.[22] If the district which they passed through happened to be holding an electoral assembly, the commissioners delivered speeches and even tried to obstruct the election of moderate candidates. This was especially true in the case of Momoro and Dufour at Bernay. Upon arrival on the evening of 7 September, they found the electoral assembly of the Eure holding its election of candidates to the Convention. Momoro distributed to a certain number of electors copies of a pamphlet he had written entitled, *De la Convention Nationale. Déclaration des droits.* As soon as the local authorities discovered what the commissioners were up to, they were arrested, taken to the municipality and finally escorted out of town.[23] Buzot recorded that he had even saved them from being hanged by the electors at Bernay while he was presiding over the electoral assembly.[24]

In an attempt to counteract the executive council's missions, which were controlled by Danton, Roland, from the end of August, organized his own missions which he called 'patriotic missions'. The purpose of these missions, according to the official statement, was to disseminate the decrees and writings of the Legislative Assembly throughout the departments to ensure the security of the state against the invasion of enemies.[25]

Roland first exposed the activities of Danton's commissioners in a letter to the Assembly on 13 September. He referred to numerous incidents, such as the one at Rouen, where commissioners overrode the decisions of city officials and challenged the commissioners sent by the executive council to bring stability and order. This letter was sent to the extraordinary commission for examination that evening.[26] When the Assembly heard about the activities of the commissioners, it ordered a prompt investigation. Vergniaud presented a report on 14 September in the name of the extraordinary commission, which intended to limit the power of the commissioners sent from both the executive and the commune. Concerning those from the executive, he told the Assembly that they should keep within the limits of their powers and that they must provide proof of their powers to the constituted authorities. He was even more critical of the commune's commissioners, reporting the 'complaints we have received from the departments against some so-called commissioners from the city of Paris'.[27] The first decree that the Assembly passed, which Vergniaud had suggested in his report, was designed to protect the commissioners sent out by Roland, who had been authorized by the Assembly, while the second was a direct attack on the commune. It forbade municipalities from sending commissioners outside their jurisdiction; it prohibited local authorities from obeying those who had already been sent and lastly, it annulled and revoked everything they had done. If the municipality's commissioners did not obey the law, they would be arrested.[28] Although Roland sent a circular to all of the departments announcing the new laws, these regulations were almost impossible to enforce. Commissioners of any type, whether sanctioned by the Assembly or not, were very unpopular in the provinces. On 22 September, Roland recalled all agents. In the end, he lost out, as in order to stop the Paris Commune's missions he was forced to recall his commissioners as well.[29]

ARREST WARRANTS AND MASSACRES

On 28 August, with foreign armies rapidly approaching the capital, the Assembly, at Danton's insistence, authorized the Paris Commune to search private homes for concealed weapons. Prisons were filled to capacity with suspects. Girey-Dupré, Brissot's deputy editor, writing in the *Patriote Français* of the same day, implied that these household visits were intended to terrorize the community.[30] When summoned to appear before the commune to explain himself, he refused, and instead replied with a letter of protest arguing that patriotic writers were under siege from the members of the commune and that the liberty of the press was being threatened. Girey-Dupré had been accused by the commune of having printed falsehoods about it.[31] Reaction among deputies was similar. Condorcet condemned the commune's actions as a 'violation of individual freedom'. Vergniaud, in the name of the Assembly's extraordinary commission, presented a draft of a decree concerning the commune's order against Girey-Dupré. The Assembly adopted Vergniaud's suggestions that they quash the summons which was contrary to the liberty of the person and of the press. Moreover, it ordered the dissolution of the revolutionary commune.[32] Upon hearing the intentions of the Assembly, a meeting of the General Council of the Commune was held which lasted throughout the evening of 30–1 August. It was at this meeting that Robespierre denounced Brissot, Girey-Dupré, Condorcet and Roland, who were said to have circulated libels against him. Robespierre claimed they had been produced in Roland's offices.[33]

Carra, who had not written a word against the Paris Commune, – he continued to praise its zeal – now thought it had gone too far in 'setting up a tribunal and wanting to suspend patriotic presses'. This is a clear defence of press freedom without an outright condemnation of the commune.[34]

Tallien, on 31 August, representing the commune, spoke to the Assembly to protest against its slandering of the commune. The commune, he declared, had come to demand justice. It was the commune that had saved the country and everything it had done had been sanctioned by the people. Once again, the commune purported to represent the general will of the nation: 'Called by the people during the night of 9 to 10 August to save the fatherland, they did what they had to do. The people have not limited their powers; they said to them: Act in my name and I will approve of what you have done.' Lacroix, president of the Assembly, repeated the Assembly's position, already expressed by numerous deputies, that the formation of the commune had been contrary to the law; that it was the result of a crisis and as soon as the perilous circumstances had passed, the provisional commune would cease to exist.[35]

Couthon, in his report of the conflict, reiterated the Assembly's line. He denounced the 'provisional municipality' as being run by 'some dangerous men'. He continued to resent the commune's encroachment of the Assembly's power, and expressed the general feeling of the Assembly when he wrote: 'I hope that the Municipality of Paris will cease to believe it is the municipality of the whole Empire.'[36]

In his address to the sections of 1 September, Robespierre repeated his denunciation of 'articles by journalists attached to the same faction', which included those by Brissot and Condorcet. In addition, he recalled the manoeuvres of 'Monsieur Louvet' and the incident of Girey-Dupré. However, he continued to put his faith in the 'incorruptible mayor of Paris', Pétion.[37] During the evening of 1 September, Robespierre denounced his enemies in the Assembly: Brissot, the faction of the Gironde (meaning the deputies from that department) and the villainous extraordinary commission, to the commune on a specific charge of treason. This accusation was repeated by him with Billaud during the session of the next day, while massacres were taking place in the prisons and the commune's Surveillance Committee issued arrest warrants for Brissot, Roland and eight others.[38] The names of those intended for arrest have never been published. Although they may not be entirely reliable, Louvet provided some indication in his memoirs. He thought that responsibility for the warrants lay with Marat, who had joined the Surveillance Committee on the afternoon of 2 September, even though he was not a member of the commune's general council, and he noted that the punishment of Brissot, Vergniaud, Guadet, Condorcet, Roland and his wife, his wife and finally himself, had been decided.[39] There were others destined for death whose names Louvet did not mention. On a poster dated 28 August, Marat denounced the men referred to above with thirty other members of the Assembly. They were accused of writing to the departments that the Assembly was under the knife of the commune and advising provincials not to elect members of the commune to the forthcoming National Convention.[40]

Only Danton's intervention the next day prevented the execution of these warrants which presumably would have sent Brissot and a number of his friends to their deaths in the prison massacres.[41] On 4 September, Danton and Robespierre were received by Pétion at the mayor's office to discuss the warrants. Pétion's later recollection of the conversation he had with Robespierre reveals that Robespierre had convinced himself of Brissot's betrayal. When Pétion asked Robespierre 'what is bothering you, what do you think?', Robespierre replied, 'Well then, I believe Brissot is with Brunswick.' (The Duke of Brunswick was the Commander-in-Chief of the Prussian army.) Pétion explained that neither Danton nor Fabre agreed with his plans to arrest Brissot and a number of his friends. They thought that everything between Brissot and Robespierre was the 'result of vanity and personal animosities'.[42] Chabot, in a defence of the deputies in the Assembly, also disagreed with Robespierre's suspicion of treason on the part of Brissot: 'You are ignoring that our enemies are looking to disrupt all constituted authorities, that they are even trying to depopularize the National Assembly to replace it with a usurping authority.'[43] Since this speech was contemporary, it placed Chabot firmly against the Paris Commune.

On the morning of Sunday, 2 September, Parisians learned that Verdun, the last fortress blocking Brunswick's entrance to the capital, had fallen to the Prussians. Roland, upon hearing this news, suggested moving the capital to Blois. According to Fabre, this proposition was supported by other ministers such as Clavière, Servan and Kersaint. They interpreted leaving Paris as a necessity given their belief that Brunswick would be in the city within a fortnight.[44] As this resolution was about to be adopted, Danton intervened, expressing with vehemence his opposition to it: 'Before the Prussians enter Paris, I want my family to perish with me.' Turning to Roland, he exclaimed: 'Watch out that the people don't hear of this plan to flee.' Pétion tended to agree with Danton. He was in no hurry to leave Paris and Danton praised him for his courage and composure.[45] The significance of this incident is that it augmented the growing tension between Roland and Danton, who had already quarrelled over the missions. In addition, Roland was extremely jealous of Danton's growing power. Danton a stronger character than Roland, was much more adept at leadership during this perilous period. Not surprisingly, this led to resentment on the part of Roland and his wife. Danton was officially Minister of Justice, and Roland of the Interior; in other words, it was Roland's job, not Danton's, to organize national defence. It was Danton rather than Roland who delivered the famous rousing speech to the Assembly on 2 September which called citizens to arms: 'Gentlemen, we must take great measures. We demand that you declare that each citizen who refuses to march against the enemy or to take arms will be punished with death. To defeat them, we must have audacity, again audacity, always audacity until France is saved.' Even though Danton had saved Roland's life, Roland foolishly turned against him.[46]

There is no evidence that the Jacobin club was involved in the prison massacres. Nor did the club approve or disapprove of them. Its proceedings are mute on the incident until long afterwards. The first mention of them is not until 19 September. On the other hand, individual club members, such as Danton, Robespierre, Pétion, Billaud, Manuel, and Santerre (commander of the National Guardsmen), all of whom held prominent positions in the Parisian and national governments, and who had moral authority in the city of Paris, did nothing to prevent them from proceeding.

It is almost impossible to discern who actually planned the massacres. According to a report in a contemporary newspaper, the *Feuille de Paris* – the only journal which provided an account of the general council of the commune's deliberations on 2 September – Billaud had recommended in that meeting that the commune send two commissioners to the Abbaye prison to have a look at its registers and that those held in connection with the crimes of 10 August 'should be handed over to the people'. In spite of the protests of 'a member', the council adopted Billaud's motion, and it was decided that two members would go to the Assembly to inform it of this measure and to ask it to nominate some of its members to accompany those from the commune.[47] The evidence presented here is corroborated by the information contained in the register of deliberation of the section of the *faubourg* Saint-Denis.[48] Since there is no other contemporary account stating Billaud was responsible for this motion, it must be read with some caution. It does, however, seem probable from the evidence that at least a majority of the members of the commune's council were in favour of taking action against counter-revolutionaries in the prisons of Paris.

On 3 September, a circular produced by some members of the Surveillance Committee of the Paris Commune, Duplain, Sergent, Panis and Marat, addressed all municipalities, inviting them to massacre suspects in their prisons. Apparently, it was sent to the Ministry of Justice for countersigning, which Fabre arranged. Fabre not only justified the prison massacres, but said that they were entirely necessary.[49] He recommended further massacres if his friends, Marat and Desmoulins, were not elected to the Convention.[50]

Marat later wrote that he was 'at the Surveillance Committee when it was announced that the people were going to tear off the hands of the guards and kill many refractory priests'. He and Panis did not seem to mind the massacring of counter-revolutionaries, but 'Panis and I cried: Save the poor debtors, the brawlers and the delinquents.'[51]

Although the organizer of the prison massacres is unknown the reaction to them by the radicals clearly confirms that not one of them was averse to violence of this magnitude. Gorsas, in his newspaper, openly advocated the massacres in August. On 18 August, he wrote that the deaths of citizens on 10 August ought to be justly avenged. Then, on the 29th, he repeated his demands for vengeance: 'We are intimately persuaded that virtue should be recompensed and crime be punished.'[52] None of the radicals, including Brissot, Pétion, Condorcet and Madame Roland, protested against the massacres. Nor did they make any attempt to stop them until several days after they had begun. Madame Roland was aware of the massacres on the afternoon of 2 September and her letter to her friend Bancal indicates an attitude of acceptance rather than one of repugnance.[53] Her first hostile reaction to the massacres was on 5 September when she received knowledge of the arrest warrant against her husband, and wrote: 'We are under the knife of Robespierre and Marat. These people are doing their best to excite the people and turn them against the national assembly and the council. Can you believe that they have issued an arrest warrant against Roland and Brissot, as spies of Brunswick?' In addition, she expressed, for the first time, her indignation against Danton, whom she referred to as, 'the leader of the pack'. She denounced Robespierre, Danton and Marat in her next letter, dated 9 September.[54]

Roland's letter to the Assembly dated 3 September was equally moderate. This letter, the source of Roland's immediate attitude, has been often misinterpreted. Roland did not denounce the massacres, rather he admitted they were 'necessary' given the circumstances. He said that 'a veil should be drawn over the day's events'. He reproached the commune of 10 August for its abuse of power, but he also recognized that it had rendered services. He described the men of the commune as 'zealous men of great ardour who are only lacking in knowledge and moderation'.[55] These comments seem to contradict those made just a few days previously when he had attempted to have the commune dissolved on the occasion of the summoning of Girey-Dupré. Roland, in the defence he published against Marat on 13 September, stated that he had learned some days after

2 September that he had been the object of an arrest warrant issued by the Surveillance Committee and that Pétion, Santerre and Manuel had seen the warrant.[56] It was not the massacres themselves which Roland opposed, but their extensions to '*l'homme juste*', presumably himself and his friends.

Condorcet's reaction in his journal was almost a carbon copy of what Roland had said to the Assembly: 'We pull a curtain over these events of which, in these difficult moments, it is very hard to calculate the ramifications. It is an unfortunate and terrible situation in which the character of a people who are naturally good and generous, is forced to take such revenge.' In other words, the people had no other choice: they were compelled to take vengeance into their own hands. Even this man of the law, who consistently abided by the constitution, was justifying the massacres.[57]

On 3 September, the *Patriote Français* did not express any opinion, but merely reported the facts. Brissot's paper provides the fullest description of what went on, but without comment. The next day, it presented a brief summary of the events, and expressed regrets at what Brissot now called, the 'terrible event'. He supported the motive behind the massacres calling them a 'praiseworthy project', but thought that they could have been more moderate. He referred to the commissioners from the Legislative Assembly whose efforts to stop the massacres had been, sadly, futile. By 7 September, he interpreted the massacres as a political plot.[58] It was therefore only when Brissot and some of his friends learned that their own lives were in danger that they began to denounce the massacres.

Gorsas, in an article drafted at 9.00 p.m. on 2 September, at the very moment when the 'torrent of the people took itself to the door of the Conciergerie and demanded guilty heads', approved wholeheartedly of the violence. The people had carried out 'dreadful but necessary justice'. To Gorsas this was open warfare against the enemies of liberty and there was only one choice. 'Either we perish at their hands, or they at ours.' He linked the massacres with foreign invasion and compared the expeditions to the prisons with fighting a foreign war. He did not raise his pen against them during this period. His last reference, on 12 September – 'There is no property more sacred than the life of citizens. We are strong; we fight, but we will not massacre.' – does not condemn them.[59]

Carra's explanation was similar. Things were black and white: the guilty would perish and the innocent would be saved. All those who had perished had provided 'proof of anti-patriotic behaviour'. It was their own fault and they were getting what they deserved. On 5 September, he rallied to the commune's theory of a 'prison plot'. When he wrote that the lives of the innocent had been spared, perhaps he was referring to his own, as well as those of his friends. As with Gorsas, he did not denounce the prison massacres at this time.[60]

The responses of Couthon and Louvet were identical to those of Gorsas and Carra. They were a result of the people's vengeance.[61] Pétion was applauded by Couthon, calling the mayor, 'brave and virtuous'. Louvet's *Sentinelle* did not appear between 2 and 8 September. On 8 September, although he thought it was time to stop them, he nevertheless labelled them as a 'beautiful movement'. On 6 November, he was still referring to the massacres as 'that terrible necessity of vengeance'.[62]

Neither the Paris Commune nor the Assembly acted to stop the massacres. This is understandable as it would have meant calling out the National Guard and quite possibly could have resulted in a second Champ de Mars massacre. Pétion said he knew nothing of the massacres when they began on 2 September. Between 2 and 8 September, he wrote twice to Santerre, commander of the National Guard, to intervene, but the massacres continued. This was the only action he took until he visited the general council of the commune, and with a deputation from it visited the Force prison on 6 September. For his part, Santerre replied to Pétion that the guardsmen

The massacres of September at Nantes. (Bibliothèque nationale de France)

were understandably too frightened to intervene.[63] Perhaps Pétion was frightened too, but with the elections to the convention occurring simultaneously, it is not unreasonable to wonder if the popular mayor did not want to lose his support from the people of the sections at this crucial time.

Manuel, Pétion's deputy, visited the Abbaye prison twice: on 2 and 3 September at the head of a delegation from the commune. Tallien reported to the Assembly that Manuel was not made welcome. Manuel himself told the Assembly of the 'sad spectacle which took place before his eyes', and that the efforts of the twelve commissioners from the Assembly with their colleagues from the commune were powerless in saving any criminals from death.[64]

At the time they occurred, the September massacres were less important than one would expect in dividing the radical revolutionaries. They were more of a pretext than a cause for division. No one was immediately outraged. Brissot and his friends only developed the argument that the massacres were the work of a fanatical minority that dominated Paris much later in the Convention, after they had lost the elections in Paris.

ELECTIONS TO THE NATIONAL CONVENTION

Although the elections to the French National Convention did not begin until 2 September, preparations such as tentative lists of possible candidates for Paris had been printed as early as the middle of August. Louvet published his list of candidates on 21 August which proposed most of the major radical figures who are under consideration here: Robespierre, Pétion, Buzot, Barère, Danton, Billaud, Collot, Robert, Brissot, Condorcet, Guadet, Vergniaud, Carra, Gorsas, Mercier and Manuel.

)ther radical figures whose election he endorsed were: Chaumette, Tallien, Audouin, Antoine, .ersaint, Bancal, Girey-Dupré, Lanthenas, and Garat. Conspicuously absent from the list were Marat nd Desmoulins. Marat replied with a list of his own. He recommended Robespierre, Danton, Billaud, Merlin, Chabot, Panis, Desmoulins, Manuel and initially Tallien, although he was struck off the list a w days later when Marat learned that Tallien was a partisan of Roederer.[65] Always a loose cannon, 1arat only recommended men from the commune. In addition, Marat produced a 'critique of ouvet's list', composed of Carra, Gorsas, Lanthenas, Girey-Dupré, Barère, Louvet and Réal. He escribed Barère as a 'nobody, without virtue or character . . .' Brissot, Guadet, Lasource, Vergniaud, ondorcet and other 'unfaithful deputies' left unnamed, were not worth discussing.[66]

Gorsas reacted bitterly against Marat's description of him as a 'flatterer of Necker, then Bailly and fterwards Motier' (meaning Lafayette). In an article published the day after Marat's placard, iorsas replied with an article in which he rebutted Marat's comments about him by claiming his upport in the numerous sections and popular societies. He specifically referred to the section of ontrat Social which had named him with a majority of votes at the same time as Marat was alling him a partisan of Necker. Here Gorsas was pointing out to his readers that the people of 'aris were championing him in spite of what Marat was writing in his journal.[67]

What these electoral lists of proposed candidates reveal is the personal preference of the ournalist drafting them rather than any 'party' line. Louvet proposed the men he considered to be is friends and supporters rather than men of any particular faction. This is equally true in Marat's ase. The major difference in the lists is that Marat only recommended men from the Paris Commune, while Louvet proposed a broader group composed of men from the Commune, the Assembly and radical journalists.

Although the Jacobin club had been neither particularly active nor effective throughout the veeks after the king's dethronement, some individual members, most notably Robespierre, Collot nd Danton, went much further than the journalists in influencing the elections.[68] The club had egun preparing for the elections to the Convention as early as 22 August when the society decided hat it would send to affiliates the results of the seven roll-call votes in the Legislative Assembly to nform departmental electoral bodies of the political positions of the candidates. It was pointed out o provincial clubs that the vote on Lafayette was the most significant to consider when re-electing nen from the Assembly. A significant number were standing for re-election. It was particularly mportant not to re-elect men who had voted against Lafayette's indictment which had been lefeated by 406 to 224 votes.[69] In addition, the society singled out support for members, some of vhom had been deputies to the Constituent Assembly: Antoine, Buzot, Coroller, Dubois-Crancé, :ollot (referred to here as 'le bon père Gérard', after his almanac of the same name), Grégoire, .e Pelletier, Pétion and Robespierre. The majority of names on this list were those men who had een instrumental in saving the club from extinction at the time of the Varennes crisis.[70] The lissemination of these lists was approved by the club which had finally written an important :ircular, the first since 10 August, dealing principally with the elections. In addition, it endorsed he democratic legislation which had been passed by the Assembly since 10 August.[71]

The general council of the Paris Commune, dominated by Robespierre, was even more significant n controlling the elections. Before the actual voting began, Robespierre took a number of measures o ensure that the candidates he favoured would be elected or re-elected. He suggested that the lectoral assembly be held in liaison with the Jacobins, who, meeting in advance of the elections, vould designate those candidates to be elected.[72]

Several radicals were nominated electors from their sections, the largest number representing the Théâtre-Français section, now called Marseilles. These included Billaud, Danton, Desmoulins, Fabre, Manuel, Marat and Robert. Carra and Collot were electors from 1792, formerly Bibliothèque, which was also Brissot's section, although he was not an elector, while Louvet (Lombards), Pétion (Pont-Neuf, formerly Henri IV) and Robespierre (Place-Vendôme, formerly Picques) were also electors from their sections.[73] All of these men, with the exception of Louvet, Pétion and Carra, were successfully elected from Paris, and Pétion only had himself to blame for not being a Paris deputy. He withdrew from the Paris elections after he was elected second to Robespierre's first. Brissot, however, was not an elector from his section even though he had been one in the past two elections of the French Revolution. A possible explanation for his absence was his growing unpopularity with both the Jacobins, where he seems to have stopped attending at least since 10 August, and the commune, which had sent out an arrest warrant against him immediately before the massacres. As noted above, early in August, a member had called for his expulsion from the club. One day before the elections started, on 4 September, Brissot had denounced the commune in an article in the *Patriote Français*. It appears that the article was written by Brissot and not by his editor-in-chief, Girey-Dupré, because it is entitled, 'J.P. Brissot à ses concitoyens'. Brissot must have been aware of his personal unpopularity in Paris. The fact that the elections were stage managed by certain members of the Paris Commune, and to a lesser extent, the Jacobins, surely meant that anyone unpopular with both institutions would be excluded. On the other hand, Carra, Louvet and Pétion in addition to the future 'Mountain' deputies, although they did not attend Jacobin meetings regularly either during these six weeks between 10 August and 20 September, nevertheless remained popular.[74]

Sixteen out of the twenty-four Paris deputies were members of the commune and if Tallien had not been critical of Robespierre, there would have been seventeen. Eleven out of the twenty-four were residents of the Marseilles section, home of Danton's Cordeliers.[75] However, only thirteen out of the twenty-four were Jacobins and only seven were active members. Carra criticized Robespierre's domination of the electoral assembly, calling it a 'scandalous empire'. He demanded that Robespierre support a recount of the votes.[76] Louvet later wrote that the elections in the provinces had made up for those in the capital. Men who had been rejected by the 'Parisian faction' had been elected by the people of the provinces. He provided the names of Pétion, Sieyès, Thomas Paine, Condorcet and Guadet.[77]

Brissot and Pétion were not pleased with the manner in which these elections had been conducted. They came out on the side of the sections, which had been prevented from having a voice in the selection of the candidates. On 17 September, Pétion wrote to the general council of the Paris Commune expressing his dismay at the outcome of the elections. He wrote that he 'watched with as much pain and worry the clash between the general council and the sections and between electoral assembly and the sections'.[78] Brissot was more explicit in his explanation of the quarrel which broke out between the sections, the municipality and the electoral body, presumably because he had not been an elector. According to him, the sections were forced by the 'charlatans who played the people by boasting of their sovereignty' to revise their choice of candidates before the elections and submit to a 'purification ballot'. Although the sections asked for a recount, the 'furious orators', fearing its results, refused.[79]

A new division had occurred as a result of these elections. The radicals were now split between the deputies from Paris and Brissot's friends, who were on the whole rather more genuinely

arisian than Robespierre, Danton and the group elected as Parisian deputies. With their failure to
e elected as Parisian deputies, Brissot and his Parisian friends were forced to turn to the provinces.

While the Parisian deputies had fixed the elections to elect their chosen men, there is evidence to
upport the premise that Brissot and others kept out of Paris operated in a similar fashion in the
rovinces. This was the case in the elections of Brissot, Condorcet, Carra, Gorsas, Buzot, Louvet and
arbaroux. All of them except Barbaroux had received some votes in the Paris elections. Alison
atrick has cited a dozen departmental assemblies in which there was a faction operating to control
hese elections. She cites strange goings on in the elections in the departments of the Somme,
ouches-du-Rhône, Loiret, Eure, Orne and Rhône-et-Loire. There is apparently a case for the
xistence of a cabal in the voting procedures in the elections of Carra and Gorsas in the Orne.
lthough Carra and Gorsas were not known in the department, they were elected on the first ballot.

There were also irregular developments in Loiret. The local assembly had resolved to elect local
andidates; however, Brissot and Louvet, who were not locals, were elected at the exclusion of two
ocals on the first ballot. Louvet's election prevented that of two local men who had already been
hosen as substitute deputies. Garran Coulon, a deputy to the Legislative Assembly from Paris, was
ot re-elected in that department. Instead, he was elected in Loiret, where he was an unknown
uantity. His home department was Deux-Sèvres which did not elect him.[80]

Brissot, Carra and Condorcet, all of whom were friends of Buzot, were elected in his home
epartment of the Eure, even though none of them were known there. Buzot was president of the
lectoral assembly in this department and had considerable control over it. Buzot himself, who
bviously was a local notable, was elected first deputy.[81] Both Brissot and Condorcet refused their
nandates here and opted to represent their home departments of Eure-et-Loir and Aisne respectively.

There is no evidence that irregularities occurred in the elections of Barère, Saint-Just, Fouché,
'outhon or the Bordelais. All were elected, or re-elected in their native departments of Hautes-
'yrénées, Aisne, Loire-Inférieure and Puy-de-Dôme respectively. There is no evidence that Barère
ttempted election in Paris, but he was elected by the neighbouring department of Seine-et-Oise,
nd after much thought, decided to represent his own department where he was a well-respected
otable.[82] The electoral college of Soissons met on 2 September. Saint-Just, the youngest man there,
vas chosen secretary of the provisional office, and two days later, president of the first office, who
ounted the votes. On the next day, he was elected fifth representative, with 349 out of 650 votes.[83]
'ouché was elected sixth deputy on 8 September, the fourth day of voting, with 266 out of 405
otes.[84] As soon as the Legislative Assembly passed the legislation for the forthcoming elections, he
uit the Oratorians. He was known locally through his association with the Jacobin club and as
rincipal of the college. Vergniaud, Guadet and Gensonné were all returned by the department of
he Gironde, along with nine other deputies which represented this department.

The major conflict during the period after the insurrection of 10 August 1792 occurred between
he Legislative Assembly and the Paris Commune, with the latter assuming that since it successfully
verthrew the monarchy, it now represented the entire country. Deputies to the Assembly quite
easonably rejected this attempt to undermine their legitimate power. They had been legally elected
o represent their constituents, unlike the men of the commune who had illegally overthrown the
lected Paris Commune and put themselves in power. The conflict during these six weeks did not
esemble what would emerge in the National Convention.

Radical politicians were divided between those who were members and supporters of the
'ommune, or the Assembly. Some, like Danton and Fabre, were neutral. They were preoccupied

with the Justice Ministry. Still others, such as Carra, Robert and Gorsas, who were not members of the commune, Assembly or government, were simply not involved. The position taken by Pétion is unique in the sense that he was a member of the commune as mayor of Paris, yet he defended the power of the Assembly. Other tensions between radicals occurred over the question of patronage in terms of propaganda money. The allocation of funds for newspapers would become a further source of tension between some of these men once the Convention began its sessions.

Manuel supported both the commune and the Jacobin club. Throughout these six weeks, the Jacobin club was a weak and leaderless institution. It seemed to have lost the momentum of the pre-insurrection period. Attendance was poor, strong policies and influence were lacking. Its most prominent members were engaged elsewhere either at the Paris Commune, the Assembly or the Ministry. Only during the latter part of August with the onset of important national elections and under Robespierre's leadership, did the club appear to have an impact on politics.

Members of the Paris Commune not only attempted to deprive the Assembly of its rightful power but a few, such as Billaud and Robespierre, tried to have some deputies, such as Brissot and Condorcet, and a number of deputies from the Gironde, arrested at the time of the September massacres. Only Danton's intervention saved their lives. The relationship between Brissot and Robespierre, which had first deteriorated over the war issue, had now gone beyond the realms of reconciliation. Robespierre no longer trusted his old friend: Brissot was an enemy who had abandoned the true cause of the revolution in the name of power, which Brissot had equated with office too many times. He would henceforth be considered a counter-revolutionary and suspect by Robespierre.

Although the initial reaction to the September massacres was similar among those inside and outside the Assembly, the threat of massacre to Brissot and a number of his friends increased the former deputies' hostility towards the commune. Some became critical of the massacres, which they would later use as a weapon in the Convention.

By the time of the opening of the Convention, then, to what extent had the republican movement which had successfully overthrown the monarchy fragmented into two warring factions? For the most part, the basic division between politicians appears to be what it had been shortly after 10 August: a division between the Paris Commune and the Legislative Assembly, with some exceptions. Pétion had turned against the commune and Jacobins when he failed to get elected first deputy for Paris on 5 September. However, the great majority of deputies – still sitting until late September and some re-elected – had not forgotten the commune's bullying.

Brissot and a number of his friends had not stood for election in Paris. Brissot himself had failed to become an elector. He had lost influence in the Jacobin club and he had personally fallen out with Robespierre, who was influential in both the club and the commune, which controlled the elections. Brissot must have realized his unpopularity in Paris, especially after having denounced the city's government both in his newspaper and in the Assembly. It is therefore not surprising that he did not attempt election from this department. It appears that he had become estranged from the radical popular movement in the capital. The reasons why Louvet, Carra and Gorsas did not stand for election in Paris are less apparent. Carra and Louvet had been electors and with Gorsas, prominent Parisian journalists since 1789. Both Carra and Louvet had been recently praised at the Jacobins. A possible explanation is that their personal tie with Brissot was a stronger bond than that of the club. The tie with Brissot may have worked to their detriment in preventing their election in Paris. At any rate, they turned to the provinces for support before the opening of the Convention, and in this sense had sorted out their affiliation and had come down on the side of Brissot rather than Robespierre.

6

THE FRENCH REPUBLIC

THE NATIONAL CONVENTION

The French National Convention opened on 20 September 1792, the day of the French victory at Valmy when the Prussians began their retreat. Enormous problems confronted France's first republican assembly. Deputies had to deal with issues which had been unresolved since the Constituent Assembly, such as the *émigrés* and the counter-revolutionaries, both internal and external; added to these were the foreign war, a financial crisis and the threat of violence from radical Paris sections. It was against this background that the Convention became a violent struggle until death, 'an arena of gladiators'.[1]

During the autumn of 1792, a good number of the radicals began to sort out their political affiliation. This chapter will seek to discover the nature of the factions to which these men began to adhere. What prompted men to support the anti-Parisian line taken primarily by Buzot, Barère, Barbaroux and Brissot? Who supported whom and for what reasons? And finally, which men were not part of any faction, and who sought to reconcile the growing differences between the once cohesive group of radicals?

LAW AND ORDER

Harmony reigned throughout the first few days. There was reason for celebration with the French military victory at Valmy. On the same day, 21 September, following Collot's proposal, all deputies voted in favour of declaring France a republic. Unity was, however, short-lived. From here, things went consistently downhill.

Kersaint's demand for a commission to present measures to be taken against brigands and assassins brought about the first confrontation in the Convention. Garran Coulon, Gorsas, Buzot, Brissot, Vergniaud and Barbaroux all supported Kersaint. On the other side, opposing the issue were Billaud, Fabre and Collot.[2]

Buzot's request for a departmental guard to protect the Convention from Parisian insurgents at the session of 24 September, supported the insistence for law and order made by Roland, Minister of the Interior. This proposal further divided the Convention, which was already split between those who supported and those who opposed Kersaint for a law against those who 'provoke anarchy', but not simply along the lines of Parisian deputies versus those from the provinces. A number of provincial deputies those who opposed the measure for a departmental guard. The deputy Monestier explained: 'This armed force is demanded with great cries by members who were from

Triumph of the French Republic, one, indivisable and democratic. (Musée Carnavalet)

he constituent and some from the legislative. It is uncompromisingly rejected by one part of the same legislature, and by a large number of my newly elected colleagues, by the Jacobins, by many Paris sections, in general, by all the men of 10 August.' He did not support the guard since it gave rise to 'diverse reproaches', and 'hinders our work very much'.[3] Some deputies who initially supported Buzot's proposal, later changed their minds. This was the case with Condorcet and Couthon. Condorcet urged the union of all Frenchmen in the face of the grave problems confronting the new republic: foreign war, counter-revolution and economic crisis. He interpreted the measure as one which would unite rather than disunite the empire against the enemy armies.[4] Later, along with Barère, Couthon and Carra, he would oppose the plan, but for different reasons. For Barère, Condorcet and Carra, it would be a matter of principle, while for Couthon, it was a matter of changing personal loyalty after he was not made a member of the Convention's Constitution Committee on 12 October.[5] By the end of October, Buzot had lost the support of Condorcet for his guard. Condorcet argued that it could only create conflict between Paris and the departments and he feared that such an armed force would be capable of dissolving the Convention if conflicts became insurmountable.[6]

The creation of a departmental guard dominated several Jacobin meetings. Billaud, Marat, Fabre and Robespierre were among those who opposed the guard. Robespierre's objection rested on the basis of the principle that it would divide Paris from the departments rather than unify them. He interpreted the project as an attack on the citizens of Paris and many deputies representing that department. He denounced the members of a new commission of nine, which was charged with preparing a report on Paris. The commission included Buzot, Delacroix, Manuel, Thuriot, Lesage, Mathieu, Garran Coulon, Reubell and Royer. Other Jacobins who were opposed to the guard were Dufourny, Bentabole, Laurent, Tallien and Saint-Just, none of whom were Paris deputies.[7]

Saint-Just also remained entirely outside the personality and factional conflicts. He confined his speeches to the issues and consistently sought a question of principle behind the issue he discussed. His maiden speech was on 22 October at the Jacobins, rather than at the Convention, and it concerned the departmental guard, which he opposed for reasons similar to Condorcet's: it was unnecessary and would only lead to the provocation of agitators in Paris. At the same time, he upheld Buzot's vision of a republic, in which all men saw each other as brothers, and their only leader was 'the law that emanates from the general will, freely expressed by the representatives of the nation as a whole'. He was able to acquire the respect of both sides in the Paris versus the provinces conflict by saying that although Paris was responsible for 10 August, it had only been possible with the support given by the provinces.[8] To sum up, on the issues of law and order and the departmental guard, Saint-Just, Carra, Fabre, Collot, Condorcet, Billaud, Robespierre, Barère, Desmoulins, Couthon and Marat opposed them, but most did so without attacking personalities. The exceptions were Desmoulins, Couthon and Marat. Pétion was non-

Pastel of Louis Antoine Saint-Just, by Phillipe le Bar. (Musée Carnavalet)

committal, but defended Buzot. Barbaroux, Buzot and Gorsas, advocates of the guard, were more apt to attack individuals than Brissot, Garran Coulon and the Bordeaux deputies Vergniaud and Gensonné.

ATTITUDE TOWARDS THE PARIS COMMUNE OF 10 AUGUST 1792

The relationship between the revolutionary commune and the September massacres stirred up much dissension during the opening sessions of the Convention. Barbaroux denounced the commune of 10 August, its commissioners sent to the departments and the arrest warrants against the deputies from the Legislative Assembly drawn up by the commune's Surveillance Committee. He repeated his accusation of Robespierre aspiring to be a dictator at the time of 10 August, but maintained he 'esteemed and liked' him. All Robespierre had to do was 'recognize his mistake' and all would be forgiven. Barbaroux resented what he saw as Paris' domination, writing that 'in a word, Paris wants everything for itself and ignores that there are eighty-two other departments'.[9] Previous deputies to the Legislative Assembly were equally hostile to the Paris Commune of 10 August and its tendency to dictate policy for the nation. Among the most critical was Cambon. He vigorously attacked Marat and reminded deputies of the crucial role the Assembly had played during 10 August. Finally he repeated the charge that the commune had 'relentlessly insulted the representatives of the people'.[10]

Brissot accused Panis, now a Paris deputy, but at the time of the massacres he was on the commune's Surveillance Committee, of wanting to have him killed. In addition, Brissot recalled Robespierre's condemnation of him at the session of the commune on the eve of the massacres. Barère demanded an apology for 2 September from the Paris Commune of 10 August.[11] Marat could not allow himself to forego a chance of getting at his enemies, and protecting his Parisian friends, Danton and Robespierre. He replied that Brissot had many personal enemies in the Assembly, and he denied the charge Brissot had made against himself, Danton and Robespierre of scheming to be dictators. Gorsas did not say anything about the massacres until 12 October when he accused Marat of provoking them. It was at this time that Brissot was expelled from the Jacobin club. There may well be a relationship between the two issues. Carra's first word against the massacres was not until 26 October at which time he wrote that they were 'popular atrocities that every good citizen should delete from his annals'. He denied any relationship between the Paris Commune of 10 August and the massacres.[12]

At the Convention, there appeared to have been two groups operating at this time: a minority of anti-Paris men, including those following the lead of Roland, composed of Barbaroux, Cambon, Barère and Buzot, lashing out against the Paris Commune and those who could be called the conciliators, who included Danton, Pétion, Fabre, Manuel and Condorcet, who were attempting to bring together those who were at odds. These men believed that the Convention should not occupy itself with personalities when the issue involved principles. In addition, there were men like Fouché and Saint-Just who contributed little to the early debates and remained entirely outside the factions. Fabre noted that if there appeared to be two parties in the Convention, it was because of the accusations that had been made against Paris. Pétion replied in a most conciliatory fashion and repeated his maxim that everyone desired liberty. He said that now that the monarchy had been abolished, it was in no one's interest to have divisive factions. Once again, the Rousseauist notion came through in that 'if everyone was working for the public good, private interests could not exist'.[13]

OFFICES AND COMMITTEES

The first president of the National Convention was Pétion, receiving 235 out of 253 votes, while Brissot, Condorcet, Vergniaud, Camus, Lasource, and Rabaud Saint-Etienne were made secretaries.[14] Marat denounced these choices as those of the 'faction Brissot-Guadet' which had long since sold out to Motier, meaning Lafayette.[15] Desmoulins denounced a faction which he called the 'Phlegmatics'. It was composed entirely of men who held office as secretary or president or both.[16] This faction contained neither Brissot nor Guadet, two of the men he later accused of monopolizing offices. The personnel composing his factions changed frequently. Desmoulins' remarks may well be an indication of his own bitterness at having failed to be elected to a committee or an office during these months. Marat wrote of a 'cabal' from the two previous assemblies, headed by a clique from the Gironde and Bouches-de-Rhône. The centre of the clique was composed of Buzot, Delacroix, Guadet, Brissot, Gensonné and Rabaut. These men either held an office or sat on a committee. He also denounced another group, again composed primarily of committee men.[17] Of the men who are the subject of this study, only Desmoulins, Marat and Billaud did not sit on a committee or hold an office from September to December.

The perspective that a 'Brissot-Guadet' faction was operating to pack the committees of the Convention and to dominate the offices of the presidency and secretaries, was later adopted by leading twentieth-century French historians of the revolution.[18] Their view was accepted until M.J. Sydenham challenged the interpretation based on the personnel of only one committee, the Constitution Committee, because it was supposedly composed of a 'Girondin' group. He did not examine the other important committees of the Convention, such as the Committees of General Security, War, Diplomacy, Legislation and Finances.[19] When one investigates the personnel of these committees, a picture emerges very different from the traditional one.[20] It appears from the personnel of the offices and committees that the deputies representing provincial constituencies were well represented, but that they did not necessarily adhere to any particular faction, as Desmoulins alleged. Most of the Parisian delegation sat on a committee either as a full member or as a substitute. Personal popularity may have played a role in determining who got elected to a committee. Marat was not particularly popular with anyone, receiving only one vote out of a possible 258 in the elections for president on 13 December.[21] Concerning the men who are the subject of this book and who were elected to both committees and offices, most had previous legislative experience and/or had newspapers with an excellent circulation in the provinces. If one looks at who was president of the Convention between September and the end of November 1792, two conclusions may be made: firstly that all men who sat in the president's chair had been members of previous French revolutionary assemblies, either the Constituent or Legislative Assemblies, and second, they were all provincial deputies.[22] When it comes to the secretaries, with the exception of Saint-André, Carra and Saint-Just, all had been deputies to previous assemblies. There is nothing to prove that a faction was controlling these offices. Barère was the only man who was president, secretary and a member of three committees. If anyone monopolized offices in the Convention, it was him rather than a faction.

PERSONAL ANTIPATHIES

Much of the responsibility for stirring up personal antagonisms can be attributed to the Rolands, two people who were not deputies, but personal friends of men like Brissot, Buzot and Barbaroux. Roland was not particularly liked by many in the Paris delegation. This may be explained by his refusal to grant some of the journalists or would-be journalists funding for prospective newspapers in August and for his attack on Paris at the Convention. The Rolands focused their attack on one individual representing Paris: Danton. Madame Roland was particularly hostile to Danton, and much of her husband's behaviour can be attributed to her influence, as well as Roland's jealousy. Danton was an enemy of no one, and had stayed outside the bickering over Marat, the massacres and the Paris Commune. He would have been quite willing to work with Brissot and his friends had it not been for the Rolands, who quite openly antagonized him. Their attacks on him began during the crisis in early September when, as Minister of Justice, he quite inappropriately intruded into Roland's jurisdiction as Minister of the Interior, and proved himself to be the man of the hour, who had the strength of character to take upon himself a leadership role for which Roland seemed incapable. Madame Roland then proceeded to attribute responsibility for the September massacres to Danton, even though he had presumably saved their lives by quashing the arrest warrants. The next tactic of the Rolands was to accuse Danton of aspiring to a dictatorship with Robespierre and Marat, to which Danton replied there was absolutely no truth in such vague and indeterminate claims. He openly declared himself to be no friend of the 'people's friend'.[23]

Danton, quite understandably, retaliated during the debate over the question of whether or not an individual could hold the positions of minister and deputy simultaneously, in which he publicly insulted Roland. Although he stated that he had not doubted the services that Roland had rendered to his country, which may have been intended as a sarcastic remark, he accused Roland of cowardice in advocating the desertion of Paris when enemy forces had broken down the last remaining fortress before the capital. Even more insulting was Danton's reference to Madame Roland's powerful influence in her husband's ministry: 'If you invite him, then invite Madame Roland as well, as everyone knows that Roland is not alone in his department.' When Roland had recommended transferring the capital to Blois, Danton alone opposed this measure and described Roland as 'an old driveller who sees ghosts everywhere, and who is frightened by the slightest popular demonstration'.[24]

In this case, Brissot was furious with Danton for his comments against his old friend Roland and his wife, calling his reproach 'vile'. He asked if it was a 'crime for a minister to be fortunate to have a friend and a helpful counsellor in a wife'.[25] Gorsas also took Roland's side when he wrote that by staying in his job, Roland had outwitted all manoeuvres, had fulfilled the wishes of all good citizens and reduced to silence the political agitators.[26] In this instance, the source of commitment was personal rather than political. Gorsas rallied to Roland's defence, as did Buzot who publicly called Roland his 'friend'. Gorsas' support for Roland may have been self-interested. Roland had helped to fund his newspaper through his *Bureau de l'esprit public*.

The tension between the Rolands and Danton escalated over the question of Danton's secret expenditures while he was Minister of Justice. Danton claimed that he did nothing during the ministry except what had been ordered by the executive council, which was only accountable as a whole. He invited his audience to recall that when the enemy had laid siege to Verdun, the Assembly instructed the council not to make expenditures, thus it had been forced to use extraordinary money. Danton confessed that he did not have the legal receipts for the majority of these expenses, but justified this in the light of the extraordinary circumstances. Roland's charge of corruption forced Danton – whose career could have been ruined – to turn to his colleagues in the Paris deputation for protection, and later alienated independents. In this case, personalities proved to be more important than the issues. A letter addressed to Madame Roland by Gadolle, one of

Roland's agents, indicated the effect which Roland's account of his own expenditures and Danton's lack of accountability were supposed to have had: 'The patriarch [Roland] killed his enemies by the honesty of his accounts, and Danton remained suspended in a state of suspicion which was disheartening for his friends; this state of affairs intensified the rage of his barkers.'[27] The Rolands were entirely responsible for this alienation of Danton. Brissot and many of his friends, such as Condorcet, were quite happy to have Danton on their side, and considered him an asset rather than a liability. However, Brissot's persistent defence of Roland, a close friend and one of his employers before the revolution, eventually cost him Danton's friendship. Danton commented that on the one hand, Brissot continually cried out against revolutionary ministers who had not provided an account of their expenditures, but on the other hand, he seemed inclined towards indulgence for an ex-minister, meaning Roland. Garat, who later eulogized Danton, wrote that Danton had told him: 'Twenty times I offered them peace; they did not want it.'[28] Losing Danton as an ally would later prove to be an important mistake.

JACOBIN VERSUS REUNION CLUB

After 10 August, the Jacobin club had been relatively inactive and lacking in influence. Its debts had grown, and correspondence with provincial clubs had stopped. During the first few weeks of the Convention, leading Parisian deputies rarely spoke at the club. Danton, who was named president on 10 October, did not appear before that time, while Marat did not make his appearance until 12 October when he at last joined the club. Interestingly, that was two days after the club voted to expel Brissot. As for Robespierre, he only appeared about five times within the first month of the Convention. His attendance was irregular because of illness. Until the change of offices early in October, Pétion, who had been recently elected on 23 September, remained president. The deputy Réal and future assistant of Chaumette at the Paris Commune, held the office of vice-president. The majority of the Jacobins wanted a reconciliation with the Reunion club, just as they had with the Feuillants in 1791.[29] C.J. Mitchell maintains that the Reunion only met when the Jacobins were not in session, which meant members could attend meetings of both groups. Apparently when the Reunion group stopped meeting in the autumn of 1792, it had at least 200 members.[30] There is some evidence to suggest that the Jacobins may have been experiencing problems attracting members to their meetings. This phenomenon had been occurring since immediately after the insurrection of 10 August, when many Jacobins were engaged elsewhere, either at the Paris Commune, the executive council, or the Assembly. The question of diminishing attendance was raised at a meeting on 18 September and again on 23 September when the member Deperret suggested that the society should compose a list of deputies to the Convention who were members of the club, and hold regular meetings as a means of increasing attendance.[31]

Thuriot declared that the Reunion club had been formed by patriotic deputies, 'who believed it was in the public interest that they unite to strengthen themselves against the aristocrats'. He demanded that the Jacobins should not reject any members who also attended meetings of the Reunion club. Thuriot's statement that the Jacobins were depriving themselves of 200 'enlightened members' by insisting on expelling all those who attended the Reunion, illustrates the importance of this club in terms of numbers.[32] The fact that Collot, Chabot and Baudouin appealed to the Jacobins to end 'private meetings and private intrigues', also demonstrates how perturbed they were about the popularity of the rival club. Although Collot was critical of patriotic meetings other than the Jacobins and concluded that, 'whoever is unfaithful to the Jacobins is unfaithful to the Republic', the society adopted Bourdon's proposal to delay the renewal of the Correspondence Committee until the members of the Reunion club had returned in order that the committee might be drawn from all members of the society.[33]

The Reunion continued its meetings until 1 October when Calon, president, announced that its members had decided to return *en bloc* to the Jacobins. Mathiez likened the return of the Reunion members to the Jacobins on 1 October to that of the Feuillants during the period following the Varennes crisis in August and September 1791. He claims that about half the Reunion members refused Calon's invitation.[34] What is important is that, at this stage, there seems to have been a club composed of many deputies, both from Paris and the provinces and that the Jacobins, which had been suffering from a loss of members to the Reunion, had both Parisian and provincial deputies urging unity and the winding up of the Reunion club.

BRISSOT'S EXPULSION FROM THE JACOBIN CLUB

Brissot's expulsion from the Jacobin club was initiated by the deputy Chabot, a former ally, whose attack on Brissot was based primarily upon articles in the *Patriote Français* rather than anything Brissot had said either at the Convention or the Reunion club. Chabot attacked Brissot for the remarks he had made in the 23 September issue of his newspaper in which Brissot had denounced a small group of 'anarchic, demagogic deputies'. Chabot also denounced Brissot's friends, presumably meaning Roland and his group, whom he referred to as 'that conspiracy which appears to have been formed to make Danton, Robespierre and Collot unpopular'. He demanded that Brissot explain his remarks concerning the 'disorganizing party'. If Brissot failed to appear at the club's next session, then his name should be struck off the list of members. Chabot reiterated this demand at the next session when Brissot failed to appear, and Chabot sent a letter in which he expressed his desire to explain himself to his colleagues and promised to do so that evening. Pétion, president of the club, urged unity and stated that if Jacobins continued to be divided, 'all would be lost'. He beseeched his fellow members to 'forget all hatreds, forget personalities and focus on the issues for the good of all'.[35]

On 10 October, the society moved to strike Brissot's name off its list of members if he did not appear to exonerate himself. The member who proposed this, Moras, remarked that it had been twelve days since the club had passed this decree and Brissot had not kept his word. Yet Brissot was supported by Collot who insisted that his principles commanded him to take Brissot's side. He urged his fellow Jacobins to 'try to defend Brissot'. Manuel demanded that the club give Brissot a chance to be heard in person.[36]

When Brissot had still not appeared by the next meeting, two days later, Collot had run out of patience and he rose to deliver a scathing attack on Brissot. As with Chabot, Collot's attack was based entirely upon articles Brissot had written in his journal throughout the month of September. This demonstrates both the danger in being a journalist and that the Jacobins were still carefully reading Brissot's paper. Many of Collot's criticisms concerned Brissot's negative remarks about the Paris Commune. Collot reproached Brissot for advocating an offensive war, for having supported Narbonne, and, although he admitted that Brissot had denounced Lafayette once at the Jacobins, contradicting himself when he praised him in his newspaper.[37] It seems that the Jacobins considered the expulsion of Brissot as a measure to be taken only as a last resort. Not only had they appealed to him to come to the club to defend himself at their meetings, but they had even asked Desmoulins to write to him for that purpose. According to Desmoulins, he had done so, but Brissot, 'preferred to reply that he would come when he had the time, and he had not found any in the fifteen days since the invitation'.[38] Due to these transgressions, the Jacobins felt they were left with no option but to expel Brissot. When the vote was taken, it was almost unanimous in favour of expelling him from the club even though many Jacobins had wanted to prevent his expulsion.[39]

Why had Brissot been so reluctant to come to the club? He did not provide reasons for his silence in his journal, his private papers, or in his *Mémoires*. Perhaps he thought that his voice no longer carried any weight at the club, and no matter what he might say, he would not be believed. It is true that Brissot had not attended meetings since 10 August, but this was also true of men like Danton and Robespierre. Since the Jacobin club had been rather weak after 10 August, Brissot may well have thought its meetings were not worth attending. He may have felt that the centre of real power was now at the Convention and in the ministry. Explaining himself before the Jacobins might have saved him from being expelled at least temporarily, as he still had plenty of provincial supporters.

Three days after his expulsion, the society printed a formal justification of its actions in the form of a circular letter to its affiliated societies. What it amounted to was a Parisian interpretation of Brissot's activities from the beginning of the revolution to the present day. He had supported Lafayette after the Champ de Mars 'massacre', he had rashly advocated war without taking any measures to prepare for it. Brissot had his friends made ministers. During the period of the question of the king's dethronement, he and his friends had rarely appeared at the Jacobins, rather they had formed their own club, that of the Reunion. The demonstration of 20 June was attributed to Brissot's faction united with the deputies from the Gironde in an attempt to get their ministers back in office. Brissot had taken no part in the insurrection of 10 August, but instead had tried to stall it by doing a deal with the king. After 10 August, Brissot and Roland, with the help of Roland's secret funds, produced incendiary pamphlets and placards which incessantly attacked the commune, especially the best patriots, and spread rumours that Robespierre had been designated as dictator. The September massacres were used by Brissot and his friends to inspire a 'really perfidious party' against Paris. Although the circular was intended as a justification of its action against Brissot to provincial societies, the Paris club also attacked some of his friends, such as the ministers Clavière and Roland, together with Condorcet. It specifically isolated Condorcet's journal as a slander sheet against the commune. In some ways, this is ironic since Condorcet was one of the conciliators rather than someone on the offensive. Nor was he a particularly close friend of Brissot.[40]

The letter is a perfect example of Parisian propaganda designed to turn the provincial societies against Brissot. It did not always prove effective. The clubs in Chartres, Pont-Rouge, Riom, Meaux, Châlons-sur-Saône, Puy and Granville all wrote letters to the mother society defending Brissot. As a result of Brissot's expulsion, the Pont-Rouge club severed its relations with Paris. The behaviour of the Pont-Rouge society was probably a reflection of the decision of the Paris Jacobins to expel not only Brissot, but his friends towards the end of November.[41] Other clubs which responded in a hostile fashion to Brissot's expulsion were Cherbourg, which denounced Marat and his newspaper at its session of 21 October, and the society of Morlaix, which demanded the expulsion of Marat on 8 November. The Récollets society (the Jacobins of Bordeaux) made him an honorary member. It asserted its antipathy to the 'insolent and anarchistic principles' found in the circular of 15 October.[42] Brissot's popularity in the provinces was related to the success of his newspaper which ranked fourth in the standings of the most subscribed newspapers by Jacobin clubs.[43]

The expulsion of Brissot from the club marked a turning point in the disintegration of relations between a formerly homogeneous group of radical politicians. During the previous week, the society had renewed its Correspondence Committee, which was composed of Chabot, Collot, Dufourny, Deperret, Isambert, Merlin and Augustin Robespierre, or Robespierre jeune, Robespierre's younger brother. It was changed only four days after the apparent closing of the Reunion.[44] Danton took over the presidency on 10 October, the same day that Collot denounced Brissot and demanded his expulsion. It was about this time that relations between Danton and Roland had broken down. It appears that the change in the members of the Correspondence Committee, the president and secretaries and the attacks upon and expulsion of Brissot occurring within such a short space of time were not coincidental, but amounted to a concerted effort to eliminate Brissot and his closest friends from any kind of influence in the club.

Nor does it seem coincidental that Brissot and friends had lost the support of two previously sympathetic deputies Thuriot and Couthon on exactly the same day. In his initial speech against Brissot and his group, Thuriot spoke about an insurrection at Lorient. He proposed the suspension of all criminal trials related to popular movements which had occurred since 10 August. He advocated this because he feared that 'good patriots had perhaps been the victims of an exaggerated zeal.' Condorcet criticized Thuriot for having proposed an amnesty for crimes committed on 10 August. Réal supported Condorcet and proclaimed that Thuriot had forgotten what the last revolution was all about. Thuriot seemed to think the whole affair was a concerted effort by Brissot and his friends, which it probably was not. He claimed that it amounted to a tactic on the part of Brissot and his forces to discredit him.[45] The denunciation of the so-called 'Brissotin faction' must have been considered important by the officers of the club, as Thuriot's name was mentioned in the Jacobin circular as one of those who had contributed to saving the republic on 10 August.

The Paris Jacobins took note of both Thuriot's and Couthon's turnabout on the departmental guard question and rewarded them with places on their 'auxiliary constitutional committee', which had been formed on 19 October. Brissot's friends were conspicuously absent from the committee. There was now a dominance of Paris deputies on the Jacobin Constitution Committee: Robespierre, Danton, Antoine, Bentabole, Cloots, Robert, Saint-Just, Saint-André and Chabot.[46] The prickly Desmoulins, who was pleased to get at Brissot, expressed his satisfaction at Couthon's outburst in the Jacobins. 'Couthon', Desmoulins declared, 'had risen against the party of intriguers who dominate the convention.' He continued by arguing that Brissot had a 'party' which Couthon called 'brissotin', and which was synonymous with 'intriguers' and 'aristocrats'. According to Desmoulins, they resembled a coalition of many, or a faction.[47]

It took Brissot a fortnight to respond to the Jacobins in the form of a pamphlet, dated 24 October. He did not appear before the club as he had been requested to do. It was a defence of his revolutionary career, his war policy and an attack on his enemies, whom he called the 'disorganizers'. His most prominent enemy was the Paris Commune after 10 August, which had committed numerous crimes. It had invested a municipality with national powers and raised the stature of Paris well above the rest of the country. It had conducted missions in which the representatives had been charged with 'making inflammatory statements, preaching agrarian law and pillage and familiarizing the people with the effusion of blood and the spectacle of decapitated heads'. He specifically named Marat, Robespierre, Chabot and Collot as his enemies. Brissot insisted that the club had stopped being important or useful since February at which time a radical 'clique' overwhelmed the majority of moderates such as himself. He did not recommend the club's closure, but its renewal and reformation. Brissot seemed to be saying that the Paris club should not have a more important role than the provincial societies, as he wrote that the Paris club was just one of many popular societies in France. He had definitely switched allegiances and for Brissot, Paris was no longer the centre of the revolution: 'There is only one republic in France; there cannot be one church of Jacobins and one of republicans. I belong to the republic, to that church: it is no longer in Paris alone.'

He discussed Robespierre's denunciation of himself and his friends at the commune, and the 'massacre warrants' issued against them by the Surveillance Committee. On the subject of the September massacres, which he now abhorred, he referred to 2 September as 'a day of shame for Paris and one of mourning for humanity'. Brissot asserted that the butchering of the prisoners was only an accessory to a greater plan, a conspiracy directed against the legislature, the ministry and its defenders. On the other hand, he did not reproach Danton; rather, he seemed to lament the loss of a good man who had been lured to the other side by Robespierre. It is typical of Brissot's impudence to comment on how he disliked divisions when, in many ways, he provoked his own expulsion. In addition, he protested against the electoral assembly of Paris which had 'prostituted itself to the most vile of factions', and added that he had been condemned because he held principles contrary to it and to the Paris Commune.[48]

Gorsas, who had openly spoken against the Jacobins immediately after Brissot's expulsion on 12 October, came out strongly in support of his friend in his review of Brissot's pamphlet. He proclaimed that Brissot had been the first republican in France and he defended him as the apostle of offensive war. This is a curious remark coming from a writer who, throughout the war debates, had remained non-committal, and if he had swayed either way, it had been towards Robespierre. It seemed to indicate a complete turn-around in his attitude. The expulsion of Brissot turned him against the club which he 'esteemed', which contained 'a great number of my dearest friends', yet this club 'listened to the one you call atrocious, maniac and bloodthirsty'. Gorsas, who had openly supported the massacres while they were being committed, now with Brissot, condemned them and those whom he believed to be their authors, Marat and his associates, who had issued arrest warrants against his friends.[49] When it came to taking sides, Gorsas was motivated by personal friendship for Brissot, rather than political principles. It is true that he had no use for Marat, but neither did many other deputies, including Parisians, yet they did not back Brissot in this case. The expulsion of Brissot from the Jacobins forced him to decide whom he would back. It was only after he had made this decision that he revised his stance about the issues: the war, the Paris Commune, the prison massacres and the Jacobins.

Shortly thereafter, Desmoulins turned against Gorsas and implied that Pétion was not a Jacobin, simply because he was a friend of Brissot. Concerning Gorsas, he inquired as to the reasons 'why this relentlessness by our old friend Gorsas against those he falsely accuses of having presided over the massacres of 2 September?' Desmoulins found the answer in Gorsas' bitterness at not being elected by the electoral assembly of Paris. This was also true of Louvet whose 'jealousy and hatred of our deputation has no other foundation'. Desmoulins also pointed out quite justifiably the hypocrisy of both Brissot and Gorsas' attitude towards the September massacres.[50]

The expulsion of Brissot from the Jacobins polarized loyalties. Some of Brissot's friends supported him even though they had disagreed with his policies. Others, such as Couthon, had their own personal reasons for deserting their previous friends.

LOUVET'S 'ROBESPIERRIDE' AND ROBESPIERRE'S REPLY

The same day that Gorsas wrote his polemic against the Paris deputation to the Convention, 29 October, Louvet rose in the Convention to deliver his 'Robespierride'. Keeping in mind that it had only been four days since Brissot produced his pamphlet against the Jacobins, this looks very much like a concerted effort on the part of Brissot, Louvet and Gorsas against the Jacobins. Louvet's speech had been prepared for more than a month, and Brissot, Madame Roland and Guadet had read it beforehand and had probably agreed as a group what Louvet should argue.[51] The differences between Louvet and Robespierre were much more a matter of personal dislike and personal loyalty than a division over the issues. The content of Louvet's speech did not differ significantly from Brissot's brochure. The major difference was that Louvet, presumably under the influence of Roland or Madame Roland, attacked Danton as well as Robespierre and Marat (Louvet demanded Marat's arrest), while Brissot had shown a reluctance to oppose Danton. Louvet posited that Robespierre was aspiring to be a dictator while Danton had not done his job on 2 September.

   More significant than the actual content of the speeches by Robespierre and Louvet – Robespierre replied to Louvet on 5 November – were the reactions of the Jacobins and of Brissot's friends. Clearly, politicians who had not previously done so were sorting out their political affiliation. The Jacobin session of 29 October was entirely preoccupied with Louvet's speech. It began with a member (not named) proposing to expel him. The president, La Faye, replied by summarizing the most important element of Louvet's speech: that Louvet had accused Danton, Robespierre, Marat and Santerre. Fabre immediately asked members to delay this motion, as they had done with Brissot. He closed with the proposition that Pétion act as arbiter between Robespierre and Louvet. In his speech, he commended Pétion, who was 'always pure and sincere'.

Robespierre speaking at the podium, by anonymous artist. (Bibliothèque nationale de France)

Fabre urged the club to be 'tolerant and generous'. At this juncture, Pétion could still be trusted, as was illustrated by Fabre's statement that whatever the liaisons were between the 'intriguers' and Pétion, he did not question Pétion's integrity. Legendre, who spoke after Fabre, seemed to imply that Louvet's timing had been deliberate as his speech had been prepared for some time. It had been just sitting in his pocket, waiting to profit from the effect of Roland's report and Brissot's pamphlet. It was a concerted party effort. Merlin, who called Louvet 'the dignified champion of intrigue', disagreed with Fabre's designation of Pétion as a judge because Pétion was friendly with Brissot, and he 'sees Roland, and receives Lasource, Vergniaud and Barbaroux'.[52]

   Robespierre's response was highly defensive. He rejected all of Louvet's accusations. He denied having any contact with Marat: he first spoke with Marat during the summer of 1791, and told Marat that his continual demands for heads 'revolted the friends of liberty'. He defended his behaviour at the electoral assembly: all decisions were unanimous and were ratified by the sections of deputies. As for having designated Marat as a deputy, (which he had), Robespierre replied that he had not recommended Marat any more than other 'courageous writers who had fought or suffered for the cause of the revolution'. Concerning the events of 2 September, far from provoking them, the general council of the commune did everything in its power to prevent them.[53] In regard to his leadership role at the Jacobins, he claimed that he never sought to dominate the club and had rarely attended meetings since 10 August.

Robespierre's inclusion of Condorcet's *Chronique* among the 'Brissotin' newspapers was curious, for by that time, without attacking individuals, Condorcet had clearly distanced himself from that group. He had changed his mind on the issue of the departmental guard in October, fearing that its creation would risk a conflict between Paris and the provinces and might even lead to the dissolution of the Convention. He rejoiced in the Convention's decision to adjourn its creation and supported the right of the sections to send an address to the provinces against this armed force. Moreover, he urged unity and he disapproved of Louvet's speech against Robespierre, or 'Robespierride', saying that it was not what the 'public good required'. Finally, he did not attack Robespierre after his reply to Louvet, but merely urged everyone to put disputes aside for the good of the country.[54] He seemed to be in good standing at the Jacobins. Chabot had recently spoken of Condorcet as a friend when commenting on the Convention's Constitution Committee at the Jacobins.[55]

Vergniaud and Gensonné also opposed Louvet's denunciation. They thought the timing was bad and the speech would only enhance divisions. Danton, who shared Vergniaud's trepidation that disagreements would ruin the republic, intervened with a plea for understanding and reconciliation.[56]

Barbaroux demanded that Robespierre be denounced and that his denunciation be engraved in marble, while Barère eloquently begged deputies to end 'these political duels, these single combats of vanity and hatred'. He urged deputies to get down to the important business at hand: public security, the colonies, public instruction and the constitution. Matters of policy rather than personality should be the concern of deputies.[57]

The Jacobin meeting of 5 November was devoted to a discussion of Louvet's attacks against Robespierre and the deputation from Paris. Manuel initiated the debate by announcing that Robespierre was no longer his friend. Yet he added that Pétion and Robespierre were the 'two twins of the revolution'. Robespierre, the 'austere philosophe', had lost out to the 'cheerfulness of an honest man' (Pétion). Collot, in his reply, began saying that Manuel's errors necessitated a reply. He agreed that the 'two stars', like Castor and Pollux, had 'raised themselves to the sky of liberty, but it seems that Robespierre should be the summer star and Pétion the star of winter'. Concerning the events of 2 September, he regretted the innocent who had suffered, but they must be interpreted in the light of the general good they had accomplished. They were the necessary corollary to 10 August. He insisted that Manuel had cooperated on the day and that citizens could not allow women and children to come under the knives of conspirators.[58]

Fabre assured members that it was the 'men of 10 August' who had forced their way into the prisons in Paris, Versailles and Orléans, who were now condemning the massacres. Fabre demanded that the society send a 'historical memoir' of these days to the affiliated societies. Panis, Tallien, Danton, Chabot, Basire, Collot and himself were assigned the task of writing it.[59] Barère took a similar line on the massacres to Collot: morally, the *journée* of 2 September was a crime, but in terms of politics, it was an advantage for the revolution since it destroyed the 'remainder of those

The *machine* of Dr Guillotine presented to the National Assembly, 1789. (Bibliothèque nationale de France)

impure people who could not be dealt with by the law'. Deputies should no longer speak of this day. There was no need to put the revolution 'on trial'. Chabot took a slightly different view by reproaching the Surveillance Committee for not stopping the blood-letting.[60]

Pétion finally broke his silence when he addressed a letter to the Jacobins two days after Robespierre's speech. The letter was most of all a justification of his own behaviour, and a demonstration of his support for the Jacobins, which he defended with all his strength. Pétion claimed to have taken responsibility for the Jacobins at the time of the Champ de Mars massacre. Unlike Robespierre who was so was terrified that he would not attend sessions at the Assembly, Pétion claimed: 'I saved Robespierre; he wanted to flee. I saw him trembling from persecution when everyone had abandoned him.' On this occasion, Robespierre did not live up to his reputation as a patriot. Pétion protested that he did not know of a 'faction Brissot', to which Chabot replied, 'when Pétion tells you that he does not know a Brissot party, I start to doubt his virtue'. He added that Pétion had not tried to prevent the demonstration of 20 June because its true intention was the return of the ministers Clavière and Roland to office.[61] Chabot's speech is another example of how events were distorted to suit the present political ammunition.

Pétion's letter of 7 November was followed by a speech in the Convention three days later. In his opening statement, he declared that he could no longer keep his silence on the events that had occurred since 10 August. Initially, the new commune was reproached unjustifiably, but it soon merited criticism for prolonging the revolutionary movement beyond its term and for rivalling the Convention as the national power base. At the first session of the new commune, he discovered that it was no longer an administrative body deliberating on city business, but a political assembly which believed itself to be vested with national powers. He contrasted his own position with that of Robespierre. While the mayor no longer held a position of influence, Robespierre had become all-powerful. He said that he rarely came to meetings and that Robespierre took control. He went on to repeat much of what had already been said by Brissot and Louvet about the September massacres, the missions and the elections to the Convention. Robespierre, in his reply to Pétion a few days later, noted this fact. Pétion reviewed his personal experience as a powerless mayor which he called 'a useless title'. What Pétion's speech revealed was that when he was finally forced to make a decision between Robespierre and Brissot, he chose Brissot. Torn between his former colleague and good friend from the Constituent Assembly and his old school friend, Pétion strongly defended Brissot for the following reasons: he had known Brissot since childhood and he believed his 'principles to be pure'. Friendship in the case of Robespierre and Pétion could not resist division over issues. The idea of Brissot as the head of a party, as Robespierre had alleged, was completely absurd, as Brissot did not possess 'the reserve, the duplicity, or the influence to be the leader of a party'. When Robespierre had denounced Roland, Brissot and several others at the commune on the eve of the September massacres, Pétion explained how he had reacted: 'I had a lively explanation with Robespierre. I told him that you have done wrong; your agitations, your alarms, your hatreds, your suspicions agitate the people; but, finally, explain yourself; do you have facts? Do you have proof? I fight alongside you; I love only liberty.'[62] Pétion's speech illustrates that personal friendship for Brissot was the vital issue. In a revealing letter printed by Condorcet, Pétion perceptively summarized the source of the divisions between these revolutionaries: 'Jealousy is the principal passion which devours mediocre men and the most active of all divisions, of all disorders. It is necessary that those who deserve to be truly free men, those who have perfected their reason, who have acquired useful knowledge, unite to show an untiring zeal to enlighten their fellow citizens.'[63]

During these initial months of the Convention, cleavages developed, but they did not entirely resemble the line-up which would exist at the end of May 1793 when a group of twenty-nine deputies was expelled from the Convention. Divisions which existed between individuals resulted either from differences over particular issues, such as the departmental guard, the role of the Paris Commune after 10 August, the failure to be elected to a committee or an office, or because of personal dislike. Most deputies, regardless of faction, avoided defending Marat if possible, and it was the deputy Boileau rather than Brissot, who first called for his expulsion from the Convention.

Brissot, Barère, Buzot, Barbaroux and Gorsas, in addition to a number of former Legislative Assembly deputies, were on the offensive during these first few days of the Convention, attacking the Paris delegation and the commune's actions after 10 August, including its supposed role in the September massacres. This indicates a continuation of a pattern established during the post-10 August Assembly. Brissot's behaviour is more understandable than the others since his name had been on the arrest warrant issued by the commune at the start of the massacres and he had been a personal enemy of Robespierre for some time. They had fallen out earlier in the year over the issue of war. Gorsas allied himself with Brissot for reasons of friendship. Buzot and Barbaroux's actions are more puzzling. Buzot incessantly denounced Paris and the project for a guard was his personal idea. There is no evidence that Buzot and Barbaroux had been intended for death during the massacres. Nor did either seek election in Paris. Carra's denunciation of Robespierre was in reaction to the latter's criticism of his newspaper.

Many of the deputies who were elected to a committee or office were denounced by Marat at the time. Control of committee membership seems more evident at the Jacobin club after Brissot's expulsion than in the Convention. Couthon resented not gaining a position on the Constitution Committee, although he was elected a few days later to the Legislation Committee. Couthon's disappointed ambition could be compared to that of Robert, who had attacked Brissot after the latter was unable to secure a diplomatic position for him the previous March when the first Roland ministry was appointed. Although Desmoulins was not elected to a committee or office either, he did not complain about this until months later. Nor did Billaud have anything to say at the time about not being on a committee. There is no evidence that a faction working to get its own people on committees or in offices, was operating at the time.

Mercier and Saint-Just remained entirely outside any faction fighting at this juncture. Robert remained silent both in the Convention and at the Jacobin club. Fouché, who had been elected a moderate deputy from Nantes, was far closer to Vergniaud than Robespierre with whom he had quarrelled and personally disliked.

Pétion, Condorcet, Manuel, Gensonné and Danton were the major conciliators, repeatedly urging their colleagues to forget personalities and focus on the problems facing the new republic. The Bordelais, especially Vergniaud and Gensonné, tended to stay outside the personality contests, although Vergniaud denounced the Paris Commune of 10 August, but not the Paris delegation to the Convention. Roland, and his wife, who resented Danton's strength of character particularly during times of national crisis, such as the September massacres, alienated Danton by trying to prove that he was dishonest with funds while serving as Minister of Justice. Roland played an important role as an agitator and practitioner of patronage politics by funding Louvet, Gorsas and other newspapers. Brissot's persistent defence of Roland, his former employer and close friend, cost him Danton as a valuable ally. Louvet, whose allegiance lay with Roland for financing his paper, denounced Robespierre. Pétion, when forced to decide between Brissot and Robespierre, defended

Brissot, his childhood friend. Condorcet, who has been traditionally associated with the 'Brissotins', clearly distanced himself from men like Barbaroux, Brissot and Buzot, and was really a member of no party as he said himself in a letter to his electors in Aisne: 'I joined some members of the Constituent . . . but we were of no party . . .'[64] Condorcet viewed the onslaught on Marat, Danton and Robespierre as petty and dangerous.

Brissot was reluctantly expelled from the Jacobin club and only had himself to blame, as he was asked many times by fellow members to explain himself before them. Prominent members like Fabre and Collot clearly wanted to prevent Brissot's expulsion. Louvet, understandably, was expelled a short time after his personal attack on Robespierre, but except for him and Brissot, all the others continued to be members. Brissot, Barbaroux, Gorsas and Buzot were particularly hostile to the Paris Commune, but so were Barère and lesser-known provincials such as Cambon, who had been a deputy to the previous assembly. The major bone of contention, apart from personal rivalries, was the September massacres, which, as Desmoulins pointed out, no one had condemned at the time. Brissot had not forgotten Robespierre's denunciation of him on the eve of the massacres. The effective control of the Paris elections by Robespierre caused much dissension as did the behaviour of the Paris Commune after 10 August.

The months from September until the end of November were crucial in determining how the two sides of the Convention were coagulating. It would take the important issue of what to do with the dethroned and now imprisoned king for the formerly homogeneous group of radical politicians to sort out their political affiliation.

7

New Challenges to the Republicans

Between January and March of 1793, increasing tension mounted as the challenges confronting deputies grew more complex and difficult. On 21 January 1793, the king was executed after a trial drawn out over many months. At the same time, the war was putting new pressures on the young republic. What follows is not a chronicle of events, but an examination of how, if at all, the important circumstances and issues of these months affected the groups which had already developed by this time.

The Trial of Louis XVI and the Convention

Charcoal drawing of Louis XVI, 1793, by Joseph Ducreux. (Musée Carnavalet)

Deputies were unanimous about the question of Louis XVI's guilt when the Convention voted him a traitor on 15 January 1793. Not one of the republican politicians who are the subject of this book voted against this question. However, the issue of putting the king on trial raised all sorts of new problems for the revolutionaries. Was the king not covered by his constitutional inviolability for everything that he had done up to 10 August? Who should try him? Should there be a referendum on the verdict? These questions would occupy the business of the Convention for a number of months. What is of importance to this book is not to analyse how the entire Convention voted – this has been more than adequately done by Alison Patrick[1] – but to examine how the men who are under consideration here conducted themselves and provide reasons for their political behaviour.

Buzot, Barbaroux and Pétion took the initiative in introducing the questions relative to the trial. The trial itself opened on 7 November, but Barbaroux, back on 16 October, had demanded that the Convention should form a judicial committee and that discussion on the trial be opened. On 7 November, the deputy Mailhe presented a report, which concluded that the king, whose reign had been overthrown by the nation, could be judged by the representatives of the nation.

Discussion of Mailhe's report began on 13 November. Pétion put forward the question of whether or not the king could be judged. He argued that the king was not inviolable.[2] Robert, in complete agreement with Pétion, denied the validity of the constitution of 1791 because it was a monarchical constitution. Following Pétion's motion on 3 December, the Convention decided that Louis could indeed be judged.[3] A day later, the deputies decreed, again on Pétion's motion, that the Convention occupy itself with the king's trial every afternoon. On Buzot's suggestion, the Convention voted that anyone who proposed to re-establish monarchy in France would be put to death.[4] Barbaroux read the list of Louis's crimes on 12 December. Upon Guadet's proposal, the Convention decreed that it would deliberate on the questions which dealt with the king's guilt, the ratification of the Assembly's vote by the people and the type of punishment to be inflicted.[5] Clearly, it was those later accused of wanting to save the king, and thus considered to be moderate, rather than the Parisian extremists who took the initiative on the king's trial.

Saint-Just, in response to Pétion's question on whether or not Louis could be judged, declared that Louis should not be judged as a citizen, but as an enemy. He, Marat and Robespierre did not think that a trial was necessary. Brissot praised both Saint-Just's speech as well as the man himself, welcoming him as a 'talent which could one day honour France'. Condorcet endorsed Robespierre's argument that the king could not be judged by the Convention because it was a political assembly, rather than a court of law. Believing in the separation of powers, he wrote that the Convention 'could not be a legislature, a court of law, and a judge'. In fact, Condorcet warmly praised Robespierre's speech of 3 December.[6] Condorcet did not play a significant role in Louis' trial: he would intervene only at voting time. His biographers maintain that he behaved more like a *philosophe* than a politician. He remained isolated from both factions, and during the vote on Louis' punishment, he even encouraged the Assembly to abolish the death penalty except for crimes against the state. When the time came for him to vote, he simply stated: 'I have no voice.'[7] In terms of the question as to whether or not Louis could be judged, deputies conducted themselves in a gentlemanly fashion. Factional squabbles were absent as politicians focused on this issue.

THE REFERENDUM

The king's trial involved the question of whether or not the people of France should ratify whatever decision deputies made, known at the time as the *appel au peuple*. The vote on the referendum was significant because it became the issue which would divide some deputies on principle, and be used by others to attack their opponents, perhaps in the hope of persuading undecided voters to their viewpoint. Moreover, two months after the king's death, the controversy over the referendum would be kept alive by the petition from the Marseilles Jacobins, which demanded the expulsion of those who voted in its favour.

The referendum has long been considered a political manoeuvre by the 'Girondins' to gain ascendancy over the 'Mountain'[8] in the Convention, but this is not necessarily the case since it was not originated by 'Girondins' and many non-'Girondin' deputies endorsed it.[9] Moreover, not all 'Girondins' voted in favour of it, and for those who did, it did not turn them against radicals such as Saint-Just, Carra and Barère, who voted against it.[10]

Many deputies spoke in terms of personalities and used their speeches as a pretext to attack their opponents. This was particularly true of Gensonné, Barbaroux and Marat. Gensonné, who was in favour of the referendum, used it as a excuse to attack the '*faction maratique*' and Paris, but not Carra. Gensonné maintained that the referendum was a way of uncovering factions and of preventing the usurpation of the people's rights. He felt that it would stop one faction from dominating the Convention. He reproached Robespierre for opposing this measure in the hope of robbing the nation of its sovereignty and for speaking incessantly about the 'intriguers' who dominated the Convention. He attacked those who had approved of the September massacres and advocated new massacres.[11] This marks a change in Gensonné's attitude. Previously, he had not been on the offensive.

On the other hand, Carra was irritated by the endless denunciations directed against the Paris Commune. This was precisely the theme of a letter written by Robespierre and addressed to Brissot, and the three Bordelais, at this time. The principal subject of the letter was the referendum, but Robespierre used the letter to praise Paris, attack Brissot for identifying him with Marat, and repeat his old indignation at Brissot's reckless launching of a war to be run by a 'perfidious court'. He defended Marat and his journal, but with qualification, writing that 'his paper . . . is not always the model of style and wisdom'. In addition, Robespierre denounced the Bordelais for their compromise with the king in July 1792.[12]

Brissot too spoke in terms of personality, but in a positive rather than a negative fashion. Although he was very surprised at Carra opposing the referendum, this did not affect their relationship.[13] Brissot's attitude towards Carra demonstrates that one could disagree on a matter of principle, but remain friends. Carra and Brissot would often find themselves on opposite sides of an issue, yet they did not become enemies. Presumably this must mean that there was more involved here than merely political principles. Often a conciliator during these months, Carra urged his colleagues to 'speak impartially and not about personalities'.[14]

The question of taking the monarch's fate to the people involved the fundamental principles of democracy, representation and sovereignty. Was sovereignty located with the people themselves, or with their representatives? Many deputies, especially those from Paris, felt that it was dangerous and inadvisable to extend sovereignty to the ordinary people. Every Paris deputy who spoke on the issue of sovereignty, argued that it rested in the Convention, i.e. with the people's representatives, and not with the people themselves. Fabre used the Rousseauist argument that each citizen could not exercise his sovereign will because that would mean voters would be divided into particular wills. In other words, there would be opposition. The general will of the French people was represented by the Convention. Billaud employed the same sort of language: 'Sovereignty is nothing more than the expression of the general will . . . in its essence, it is one and indivisible. Should one claim that the Convention does not have sufficient powers? That would be to negate its competence.' Since the Convention had been elected by the people, it had the right to speak for it. Robert declared that as deputies they were called to represent the people, but not to consult it. 'To consult the people rather than to work on its behalf, meant to betray it.'[15] Couthon shared the same ideology as the Paris delegation on this matter. He believed the referendum was 'a violation of sovereignty'. It would destroy 'national representation and save conspirators'. He explained that although the people were sovereign, in an established society, it could not turn primary assemblies into tribunals.[16]

Taking an entirely different and arguably a more democratic stance on this issue were Barbaroux, Brissot and Louvet. Barbaroux insisted that it was time for the 'people of the

84 departments to exercise their sovereignty'. Barbaroux's speech can be contrasted with Marat's of the same day. Although Marat paid homage to the sovereignty of the people, he argued that the people could only exercise this sovereignty in the case of the declaration of rights, and 'extending the restricted sanction of the people to important decrees would overturn the state and make it into a desert'. Marat continued to state that ratification by popular assemblies 'meant wanting to tear the merchant, the artisan and the labourer away from their occupations to make them into statesmen. This would be to reverse the order of things.' Robespierre spoke in similar terms as the 'people's friend'. Both seemed to imply that the ordinary citizens of France had neither the capacity nor the inclination to participate in the referendum: 'If the people had the time to meet to judge the trial or decide questions of state, they would not have entrusted their interests to you . . . Virtue is always among a minority on earth.'[17]

Barère favoured a trial and, initially, banishment rather than death. He argued brilliantly against the referendum in an evidently moderate speech by subtly stating that a direct appeal to the people was an act of defiance against the principle of representation on which the constitution was based. Although Brissot disagreed with Barère, he praised Barère's 'patriotism and talents'.[18] Couthon, holding the opposite view from Barère, in terms of the need to hold a trial, also praised his speech. Couthon did oppose the appeal to the people on the grounds that it was not practical.[19] It could be surmised from these arguments and attitudes that at the time of the debate on the king's trial, one's attitude on the issues did not make friends into enemies.

Those who voted for the referendum were later accused by their enemies of wanting to save the king's life. Based on the contents of the deputies' speeches, it could be argued that rather than an attempt to save the king, the referendum was their method of discharging the Convention of the responsibility for the king's death. During the discussions which took place between 26 December and 7 January, the group which opted for the referendum all declared that Louis should be condemned to death. Their speeches were as violent as their opponents who voted against the referendum.

Barère was not the only deputy who was inconsistent during the king's trial. The case of Fouché is particularly interesting. Fouché's principal biographer, Madelin, has posited that for reasons of ambition, Fouché changed his mind on the death vote at the last minute. Using statements from contemporary memoirs, Madelin argued that Fouché had promised his colleague Daunou that he would vote against the death verdict, but when the day of the vote arrived, Fouché uttered only two words: '*la mort*', to Daunou's amazement. Madelin claims that Fouché voted this way in order to be 'on the winning side'.[20] More recently, Patrick has skilfully re-examined the evidence to demonstrate that Fouché could not possibly have known which way the majority was going to vote when he cast his ballots and therefore did not change his mind at the last minute. She explains that when Fouché voted against the referendum, there were sixty-seven votes in favour and forty-seven against, so he was voting against the trend. Second, concerning the death vote, there was no clear trend: fifty-six unconditional votes and forty-one for mercy. She concludes that whatever Fouché's motives may have been, he could not have known how the majority would vote.[21] Another writer has suggested that Fouché's mind was changed in a club which he attended, but he does not say which one, or provide any substantiation for this claim.[22] Although the question of Fouché's motives will never be resolved, what is clear is that his radical vote in the king's trial marked a complete change in his previously moderate politics. This does not mean, however, that he became partisan in his attitude. His one remaining pamphlet on the king's trial is devoid of factional rhetoric. The pamphlet is entirely about the referendum. Fouché clearly indicated the disadvantages of a referendum: a 'violation of the principles of our representative government', and advised those in favour of the referendum to 'abandon their honourable abstractions and reflect on this dilemma'.[23]

THE JACOBINS AND THE KING'S TRIAL: A FORUM FOR DENUNCIATIONS AND EXPULSIONS

The debate concerning Louis XVI's trial was played out in much stronger factional terms at the Jacobin club. Other issues were at work, however, and while the Convention concerned itself with endless speeches on Louis XVI, the Jacobins were preoccupied with personalities, the extraordinary influence of the 'Brissotin' press in the provinces, and the means by which to curtail it.

Although by mid-November the club tended to be a predominantly Paris-dominated institution, Carra, Gensonné, Buzot and Pétion continued to attend meetings of the Jacobins after the expulsions. During the debates on the king's trial, a new round of denunciations and expulsions of former colleagues and friends took place at the club. On 26 November, Roland, Louvet, and Girey-Dupré (Brissot's editorial assistant), were expelled for their propaganda against Robespierre and the deputation from Paris.[24] They were expelled after almost no discussion – a marked contrast to the agonizing over Brissot's expulsion. These expulsions were denounced in the presses of Brissot and Gorsas. Brissot wrote that the Jacobins had begun their 'purification vote', but in the reverse sense by expelling their best members, while Gorsas questioned the motives of such an action. He printed several letters from provincial societies, such as Pontivi (Haute-Vienne), and Rheims, expressing indignation. Nantes and Villeneuve-sur-Yonne demanded the expulsion of Robespierre and Marat. Brissot reproduced a letter from the Bordeaux society which announced its intention to sever all relations with Paris as long as Danton, Chabot, Marat, Merlin, Panis and Robespierre remained members.[25]

Manuel, a Paris deputy and someone who was not part of the Roland group in terms of journalistic patronage, was also denounced at this time and expelled from both the Jacobin and Cordelier clubs. He no longer deserved to be a member of the Jacobin club for his 'anti-patriotic conduct in defence of Louis XVI'. In addition, he had proposed that a court be established to distribute justice to guilty '*septembriseurs*'.[26] Fabre proposed that Pétion also be expelled from the Jacobins, but on Albitte's motion the society adjourned his removal from the club's list of members and members turned their attention to the king's trial.[27] The Bordeaux deputies were expelled from the club in January for their negotiations with the king the previous July.[28]

There is some evidence to suggest that individual Jacobin members were under pressure to vote for the radical line on the issue of Louis XVI. Curiously, Robert, who would later vote for the king's death without reprieve with almost the entirety of the Paris delegation, demanded on 27 December that the club 'grant a delay to Louis Capet'. This moderate proposal was immediately denounced by members such as Saint André who expressed surprise that 'such a proposition could come from the mouth of a patriot'. He declared that Louis must be 'heard and judged in the same session'. Robert 'justified' himself at the next meeting. Robert's moderate proposal suggests that initially there were differences of opinion among Parisian deputies, but that they were pressed to vote for the party line, or be denounced, or even expelled. From this time forward, Robert preached the radical line, speaking against the referendum, voting for death and no reprieve. Never again did he utter a word of moderation.[29]

There is also evidence to suggest that Carra was also under some pressure from the club. He was expelled and later readmitted as long as he voted for death. He had been outraged by the Jacobins' behaviour, writing that 'the mother society was concerned with nothing other than excommunications'. He was silent on the reasons for both his expulsion and reintegration, and the only reference to his problems with the club is in the *Journal Français*. It claimed that Carra was reproached for not having 'spoken clearly enough' about the massacres and that he was biased in his opinions of Robespierre and Marat. It compared the rift to the sulking between a lover and his mistress. As long as Carra promised to vote for death, he would be reconciled to the club. This is further evidence of Jacobin pressure to vote in favour of the radical line, which Carra did, perhaps because he was forced to do so.[30]

It is no wonder after these denunciations and expulsions, that Pétion wrote a letter to the president of the club, Saint-Just, on 21 December. The letter was written in response to a complaint made by a member that Pétion had prevented Jacobin letters from reaching the department of Eure-et-Loir, the department that Pétion represented. This pretext provided Pétion with the opportunity to urge members of the society to no longer 'suffer vague denunciations and calumnies'. The true friends of the society were those who wanted it purged. 'Why', he asked, 'were there so few patriots in attendance?' Because the distressing scenes made them ill and when they did get up the courage to speak against those who dominated, they were not heard. The patriots no longer attended meetings because they were treated like 'enemies of liberty and of the public good'. He compared the club to a 'scandal shop where denunciations and petty quarrels took precedence over serious discussions of public policy'. Presumably this was Pétion's reason for sending a letter, rather than speaking in person to the club. At the close of his letter, he implored members to concentrate their energy on the business at hand, rather than personalities.[31] Interestingly, Carra had been expelled the day Pétion's letter was read to the society, but he was readmitted on 9 January.

THE JACOBINS AND 'BRISSOTIN' NEWSPAPERS

The popularity and influence of journals funded by Roland at the provincial clubs had been the source of much vexation for the mother society for some time. With Roland's financial backing, a good number of his friends were successful in creating a distribution network throughout France. Those who received funding for their newspapers included Brissot, Louvet, Gorsas, Condorcet, Dulaure, Lemaire and Guinguené. In addition to his expenditure on journals, Roland also paid for the printing and distribution of speeches by Pétion and Louvet against Robespierre.[32] This was a formidable machine against which the Jacobins had to fight. To defend its declining reputation, on 5 November the society voted, on Fabre's motion and supported by Chabot, to draft an address to affiliated societies. It would contain the Jacobin rather than the 'Brissotin' version of events since 10 August. A committee composed of Fabre, Tallien, Danton, Chabot and Basire was struck to write it. Curiously, it took them almost a month to accomplish this task, and in the end only Robert and Chabot wrote it, rather than the entire group. In the ensuing three weeks, the most discussed topic at debates was 'Brissotin' propaganda. Not only were the departments inundated with the newspapers of Brissot, Louvet, Gorsas and others, they were also receiving copies of pamphlets such as Brissot's *A tous les Républicains*. This pamphlet was written by Brissot after his expulsion from the Jacobins in October.[33] The major issues dealt with in the club's circular at the end of November were 'Brissotin/Rolandin' propaganda and the attacks made against both the Commune of Paris and its deputation by the agitators: Roland, Brissot, Barbaroux, Buzot, and Louvet. Not only was Roland spending enormous sums of money on journals, libels and papers, he was intercepting Jacobin correspondence. The September massacres, intrinsically connected to 10 August, were defended as a necessary measure to exterminate France's enemies.[34]

Denunciations of 'Brissotin' newspapers continued throughout December. Robespierre, who had not taken a leading role previously, was now taking the initiative. He delivered powerful speeches on the 7th and again on the 12th of this month, He repeated the now common criticisms of the 'Brissotin' press, and summarized his major complaints: their goal was to raise up the departments against Paris, to save Louis, to spread alarm over Parisian food supplies. It was time for a counter-offensive by the Jacobins and this meant 'clarifying public opinion by all possible means'. He demanded on the 12th that the two worst newspapers he could name, those of Brissot and Condorcet, be read at the club. He ordered the same of Carra's and Gorsas' journals, but this was rejected.[35] It is curious that the journals of these men would be linked together, especially those of Carra and Gorsas, which often took opposing sides on the issues. Gorsas was much more hostile to Robespierre personally than Carra. Carra's journal was not funded by Roland. The only similarity between them was that their circulation among the departments was extensive. This was particularly true of Carra's *Annales*, which was read at the opening of most provincial Jacobin meetings.[36]

Jacobin anxiety about their lack of popularity among the provincial societies was not unfounded. As stated previously, the Correspondence Committee had not been doing its job of writing to provincial clubs. Several now complained about not getting mail from Paris.[37] Demands for the expulsion of Robespierre and Marat from the club had started after Brissot's expulsion in October and continued into early January. On 1 January, a member identified as 'C' remarked that the demand to expel Robespierre and Marat was coming from many clubs. He accused the Correspondence Committee of neglecting to do its duty of presenting the two men in glowing terms to the affiliates. At one point, the society decided to send missionaries to clubs where loyalty was wavering. A member was endorsed on 1 January to carry out this mission.[38] Some clubs were still calling for the expulsion of 'Robespierre, Marat and all the agitators' on 13 January. The club was clearly troubled by these demands.[39]

In addition to attempting to counter the powerful impact which the 'Brissotin' press had made in the provinces, the Jacobins made important changes to their own publications. The society was dissatisfied with the editorial policy of Deflers, editor of the club's *Journal*. Members felt that his transcription of debates made them look more radical than they were to the provinces. Robespierre had reminded colleagues that it was their 'duty to oppose insurrection'.[40] On 21 December, Deflers was denounced for his inaccurate reporting of both the club's discussions and Marat's speech on 16 December. Deflers, who had become the editor of the club's official journal in January 1792, had received funding from Roland from the end of September to the end of October. Roland cut the funding not long after Brissot's expulsion.[41] It is not surprising that with Roland's money Deflers was not reporting debates entirely accurately. Feelings against Deflers were so strong that he was physically removed from the hall on the rue St Honoré on 23 December. On the same day, he was expelled unanimously. In his transcriptions of that day's proceedings, he wondered how his voice could be heard in a society where wise advice by men like Pétion was lost among the 'murmurs and clamours of prejudice, and even slander'.[42] The Jacobins decided to publish their own journal, but lack of funds prevented this for six months. Lack of funds remained a persistent problem for the Paris Jacobins throughout this period. Membership dues had been spent by October. In December, a fund was opened for donations which would pay for the printing and distribution of propaganda, which included members' speeches on the king's trial.[43] Interestingly, the club never issued a circular on the subject of the king's trial. The only circular during this period, the one dated 9 January, did not refer to the trial at all. Saint-Just, as president, reminded members that the office was open where everyone should pay fifty *écus* to enable the club to publish and distribute Robespierre's pamphlet on Louis XVI. It would assist the club in 'dissipating the errors made by the Roland/Brissot faction'.[44]

The question of the newspapers of Gorsas, Carra and Louvet was raised again on 27 December when the society decreed that Tallien should edit a newspaper reporting the sessions of the Convention. This was suggested by Robespierre jeune who denounced the 'Brissotin' corruption of public opinion. It would be distributed throughout the provinces to counteract the influence of the 'Brissotin' journals. Maximilien Robespierre had already demanded that Brissot and Louvet's papers be read at each session; however, this was never carried out. At the same session of 27 December, in a further effort to fight the 'Brissotin' control of public opinion, the society decided to draft another circular. This was the circular of 9 January, which summarized club policy that had evolved over the past few months. Societies which supported Brissot were chastized. The Jacobins were in Paris, not in the provinces. Parisian interpretation of events was the only interpretation. Jacobin principles were 'pure and uncorrupted' by patronage. The circular focused its attack on Roland. He had intercepted Jacobin mail and this prevented the circulation of 'patriotic' writings in the provinces, he had failed to provision Paris, and he was accused of criminal negligence or criminal complicity with the court for his handling of the secret royal papers discovered at the Tuileries palace.[45]

SIGNIFICANCE OF THE TRIAL IN TERMS OF FACTIONS

The king's trial did little to change the factions and suspicions which were already in place. The same men continued their attacks and used their speeches on the king's trial to do so. It could be argued the trial intensified suspicions and hatreds which been developing over the past few months. The case of Robert demonstrates this clearly. It was during the period of the king's trial that he publicly denounced both Roland and Brissot, but before the voting took place and for reasons that had nothing whatsoever to do with the trial.

It is true that the most consistent voting can be found among the Parisian deputies, but this may well have been achieved under pressure. All Parisian deputies with the exception of Manuel, Danton and Collot voted against the referendum, and twenty-one out of the twenty-four voted for death. Danton and Collot did not vote because they were away on mission at the time. Robert, who had shown some moderation towards the king, was reprimanded for this at the Jacobins and immediately modified his view. Carra, not a Paris deputy, who had been expelled from the Jacobins, was readmitted on the stipulation that he voted for the king's death. There may well have been others like him who felt pressured to vote along the radical line. The trial did bring out tensions even between those who were apparently on the same side, such as between Marat and Robespierre, with the Jacobins divided between the two men. At the same time, men could disagree on an issue and not become enemies. This is true in the case of Carra and Gorsas, who were on

Louis Capet, his wife, sister, son and daughter dine together in the Tower of the Temple, 1793. (Bibliothèque nationale de France)

opposing sides in the referendum and sentencing votes, yet they remained friends. The same can be said for Brissot and Carra. Brissot acknowledged that Carra's speech 'surprised those who know his ideas and political views'.[46] Saint-Just, Barère and Fouché voted with the Paris deputation, but they did not personally attack those who voted the other way.

Although Louis XVI's trial did not produce a significant change in the suspicions which were already in existence, it did give rise to important changes in the Convention and in the Jacobin club. In the Convention, the major consequences of the trial were the resignation of Manuel on 18 January and the radical votes of Fouché and Barère. Manuel's letter of resignation, dated 18 January, was written in objection to the death sentence. He and Gorsas, both secretaries at the time, had been censured for not being present when the voting on the king's sentence began. Gorsas explained that he had worked thirty-six hours on the drafting of the proceedings and was held up getting some of them to Manuel. His censure was later lifted.[47] Condorcet grew increasingly apart from Brissot and his friends, to whom he had been particularly close at the time of Varennes. He now appeared to be an isolated politician, adhering to neither faction and staying entirely outside the personality contests. He had, however, accepted funding from Roland for his newspaper. Barère and Fouché, who had previously behaved very moderately, voted radically. Barère's biographer points out that the king's trial was a major turning point for him in that he had turned his back on his moderate past. When the time came for Barère to cast his vote, which he did in favour of the death penalty, he declared: 'The law tells me that between tyrants and peoples there are only struggles to death . . . As a classical author said, the tree of liberty grows only when it is watered by the blood of all tyrants. The law says death and I am only its voice.'[48] This was the case for Fouché as well; however, it did not mean that he made new enemies.

At the Jacobin club, which had been on the defensive against the powerful propaganda machine of Roland since 10 August, a change occurred after the middle of January. Provincial clubs which had supported the 'Brissotins' against the Jacobins, began to swing back to the mother society. This shift of opinion occurred towards the end of January. Although different clubs had varying reasons for turning against Brissot and friends, the change may well have been the result of the strengthening of the Jacobin propaganda machine with the circulars in December and January, and the weakening of the Roland/Brissot publishing enterprises. Roland's resignation meant the end of subsidization for the 'Brissotin' papers. Louvet announced that he was no longer publishing the *Sentinelle* at the end of November, stating that he wished 'to avoid all outside influences'. He began working for the *Bulletin des amis de la vérité* which was published by the Cercle Social.[49] The vote on the referendum may also have been important in some clubs. It appeared to many to be a delaying tactic in the king's execution. This was what the Marseilles Jacobin club believed when it justified the expulsion of Barbaroux and Rébecquy who both voted for the referendum.[50] This gradual change does not mean that the 'Brissotins' had been entirely abandoned by provincial societies. Gorsas noted favourable letters he received from 'many societies declaring that Roland merited the nation' on 6 February.[51]

When the deputy Lepelletier was assassinated by a royalist fanatic for voting in favour of the king's death, every deputy attended his funeral on 24 January. Vergniaud delivered the funeral

Engraving of the execution of Louis XVI, 21 January 1793, by Helman/Monnet. (Musée Carnavalet)

oration. No doubt the lives of others were also threatened, such as that of Jean Debry. Vergniaud's only letter written during the period of the king's trial, immediately after Lepelletier's murder, reveals that his house staff felt that his life too was in danger. The assassination at the end of Vergniaud's term as president of the Convention, on 25 January. Vergniaud did acknowledge that he had many enemies among the 'aristocrats and false patriots'.[52]

The deaths of Louis XVI and Lepelletier appeared to have given the Convention a new life and it entered a new phase. On the day of Louis' execution, Pétion invited deputies to forget their divisions, but Collot accused him of having slandered the electoral assembly of Paris.[53] Deputies found themselves confronted with serious issues to resolve. These included the problem of food supplies, the conduct of the foreign war, and the writing of a constitution, the reason the Convention had been elected. It would take real threats to the Convention to bring deputies together.

FIRST THREATS AGAINST THE CONVENTION

By September 1792, the economic situation in France was in a serious state. Although there had been a good harvest the previous summer there was little grain on the market. Prices were rising, inflation was rampant and the *assignat* was rapidly losing its value. The Parisian economy had been depressed by the collapse of the luxury trade. When the Paris Commune petitioned the Convention for price controls at the start of November, clearly something needed to be done. The deputies' response was a traditional one: the joint Committees of Agriculture and Commerce delivered a twenty-five-article decree recommending the requisition of grain by municipalities. Roland, as Minister of the Interior responsible for food supplies, addressed two letters to the Assembly, on 18 and 27 November, appealing for free trade as the solution. His case was that there was plenty of grain; the problem lay in France's restrictive laws impeding its circulation. He demanded that those who prevented the freedom of circulation be arrested. In addition, he criticized the Paris Commune, which would ruin people and expose them to famine if it forced merchants to sell necessities at cost price.[54]

The situation was particularly serious in neighbouring departments to Paris, where there had been rioting. This issue brought members of the Convention together, although Roland, who reassured members of the Convention that food was in abundance in Paris, used the food shortages and troubles in the neighbouring departments of Eure-et-Loir, Loir-et-Cher and Loiret, as a pretext to denounce Paris.[55] But among deputies, there was general agreement on what measures should be taken to resolve the problem. Barère proposed sending commissioners from the Convention into the troubled departments to re-establish the freedom of grain circulation and to discover the reasons why the laws of the Convention were not being executed. On 26 November, nine commissioners, including Couthon, were dispatched to these departments. Couthon went to Loir-et-Cher, where he claimed to have re-established the free circulation of grain and to have suppressed arbitrary price controls.[56] On 29 November, the commune presented a petition against the freedom of commerce and it demanded administrators to control the price of foodstuffs as a way of avoiding famine. It was at this point that Saint-Just delivered his famous speech on the economy, which was praised by Brissot: 'Saint-Just treated the question of food supplies in its entirety, in all its moral and political aspects; he deployed spirit, warmth and philosophy, and honoured his talents in defending the freedom of trade.'[57]

Since revolutionary circumstances were by no means ordinary, revolutionaries had to take extraordinary measures. Saint-Just's solution was a modified version of free trade: the state would have some control, but for the most part he sanctioned a system whereby the economy would run on the principles of free trade. He advocated limiting the issuance of paper money, the sale of *émigré* goods, paying the nation's creditors in land or annuities, and the freedom of navigation on the rivers. Although Saint-Just's speech was acclaimed by all in the Convention, it did not act upon most of his suggestions. It passed a decree, which prohibited grain exportation, but made sure that there was free circulation within the country's borders. What the speech did do, however, was to enhance Saint-Just's prestige among both factions. He was made president of the Jacobin club on 9 December and a secretary in the Convention at the end of November.[58]

Pétion also spoke against price controls on wheat and recommended sending a major force into the department of Eure-et-Loir to ensure the free circulation of grain and to prevent people from stealing it. Danton seconded this opinion and added that those who violated the Convention's law would be severely punished. Buzot, Pétion and Robespierre made similar arguments. Interestingly, this important matter of food shortage, which had brought out petitioners threatening the Convention, brought the splintered factions together. There was unanimity concerning the measures to be taken and Robespierre, in particular, defended the sovereignty of the deputies. He stated in no uncertain terms that the 'sacred character' of the representatives of the people should not be insulted. 'The Convention', he declared, 'is the supreme power. Anyone who attacks it should be severely punished and this punishment was for their own good.' He closed his speech with a call for unity and concord in the Assembly. Danton reiterated Robespierre's position. When the Convention was threatened, the battle was no longer between its members, but between it and the 'people', the sans-culottes, who had attacked it. It was acceptable for members to attack each other, as they had throughout the king's trial and during the month of November, but when the Convention itself was attacked from outside, that was totally inappropriate. The deputies could be compared to a quarrelling family. When threatened from the outside, it would pull together and support all members. This is what Robespierre and Danton urged.[59]

Throughout the next few weeks, the economy continued its downward slide. Deputies had focused on the king's trial. On 12 February, the Convention was once again faced with a hostile group of petitioners; this time it was representatives from the forty-eight sections of Paris. They demanded a maximum price for grain, a low price for bread and a penalty of six years in irons for administrators who carried out commerce in grain. The petition caused general indignation among deputies. The usually radical Marat responded in a most conservative manner. The first to reply to the petitioners, he retorted that the measures proposed by the group were 'so foreign, so violent and so subversive of all principles, so contrary to the free circulation of food supplies and intended to cause disorder that they would lead to famine and anarchy'. Since the petitioners appeared without the mayor of Paris, as was traditionally done, Marat condemned their deputation as illegal. He demanded that the petitioners verify their powers and be pursued as disrupters of the public order. Buzot, Carra and Billaud supported him.[60] Barère remarked that they should be denied the traditional 'honours of the session' because they were 'doubly reprehensible': they had written a petition of the rich under the guise of the poor, and they had demanded something contrary to the law which had been passed by the Convention only three weeks previously: the freedom of grain circulation. Barère's proposal was adopted. Marat and Louvet, in unison, demanded that no further petitioners be admitted to the podium. Marat ordered that each petitioner provide his name and address on his way out. He demanded the arrest of two petitioners and that they appear before the Committee of General Security.

Although Robespierre paid lip service to the goodness of the 'people', he condemned their violence and disorderly behaviour as much as anyone else in the Convention. At the session of the Cordeliers on 25 February, Robespierre openly attacked Chaumette on the subject of the agrarian law, which Robespierre called 'a law of murder and blood'. Finally, at the beginning of March, Robespierre drafted a very moderate circular to justify the Jacobin club's position and behaviour. In the circular, he repudiated violence and the pressure for price controls and he stressed the club's continued attempt to prevent unrest on the streets of Paris. He was thus condemning the people's violence and anarchy as much as his opponents in the Convention.[61]

Carra's speech on the subject of food supplies further demonstrates the unity among deputies on this issue. He demanded that the administrators and financiers should be subject to declarations of their entire fortune. He proposed that a commission should be established to arrest, if necessary those who did not cooperate. His words were heartily applauded.[62]

The deputies representing Paris felt the issue to be serious enough – the petitioners did threaten to revoke the Paris deputation – to warrant a letter directed to their constituents. The letter was very much a defence of Paris in addition to an attack on the petitioners. The deputies from Paris called the intentions of the petitioners 'perfidious', their methods 'seductive' and their pretext 'on the surface, good'. The orators claimed to speak not merely on behalf of Parisians, but in the name of the entire people of France. The 'intriguers' had abused the 'good faith' of the patriots. In addition, the deputation used this opportunity to attack the 'leaders of a guilty machination' (presumably Brissot and friends), who had called up the *fédérés* from Marseilles as an anti-Paris measure.[63]

All deputies demanded that the law be upheld. Saint-Just ordered the petitioners to calm down and stop their violence. Intimidated by the petitioners, he told deputies that there was a publication circulating around Paris on the subject of food supplies which denounced him. All were speaking in support of law and order, not just a section of them.[64] Louvet summed up the general view of the deputies in the light of the threatening petition. He asked if there were not two Conventions in France, and two national representations. And if the petitioner was the representative of the departments, then who were the deputies and what were their powers?[65] Although there had been plenty of personality clashes in the Convention, deputies were indistinguishable from those outside it.[66]

The Jacobin club was also under threat from the people from the sections. On 22 February, a group of women from the section of Quatres-Nations demanded that the Jacobins lend their premises to them to discuss food hoarders and monopolists. The club as a whole refused their demand. Billaud, president at the time of this incident, was forced to run for cover. Although the member Dubois-Crancé tried to explain to the crowds that they had to conquer liberty first and then deal with supplying necessities at a good price, this did not satisfy them. Finally, as president of the Convention, he rejected the petition, demanding a tax on foodstuffs, with horror.

PRESSURES OF FOREIGN WAR

In addition to dealing with pressing internal issues, there was the problem of conducting a foreign war, which tended, initially, to unite, rather than divide the two factions. During the period between January and March, there was a good deal of cooperation among those who had quarrelled personally. Factional fighting was predominantly absent during the debates concerning the conduct of the war during these months, including the declarations of war against England and Spain and the reorganization of the army.

Barère was instrumental in attempting to keep peace between those deputies who had quarrelled throughout the autumn of 1792. Two days after the king's execution, on 23 January, he delivered the first of his many 'Reports to the French Nation'. He showed himself to be 'impartial', the name Robespierre attributed to him. He believed that 'bitter prejudices and deep fears had pitted deputies against each other'. The time had come, however, for them to forget about the differences of opinion. 'Henceforth', he declared, 'the National Convention and the French people will have only a single thought, a single feeling, liberty and civic brotherhood . . . The time has ceased for disputes; we must act.' He then pleaded for patriotic unity in the face of a common foreign enemy: 'The despots of Europe can be strong only if we are divided . . . Let us rise before an astounded Europe . . . let the entire nation rise again in the defence of the republic. This is the cause of Frenchmen; it is the cause of all mankind.'[67] Couthon praised Barère's speech in a letter to his constituents, describing members of the Convention gathering around Barère after his speech, promising union in the war effort.[68] Brissot spoke in similar terms a few days later, imploring everyone to concentrate on the war: 'The great French family must be nothing more than an army, France nothing more than a camp where only war is discussed, where everything is directed towards the war.'[69]

A Committee of General Defence was created on 1 January on Kersaint's proposal. It would later become, in amended form, the famous Committee of Public Safety. Initially, it met three times a week, in the evenings, but this changed to daily after 22 January. Its purpose was to coordinate military and diplomatic operations and to assist ministers in making decisions concerning urgent military matters. The twenty-four members were chosen from the already existing Committees of War, Finance, Colonies, Navy, Diplomacy, Constitution and Commerce. The first members included Brissot, Guadet, Gensonné and Barère among others.[70] Although this committee has been criticized by historians for its inefficiency due to its size and its publicly held meetings, the Convention very often voted decrees based on its reports.[71] The declaration of war against England and Holland was considered at the committee's session of 10 January.[72] At the Convention's session of 12 January, Brissot presented, in the name of the committee, a report on the British government. After hearing Brissot's report, the Convention decreed the measures he proposed.[73] Sieyès' important report on the reorganization of the war department was first read at the committee at the session of 13 January before it was heard at the Convention two days later. Similarly, the first of Dubois-Crancé's two reports concerning the army was presented and discussed at an extraordinary session on 21 January before it was read to the Convention on 25 January. On 30 January, the committee put Brissot in charge of a report on England and Barère on Spain. Brissot reported on the following day to the committee and to the Convention on 1 February. On 3 February, Fabre, in the name of the committee, presented a list of nine commissioners to visit the northern and eastern borders to assist the armies. The measure was passed.[74] Barère was charged with a report on Spain again on 26 February and he presented his report on the hostilities of the Spanish government and the necessity to declare war against it to the committee on 4 March and to the Convention on the following day. It was upon the committee's recommendation that France declared war on Spain.[75] The committee appeared to be working well and carrying out its mandate.

Brissot spoke again on the subject of England on 1 February, arguing that the English court had desired war for a long time, that Pitt had dismissed the French ambassador and secured from

Parliament a large increase in the armed forces. George III had secretly 'meditated against your liberty'. His proposal, this time in the name of the Diplomatic Committee, to declare war against the king of England and the Stadtholder of the United Provinces, was unanimously passed.[76] Fabre proposed an 'Address to the English people', in the name of the French nation. In addition, Fabre suggested that the Convention decree that the English and Dutch people in France were under the protection of French law. Barère wholeheartedly supported Fabre's first proposal and declared that the war which had just been declared, 'resembled no other war. It is not one king against another or one government against another. Ordinary measures should not be employed.' He felt that Brissot's speech sufficed for the act of one government against another, but the French nation had not spoken and must be heard. Marat consented to the address on the grounds that it served some purpose for the French. As someone who had lived in England for a time before the revolution, he considered himself to be an expert on the country. The Convention decided that the address would be written by Condorcet, Barère, Thomas Paine and Fabre. Condorcet, who had already composed an address of this type to the Dutch and the Spanish, against the 'scourge of the war and of the advantages of liberty', drafted it. Barère spoke of the address as 'a masterpiece of reason and of the wise and philosophical talent which characterized the works of Condorcet'. Fabre rejected the draft for Condorcet's remarks about the massacres and demanded that they be changed. The address was never sent, however, because of the 'changing circumstances and torrent of public affairs which preoccupied the Convention'. Following Condorcet's advice, Barère retained it, and said it was 'kept religiously, as the production of a genius and a persecuted *philosophe*'. He was later forced to burn the speech when his papers were seized by the Paris Commune.[77]

The Convention's War Committee drafted a complex bill in fifty-eight articles which was designed to reorganize the army to cope with the newly declared war. It proposed a levy of 300,000 men – this had been initially suggested at the Committee of General Defence – and an amalgamation of the voluntary and regular forces. The bill, which also called for the election of officers, was presented by Dubois-Crancé on 7 February. At the discussion which ensued, there were a variety of opinions presented, both for and against the decree, but personalities and factionalism remained outside the debate. Barère, for example, opposed both the election and unification, but he did so without malice. He had advocated competition between the corps. In addition he felt it was too expensive for the state to pay volunteers. They should be rewarded with 'civic recompense' in the form of oak leaves. He thought that it was not the right time to be concerned with restructuring the army. The country was in too much danger.[78] Saint-Just, who also spoke on 11 February, was generally well disposed to the report, although he thought that the generals should be appointed by the deputies and he attacked the proposal which would increase volunteers' pay if they served on more than one campaign.[79]

The issues that arose during the first months of the Convention – priests, *émigrés*, the extension of the war, the resistance to popular demand for price controls – found the deputies fairly united. They all agreed in proclaiming France a republic and Louis XVI a traitor. The decision to try the king, the manner in which to effect this and the question of a referendum, divided deputies in all sorts of ways. An important difference in terms of principle between the Paris deputation and the provincials was over the question of sovereignty. For Brissot and his group, it lay with the people rather than its representatives, while for Robespierre and the Parisians, it was the other way round. Men united by friendship could disagree without affecting their long-term relationship.

On the subject of factions and how they were forming at the Convention, little had changed since the previous November, with the exception of the ramifications of the king's trial as discussed above. The food shortages, which caused the people of Paris to petition and even threaten the Convention, united deputies against a common enemy. When Pétion printed his 'Avis . . . à ses concitoyens' in the *Patriote Français* on 8 February, he had nothing new to say. He repeated much of the content of his speech against Robespierre from the previous November. It is clear that he remained very bitter over the outcome of the September elections, referring to 'an intimate liaison which existed between almost all of those who had been chosen' and the rejection of 'esteemed citizens'. One new item, however, appeared, which was the result of the king's trial: the resignation of Manuel because of the 'scandalous and lively complaints' against this member from Paris who would not be 'compromised in suitable arrangements'.[80]

Things were clearer cut at the Jacobin club where factions were coalescing. The expulsion of a good number of those men associated with Brissot made the club a much more Paris-dominated organization than the Convention. With the demise of the Roland propaganda *Bureau*, the mother society started to regain some support from provincial affiliates. Gorsas remarked on 5 February that he was still receiving many letters from provincial societies, although some were reproaching him for not inserting them in his paper. Others accused him of partiality and still others were asking for direction as to which side they ought to take.[81]

There seems to have been a hardening of attitudes among those who were already enemies. Many in the club hoped to bring into the debates emotions concerned with attitudes towards the king's trial, to reinforce opinions that had taken shape over different issues. The exploitation by prominent Jacobins of the revelation of the Bordelais' negotiations with Louis XVI on the eve of 10 August, and the inundation of the provinces by 'Brissotin' propaganda were powerful tools used by the club to win back provincial clubs which had previously sided with Brissot. They had attacked his expulsion back in October and some had even demanded the expulsion of Marat and Robespierre. From the end of November, the Jacobins were on the offensive against 'Brissotin' propaganda.

8

THE DISASTERS OF MARCH AND THEIR CONSEQUENCES

By the spring of 1793, two rival factions could be identified in the Convention. One faction, which was composed of Brissot and his group, was more or less in control of the government, while the other group, led by men like Robespierre, Collot and other Jacobin deputies was challenging them. The Jacobins were divided between the militants advocating violence as a means to achieve their demands and the moderates who would not go beyond the law. These groups were not well defined but the conflict between them was becoming increasingly bitter. Onto this political struggle were superimposed several external crises which threatened both sides: sans-culottes agitation in Paris over the price of food and other necessities; the Catholic and royalist insurrection in the Vendée; and the defeat on the Belgian front leading to Dumouriez's attempt to march on Paris. The *émigré* problem also continued to vex the Convention. The question under investigation in this chapter is would these external threats to both political groups unite them, would they unite some people from each side, or would each side pretend that the threats were really concealed moves by the other?

FACTIONAL STRUGGLES ON THE EVE OF THE MARCH UPRISING

Quarrels between Brissot and his supporters on the one hand, and many deputies who were members of the Jacobin club on the other, heated up at the start of March. Brissot and his group continued to wage their battle in the press. Brissot published a lengthy article denouncing radical demagogues and their mob followers. Manuel followed by attacking the Paris Jacobins for their extreme radicalism.[1] Support for Brissot remained fairly strong among several provincial clubs. Copies of Condorcet's draft constitution were sent to provincial societies in February. The Bordeaux club read Gorsas' accounts of the Paris Jacobin sessions.[2] Meanwhile, the Jacobins continued to fight back. In February, the club had decided to write a circular denouncing the 'Brissotin' press, but it only appeared a fortnight later, in response to the riots, which it condemned.[3] Extremist members who were not deputies, such as Varlet, Desfieux and Lajouski,[4] made incendiary motions. Pétion, expelled from the club on 28 February, was denied the chance of defending himself. He had stopped attending meetings some time in December 1792. There is no record that Robespierre, who was present at the session, uttered a word on Pétion's behalf. No reasons were given for Pétion's expulsion, except that he had been enjoying life while the masses were suffering. Presumably his relations with Brissot and those who had been expelled the previous autumn did not help him.[5]

The Paris Jacobin club had become increasingly radical during the spring of 1793. Desfieux, who was president of the Correspondence Committee, issued threats of expulsion against men who had not renewed their membership. All Jacobin deputies who voted in favour of the referendum and against the death penalty during the king's trial would be expelled. To be readmitted, members would be required to prove that they had contributed to 'patriotic writings' on 2 September and during the February riots. Robespierre, in a much more moderate tone, urged the popular societies not to insist upon recalling their deputies.[6] The extremist contingency composed of Desfieux, Roux, and Varlet, had far more in common with the sans-culottes than the 'Mountain' deputies who were opposed to popular violence especially when it was directed their way. Now that the 'Brissotins' had been expelled, these radical members who were not deputies were putting a good deal of pressure on 'Mountain' deputies, who although not included in this planned purge, were criticized. Bitter complaints were directed against them for their frequent absence from Convention sessions and for allowing Gensonné to be elected president on 8 March. Threats against 'Mountain' Jacobins were issued at the session of the same day, when several radicals proclaimed that those deputies who did not attend Convention meetings would be first censured, followed by their names being posted in the Jacobin hall and finally, if they still did not comply, they would be expelled from the club.[7]

In this atmosphere of threatened purges, Jacobin deputies responded by attacking the 'Brissotins'. Robespierre denounced the presses of Brissot and those funded by Roland for corrupting public opinion'.[8] The funding of newspapers from the public purse was a common theme for many prominent Parisian and Jacobin deputies. This propaganda war had been a serious bone of contention since the previous summer and continued throughout the autumn of 1792, and now it was reaching its climax during the spring of 1793. Robespierre, as a means of retaliation, proposed that the Correspondence Committee, together with the club's president, take appropriate measures to enlighten the departments on the conspiracy which had been in operation since 10 August against 'public opinion'. He advocated the formation of a close alliance between all popular societies against the 'faction which wants to divide the republic and hand it over to the horrors of civil war and the furore of despots'.[9] The result was the circular of 6 March, in which familiar grievances were put forth in clear terms to affiliates. The 'traitors' continued to dominate committees, control the ministry and have all methods at their disposal to run the government. Journalists who had 'sold out to intrigue' continued to spread their venom throughout the departments.[10]

Brissot denounced Collot's report and his demand for a decree of accusation against Roland in his newspaper.[11] Billaud equated the presses of Gorsas with those of the abbé Royou; in other words, they were royalist.[12] The verbal assault was extended from the Jacobins to the Convention by the deputy St André. He led the attack on 8 March, declaring that he had nothing against the liberty of the press, but that he opposed journalists who 'led astray public opinion concerning the best patriots'. He denounced the presses of Brissot and Gorsas and other journalists whom he did not name, and who claimed to be 'impartial'.[13] Perhaps the reason for expanding their attack outside the Jacobin club was due to the fact that it had been largely unsuccessful in restricting the influence of the 'Brissotin' press. Leading Jacobins may have believed that denouncing the press to a wider and more moderate audience composed primarily of provincial deputies, would also give the club more credibility in the provinces where it had been fighting a tough battle. The result was a law passed by the Convention on 9 March, which partially restricted press freedom. It prohibited a deputy from exercising both professions simultaneously.[14]

Military Setbacks and the Uprising of 9–10 March[15]

During the first few days of March 1793, France's military situation deteriorated considerably. Afte
the French declaration of war on England and Holland, the Convention had sent Genera
Dumouriez into the Low Countries where he had led an offensive. On 5 March, deputies received
news of the French defeat at Aix-la-Chapelle. The defeat doomed the invasion of Holland and had a
demoralizing effect on the army. Dumouriez had faced the army of Cobourg and the Austrian
when the Prussians threatened his lines of communication with a flank attack in Belgium
Although Dumouriez had entered Holland successfully, he was forced to retreat. On 6 March, a
letter from the Liège commissioners, Delacroix, Merlin de Douai and Gossuin, was read at the
Convention. It informed deputies that almost the entire army had deserted. Danton, who had been
with Dumouriez's army, expressed the seriousness of these circumstances at the Convention on
8 March in a rousing, patriotic speech reminiscent of his oration on the eve of the Septembe
massacres. He told deputies that they 'must save their brothers in Belgium'. As well as praising
Dumouriez's character, he urged his colleagues to nominate commissioners to go that evening into
the sections to explain the army's situation in Belgium and raise up new recruits.[16] Robespierre
and Billaud visited the section of Bonne-Nouvelle during the evening of the same day to carry ou
the Convention's decrees. Brissot claimed that Billaud and Robespierre went far beyond thei
mandate of informing and recruiting and had called upon the people 'to rise up against those
called intriguers or the moderates'. If Brissot was telling the truth, then the section proceeding
had misrepresented the meeting. The section's proceedings do not provide any evidence of them
having issued this call to insurrection.[17] In view of what followed, it appears as though Brisso
invented this tale of Robespierre and Billaud inciting Bonne-Nouvelle to revolt to make them look
more radical than they were. Again, according to Brissot, Chabot, Panis and others went to othe
sections where they were not commissioners and spoke in a similar fashion.[18]

The failure of Dumouriez's campaign combined with the persistent economic strife elevated the
bitterness of the working people of Paris. The deputies had done very little to respond to the high
prices of necessities, which had sparked the February riots. From 9 to 10 March, a group o
militant Parisians led an attack on the moderate press. However, a good number of deputies were
convinced that there was more to the latest uprising than an attempt to destroy a few presses, tha
it was an assault against the entire Convention. Barère, speaking after the failed insurrection
declared that the insurgents had 'wanted to destroy the life and existence of the republic'.[19] Boyer
Fonfrède, writing to the Jacobins of Bordeaux after the incident, spoke in similar terms: 'The
present state of our country proves to you what dangers we have escaped and undoubtedly liberty
would have been lost if the Convention had been dissolved.'[20]

Unfortunately, the press law did not pacify the masses who smashed the presses of Gorsas
Courrier des 83 départements, the *Journal Français* and Condorcet's *Chronique de Paris*. Surprisingly
Brissot's press was left alone even though it had been denounced with Gorsas' paper at the Jacobins
by Hébert at the session of 8 March.[21] Also intended for destruction was Prudhomme's press
publisher of the *Révolutions de Paris*.[22] A combination of the smashing of Condorcet's press and the
law passed by the Convention stating that a deputy could not be a journalist, marked the end of his
journalist career. In his final articles, Condorcet did not stop calling for unity amongst the
patriots.[23] With the loss of his newspaper, Condorcet lost his principal means of expression since he
rarely attended the Jacobins, and seldom spoke in the Convention. This law had been primarily

directed against Brissot, who obeyed the law and turned over the editorial duties to Girey-Dupré. Brissot remarked that only Marat placed himself above the law and continued to work as both a journalist and a deputy.[24]

The chief theatres of preparation for this uprising were the popular societies, a small group of radicals at the Cordeliers and in some sections. There is no remaining evidence to prove that the Jacobin club was not involved, although Vergniaud would later accuse some members, who were not deputies, of assisting in the organization. Only four sections, those of Mauconseil, Bonne-Nouvelle, Lombards and Théâtre-Français adhered to the Cordeliers' invitation and adopted the following address: 'The evacuation of Belgium is the work of an impious faction that paralyses the Convention. The success of the enemies of France is due to the traitor Dumouriez and the odious intrigues of Brissot, Roland and their friends. They ought to be eliminated at any price.'[25] The linking of Dumouriez with Brissot would be later adopted by more important politicians such as Danton and Robespierre in their struggle for control of the Convention. In common with the insurrection of 10 August, the big men tended to stay out of the street fighting. Vergniaud alleged afterwards that an Insurrectionary Committee at the Jacobin club was in existence, although this was denied by the Minister of Justice Garat in his report on 10 March to the Convention. But he did admit that there were twenty to thirty 'dangerous men' involved. Gorsas wrote extensively about the failed uprising once he resumed publishing on 19 March. His paper did not appear between 9 and 19 March because everything had been destroyed. He claimed that the plot had been planned by Varlet, Martin and the Cordeliers, who met at the café Corazza, and that it was Varlet who drafted the threatening petition. The group's intention was to dissolve the executive, then march to the Convention, 'dissolve and inundate Paris with carnage and blood'.[26]

At the session of 8 March, Desfieux proposed the extermination of all 'Brissotins and Rolandists'. The next day, he demanded the renewal of the committees, which he claimed were filled with counter-revolutionaries, the arrest of ministers and post office administrators and the immediate establishment of a revolutionary tribunal.[27] The group of radicals left the Jacobins, without its support, en route to the Cordeliers where they proposed insurrection and from there went to the commune and sections. The Cordeliers issued a call to the electoral assembly of the Department of Paris 'to convene the electoral body to replace the members who were traitors'.[28] Even the official leadership of the Cordeliers, including Hébert, disclaimed any link to the order produced by the more militant members. The member suspected of drafting it was expelled from the club.[29]

Other than for the destruction of certain presses, which very few sections participated in, the tocsin did not sound, and the insurrection dwindled into a minor riot. When the rioters reached the presses of Brissot and Prudhomme, the workers were able to chase them away. Without support from the commune, the insurrection collapsed on the night of 10 March. Other reasons cited for its failure include the support of the Brest battalion, which was ready to defend the deputies, and the rain! The officials from the commune, Pache and Santerre, blamed the troubles on a royalist plot which involved putting the duke of Orléans on the throne. They announced to the Convention on 10 March that the troubles were over.[30]

Although the Jacobins officially opposed this kind of violent behaviour and there is no evidence that leading Jacobin deputies were involved in the rising, their persistent verbal assaults on the 'Brissotin' press may well have helped to provoke those who carried out their attempted destruction. Dulaure, whose press was pillaged, could not have been clearer about the intentions of the Jacobins in his report of the newspaper attack. He claimed that 'deputies from the mountain provoked diverse decrees threatening press freedom, but not against the Jacobin press'. He alluded to complicity between the leaders of the plot, presumably the populists, and 'some Mountain deputies who must have been duped by the leaders' fanaticism'.[31] The Jacobins had been largely unsuccessful in combating the power of the 'Brissotin' press through propaganda and perhaps felt that more direct intervention was necessary, but that the radicals went beyond their mandate to threaten a few presses by threatening the entire Convention. This was made clear in the speeches made by all deputies in the Convention in the days following the violence.

In the debates that followed the March rising, what emerged was a consensus, regardless of faction, that the militants who had provoked the troubles should be punished and that the sanctity of the Convention should be defended. There were minor variations in the details provided by different speakers. Vergniaud, on 13 March, delivered the fullest account of the uprising in a very long and revealing speech. He read out the address issued by the Quatre-Nations section, which blamed the military reverses on Brissot et al. and called Dumouriez a traitor (before he actually was one). He denounced the men whom he believed to be its instigators, the Revolutionary Committee sitting at the Jacobins composed of Desfieux, Fournier and Lajouski, and demanded that they appear before the newly created revolutionary tribunal, of which he had disapproved just a few days earlier. These were idle men and foreigners who had infiltrated the sections. In addition, he proposed that the Cordeliers hand over their proceedings to the Convention. Thanks to the commune, which had not cooperated with these men, the barricades had not been closed and the ringing of the tocsin had not taken place. Vergniaud also credited the Brest battalion, which was ready to march against the conspirators, for the failure of the rising.[32] As it turned out, only Fournier, who appeared at the podium and denied having wanted to assassinate Pétion, and Lajouski were arrested. Apparently Pétion and some ministers had been threatened outside the Convention.[33] The Convention, on Thuriot's proposal, decreed that Fournier be freed from prison after he had explained that he had had nothing to do with the uprising. At the same session, Marat insisted that he had gone to the popular societies where he had preached moderation and obedience to the laws and encouraged the people to defend the Convention if it was threatened.[34]

To summarize, the reaction from the Convention to the rising of 9–10 March was unanimous. When Isnard demanded a decree of accusation against the Poissonnière section, Marat endorsed him. From all sides of the Convention, there were shouts of 'unity, unity'. Maure at the Jacobins reported that members of the *côté droit* agreed to unite with the 'Mountain' to save the nation.[35] Perhaps because of the failure of the insurrection, everyone condemned it afterwards, or perhaps there was a genuine desire to put personal feelings aside and work together for the survival of the republic.

On the other hand, the Jacobins were not nearly as united. Varlet praised the men accused of preparing the riots and called for a new insurrection against the moderates. He also denounced Dumouriez.[36] Varlet's position can be contrasted with that of Robespierre who had supported Vergniaud and Buzot in his condemnation of the 'deep plot'. Once again, he stated that it was with public opinion that one 'combats the men who have betrayed the rights of the people. Partial insurrections are harmful to the Jacobins.' He blamed the riots on 'women who had come from distant neighbourhoods to mislead the good and vigorous citizens'. The rioters, he insisted, 'were not the true people of Paris'.[37] Billaud and others such as Saint-André blamed the rising on Varlet and Fournier and defended Dumouriez.[38] Varlet, who complained about Fournier's arrest, and had spoken before Billaud, continued to preach insurrection and when he tried to speak a second time, he was prevented from doing so.[39] Although he was cheered by radicals in the audience, the leading Jacobins who were also deputies, condemned what they interpreted as irresponsible *enragé* radicalism. Dufourny's speech summed up the club's prominent and more moderate members' attitude: the Jacobins should never participate in an insurrectionary movement and they should be careful not to be compromised in the eyes of affiliates by being too closely connected with popular violence. Robespierre spoke in a similar manner when he condemned proposals for a radical petition from the sections: 'The sections of Paris should be very reserved in petitioning; these petitions almost never have a serious goal in mind; rarely do they embrace the interests of the republic . . . under the pretext of petitions, intriguers slide in the sections and spread trouble there.' In addition, Robespierre told members that violence should not be directed against members from the Gironde, that legal means should be employed to 'secure a victory of the left over the moderates'.[40] The Jacobin deputies were sounding moderate and conciliatory through their condemnation of violence and their advocacy of restraint to the sections. The Jacobin circular of 5 March, which had informed provincial societies of the military reverses and denounced journalists who had 'corrupted public opinion', was revised and updated to include a condemnation of the riots as futile. It was 'ill-directed popular violence stirred up by counter-revolutionaries to blacken the name of the Jacobins'. In addition, the authors of the circular were opposed to demands for a recall of leading deputies. The circular was signed by the Correspondence Committee, which was composed of many smaller fry, non-deputies: Desfieux, president, Lafaye, vice-president; Fouquier-Tinville, Ovrest, secretaries. The suggestion to draft this circular had been originally proposed by Robespierre in February in response to the riots.[41]

Jacobin hostility to popular violence at the time of the March uprising was consistent with its attitude during the riots in February, led by similar radicals who were not deputies. When the Marseilles Jacobins had demanded the recall of moderate deputies, men like Saint-André and Thuriot argued strongly against it and the club accepted their position. Chabot spoke in a similar manner. He reminded fellow Jacobins that only recently provincial clubs had made similar demands against Robespierre and Marat. Robespierre made the argument that the 'Brissotin' replacements could be worse, that new elections could 'agitate' the electoral assemblies needlessly. It was enough to drive moderates out of popular clubs. No further measures were necessary.[42] What this meant was a rejection of the two major elements of the sans-culottes' aggression during the months of February and March: violence and the recall of moderate deputies.

Once again, insurrectionary activity in Paris was inextricably linked to a deterioration in the state of the war as well as the economic problems linked to the war. When the Austrians were threatening and things were going poorly for the French, the people tended to rise up. This time, the rising failed and deputies were united in their condemnation of a possible threat to their lives and the safety of the Convention. For a short time, the personal attacks and accusations had ceased.

REPRESENTATIVES ON MISSION

On the very same day as the March riots, Carnot, in the name of the Committee of General Defence, delivered a report to the Convention on measures to accelerate recruitment for the army. Danton and Delacroix had made various proposals on the previous day at the committee's meeting. The result was the nomination of eighty-two deputies who would carry out this mission in the departments, known as representatives on mission. After the nomination of these men, there were fears expressed by a number of radicals concerning a Convention without eighty-two 'Mountain' deputies. Marat, in his newspaper, wrote that 'when our commissioners have left for the departments, the *hommes d'état* will revolt against the patriots of the Mountain'.[43] The Jacobin circular of 6 March voiced similar fears about the loss of representation in the Convention.[44] Danton, however, commented in his speech of 10 March that 'we seem to fear that the departure of the commissioners will weaken one or the other parties of the Convention. Vain fears.' These remarks by contemporaries raise the question on what basis was someone considered to be a 'Mountain' deputy and whether it was some sort of factional tactic to exclude eighty-two opponents from the Convention by sending them *'en mission'*. Were Brissot and his group involved in the selection of the deputies? The proceedings from the Convention indicate that there was some debate in deciding the representatives on mission, but neither Brissot nor any of his friends intervened in either the debates or the decision. Saint-André proposed that the list be drawn up by the secretaries.[45] Collot was opposed to nominating commissioners who had voted in favour of the referendum, but he had no problem with the secretaries making the decision. Likewise, Billaud supported Danton's suggestion for departmental commissioners, but felt that they should not be men who had voted for the referendum.[46] It appears that Collot's wishes carried the day. Among the men who are under consideration here and who were appointed representatives on mission by this decree, Carra, Saint-Just, Fabre and Fouché were not particularly hostile to Brissot and his friends, while Billaud and Collot were. Fabre had shown some discontentment when he had not received funding from Roland for a newspaper, but generally he stayed out of the most acrimonious arguments. Carra was closely associated with Brissot and neither Saint-Just nor Fouché had taken part in faction fighting. Billaud and Collot, however, had spoken against their opponents on several occasions. What they had in common was that, with the exception of Collot, who was away on mission, they had voted against the referendum during Louis' trial. Based on the evidence, accusations made by Marat and other radicals that there was some sort factional manoeuvring at the choice of representatives on mission with the goal of weakening one group's influence seem to be false.

UNITY AND ATTEMPTS AT RECONCILIATION

After the March uprising and before news of Dumouriez's defection reached Paris, several deputies made genuine attempts at reconciliation. Personal gestures were made by Guadet who tried to reconcile Danton at the Committee of General Defence, and this was continued by Boyer-Fonfrède at the Convention on 13 March. The Jacobin Maure reported at the club's session of 17 March that there had been a general attempt at reconciliation among deputies of the Convention. There had been a meeting at the Committee of General Defence where he had approached the president, Pétion, 'with all the respect which this serious person deserves', and told him of his anger at the divisions which reigned among them and proposed a remedy: colleagues should put an end to the plotting in the committees to prevent good decrees. This conversation led to a very 'friendly understanding' between Buzot and Robespierre.[47] Aulard's summary indicates that Maure had indeed approached Pétion about a reconciliation between the two sides in the Convention and that the remedy was for the 'Girondins' to end their intriguing in the committees and their propaganda programme. This conversation led to a positive discussion between Robespierre and Pétion, but a reunion ended in failure.[48] Presumably, Pétion and his group would not agree to Maure's plan of equal numbers of deputies from each side being represented on the committee, and therefore the reconciliation was doomed to failure. As in 1792, the 'Brissotins' were equating power with office, this time, with control of the committees.

The ever suspicious Marat considered a union of deputies to be desirable but wondered if the 'patriotic party' could accept this olive branch from the opposing side when it 'seems to be loathed in most departments and in a moment when the unfaithful general has just lifted his mask and usurped sovereignty in Holland and Belgium'. However, he did write that without unity the Convention was powerless to pass wise laws and that scandalous scenes would lose the confidence of the people. Directing his comments to Brissot and his supporters, whom he referred as '*hommes d'état*' to, he argued that if they voted with the patriots of the 'Mountain', they could all save the country.[49] Jean Debry, also desiring unity among members, insisted that a great conspiracy existed against the Convention and told his colleagues that there had not been one deputy who had not trembled with fear. Everyone had voted to break up the plot.[50]

Brissot's newspaper, commenting on the past few sessions of the Convention, remarked that with the exception of Marat's outbursts, they had been satisfactory. Calm and the interests of the nation had dominated them. He added that the absence of so many 'effervescent heads' had permitted the good debates and decrees. At his trial, Brissot testified that he had been in favour of reconciliation and reported two meetings with Danton, which had gone very well. Apparently Robespierre refused to meet Brissot.[51]

DUMOURIEZ'S DEFEAT AND ITS CONSEQUENCES

News of the French defeat at Neerwinden reached Paris on 21 March. The insurrectionaries renewed their threats and activities. At the evening session of 22 March, representatives of the Marseilles Jacobin club presented a petition in which they denounced those deputies who had voted for the referendum and blamed the military defeat on their 'betrayal'. They only recognized the deputies of the 'saint mountain' and demanded the convening of primary assemblies. This petition was intimately connected to the declining fortunes of the French revolutionaries on the battlefield and in their own western departments. On 16 March, five letters had reached the Marseilles Jacobin society informing the club of Miranda's[52] defeat in Belgium, of the civil war in the Vendée and of continued plots by the 'Rolandists'. The Marseilles deputy Bayle reported Parisian preparations for a third insurrection and asked for help from the Marseillais. In his journal, Gorsas mentioned a movement in preparation by certain Jacobins.[53]

No one defended the sanctity of the Convention more passionately than Barère. He condemned the address as criminal and that to attack national sovereignty would be to open the door to the enemy. He even declared that 'the convention is not the mountain'. The next day he avowed that the only way to remove deputies from the Convention would be to kill them. Guadet demanded the arrest of those who had signed the petition, while Barbaroux and Pétion demanded the convening of primary assemblies. Barbaroux, as a Marseillais, took a line of his own, defending the Marseillais' contribution to the revolution. Pétion did feel that a plan was in place to destroy the Convention. But, like Barbaroux, he presented the argument that with new elections deputies would be certain to know that they had the confidence of their constituents. On Lasource's suggestion, the Convention decreed that the address be disapproved and the decrees of the sections and administrative bodies of Marseilles having the purpose of destroying the Convention, be quashed.[54] This petition was read at the Jacobins the next day. The club neither sent a copy of it to the sections as proposed by Desfieux, nor approved of it as a society. Marat wrote to the sections and popular societies urging moderation. Robespierre praised the contributions of the Marseillais to the revolution, and with regard to the petition he remarked that they had 'consulted nothing more than the ardour of their republicanism'. However, he urged caution and opposed vigorous measures.[55] The official reaction of the club was consistent with previous behaviour when confronted with menacing petitions. The deputy-Jacobins were united in their view that the sections should avoid counter-productive violence.[56]

DANTON AND DUMOURIEZ

Dumouriez had written a letter to the Convention on 12 March, which was a virtual declaration of war against the republic. He denounced the representatives on mission as thieves and men of blood and violence, and claimed that the cause of French defeats was avarice, injustice and oppression meted out by the Belgians. Barère and Robespierre demanded that the letter be read to the Assembly. Delacroix opposed and said he would rather 'lose his own head than have the general lose his'. Danton forcefully supported Delacroix. He acknowledged that Dumouriez had lost his political sense, but that he still maintained all of his military powers. The letter was received in Paris on 15 March, but the Convention's president, Bréard, did not make its contents general knowledge and was turned over to the Committee of General Defence. It was not made public until 24 March when it appeared in the *Chronique de Paris*.[57] At the committee, Barère demanded Dumouriez's arrest, which Danton opposed while enemies were still present and Dumouriez still directing the army's retreat. To avoid any suspicion, Danton suggested sending commissioners drawn from 'both parties of the Convention', naming Gensonné and Guadet because they had been friendly with the general.[58]

Danton managed to convince the Committee of General Defence to allow him and Delacroix to try to reason with Dumouriez. At this committee meeting, they not only guaranteed his military competence, but assured members that Dumouriez was still attached to the republic. Danton and Delacroix met the general on the evening of 20–1 March and interviewed him until 3.00 a.m. They begged him to retract his letter, but Dumouriez refused. His only concession was to write to the president of the Convention a note of six lines, which, without being precise, appeared to foreshadow a retraction: 'Circumstances might permit him to modify the measures he proposed in his letter of 12 March.' He beseeched the Convention to delay any report until it had received knowledge of the outcome of his meetings with Danton and Delacroix. They were to return to Brussels the next morning. Danton was supposed to return directly to Paris, but disappeared for a few days. No one knows where he went and what he did during these days. Delacroix went to Lille to assist with the army's retreat. He wrote to Danton on 25 and 28 March. In both letters, he expressed his fears of the dangers Dumouriez posed to the republic.[59]

At the first session of the newly organized Committee of General Defence,[60] now called the Committee of Public Safety, Robespierre called for Dumouriez's resignation while Danton avoided saying anything for or against Dumouriez. At the committee's meeting on 29–30 March, the general was condemned. Camus suggested presenting a report on Dumouriez's operations in Belgium and Holland and on the conduct of the generals. Pétion stated that he had gone to see Miranda with Bancal the previous day and reported an important interview between himself,

Bancal and Miranda in which Miranda confirmed their suspicions that Dumouriez was a traitor and predicted his march on Paris. Miranda urged them to warn all administrative bodies. Pétion promised to communicate these details to the committee and he did so the very next day.[61] Pétion, who corresponded regularly with Miranda, had expressed confidence in Dumouriez on 23 February, but on 13 March before he could possibly have known the contents of Dumouriez's letter, Pétion warned of 'treason in our armies and that this treason is linked with a large plot against the republic . . .'. He demanded information about the generals commanding the armies from Miranda, whose reply on 21 March was highly critical of Dumouriez.[62] Beurnonville, Minister of War (February–March 1793), read a letter from Dumouriez dated 28 March in which he announced to the minister the arrival of Dubuisson (one of those who had accompanied Dumouriez's army to Belgium) and censured the Convention. He belittled the methods of the republic and only saw brigands and deserters in the French troops. At the same time, he referred to France as a kingdom twice, bitterly denounced Brissot for declaring war on England, decried Condorcet's draft for a republican constitution, attacked the Jacobins and praised the moderation of the Austrians and proposed a treaty with them. It was decided that Dumouriez should be arrested and that Beurnonville and four commissioners, Camus, Lamarque, Quinette and Bancal, would travel to Belgium to carry this out.[63]

On 27 March at the Jacobins, Marat called up the sections to meet and inquire as to whether or not the Convention 'has the means to save the country'. If the Convention replied in the negative, he threatened that the 'people would be forced to save themselves'. This marked a change in Marat's attitude – he now sympathized with those whom he had denounced only a few weeks previously. As usual, Robespierre advised caution against an uprising, and urged members to occupy themselves and the sections with ridding Paris of traitors and counter-revolutionaries.[64]

At the Convention on 29 March, Marat protested that Danton had still not explained his behaviour and condemned Dumouriez. Marat insisted that Danton be heard immediately. Meanwhile, Buzot took the opportunity to denounce Marat and the left side of the Convention which he considered to be responsible for all of France's ills.[65] The next day, Danton spoke but revealed nothing of what really went on in Belgium. At the close of his speech on 30 March, he urged union and reciprocal confidence, and stated that after a report from the executive council, he would explain what went on in Belgium. Lasource demanded the adjournment of Danton's proposal until Dumouriez appeared at the Convention. He considered the 'disorganization' in the army of Belgium as the follow-up to a plan of conspiracy and demanded an account. He complained that up until the present time, deputies had heard only partial reports from the commissioners and Dumouriez's correspondence, described as 'insignificant bits and pieces which only led to conjecture'. The Assembly adopted Lasource's proposal, rather than that of Danton.[66]

Two days later at the Jacobins, Marat, still not satisfied, demanded that Danton explain his behaviour. Danton finally denounced Dumouriez, apologized and was forgiven. Marat did not question Danton's patriotism, but his lack of anticipation of Dumouriez's actions. Danton demanded the general's arrest and connected him to the 'moderates of the Gironde'. He urged fellow members to 'summon public opinion to require the Convention to purge itself of the weak and undesirable elements'.[67] Gorsas noted a great contradiction in Danton's attitude. Only a few days before, Danton had been 'the ardent apologist of Dumouriez'.[68]

On 1 April, desperate to defend himself against charges from Lasource concerning his associations with Dumouriez – Lasource accused him of entering into a conspiracy with Dumouriez to re-establish royalty in France – Danton repeated his attack of the deputies of the right. Deputies had plenty of reason for being suspicious of Danton's behaviour concerning Dumouriez. It was Danton who had prevented Dumouriez's threatening letter of 12 March from being read at the Convention. Then he persuaded the Committee of General Defence to send him and Delacroix one more time to Belgium to meet the general. He disappeared for two days on his return from Belgium and he was still defending the general on his return. At the first meeting of the newly constituted committee on 26 March, Beurnonville read Dumouriez's letter which proposed the evacuation of Belgium. Robespierre declared that the general ruled like a dictator in Holland and his political opinions should be of alarm to the 'friends of liberty'. They should do their best to remove Dumouriez from his command. Upon hearing this, Danton and Camus protested. Danton roared: 'Dumouriez has made serious mistakes; he wanted to raise Belgium and Holland as his own children, but he is our only man of war.' When he did speak to the Convention on 1 April, he omitted any mention of arresting him. Rather, Danton directed the violence of his attack towards the so-called enemies of the interior, such as Roland, as a way of diverting attention away from his own delicate situation. He insisted that Roland had written to Dumouriez advising him to 'annihilate the Paris party'. Only four days before, Danton had been endeavouring to reconcile the Convention. Now he was denouncing one half of it. In no part of his speech did he deal with exactly what he had done in Belgium, unlike the three Jacobins, Proly, Dubuisson and Pereira, who, after their meeting with Dumouriez, had reported its details to the Committee of General Defence. These three had informed the committee that Dumouriez had told them of a plan to march on Paris and seize the Convention and the Jacobins and re-establish the monarchy and the 1791 constitution. Surely Danton must have been aware of Dumouriez's intentions, but he never once uttered a word of them to anyone in Paris. Another odd occurrence was that Danton's disappearance coincided with Dumouriez's first utterances of defection. Deputies were also suspicious of his use of the 200,000 *livres*, which had been placed at his disposition for the Belgian mission. Nevertheless, through sheer power of rhetoric, Danton was successful in getting the deputies on his side. He diverted the deputies' attention from his denunciation of Holland and his group, arguing that the patriots could no longer work with those who had 'slandered' them throughout the country. Historians are in agreement that this was one of the greatest speeches of his entire career. He demanded that a commission be established to examine the behaviour of every deputy since the opening of the Convention.[69]

There were other accusations and insults hurled about at this extraordinary session. Marat attacked the new Committee of General Defence as being influenced by Brissot, Guadet and company. The patriots, he shouted, were in a minority. Biroteau, a member of the committee, accused Fabre, who he said was very close to Danton, of proposing a king in a veiled manner, at the committee's previous session. Fabre had apparently announced to the committee that he knew how to save the nation, but would not dare say it aloud! Fabre explained to the Convention that he had said to the committee if the government did not have the means to succeed, 'that any petty church official would be better qualified than us'. The Convention concluded with the deputy Delmas that any discussion on republicanism was dangerous, given the fragile state of the provisional regime.[70]

At the Jacobin session that evening, Robespierre defended Danton from Lasource's attack earlier that day at the Convention. Robespierre stated that Lasource had found a pretext to slander Danton because he was too credulous and because he did not take it upon himself to have Dumouriez arrested. It was all part of a grand scheme. There had been rumours that the Committee of General

Security was planning to arrest Danton. Danton's speech at the club the previous day sounded very similar to the Jacobin circular of 26 March where Dumouriez's behaviour was linked to that of the three Bordeaux deputies. Had Danton been coached by his friends at the club to denounce Brissot and friends as a tactic to save his own neck? Robespierre did not mention any names in his speech, but he did remark that Dumouriez's accomplices were among them, within France.[71]

On 2 April, at the Convention, Barère condemned a central committee which had been set up at the *Evêché* by the majority of the forty-eight sections of Paris with the intention of dissolving the Convention. He claimed that it had been in existence for three weeks; he described its activities as a 'system of terror' and insisted that Marat was its prime mover. He denied the sections the right to create a Correspondence Committee and send letters to the provinces. He praised the Jacobins for reproaching excessive behaviour. Barère's proposal that the committee appear before the Convention to explain itself was decreed. As far as the treacherous general was concerned, Barère insisted that he was not well acquainted with him – he had seen him only once and written to him on behalf of a man of letters, Laplace. When the letter of 12 March was read to the Committee of General Defence, Barère said that he demanded Dumouriez's arrest and that only Danton opposed it! Danton, he claimed, had also opposed reading the letter to the Convention. Again, according to Barère, Danton told the committee that 'Dumouriez was necessary to the army.'[72] Thuriot also spoke of the activities in the sections and thought that the constituted authorities should take action to determine whether or not a movement was taking place in the sections, which would give the advantage to counter-revolutionaries. He urged the deputies to unite: 'It is by reunion that we will be able to sustain ourselves . . . Without the Convention, there is nothing; it is here one finds the salvation of France.'[73] Boyer-Fonfrède wrote of a movement planned for 28 March, of a 'terrible proscription' and of a meeting of sections.[74]

BRISSOT AND ROBESPIERRE

The defeat of the French army in Belgium and Dumouriez's treason and flight meant that a reconciliation between those who were already enemies was no longer a possibility. Brissot was accused of defending Dumouriez on 1 April in his newspaper. The article in question was written in response to the Paris Commune's petition demanding the arrest of Dumouriez. The article did not reject this. It merely stated: 'Indignation against the victor of Jemappes should be directed against those patriots who had subsequently disorganized the army.' There is no evidence that Brissot actually penned this article. The *Patriote Français* was no longer under Brissot's editorial control. He had turned the paper over to Girey-Dupré to abide by the Convention's decree of 10 March. In reply to Marat's issue accusing Brissot of defending Dumouriez, Brissot, who was perhaps in disagreement with Girey-Dupré, wrote that because of the decree of 10 March, he was no longer editor and did not dictate editorial policy: 'People think that I dictate my opinions to Girey-Dupré. One does not impose one's opinions on a free man.'[75] Although Brissot may well have been telling the truth, the fact that his newspaper was still endorsing Dumouriez on 1 April was certain to provide his enemies with a good deal of ammunition.

The real battle between the two factions began on 3 April at the Convention with Robespierre's attack on the committee and his personal charges against Brissot, whom he accused of being an accomplice of Dumouriez. He condemned the committee because he could not deliberate with those who spoke the language of a traitor (Dumouriez) and with those who slandered Paris. Robespierre seemed to have forgotten that he, too, had expressed confidence in the general in the Convention on 10 March. There was no real foundation to Robespierre's charges against Brissot to which he replied one by one. Brissot responded that if he had kept silent about Dumouriez's crimes until now, it was because he had not wanted to give in to fear. But now he was provoked. To the first charge, he stated that he had had no part in the appointment of Dumouriez to the patriot ministry. It was the king who made such appointments. He added that Dumouriez's nomination was the result of an intrigue by Bonnecarère. Although he and Dumouriez shared the same opinion on going to war, he claimed that he did not know Dumouriez before he became a minister, and four months previously he had declared himself in favour of war at the Jacobins for his own reasons. On the accusation of calumniating Paris, Brissot responded that he had always made a distinction between the inhabitants of the city and the brigands who infested it. On Robespierre's accusation that he was a royalist, Brissot brought in totally irrelevant information about his pre-revolutionary career. He was defended by Garran Coulon, who insisted that Brissot had been at the Champ de Mars and was pursued by the police after the massacre.[76] It is true that Brissot had been on friendly terms with Dumouriez in the past, but so had many others. It should be recalled that the remarks about Dumouriez, such as agreeing with his negative comments about radical clubs, were written in the *Patriote Français*, now under Girey-Dupré's control, and not spoken by Brissot personally at the Convention. Moreover, the remarks were not so much an endorsement of Dumouriez as a condemnation of the clubs in the light of recent attacks on newspaper presses.[77]

As stated above, the petition presented to the Convention on 12 March demanded the arrest of Dumouriez. Delacroix, Marat and Barère defended him. Barère glorified the 'conqueror of the Argonne and Jemappes', while Marat declared that Dumouriez was tied up with the safety of the country by his victories and to arrest him would open the doors of France to the enemy.[78] The Jacobin address to its affiliates of 12 March did not disapprove of Dumouriez. It was a call to arms.[79] Almost everyone had been associated with Dumouriez and Barère wrote a very flattering letter the previous summer. They had all supported Dumouriez except for Marat who was inconsistent in his attitude towards the general. He had denounced him at the Jacobins the previous October, but had praised him at the Convention on 12 March. The Jacobin circular of the same day said nothing against Dumouriez. Louvet noted that Fabre, Danton and Santerre had recently accompanied Dumouriez to the theatre and opera. On 8 March, Danton had told the Convention that only Dumouriez deserved to have an army. Delacroix on 15 March had stated to an orator from the Poissonnière section that only a counter-revolutionary would indict Dumouriez. Only with the news of military setbacks in the Netherlands did the Jacobins begin to turn against him. Their attitude changed around 17 March. Their tactic was to implicate Brissot and his friends with him. Marat wrote that Dumouriez was the 'creature of the Brissotin faction' and Desfieux made similar comments at the Jacobins especially with respect to his relations with the Bordelais deputies and in particular Gensonné, who had corresponded with the general up to 1792.[80] Roland was denounced at the Convention by Danton for writing to Dumouriez at the session of 27 March. A few days later, when news of Dumouriez's negotiations with the Austrians to march on Paris was confirmed, the Jacobins issued a circular which denounced Miranda, Brissot, the Bordelais and the former War Minister Beurnonville as accomplices of Dumouriez.[81]

In the recent past, no one had been friendlier with the general than Danton, yet he was forgiven his transgressions by all at the Jacobins, including Robespierre and Marat. The reason for their reluctance to turn against Danton, whose behaviour *vis-à-vis* Dumouriez had never been properly explained, was the fact that he had attacked two of the greatest enemies of Robespierre. They were Roland and Brissot. Robespierre, perhaps, had been planning such an attack on Brissot for months, but lacked a general pretext. It should be recalled that they first parted company over the war, although they had been publicly reconciled. However, Robespierre had always put much less faith in the generals than Brissot and now that one of them had turned out to be a counter-revolutionary traitor, all of his past suspicions came to a head. Robespierre demanded a decree of accusation against all of Dumouriez's accomplices. But for the time being, Brissot's reply had satisfied the Assembly and it moved on to the day's business without taking action.[82]

The extreme pressures and challenges confronting the Convention during the spring of 1793 were serious enough to have threatened the very existence of the new regime. In terms of the factional struggle, the tension had initially brought about a temporary rapprochement between those who were already opponents, with the exception of Brissot and Robespierre, who were irreconcilable by this time. Each time the Convention was endangered from an outside force whether it was the *émigrés*, the foreign war, internal civil war or from the growing popular movement in Paris, the result was a drawing together of deputies to protect themselves and save the republic from destruction. The sanctity of the Convention was defended by all deputies. Even Marat denounced the radicals who had been intimidating it.

Throughout this period of crisis, the leading Jacobins who were also deputies remained firmly opposed to purges demanded by the more radical non-deputy Jacobins who were in control of the society. The Jacobins had become dominated by the more radical members during the spring of 1793 in response to the pressures that were facing the country. Their method of solving the country's problems was through threats of violence. The more moderate members, who were deputies, were menaced by threats of purges by men from the radical popular movement if they did not agree to their demands against the 'unfaithful' deputies in the Convention. The club was not united at this stage of the revolution, although it had successfully purged the majority of Brissot's close associates. Only Carra and Mercier remained members. Their newspaper had never received funding from Roland. Mercier rarely spoke at the society if he attended meetings at all. The expulsion of Pétion, who was not defended by Robespierre, was a major turning point for the club. He had been one of its most fervent defenders just two years previously.

The war between the presses of the 'Brissotins' and the Jacobins had continued throughout March and certainly did not end there. The attempt to curtail the impact of 'Brissotin' opinion in the provinces led to a partial restriction of the press. This censorship of the press, lifted by the Convention in April, had not prevented the powerful 'Brissotin' journalists from getting their message across to French patriots in the countryside.

The news of Dumouriez's treason was a major turning point for men from both factions who had previously been supporters of the general. The linking of Dumouriez with Brissot, Roland and the Bordelais by men like Danton, who had rarely participated in the factional struggles, was an important development. Rather than uniting the two factions, the Dumouriez affair worked in the opposite direction. This could be explained by either the fear of an Austrian invasion after Neerwinden – which might have been expected to make for unity – or the fear that Dumouriez would turn his army on Paris and dissolve the Convention and the Jacobins. The former fear continued throughout the spring, while the latter, possibly more acute, was much more short-lived since as soon as it became clear that the army would not cooperate, Dumouriez fled.

A possible explanation as to why the Dumouriez affair divided the factions seems to centre round Danton. Danton disappeared mysteriously for a few days in the hope that Dumouriez's plans would come off so that he would become Dumouriez's right-hand man. This was too good an opportunity for the 'Brissotins' to miss and their attack on Danton (who previously had favoured a compromise with them) drove him, in self-defence, to denounce them as secret allies of Dumouriez. In other words, once Dumouriez himself was no longer a threat to the revolution, it was safe to use him as ammunition in the faction fight.

By the beginning of April, based on the speeches and behaviour of these men over the past few months, it seemed that Danton, Robespierre, Marat, Billaud, Desmoulins, Collot, Couthon and Robert were lined up against Brissot, the Bordelais, Gorsas, Barbaroux, Buzot and Louvet. The battle lines were much clearer by the beginning of April than they had been just one month before.

THE CRYSTALLIZATION OF FACTIONS

By the beginning of April 1793, two increasingly polarized, but not yet fixed groups were emerging in the Convention. This Assembly, which had been elected for the purpose of giving France its first republican constitution, had still not done so, and continued to occupy itself almost entirely with mutual accusations and charges of royalism and of betrayal. The major players involved in the rhetoric of denunciation at the Convention were primarily the same men who had been opponents for some time now: Pétion, Robespierre, Brissot, Vergniaud, Gensonné, Gorsas, Guadet, Marat and now, Danton, who had previously vacillated between attack and reconciliation. As a result of the Dumouriez crisis and in a desperate attempt to clear his own name, he had accused Brissot and the Bordelais of being accomplices of the general. Men such as Mercier, Garran Coulon, Fabre, Saint-Just, Condorcet and Barère remained silent, or only intervened on issues such as the constitution or the problem of provisioning. Brissot's support for men like Fabre is demonstrated in an article in the *Patriote Français* about the Jacobin meeting of 12 April, which reported that when the Jacobins recently established a 'purification committee', they had left out some 'good' men who remained in the society, such as Fabre and Chabot.[1]

Conflict within the Convention was further complicated by the growing militancy of the radical movement which had been developing in Paris for some time now. It was based primarily in certain radical or Sans-culottes sections, among one group at the Jacobins and at the Cordeliers, rather than in the commune. These militants took a rather dim view of the Convention as an entirety, and not simply one part of it, and were always ready to appeal to force in order to get what they wanted. This was demonstrated firstly in the February riots over food shortages and then again in March when the Convention united against this group which potentially threatened its existence.

Dumouriez's treason and flight to the Austrians had provoked the Jacobins into issuing their first collective statement demanding the purging of some members from the Convention. The linking of Brissot and his group with Dumouriez's defection was a new tactic on the part of men like Robespierre. The leading Jacobins had universally praised Dumouriez as late as 12 March. The Jacobin club itself was often divided between the more moderate, like Robespierre who continually denounced radical measures such as the use of violence and the more radical like Desfieux. Throughout the months of April and May, until the purging of one part of the Convention, deputies who were also members of the Jacobins supported the sanctity of the Convention.

This chapter seeks to investigate whether or not the two emerging groups in the Convention would continue to unite against a common external threat, as they had done in March, or whether growing personal animosities and suspicions were too entrenched for that. Would some of the Jacobin deputies be prepared to support, or at least accept, a popular movement with the intention of purging the Convention of some members which would not be under their control and was at risk of transferring power to people who had no respect for them?

PETITIONS AND DENUNCIATIONS

The month of April was characterized by almost continuous petitioning from the sections, both at the Jacobins and the Convention, firstly, for the removal of certain 'unfaithful' deputies who were associated with Dumouriez, and second, for a maximum price to be set on essentials such as bread. On 8 April, a petition from the Bon-Conseil section, formerly Mauconseil, demanding the arrest of 'les Buzot, les Barbaroux, les Guadet, les Gensonné and some others', was read to members of the club. The more radical members were sympathetic, but the leading Jacobins who were also deputies, rejected it.[2] While Robespierre felt that the club must adopt the petition which was 'basically good and just', he told members that the expressions employed by its editor were 'vicious' and 'indecent' and could be used by their enemies as a pretext to slander patriots. Therefore, certain passages had to be suppressed and replaced with the 'proud language of republicanism'. The Jacobins nominated four members to attend an all sections meeting for this to be accomplished.[3] This section, however, in common with a good many others, was not consistent in its attitude towards the 'unfaithful' deputies throughout the months of April and May. Less than a month later, the same section sent a petition to the Convention opposing the purge of deputies.[4] The evidence from the sectional proceedings seems to indicate that there were many battles taking place within these assemblies for leadership between the radicals and moderates.[5]

The Bon-Conseil petition was presented on the same day at the Convention. Brissot's journal indicates that petitions from the sections of Finistère and Nord supported Bon-Conseil.[6] The orator demanded that deputies 'examine severely and profoundly the conspiracy of Dumouriez' and called Brissot and friends 'his accomplices'. Gorsas called for the insertion of the petition in the bulletin and proposed that it be sent to the departments. Terrible disorder in the Convention was the response to his proposal. On Marat's insistence, the petitioners were granted the 'honours of the session'.[7]

The next day, 9 April, Pétion announced a new plot against deputies from the section of Halle-aux-Blés. It had circulated a petition to all sections demanding that Roland be turned over to the revolutionary tribunal, and that all deputies who voted in favour of the referendum be recalled. Pétion demanded that severe measures be taken against the leaders of the section: that the president and secretary of this section who signed the petition be brought before the Convention to verify their signatures and then be sent to the revolutionary tribunal. He claimed that the petition must have been written by either royalists or counter-revolutionaries. His attitude can be contrasted with that of Danton, who insisted that they discuss whether or not the petition be given 'honourable mention' because he found parts of it 'truly good'. At this point, he was certainly not in favour of a petition which demanded a purge of the Convention, but he took a more rational view of the petitioning than did Pétion, believing that Pétion was overstating the seriousness of its contents, and claiming that the Convention continually received petitions which were 'exaggerated'. Danton insisted on consistency in the behaviour of deputies concerning petitions and then asked that they move on to the business before them and not waste any more time on discussing the petition. Similarly, Fabre tried to change the subject by declaring that the enemy was at the camp de Maulde and that members should be occupied with ways of saving the country. Boyer-Fonfrède blamed the petition on counter-revolutionaries such as royalists and refractories.[8] The Assembly decreed that the newly organized Committee of Public Safety, which included Danton and Barère, would report on it.[9] The Committee of Public Safety had replaced the

Committee of General Defence. It was really a war cabinet for its primary responsibility was the conduct of the war. The composition of it is rather significant since none of the leading antagonists in the Convention were now members. Brissot and his friends had lost a good deal of prestige over the Dumouriez affair and Robespierre had stated that he would no longer serve on the same committee as Brissot.

The Bon-Conseil petition provoked a new round of mutual denunciations and accusations by the major players from the two factions. While Pétion was demanding that measures be taken against those who had signed the petition against certain members of the Convention, Robespierre believed the right moment had arrived for yet another verbal attack. Guadet vehemently protested against 'the artificial opinion which surrounded deputies' as a method of disguising the truth.[10] Vergniaud, Guadet, Brissot and Pétion all delivered long self-justification speeches to the Convention or wrote pamphlets in response to this petition and Robespierre's verbal assault. Robespierre's speech could most appropriately be characterized as the history of his interpretation of the evolution of the two factions, or the breakdown of relations between those who had not so long ago been his friends and political allies. Most of his speech was a repetition of previous allegations. What was new from the end of March were his comments about Dumouriez. In all, he made fourteen charges. Firstly, he claimed that a faction was conspiring with the tyrants of Europe to put a king back on the French throne. This faction, which was dominant in the Convention, had been formed a long time ago. Initially, the 'party' had defended the rights of the people and of patriotic societies, but this changed when it attained power. At this point, the group became moderates, 'hiding their ambition under the mask of moderation and love of order'. They called all those not enrolled under their banner 'anarchists' and 'agitators'. The faction, composed of the 'ambitious' from the start of the revolution, had slandered the best patriots. It had treated as assassins the 'most energetic patriots', denounced the commune of 10 August, provoked a departmental force, exaggerated the evils of 2 September, had wanted to save the king, had been opposed to Belgium's unification with France, and finally, it had been in agreement with Dumouriez's plan to cut out the patriots' throats. In addition, he made all sorts of wild accusations against Brissot and the three Bordeaux deputies: Vergniaud had told the king on 10 August that he would respect the constituted authorities and that the 'faction' had put Dumouriez in power. Gorsas, who published long extracts from Robespierre's speech, remarked that the reaction of the Convention to these 'calumnies repeated a thousand times', was the 'silence of contempt'.[11]

Where the opposition made its error was in replying to Robespierre's charges one by one, making itself look guilty even if it was not. Vergniaud replied to Robespierre in an equally long speech, refuting all of his fourteen accusations. Similar and often familiar material can be found in these documents. The major themes included the 'faction's' influence in the appointment of ministers, in the committees and in the Assembly; on the declaration of war, intelligence with traitors, namely Lafayette and the court, for months beforehand.[12] There seems to be little rational justification for replying in such detail to Robespierre other than perhaps Vergniaud believed he could garner support from the rest of the Convention. Since almost no deputies rose to defend him – other than those who one would expect – there seems little evidence for this. Guadet spoke after Vergniaud, adding denunciations of both Marat and the Jacobin circular of 5 April, which according to Guadet, issued a call to arms.[13]

Robespierre's attack in the Convention provoked Brissot and Pétion into publishing pamphlets in response. It is interesting that Brissot conducted his struggle almost entirely with his pen during

The Republican 'Montagnards' of 1793, by an anonymous artist. (Musée Carnavalet)

the last two months he was a deputy. After his self-defence speech responding to Robespierre's accusations that he was an accomplice of Dumouriez at the beginning of April, Brissot had gone into retreat. He almost never spoke again in the Convention. This could be interpreted as Brissot's understanding that he and his friends no longer commanded the support they once had. He wrote that he had intended to reply to Robespierre at the Assembly, but he did not want to tire it. What is certain is that the attack by the leading 'Mountain' deputies was forceful enough to keep their opponents on the defensive, either at the Convention (the speeches of the Bordelais and Pétion), or in written form (pamphlets by Brissot and Pétion). Both pamphlets are extraordinarily defensive in nature. They contain similar arguments and information: the denial of being the accomplice of Dumouriez, Miranda and Orléans. Brissot denied knowing Dumouriez before February of 1792 and having any part in Dumouriez's appointment to the ministry. After 10 August and since Dumouriez had become a general, Brissot denied having any contact with him, which of course, was not true since Brissot had written to Dumouriez on 28 November, 2 and 9 December. These letters all concerned Brissot's wish that Dumouriez release Miranda from his command in order that he could carry out a revolution in Spanish America.[14] He denied being the head of a 'party', or running a ministry: 'Robespierre accused me of governing the ministry since 10 August and I affirm that it is Robespierre, Danton and their party which has governed it and still governs by terror.'[15]

Pétion made similar remarks in his pamphlet where he explained his relations with Dumouriez, Miranda and Orléans. He claimed to have applauded Dumouriez's military successes like everyone else, and to have written to him once to encourage triumph in battle. Dumouriez had not replied. Miranda was introduced to him while he was mayor of Paris by Garran Coulon. This brave general had been sacrificed by Dumouriez at Neerwinden. Concerning Orléans, Pétion wrote that it was not he who brought him and defended him at the Convention. He had advised Orléans to leave the country after Louis' execution.[16] As stressed above, the important point of all these speeches and pamphlets is that they are all defensive in nature.

MARAT'S IMPEACHMENT AND ACQUITTAL

The Jacobin circular of 5 April, signed by Marat as president, led to demands for his arrest. The circular asserted that counter-revolutionaries were in the government and in the National Convention and urged republicans to arm.[17] Guadet condemned the circular and accused the Jacobins of having organized the failed uprising of March and Dumouriez's treason and of plotting to put the Duke of Orléans on the throne. Marat did not deny having signed the circular, but he claimed to have done so as a newly elected president, without having read it properly. Was this the first collective Jacobin statement calling for the removal of deputies from the Convention? If it was, the club was not united. Most Jacobins who were also deputies disapproved wholeheartedly of the independent action which some of the sections were taking. In addition, they denounced any violence taken against the Convention. Marat disowned a central committee which had recently set itself up at the *Evêché*. Similarly, Barère was highly suspicious of an organization whose purpose was 'to degrade national representation to subsequently usurp its authority'.[18] The Convention's Committee of Public Safety had been created to counter the growing influence of the revolutionary committee sitting at the *Evêché*.[19] The revolutionary committee was formed by militants from the sections, on the impetus of those in the Droits-de-l'Homme section, of which Varlet was secretary, and called itself a 'central committee of public safety'. This group declared itself to be authorized to correspond with all the municipalities of France and to issue orders. Twenty-eight sections were represented at the committee and their primary focus was with petitions demanding the expulsion of the moderates from the Convention. They secured support by methods of intimidation. If section members refused to sign petitions, their certificates of patriotism were revoked. Many Jacobins were opposed to their objectives and tried to convince the sections to withdraw their support.[20] Robespierre warned against premature violence that might weaken the authority of the Convention: 'the most fatal of measures', he proclaimed, 'would be the violation of national representation'.[21] But the club was not without its dissenters. The younger Robespierre had more in common with the sectional militants than his more cautious older brother. At the club, Robespierre jeune delivered a violent speech which Gorsas printed in his newspaper on 8 April: 'We will never uncover the plots of our enemies if we don't act. Roland has not been arrested; he even received honours at his section. The Convention is not capable of governing. We must attack the leaders. All good citizens should meet in their sections . . . come to the Convention and demand the arrest of the unfaithful deputies. It is by these petitions that you can save the republic.'[22]

Danton took Marat's defence by trying to divert attention away from Marat to Orléans, but to no avail. This marked a change in Danton's attitude towards Marat since the previous autumn when he had done his best to distance himself from Marat. Cries were heard from all parts of the Convention: 'To the Abbaye'. Pétion and Marat exchanged insults and then Pétion cried out: 'There is the man who has endlessly demanded despotism, sometimes under the name of dictatorship, sometimes under the name of triumvirate.'[23] Many deputies demanded a decree of accusation, including Buzot who demanded Marat's expulsion on 13 April. Danton admitted that for a long time, he did not believe in the existence of a 'faction', but now he realized that this was true. The Dumouriez affair had been a turning point for him. This does not mean that he did not continue to urge deputies to work together for the good of the nation, but he had now laid his cards on the table, publicly declaring himself on Robespierre's side. The new tactic of the Bordelais and supporters like Buzot was to demand the immediate convening of primary assemblies and elections. These elections would determine which deputies still claimed the confidence of the people. Robespierre cried that Gensonné's principles were 'blasphemous and against liberty'. Desmoulins could only see treason in them. Delaunay jeune, in the name of the Legislation Committee, presented a report on Marat's writings the same day that many were calling for his arrest. This report concluded that Marat's publications did indeed encourage the pillaging and dissolution of the Convention. The Convention voted for the printing of this report and that it be transmitted throughout the departments. Immediately after the reading of this report, Boyer-Fonfrède demanded a vote on Marat.[24]

Marat's arrest was demanded by many in the Convention, including Delacroix, Danton's colleague on mission.[25] Yet the 'Brissotins' were later to be blamed for it, even though many either abstained or stayed away on the voting day. This was presumably because Guadet had initiated the latest attack as a tactic to defend himself. The voting results were as follows: 226 approved of the accusation against him, 93 disapproved and 47 abstained. None of the Bordelais voted in favour of Marat's impeachment: Vergniaud was absent for the vote while Guadet and Gensonné declared themselves incompetent to judge Marat. Only Gorsas, Barbaroux and Mercier voted in favour of the accusation against Marat. The majority of deputies who are the concern of this book either abstained, were absent for the vote, or were away on mission. Only Robespierre and Desmoulins voted against Marat's impeachment.[26] According to the *Patriote Français*, many deputies, namely,

Lasource, the Bordelais, Brissot, Pétion and others did not vote against Marat because they had been 'personally threatened by Marat'.[27]

Although Brissot was absent from the vote on Marat, the evidence suggests that he continued to wage war against Marat through the editor of the *Patriote Français*, Girey-Dupré. During Marat's trial, an Englishman who was one of the witnesses, was asked if he was aware of the insertion in the *Patriote Français* of a paragraph stating that a young Englishman named William Johnson, who had come to France to discover liberty, had attempted suicide when he learned about Marat's attempts to destroy it. Girey-Dupré, when interrogated, admitted that Brissot had in fact given him the article, but that it was he, as editor, who was responsible for publishing it. Brissot was invited to appear at the trial, but he never did. The note was passed to the president of the Convention, who did nothing about it. This evidence seems to suggest Brissot was working behind the scenes to get Marat convicted.[28]

There appears to have been a distinct lack of party discipline on the part of the Jacobin club on this vote, unlike during the king's trial when threats of expulsion from the club were made against those who had hinted at voting in favour of the referendum. Marat spent one night in prison between his arrest and his appearance before the revolutionary tribunal. His trial was based on articles in his journal which were alleged to provoke pillage, murder and the dissolution of the Convention.[29] The tribunal acquitted him of all charges on 23 April. In his letter to the Convention, read while he was in prison, Marat declared that he would not obey the decree of accusation against him unless a similar one was launched against those he accused of being Dumouriez's accomplices: Salles, Barbaroux, Lasource, Brissot, Guadet, Gensonné, Vergniaud, Buzot, and other 'unfaithful deputies'.[30] Writing in his history of the Convention, the deputy Paganel gave the impression that the accusation against Marat was inspired by Vergniaud's speech: 'Marat had just provoked the shedding of French blood. Vergniaud hastened to the tribune; his voice launched the thunderbolt; and that faction which braved human and divine justice trembled for the first time.'[31]

THE PROPAGANDA WAR AND THE JACOBINS

Robespierre and others at the Jacobins had long accused Brissot and his friends of disseminating anti-Paris propaganda in the provinces. In the midst of the Marat affair, the 'Brissotins' discovered that their rivals at the Jacobins had also been engaged in this propaganda war in provincial France. This incident served to further alienate the two factions. At the session of 18 April, two delegates from Bordeaux were introduced to the Convention to denounce what they interpreted as a counter-revolutionary conspiracy. Garraud and Paganel, members of a quasi-official Surveillance Committee at Bordeaux, stated that this committee had arrested a special courier who had been sent to the south-western departments by the Jacobins of Paris and had seized and opened the packages he was carrying. The packages contained private letters in addition to printed speeches and pamphlets from the club intended for provincial affiliates. One of the letters spoke favourably about the purge of moderate deputies. During the discussion that ensued, Barbaroux demanded that the contents of the fifteen packages be read out to the Assembly. Fabre immediately disagreed, thinking that this would imply that the Convention did not approve of the conduct of the department, which should be denounced. Fonfrède declared that it had not been the department which had authorized the violation of secrecy, but the commissars from the Convention, Garraud and Paganel, who had established this Surveillance Committee. After much debate, and on Vergniaud's motion, the packages were to be examined by the Committees of Public Safety and Legislation. Robespierre had recommended they go to the Committee of General Security. The contents of these packages were almost entirely pro-Jacobin propaganda with many items demanding the removal of moderate deputies from the Convention.[32]

The Jacobins responded immediately to this interruption of their post by asserting that the act was a flagrant violation of privacy and violation of the mails by counter-revolutionaries. For months, they had been suspicious that their mail had been intercepted and blamed this on Roland and the deputies from the Gironde. This latest incident convinced them that they had been right all along, even though there was no proof that Roland and the Bordelais had anything to do with the interception of Jacobin mail. The following week, a lengthy Jacobin circular appeared, angrily denying that the club had been spreading seditious material and thoroughly denouncing the Surveillance Committee and its advocates in Paris for blatant violations of civil liberties.[33] The circular blamed the entire incident on the leaders from the Gironde, who may not have had anything to do with it. Although the affair died down and no measures were taken against those who opened the mail, it provided one side with increased ammunition.

Meanwhile, the war between the presses continued to rage in the capital. While the Jacobins were attacking the moderate deputies by sending hostile literature to their provincial affiliates, Brissot and friends countered through their newspapers. An article in the April issue of the *Chronique* attacked the Jacobins, while Brissot defended the moderates and attacked the left in an article in which he wrote that in order for the Convention to restore order, 'it must strike at the trunk of the power which rivals it, or this power will destroy it'.[34] Pétion published one of the most damning critiques at the end of the month. He described a phenomenon which had not existed before in any revolution: 'it is a school of slander open daily, where two thousand people without ceasing, distil envy, hate and intrigue; two thousand spectators, who every day, hear from the tribune the same defamation . . . This was the Jacobin society, which holds a remarkable place in history, which has rendered such great services to the country.' The Jacobin club was no longer an association of enlightened men, but it was now a 'coalition of envious beings, intriguers, aristocrats, disguised royalists . . . animated by the spirit of destruction, preaching and spreading licence and disorder'.[35] The club responded to this sort of anti-Jacobin propaganda by assigning three members to the task of investigating suspicious writings and reporting to Hébert at the commune for possible prosecution. Three more members were to keep a list of all provincial societies which demanded the expulsion of prominent men who voted for the referendum from the Convention.[36]

CONSEQUENCES OF MARAT'S ACQUITTAL

There were several ramifications of the Marat episode. It temporarily united the Jacobins. They had been divided since the failed uprising of 9–10 March. Marat became a rallying point for the radicals. He returned to the club in triumph like a hero in an elaborate and ceremonial session. The club's manifestation of its support for Marat was to republish the circular of 5 April which Guadet had used to attack Marat. In addition, its circular of 19 April, not issued until the 24th after Marat's acquittal, produced more material in favour of Marat. It attacked Brissot, Pétion, Barbaroux and the deputies from the Gironde and demanded the removal of 'some monsters who agitate, hinder and dishonour' from the Convention.[37] Previously, the more moderate deputy leaders were able to prevent statements like this from going into the circulars, but with so many of them away from Paris and others not attending sessions, the militants had succeeded in sending what was the most radical circular yet to the departments. This circular was read to the society by Sambat, who, on the basis of it, was named to the Correspondence Committee.[38] Even before Marat was acquitted, Dubois-Crancé warned 'moderates' that their unfair campaign against Marat would not produce a criminal, but an 'acquitted hero'.[39]

A further result of the Marat affair was an address presented to the Convention in the name of thirty-three or thirty-five sections demanding a decree of accusation against twenty-two deputies on 15 April. Buzot demanded that the petitioners be admitted to the session and sign it individually. Barère was opposed to their admission, but Buzot's motion was carried and the petition was read. Those named for proscription in the petition who are also subjects of this book were as follows: Brissot, Vergniaud, Guadet, Gensonné, Buzot, Barbaroux, Gorsas, Louvet and Pétion. To their names were added: Grangeneuve, Salles, Biroteau, Pontécoulant, Lanthenas, Valazé, Chambon, Fauchet, Lasource, Hardi, LeHardi and Valady.[40] During the discussion of this petition, two proposals which would be repeated by the proscribed deputies were made. Lasource called for the convening of primary assemblies, which had already been proposed by the Bordelais, while Guadet demanded that the Convention move its meetings to Versailles because of the frequent interruptions by the public. These motions were ignored. Understandably, those who spoke against the petition included: Louvet, Gensonné, Vergniaud, Guadet and Buzot. However, leading 'Mountain' deputies, such as Robespierre, also opposed a purge: 'When I suggest firm and vigorous measures, I am not suggesting those convulsions that do death to the body politic.'[41] Philippeaux, a colleague of Danton, did demand that deputies put an end to divisions and passions and occupy themselves with measures to ensure the safety of the country.[42] After much debate on the petition, a general consensus emerged that the petition be rejected as slanderous. However, about a fortnight later, Fabre, in a long speech on the subject of the petition, announced that 'there was no more peace between the coalition of the twenty-two and the Mountain in as much as I wish it to be possible, it appears to be impracticable and the people must know this.' He did not offer a solution to what he called 'open warfare of the twenty-two against the Mountain, the sans-culottes and the people', but he foreshadowed an uprising as a possible resolution: 'However things will turn out, a violent explosion seems to be shaping up if one side does not cede.'[43] Fabre seems to have been won over to the more militant side of the club. A violent uprising was not what Robespierre and others were advocating at the start of May. To the contrary, he was preaching moderation and staying within the confines of the law.

The tension did not let up in the weeks following the petition. On 6 May, a debate over Paris, which had for so long been the source of contention among many of these men, arose again. Although the Convention had decreed on 1 May, on Marat's proposal, that Paris merited the nation, a letter from petitioners from the Bon-Conseil section protesting their imprisonment on the grounds that they 'had the audacity to be good citizens', brought about another embittered debate on the city. Vergniaud arose against the 'perpetual usurpation of powers by the Paris commune' and demanded that the mayor explain the reasons for the arrest. He was supported by Guadet, Cambon and Robespierre, who saw in this motion, 'the reversal of all principles'. The Convention decreed Vergniaud's proposal. On the same day, Guadet called for extreme measures. He demanded that all Paris bodies be suspended and be provisionally replaced by commissions appointed by the executive council, that the sections of Paris no longer remain in permanence and that the revolutionary committees which they had created, be dissolved.[44] Chaumette, speaking at the commune on 8 May, demanded that a deputation be sent to the Convention to warn it that the municipality considered the *Patriote Français* an 'anti-patriotic paper', having a tendency to degrade constituted authorities and that Girey-Dupré in issue 1365 was impeding recruitment for the Vendée.[45]

The acquittal of Marat was a major blow to Brissot and his friends. Even if they had not voted in favour of Marat's impeachment, they were blamed for it. This only led to increased hostility and tension. This was particularly evident in the Jacobin club, which, as noted above, had issued its first circular calling for the removal of certain deputies from the Convention.

Although the Jacobins united in their praise of Marat, they continued to be a divided institution over other matters. The debates indicate that there was much dissension over the content of their circulars which were intended for provincial consumption and thus a dissemination of the Paris club's view of current revolutionary circumstances. At the meeting of 21 April, discussion centred round the next circular. The last sentence caused much disagreement. It was very violent in its wording: 'Two parties exist in the Convention. Destroy these greedy monsters with your blood. Until when will you suffer these assassins who provoked civil war, who are in contact with Dumouriez, who favour the villainous Orléans? Their crimes are well-known; why are you waiting to strike?' Robespierre, Albitte and Dubois-Crancé denounced the circular with Robespierre demanding the retraction of the last few lines. The society adopted Robespierre's recommendation.[46] Once again, for whatever reason, the leading Jacobin deputies opposed violence against their parliamentary opponents.

THE CONTINUAL PROBLEM OF PROVISIONING

Madame sans-Culottes. (Bibliothèque nationale de France)

Meanwhile, there was a more pressing problem at hand: how to deal with the growing lack of food supplies in Paris. Deputies had done little to respond to the needs of the ordinary people in the past. The rioting in February had not resulted in any concrete measures. On 5 April, the section of Quatre-Nations petitioned the Convention for an inventory of grain and forage and an additional tax on the rich. It was Danton who took the initiative on this issue, maintaining that something had to be done for the sans-culottes. Later the same day, he convinced his colleagues to vote in favour of the establishment of a paid sans-culottes militia and the imposition of special taxes on the wealthy as a way of maintaining bread prices at a fixed proportion of the workers' wages. The special tax proposal never got past the committee stage because deputies feared that it might do some harm to commerce. The deputies also added the proviso that no measure should be passed which would interfere with commerce.[47] Popular demands continued to vex the Convention. Deputies found themselves forced to give in to demands for a maximum price measure. As a way of avoiding the maximum, the Committee of Public Safety suggested and the Assembly decreed that all transactions would take place using *assignats* rather than hard currency. In mid-April, small riots took place among some of the bakeries and one was pillaged. Bread was not the only expensive food. Meat was also costly and in short supply. Some of the popular gatherings which were gaining in momentum, threatened both the Convention and the Paris Commune. The 'Fraternal society of the two sexes', formed by militant sans-culottes men and women, attacked the Jacobins for not responding to the subsistence problems of ordinary people. This group also circulated petitions at the entrance to the Convention, attacking the leaders, who they said, dined well every day while the people were starving. Their criticisms were aimed as much at Robespierre and Saint-Just as at the 'Brissotins'.[48]

On 18 April, a general meeting of mayors and municipal officers from Paris and the surrounding area took place. They demanded radical measures. They claimed that the rights of property could not extend so far as to deny food to a starving fellow citizen, for 'the fruits of the earth, of the air, belong to all men'. The petitioners asked for a maximum price for wheat, the suppression of parasitic middlemen and a general census of grain after each harvest. Although Robespierre interrupted Buzot who was condemning the petition, to declare that Buzot was slandering Paris, he did nothing to support the maximum-price measure. Vergniaud demanded that the petition be referred to the Committee of Agriculture. He thought that both commerce and agriculture would be destroyed by the maximum-price measure. Deputies agreed to Vergniaud's motion and thus continued to delay making a decision on the maximum by referring the petition to their Committees of Agriculture and Commerce.[49]

The intransigence of the Convention led the commune to take more radical measures than mere petitioning. The commune, on Chaumette's proposal, renewed its vow of 10 August: 'the sacred oath that all would act as one and die at their posts rather than submit to the last blow at the people's rights'. It followed this by declaring itself in a state of revolution as long as the means of living were not assured. When these dramatic proceedings were reported to the Convention, Gensonné denounced the decree and called for the convocation of primary assemblies. Similarly, Guadet demanded the dissolution of the commune's decree. Vergniaud obtained an order that the officers of the commune produce their minutes at the bar and answer for their conduct, but disagreed with the convocation of primary assemblies. He also discussed the petition of 15 April, which he believed was not simply in favour of the expulsion of the twenty-two, but the dissolution of the entire Convention. He reminded deputies of the incidents of 10 March and of the contents of the petitions at that time. Robespierre jeune claimed that the commune, which had contributed so much to the 'reversal of tyranny in uncovering plots', had always shown great respect for the Convention. The petition thus must have been the work of those who wanted to put Orléans on the throne. When Camboulas demanded that the municipal officials of Paris be granted the honours of the session, Robespierre jeune argued that it should be put to a vote. This motion was combated unsuccessfully by Valazé and Lanjuinais. At this point, those who sat in the centre and on the right of the Assembly departed. The results of the vote were of the 149 present, 143 voted for and only 6 against the honours.[50]

At the committee discussion of the maximum price for goods, Barbaroux declared that such a measure was unjust because it placed the economic burden on the peasant. It took no account of the increase in the price of farm implements and made no allowance for differences in soil types throughout the regions. Moreover, it would be impossible to enforce because an army of officials would be necessary.[51] Danton added that the poorer citizens should be paid to attend their section meetings to compensate for lost wages at work. Once again, other deputies applauded him, but took no action.[52]

Petitions on the subject of a maximum continued almost on a daily basis at the Convention throughout the rest of the month of April. During Ducos' speech against the maximum on 30 April, Guadet cried out that 'national representation no longer existed'. Even though women from Versailles had just presented a hostile petition demanding the maximum three days earlier, he still proposed moving the Convention's meetings to Versailles. These women also petitioned the Jacobin club. The pressure culminated on 1 May, when a group of petitioners in the name of the men of '14 juillet, 5–6 octobre, 20 juin and 10 août', from the *faubourg* Saint-Antoine, reproached the Convention for having done nothing and promising everything. It demanded a maximum price for bread and that anyone with an income over a thousand *livres* should be required to give half to the city. These men declared themselves to be in a state of 'insurrection' if their demands were not voted. They threatened the deputies sitting in the Convention that 10,000 men were at its door.[53] Although the editor of the *Révolutions de Paris*, Prudhomme, was in agreement with many of the measures proposed by the petitioners, including the maximum, he protested violently against the threats they made to the sovereignty of the Convention as did the great majority of deputies who rose in indignation at these demands including Couthon who demanded their arrest. Delacroix moved that they should not receive the honours of the session and Philippeaux thought that the orator should be sent before the revolutionary tribunal.[54] Yet the next day, the Convention finally voted the maximum law. Mathiez, one of the few historians who has directly addressed the question of the deputies' motivation, argued a number of years ago that the reason why deputies passed the maximum was to obliterate the counter-revolution. He cites closer relations between the leading 'Mountain' deputies and the commune and *enragés* after Dumouriez's treason.[55] That is one explanation. Another is that the Convention behaved the way it did only under the threat of insurrection. Deputies, who were unanimous in their belief in the free market place, only voted the maximum in response to threatening circumstances, rather than a change in ideology or sympathy for the poor. The existence of the Convention was at stake and radical revolutionaries had to be appeased. The question of price controls only divided the Convention inasmuch as some deputies, such as Guadet and Buzot, turned the debate into an attack on Paris and the Jacobins. Buzot demanded the punishment of the men who were threatening the Convention.[56] Both of these men voted in favour of the maximum.[57] As far as the basic problem was concerned, there was unanimity.[58]

What could be interpreted as closer relations between the leading 'Mountain' deputies and the sans-culottes as evidenced by the passing of the maximum, as argued by Mathiez, did not necessarily mean that these deputies supported a purge of the Convention or that they backed extremists such as Varlet. Varlet was unsuccessful in his attempt to speak to the Jacobins on 3 May, and on the 12th he was not well received. It could be argued that throughout the month of May, the club, led by prominent Jacobin deputies, such as Robespierre, tended towards the side of caution. On 8 May, he stated that there were laws to 'legally exterminate our enemies'. He preached faith in the Convention and argued that the 'gangrened part of the Convention did not prevent the people from combating the aristocrats'. Robespierre, speaking in the middle of the month, persisted in his moderate line, opposing an indictment of his opposition in the Convention. Instead, club members should focus on matters of policy such as the constitution.[59]

THE STRUGGLE FOR CONTROL OF THE SECTIONS

The sections themselves were as divided as the Convention during this crucial period. Loyalty is very difficult to gauge for it often changed quite frequently. The section of Bon-Conseil is just one

xample of this frequent movement in supporting the 'moderates' at one moment and the
Mountain' at another. Much depended upon who was in control of the sectional assemblies and
ow much violence was used to intimidate members. Often the Paris Commune tried to control the
olitics of the sections. The story reported by the Lombards section in a petition to the Convention
n 8 May is illustrative of this fact. It demanded the freedom of a member named Perrin or Permes
vho had been arrested by the commune for having protested against many arbitrary arrests by the
nunicipality. Robespierre, Charlier and others opposed giving this man his freedom, while Buzot
nd Isnard protested against the oppression of patriots. Apparently Robespierre and others confused
his man with someone called Sagnier from Bon-Conseil who had also been arrested by the
ommune.[60]

An issue which divided the sections concerned recruitment of men to fight against the insurgent
oyalist and Catholic armies in western France. The Paris Commune followed the example of the
epartment of L'Hérault which had raised 4,000 recruits. Paris intended to raise 12,000 who were
o be chosen by the revolutionary committees of each section. The commune, requiring funds for
he army, also planned a tax on all those whose income exceeded 1,000 *livres*. These measures
vere unpopular amongst the sections. People did not want to leave their homes to fight an
unknown war which meant nothing to them. Several meetings were held throughout the capital, at
he Luxembourg and even on the Champs-Elysées, protesting against conscription and against
Marat, Danton and Robespierre whom they held responsible for these measures.[61]

The sectional opposition provided Brissot and his supporters with the perfect opportunity to
xploit the enforced recruitment to their benefit. At the beginning of May, the *Patriote Français*
eported that several sections were fighting against anarchy and successfully. These were Bon-
Conseil, Mail, Théâtre-Français, (Marseilles) Unité (Quatre-Nations) and Butte des Moulins. The
aper had previously noted that Observatoire, Finistère and Panthéon Français supported the
anctity of the Convention.[62] Later in the month, Brissot's paper praised the sections of Mail,
Piques, Panthéon-Français 'and many others' for protesting against the formation of a central
issembly whose purpose would be the discussion of a war tax. He condemned men like Varlet,
vhom he referred to as anarchists for stirring up trouble amongst the sections: specifically he
eported that Varlet and his band from the section of Sans-culottes had arrived at 11.30 p.m. at the
ection of Panthéon Français where they preached insurrection. There were very few present at
hat hour and he failed to obtain their support. The next day, the section decided to end evening
essions at 10.00 p.m. and that only 200 people be admitted to the meetings.[63]

Pétion appealed to middle-class people to attend section meetings to defend their rights: 'Your
property is menaced and you close your eyes to danger. They excite war between the haves and the
nave nots and you do nothing to prevent it. There are five or six hundred men, some insane, others
teeped in crime, the majority without any means of existence, who spread themselves everywhere,
nowl in groups and clamour in the sections, threatening, speaking only of murder and pillage, who
lictate law and exercise the most odious despotism over 600,000 citizens. Parisians, rise from your
ethargy and send these venomous insects back to their holes.'[64] Pétion's letter produced important
esults in that Parisians opposed to the radicals began attending section meetings during the first two
veeks of May. On 19 May, delegations from Finistère, Gardes Françaises, Quinze-Vingts, Halle-aux-
Blés, Droits de l'Homme, Invalides and Bonne Nouvelle protested their attachment to the Convention,
ind invited deputies to occupy themselves with the constitution and stamp out anarchy. Similarly,
Brissot praised the section of Butte des Moulins in his edition of 15 May for having rid itself of the

anarchists and electing Collin, the anarchists' enemy, as president by a great majority. On 19 May,
he reported that 'republican zeal reigned in the majority of sections. Panthéon-Français, Piques, Mail
and many others have formally protested against the formation of an assembly to discuss a war tax.'
At the same time, he referred to how the 'anarchists' were engaged in a fierce campaign to win back
the lost sections by sending deputations to their meetings. Varlet, for example, accompanied by a
group from the Sans-culottes section, went to the section of Panthéon-Français, threatening a new
insurrection. Apparently, Varlet failed miserably at winning converts, but returned the next day with
a new round of threats. This was how he triumphed in Bon-Conseil and Contrat-Social where the
radicals took over the administration of the section.[65] The section of Champs Elysées demanded the
election of a new mayor and new municipality.[66] Hébert described sectional meetings as being
invaded by bankers, sugar merchants, 'shaved and perfumed dandies and hosts of other undesirables
and unmentionables, who came to kill the Mountain, the Jacobins, the mayor, the *procureur*'.[67]
Bourdon urged members to 'visit assiduously their sections to impose silence on the aristocrats'.
Maure sounded desperate on the same day when he declared that if the sans-culottes did not proceed
en masse to the sections, 'the intriguers who are in control will pass the decree for a departmental
guard and you will see the *hommes d'état* supported by bayonets'. Another member on 24 May
observed that the sections are completely 'gangrened'.[68] The sections remained divided and almost
equally so on the eve of the 31 May insurrection. On 25 May, the *Chronique de Paris* reported that
never before had the sections been so divided.[69]

By the third week of May, a majority of men who are the subject of this book, had sorted out their
political affiliation. Events which took place during the months of April and May, most significantly
the increased pressure from the working people of Paris to do something about the price of
necessities and the impeachment and then acquittal of Marat, had an important impact on the
factions. Guadet, who had really initiated the latest attack on Marat, had presumably hoped that the
Convention would unite behind him since Marat had not been very popular with most deputies. This
seemed to have backfired when only Barbaroux, Mercier and Gorsas voted for his impeachment.
Most deputies either stayed away or abstained. Now Marat had men like Robespierre supporting him
and Danton on his side, although he did not vote in Marat's favour. Marat was greeted by the
Jacobin club like a hero. The passing of the maximum law was clearly an important turning point. It
had been done under conditions of extreme pressure, and although no one had supported such a
measure in February, the leading 'Mountain' deputies yielded to the pressure for tactical rather than
philosophical reasons. This naturally made them popular with the ordinary people.

As far as individuals who had previously been uncommitted were concerned, Fabre, who had
been relatively conciliatory before, was now an open enemy of the 'Brissotins', publishing a
denunciatory pamphlet at the start of May. As a friend of Danton, presumably he was following
Danton's lead. Barère continued to be moderate and conciliatory and Saint-Just and Condorcet
stayed out of the faction fighting.

The intense propaganda war between the two sides did not let up. The discovery that the
'Brissotins' had intercepted Jacobin mail and that the Jacobins were sending intensely anti-
'Brissotin' material to the provinces helped to further alienate those who were already enemies. The
Jacobin club itself continued to be divided between the militant and the moderate, and it appeared
that, by this time, those wanting a purge in the Convention were leading the battle. The question is
whether they would be able to convince people like Robespierre and other deputies who had
consistently spoken out against illegal measures that the time had come to support them.

10

THE DESTRUCTION OF THE 'BRISSOTINS'

This chapter will endeavour to demonstrate that the uprising of 31 May to 2 June was not the decisive event in the downfall of the 'Brissotins' and the reason for their execution in the autumn. Rather, it was a combination of the illegal activities of the majority of those expelled from the Convention – twenty-one out of the twenty-nine successfully fled and rebelled – and other events, including the murder of Marat, which determined their sorry fate. An attempt will be made to explain why the snarling match was suddenly ended by a coup d'état which was almost certainly unwanted by the great majority at the time, and did not destroy the 'Brissotins', and which later became canonized by revolutionaries as one of the great revolutionary *journées*.

REVOLUTIONARY PREPARATIONS

The best modern account of the events of 31 May to 2 June is by Daniel Guérin. He demonstrates that the uprising was organized by a group of outsiders which had set itself up as a committee which sat at the Evêché. Only when the Paris Commune seized control of the movement did the leading 'Mountain' deputies support it. Contemporary evidence appears to confirm the first part of his argument; however, this author will argue that it was only under fear for their own lives, rather than explicit support for the commune, that deputies agreed to put the 'Brissotins' and the Committee of Twelve under arrest.[1] A more recent account supports the notion that the Revolutionary Committee at the Evêché, led by the leader of the Cité section, Dobsen, was crucial in planning 31 May.[2] What follows below is a summary of the events of 31 May to 2 June 1793.

THE INSURRECTION OF 31 MAY TO 2 JUNE

The successful purging of the Convention was something quite different from the factional fighting between deputies. It was a movement brought about by basically unknown and foreign men from some of the sections. What later became canonized as the famous revolutionary uprising of 31 May to 2 June, was at the time a very messy uprising, confused in terms of goals and personnel, and an almost unsuccessful coup d'état. It really began with the popular movement of 27 May. On this day, the session was tumultuous, with groups of people blocking the passageways of the Convention, insulting and menacing deputies. The arrest of radical leaders of the commune, especially Hébert, by a Committee of Twelve Deputies,[3] had served to turn some previously favourable sections against the 'Brissotins', even though none of the members of the committee were leading 'Brissotins'. They would later be grouped with the 'Brissotins' and condemned. The Committee of Twelve set to work

The 'Girondins' in the Force prison, by Marckl/Pigeot. (Musée Carnavalet)

with a vengeance, demanding section proceedings. It denounced a plot organized by the Central Revolutionary Committee of the Paris Commune – a co-ordinating committee which planned the coup – whose goal was the dissolution of the Convention, the massacre of twenty-two deputies and the suspension of the departure of a contingent of volunteers to the Vendée.[4]

Although the Committee of Twelve responded to popular protest and released the commune's leaders on 28 May, it was too late. The insurrection had already been planned. Brissot's paper on 30 May refers to a meeting of many at the Evêché, where the Jacobins and the Cordeliers had the goal of striking the major blow. The paper quoted Robespierre's speech from the Jacobins of 26 May as proof that he was involved in the organization,[5] but this was more likely an emotional response by Robespierre to Vergniaud's letters to his constituents in Bordeaux than a true call to arms. It was in the context of a discussion of Vergniaud's incendiary correspondence calling the Bordelais to rise up that Robespierre made these remarks. Robespierre's speech was contradictory. On the one hand, he ordered people to rise up, and on the other, he talked about his exhaustion and that he was 'incapable of prescribing to the people the means of its salvation'.[6] Perhaps Robespierre did not want to say anything which would later incriminate him if the uprising were to fail, but felt that something had to be done to end the impasse at the Convention. In an odd way, he was in agreement with Brissot who also felt that the Convention could not continue to function as it stood. Similarly, at the Jacobin session of 31 May, Billaud made menacing statements, claiming that the suppression of the Committee of Twelve (it had been suppressed on 27 May, and again on 31 May) was not enough: the country would not be saved until the right wing of the Convention was destroyed.[7] At the same time, Chabot and Bourdon were trying to prevent the insurrection if one can believe the account given by Hanriot's aide-de-camp, Monnin.[8]

A vote was taken on 28 May to re-establish the Committee of Twelve. Of the 517 votes, 279 were in favour and 238 against this measure. Condorcet, who had not taken part in any of the confrontation during the past couple of days, voted against its re-establishment because of the irresponsible behaviour of the committee. Danton threatened revolution if the committee continued to act in a tyrannical fashion.[9] Thus, in demanding the re-establishment of the committee, these deputies provoked an attack by force. The behaviour of the committee appeared to have made any kind of appeasement impossible.

The Central Revolutionary Committee, which prepared the uprising, was composed of unknown quantities, primarily militants from the sections. Mercier, Daunou and Garat believed that foreigners, such as Gusman, who sounded the tocsin on 31 May, were behind the uprising. Mercier remarked that the 'majority of members who composed this committee were not French'. Garat thought that it was the same group who had caused the aborted coup of 9 to 10 March: Proly, Gusman and Periera.[10] It assumed control of the National Guards and named the sans-culotte Hanriot as commander.

It took two days of uncertainty for a reluctant Convention to vote to put the twenty-two deputies plus the Committee of Twelve under house arrest. The events of 31 May and 1 June had done little to further the cause of the rebels. All that was achieved by the forces of anarchy on 31 May was the suppression of the Committee of Twelve and a promise from the Committee of Public Safety that it would report, within three days, on the committee's papers and actions. Other concessions by the Convention included the recognition of a paid revolutionary army, a uniform price for bread, and welfare measures such as care for the sick and the aged. The Convention had managed to evade the most essential of the petitioners' demands: the purging of the twenty-two. On this day, Vergniaud had praised the sections of Paris, wanting to bestow upon them the honours of the session. Chaumette also noted that the sections had been warmly received at the Convention.[11] Vergniaud's curious remark must be understood within the chronology of events which took place on this day. It was made before many of the insulting petitions were presented and after various sections such as Molière, Pont-Neuf, Gardes-Françaises and l'Observatoire had professed their faith in the Convention.[12] Vergniaud believed that victory had been achieved by the forces of anarchy by dissolving the committee. But this is not how the group sitting at the Evêché saw things. It had still not been able to get a decree of arrest from the Convention. Order reigned throughout 1 June, a Saturday. The next day, deputies arrived at the Assembly to be threatened by cannon and surrounded by 8,000–10,000 armed people. Marchand of the revolutionary committee issued the final ultimatum, the arrest of the twenty-two.[13] According to Daunou, who was present, Basire, Cambon and Barère distinguished between the satellites controlled by the troublemakers, those who were pointing their arms at the Convention, and the 'citizens of Paris' who supported the Convention and demanded a constitution. This resembles Guadet's account. On 31 May, Guadet declared that the Convention was infested with 'vile hirelings' and made an apologetic statement about the commune, which was exercising its right to petition, unlike the 'faction' insulting the people.[14] Those who surrounded the Convention on 2 June sufficiently intimidated deputies into giving in to their demands. Hanriot, commander of the National Guardsmen, ordered that no deputies leave the Convention. When deputies, at Barère's suggestion, attempted to prove that they were 'free', the majority left their meeting room for the courtyard where armed sans-culottes were blocking their passage. Only about twenty deputies remained in the meeting room including Robespierre, who feared that they would be murdered by Hanriot and his troops if they did. According to Barère, Robespierre whispered to him: 'You are making a mess of it.' Barère replied that the mess was not at the rostrum, but in the Courtyard of the Convention.[15] Delacroix complained about being insulted and degraded. At this point, the commander Hanriot called out, 'Soldiers, to your guns.'[16]

One possible interpretation was at the last minute, on the eve of the crisis, deputies understood that legal measures would have to be suppressed under the pressure of an invasion of the Convention. Deputies conceded to the demands of the petitioners in order not to lose control of events and perhaps to save their own necks. Robespierre, on 31 May, did support a decree of accusation against the twenty-two. But he said this only after declaring that the Convention was not free, as it was surrounded. On this point, Vergniaud agreed, saying that 'the Convention was unable to deliberate in its present state'.[17]

Couthon, too, seemed to yield under the pressure as he recalled: 'I was affected more than anybody by the movements which had manifested themselves in the tribunes of the Convention; I know that they can be attributed to lowly paid men, who in agreement with the odious faction, wish the dissolution of the Convention.'[18] Couthon, under the pressure of a Convention surrounded by armed men and women, on 2 June, drew up the list of deputies to be put under house arrest. House arrest merely meant that the deputies were confined to their homes and they were free to circulate in Paris as long as they were accompanied by an armed guard. At the time this decree was passed, only about twenty deputies were present. These included the members of the Committee of Twelve minus Boyer-Fonfrède and Saint-Martin, plus the three Bordelais, Brissot, Gorsas (but not Carra), Pétion, Louvet, Buzot and Barbaroux. Fonfrède and Saint-Martin were excused because they opposed the arrest warrants issued by the Committee of Twelve. Initially, Ducos, Lanthenas and Dussaulx were also included, but Marat and then Couthon removed their names.[19]

Therefore, at the last minute, those deputies present appeared to have reluctantly conceded to the demands of the insurgents. There is much evidence that the leading 'Mountain' deputies were just as frightened as the rest of the Assembly when confronted with the insurrectionaries. Delacroix and Robespierre had declared that the Convention was not free. On 2 June, Danton said that the 'French people had been outraged in the person of the representatives of the people' and that 'the head of the scoundrel who was behind such a bloody insult must fall on the scaffold'.[20] It was only under these conditions that deputies were put under house arrest. Barère agreed that they were 'in danger', that it was not 'for slaves to make laws' and that the session should be suspended and the bayonets lowered.[21] Years later, Barère, who had been very moderate during the insurrection, recalled that the arrest of the deputies occurred under 'threats and declamations'. He continued by describing the 'Convention yielding to armed force'. Those who threatened the Convention declared that they 'might mutilate or destroy the national representation with impunity'.[22] This account appears to be fairly consistent with his speeches made at the time.

It is important to stress that deputies were merely put under house arrest. A decree of accusation was not issued against them. At this point, there is no reason why they could not have been readmitted to the Convention. Billaud stressed that the Convention should not exceed its powers. He declared that, legally, the Convention did not have the power to suspend any of its members.[23]

Very few of the twenty-two deputies attended the session of 2 June. Many were held up at Meillan's house on the rue des Moulins. The group meeting there included Brissot, the three Bordelais, Buzot, Pétion, Barbaroux and others. When they received word that they had been put under house arrest, they resolved to draft a proclamation to the French people, giving their version of the events which had just taken place. Buzot's resolution, which was taken up by Barbaroux, was to challenge the group surrounding the Convention by going to their seats and shouting 'death' or 'arrest'. Barbaroux, like many others, was of the opinion that the goal of the men of 2 June was to purge the entire Convention in a single blow without distinction between the 'Mountain' or the 'right wing'.[24]

From the statements made by Danton, Barère, Couthon and Robespierre, perhaps it could be suggested that the leading 'Mountain' deputies had no more use for the movement that was prepared at the Evêché than did their rivals in the Convention, and that they were in as much fear for their lives as Brissot and many others who were too afraid to sleep in their own beds on 31 May and turn up to the Convention on 2 June. However, the 'Mountain' deputies had not wanted to lose control of the revolution to the uncontrollable masses and therefore reluctantly gave in to what could only be described as a threat against their lives in agreeing to the house arrest of twenty-nine deputies and two ministers, Clavière and Lebrun. Hence the insurrection of 31 May to 2 June that had almost resulted in failure did end with the successful purge of a good number of leading revolutionary, republican politicians and brought to a close their political careers.

However, the story does not end there. Carra, Mercier and Condorcet were still sitting in the Convention. Condorcet provided a poignant description of the events which took place that day. He made the uprising sound as if it occurred very swiftly and almost out of the blue: 'Within a moment, the freedom of the people's representatives had been openly outraged. Surrounded by soldiers and held in their seats by an armed force, they had been forced to order the arrest of twenty-nine of their colleagues, in order to prevent the greatest crime. From then on, the integrity of the national representation no longer existed.'[25] Presumably out of fear for their lives, they had remained silent throughout the crisis, as had Fabre, Saint-Just, Fouché, Robert and Collot d'Herbois.

Not everyone, however, had remained silent during the insurrection itself. Almost immediately following the purge of the twenty-nine deputies and two ministers, several deputies protested to the *Bureau* about the decree that had just been passed. They wanted to make clear that they had no part in the passing of this decree. These men included Blaviel, Ferroux, Périéres, Rouzet and Tounier. Durand-Maillane, who was a secretary, recalled that when the decree was being passed, many deputies surrounded him to indicate their opposition to it. In response, he suggested that they sign a slip of paper which he later burned out of fear.[26]

THE POST 2 JUNE CONVENTION

During the weeks that followed the insurrection, it became clear that the purge really created more problems than it had solved. It produced enormous difficulties for the Convention, not the least of which was how to deal with the behaviour of the purged deputies, the majority of whom successfully escaped from Paris in the weeks following the insurrection and incited counter-revolution in the departments of Normandy and the Gironde. Their activities will be dealt with in more detail below. The direct result of the insurrection for the Convention was, firstly, that it was inundated with protests by deputies still present, and from some of those who had been expelled, such as Vergniaud, all of whom denounced the purge; and, second, that it was very poorly attended throughout the months of June and July. Poor attendance was a form of silent protest. The proscribed deputies were treated very well. They were not dealt with as if they were criminals. They were merely put under house arrest and continued to receive their eighteen *livres* a day deputy stipend. By decrees passed by an almost empty Convention on 3 and 4 June, deputies agreed that only one policeman would guard them, they would be free to go out, and they could receive visitors.[27] The two ministers were still permitted to work. Judging from this, it appears that their confinement was intended to be a temporary one, and had they behaved differently, they would have been readmitted to the Convention. Certainly, the majority of the Convention was in their favour, demonstrating their support through either written protests or simply by staying away. The major protests against the violation of the Convention began almost immediately. Robespierre, speaking at the Jacobins, proclaimed, 'we are seized with several letters from deputies who are preaching insurrection in the departments'.[28] Although he did not sign a formal protest, Grégoire, on 4 June, insisted that that the proceedings of 2 June should emphasize the 'insults and violence against the Convention'.[29] The next day, nine deputies from the department of the Somme addressed a 'Déclaration à leurs commettants', to the Convention in protest. This address was not read to the Convention until 14 June, presumably because it was posted from the provinces.[30] An address which was not dated, from eight of the twelve deputies from the department of Aisne, including Condorcet and Jean Debry, but which was presumably written during the first week of June, also denounced the insurrection. In addition, these deputies protested against the arbitrary suppression of newspapers and the seizure of correspondence.[31] Condorcet went even further than his colleagues by writing a denunciation of his own in the form of a pamphlet entitled *Aux citoyens français sur la nouvelle constitution*. Although this pamphlet was primarily a critique of the new constitution, it contained a strongly worded denigration of the insurrection of 31 May to 2 June.[32] He was not arrested, however, until 8 July. At this time, Condorcet was denounced by Collot, and Chabot demanded a decree of accusation against him on the basis of this pamphlet.[33] Dumont, in the name of the Committee of General Security, had demanded the arrest of these deputies back on

30 June, but the Convention had hesitated. After all, one of them, Jean Debry, was a prominent republican who had voted radically, for death and no reprieve, during the king's trial. He certainly did not fit into the 'appellant' or pro-referendum category. He was elected to the first Committee of Public Safety, but had resigned for reasons of poor health. The only occurrence on 30 June was that Legendre denounced the 'perfidious deputies' including Condorcet and the petition went to the Committee of Public Safety. The Convention hesitated to attack popular deputies.[34]

Saint-Just, also a deputy from the department of Aisne, indicated which side he supported when he did not sign the address.[35] He had been added to the Committee of Public Safety with Couthon on 29 May to help with the drafting of the constitution. He was rewarded for his behaviour by being assigned to report on the purged deputies on 19 June. Interestingly, when he finally presented his report on 8 July, the day Chabot demanded Condorcet's arrest, Saint-Just did not mention the protest from the deputies of his department.

Other protests continued throughout the month of June. These included denunciations from deputies from the departments of Haute-Vienne and Hautes-Alpes.[36] The most significant of these was the one signed between 6 and 19 June by seventy-five deputies. It declared that the rights and sovereignty of the people had been 'shamefully violated from the moment the unity of the national representation had been broken by an act of violence of which the history of the nation had never furnished an example'. Mercier was one of the signatories of this poignant protest. It was never made public, but was held by the Committee of Public Safety. The initiative for this action had been taken by a friend and colleague of Barbaroux, Lauze Deperret from the department of the Bouches-du-Rhône. The signed list was seized at his home after he was arrested on 14 July.[37] Mercier also wrote a protest of his own in which he defended Brissot. His letter was denounced by Billaud at the Jacobins on 23 June. He proclaimed that 'Mercier had outraged the French people.' He demanded that all traitors and rebels be proscribed.[38]

During the first two weeks of June, there are indications that the more moderate deputies believed that the Convention could not function properly without its proscribed colleagues. On 10 June, when the deputies were discussing the constitution, Vernier protested that they should turn their attention to the purged deputies and insisted that they could not vote on the constitution without the entire Convention present. He stated that 'if the representatives are guilty, judge them and let their substitutes replace them. If the opposite is true, I don't think that we can proceed with such an important decision without their help. Our first job is to show to France that this is an act of a free Convention.' He proposed that discussion on the constitution should be adjourned until they had dealt with the detained deputies. Vernier's proposal had many supporters. In a similar vein, Coupé remarked, 'Can the people consider the constitution you are presenting to them as a free act when 32 of your colleagues are arbitrarily imprisoned without proof?' Camboulas stated that the Convention had been divided into two parties since 31 May and denounced the government of Paris. Vernier's viewpoint was also supported by Defermon and Ducos.[39] There seems to be every reason to believe that had the twenty-nine deputies remained in Paris as so few of them did, rather than provoking civil war in the departments, they would have been readmitted to the Convention.

Not only did the Convention have the problem of protests from deputies to contend with, lack of attendance was also a major concern for them. Thuriot, on 11 June, stated that the deputies not attending were in their departments preaching civil war and federalism. He demanded that they be arrested. On 13 June, a report was made by the Committee of Public Safety on the subject of these deputies. The following day, the Convention passed a decree stating that absent deputies would be considered as having deserted their post. They had voluntarily abdicated their seats and they were to be replaced by their substitutes. On 17 June, on Thuriot's suggestion, a decree prescribing that the Minister of Justice, Gohier, present a list of 'detained deputies, fled deputies and other fugitives', was passed. There were also two roll-call votes held to ascertain which deputies were still sitting in the Convention because so many had fled. These were held on 15 and 17 June. On the 15th, a good number of deputies on the right side of the Convention proclaimed that they were 'present but not free', or, as Chevalier stated, 'present to witness tyranny'.[40] Pétion claimed that on the day the Convention passed a decree of accusation against Brissot on 23 June, no more than sixty members were present. Meillan, who was present, reported around one hundred.[41] Billaud attacked the absent deputies on 24 June. He stated that they were inciting civil war in the departments and demanded that they be purged from the Convention.[42]

Although there was plenty of activity in terms of discussion and proposals, no concrete action was taken against the deputies until about a fortnight after Brissot was arrested at Moulins on 10 June and after the Convention discovered that Buzot was inciting insurrection at Caen. From Moulins, Brissot addressed a letter to the Convention begging that he be taken to Paris to be heard. He was taken to Paris, but was denied a hearing.[43] But the action that was taken was hardly severe. Brissot was accused of three offences by Le Carpentier: of abandoning his post, of travelling with a false passport (he was using a Swiss passport) and of wanting to escape from a decree of accusation. Thuriot and many others stated at the time of Brissot's arrest that his friends had escaped from Paris because they were 'torn apart by remorse'. But at the same time, he called Brissot a 'treacherous person'. On 12 June, when Brissot's arrest was discussed at the Convention, many deputies including Douclet-Pontécoulant spoke in his favour.[44] On 14 June, Saint-André, in the name of the Committee of Public Safety, presented a report against the deputies of the Somme, who, because of their protest of 5 June, were to be suspended from their functions as deputies and arrested. However, this proposal was adjourned and the Convention moved to the business of the day. On 13 June, Delacroix announced that Buzot had reached Caen where he was joined by Larivière and Gorsas. They were organizing an armed force to march on Paris. He merely proposed sending hostages to the department. Danton also suggested this measure and volunteered to go to Bordeaux in such a capacity.[45] On Couthon's demand, a decree of accusation was passed against Buzot, but no measures were taken against Louvet, Gorsas and the administrators of the department of Evreux.[46]

Robespierre made plain the 'crimes' of the purged deputies: they had fled, and they were conspiring with the Vendeans and the counter-revolutionary administrators. At the time of Brissot's arrest, the deputies decided that those under house arrest would be henceforth guarded by two rather than by one policeman and that they were no longer permitted to go out, receive visits or communicate with anyone. An exasperated Convention passed a decree of accusation against Brissot, but only after he informed them that he had incited the district of Gannat to issue a seditious protest. It voted for the arrest of Masuyer, a deputy who had helped Pétion with his escape. This did not happen until 24 June. The Convention, in response to this news then decreed, upon the proposal made by Amar in the name of the Committee of General Security, and by Saint-André, who had announced the escape, that the detained deputies be transferred not to a prison, such as the Conciergerie or the Force, but to '*maisons nationales*', which were public buildings such as convents and palaces that had been converted into detention centres.[47] According to one report of this session, fifty members rushed to the *Bureau* to protest against this decree. In response to this opposition, Hérault Séchelles, president of the Convention, presented the constitution. Ducos objected to the decree on the basis that it applied to all deputies, including those like Vergniaud and Gensonné, who had obeyed the law and not fled.[48] At the time, only Brissot was held in a real prison, the Abbaye. Even at the end of June, the Committee of Public Safety and the Convention, with the exception of a few deputies such as Billaud, Thuriot and Marat (through his newspaper), seemed reluctant to take harsh measures against the proscribed deputies. Thuriot had obtained a decree of accusation against Barbaroux on 17 June, but no other action against him was taken at the time.

Not only did the poorly attended purged Convention have protests from deputies with which to contend. Perhaps more significantly, it had almost an entire country opposed to what had just taken place. In addition to the north-west, the south-east, south-west, the cities of Lyon, Bordeaux, and Marseilles were in a state of counter-revolution. About three-quarters of the country was opposed to the purge. By the end of June, about sixty departments in the west, south and south-east were opposing Paris. This meant taking urgent measures to convince the nation that the insurrection had been necessary for the good of the country. One of these was the speedy passing of the most democratic constitution of the revolution, the constitution of 1793. It was presented by Hérault-Séchelles on 10 June and passed by the Convention on 24 June. Second, statements were sent out from both the Jacobins and the Convention justifying the insurrection. It is important to note that neither of these justifications was produced immediately after the rising. The first one sent by the Convention was dated 13 June and it was passed on the initiative of Robespierre and Couthon. It read 'in the days of 31 May to 2 June, the general revolutionary council of the commune and the people of Paris powerfully assisted in saving the liberty, the indivisibility and the unity of the republic'. Danton declared that they should finally tell the nation that 'without the insurrection of 31 May, there would not be any liberty'.[49] Similarly, the Jacobins produced a circular dated 7 June, although it was not sent to the provinces until the middle of the month. Drafted by Desmoulins, it did not stress the role of the club; rather it described the struggle for leadership which had taken place in the Convention as the final triumph of the 'Mountain', the triumph of the forces of good over those of evil, those of the 'Gironde'. It announced to provincial clubs that the purge of the twenty-nine had been a victory for the 'Mountain' and Parisian radicalism, but curiously said nothing about the club's part in the insurrection.[50] Robespierre reiterated this new version of 31 May at the Jacobins on 14 June when he stated that it was on that day 'the Convention proclaimed that it had proven it was free, that it had taken the people of Paris under its protection against those perverted by tyranny'.[51] Propaganda concerning 31 May was considered to be an important tool by the Jacobins to convince the provinces that the insurrection had been as necessary to the revolution as 14 July and 10 August. On 16 June, Fabre, still complaining that 'corrupt writings' continued to circulate in the departments, suggested that the government should finance three different types of newspapers designed for various audiences. Ironically, he used Roland's *Bureau* as his model. He proposed a journal intended for the countryside, like the *Feuille Villageoise* (which Roland had funded), one for the cities, and one for the armies. These journals, which would be free of charge to their readers, would be written by thirty deputies and cost less than 500,000 *livres*. Although the club adjourned Fabre's proposal, it demonstrates the importance revolutionaries placed upon propaganda as a means of obtaining 'converts' and the impact Roland's propaganda network had had during these years.[52]

In addition to propagandizing the departments to convince them to stop their counter-revolution, the government was also of the opinion that amnesty might appease the rebellious areas, particularly Normandy. Agents of the Paris Commune and even the Committee of Public Safety were engaged in obscure negotiations at Caen and Evreux. Saint-André told the Jacobins that he was certain the committee was 'well-intentioned' in its negotiations with the departments.[53] Garat reported that he had been involved in these negotiations as a way of avoiding civil war.[54] However, things did not always go as planned. Desfieux reported that the commissioners from the section of 1792 (formerly Bibliothèque) who had gone to Eure and Calvados, had actually joined forces with the counter-revolutionaries. Danton replied that these men had committed a crime by going beyond their mission which was to 'fraternize and to promise peace to the rebels'. A decree passed by the Convention on 26 June promised amnesty to municipal administrations who would retract their protests of 2 June.[55]

BEHAVIOUR OF THE PURGED DEPUTIES AND THE CONVENTION'S RESPONSE

Of the twenty-nine deputies who were expelled from the Convention on 2 June, twenty-one successfully escaped from Paris. Brissot was among the first to escape. He first fled to Versailles, then to his home town of Chartres, which he left for Evreux and then Caen, where he intended to meet many of his former colleagues. However, he was arrested at Moulins on 10 June, travelling on a false passport, and ordered back to Paris. Gorsas was at Caen by 9 June. Barbaroux fled on the night of 10/11 June. By 13 June, he was at Evreux where he wrote to his colleague, Deperret.[56] In this letter, Barbaroux instructed Deperret to advise Guadet and Pétion to join him where they could be useful to the departments. He warned Deperret to keep silent during the debates at the Convention, to write protests and to rally the departments against the 'Mountain'. On 23 June, following Barbaroux's advice, Guadet, Lanjuinais and Pétion fled. Guadet left his home on the rue du Faubourg Saint-Honoré to visit Gensonné. He managed to pass by the authorities guarding the city gates disguised as an upholsterer. He went on foot to Evreux and then to Caen which he reached on 30 June. Pétion reached Caen two days earlier.[57] Louvet, who had been hiding out in Paris, escaped for Caen on 24 June. He left on the advice of Barbaroux who had told him that his presence was very necessary in Calvados.[58]

The principal players in the 'federalist' revolt were Barbaroux and Pétion. Presumably Brissot would have been equally active had he not been arrested. Barbaroux wrote several letters in June to the Convention, to a colleague from his department, Deperret, and to the municipality of Marseilles. Pétion drafted a plan to create a federal republic modelled on the United States of America, complete with a Congress which would represent the new states composed of two or three departments.[59]

Vergniaud and Gensonné remained in Paris. However, Gensonné helped to raise the counter-revolution in Gironde. He drafted an address on 2 June to the sections of Bordeaux which they received on 8 June. In addition, Gensonné sent copies of his address to several other departments. He depicted himself as the victim of a popular movement and a would-be legal assassination.[60] Perhaps Vergniaud was more sensible. He merely wrote letters to the Convention, which were initially very moderate and understandable. His letter of 3 June indicated that he would obey the law and remain at his domicile and that he refused to resign his seat.[61] In his second letter, dated 6 June, he was more aggressive and demanded that the Committee of Public Safety report on the 'pseudo-plots' of which he and his friends were accused. Vergniaud claimed quite correctly that the deputies had been arrested without any proof of guilt. This time, the *Moniteur* printed parts of the letter. It omitted a section claiming that the Convention either did not have the courage to proclaim the innocence of the deputies, or 'because of its tyranny it had not the will to do so'. He also demanded the arrest of the true conspirators, L'Huilier and Hassenfratz.[62] The Convention ordered that his letter be read in spite of protests from Thuriot. After the reading of his letter, there were cries of amnesty in the corridors. Most deputies seemed to be united in their opinion that the Convention should not move too quickly in their judgement, or as Douclet stated, 'you will assassinate the republic'.[63] Vergniaud addressed a third letter to the Convention in which he indicated that he was still waiting for the report and requested permission to go out accompanied by his guard.[64] The escaped deputies also sent letters to the Convention: letters were read by Barbaroux on 3 and 7 June; one from Pétion was also read on 7 June. Pétion's letter was addressed to the president of the Convention, Mallarmé, and demanded that a report be made promptly.[65]

Under pressure to produce a report proving the guilt or innocence of the detained deputies, the Committee of Public Safety invited the mayor of Paris, Pache, to its meeting of 5 June to provide it with incriminating evidence against the twenty-nine deputies. The problem was that he could not produce any, and the Committee of Public Safety was therefore forced to announce this embarrassing news to the Convention on the same day.[66] Barère and Danton, in the name of the committee, therefore proposed measures of appeasement on 6 June. These included the suppression of the revolutionary committees, the possibility of raising an armed force, of which the 'Mountain' deputies disapproved, the dismissal of Hanriot as commander of the National Guardsmen, a stricter surveillance over foreigners, and finally sending to the departments of the arrested deputies an equal number of deputies chosen by the Convention to stay there as hostages. The hostages would guarantee the safety of the expelled deputies. The real trouble, according to Barère, came from foreigners, who would be expelled within eight days from the republic. The Committee of Public Safety decided that the solution to the problem of uniting the country was to present a constitution within three days.[67] Reaction from leading 'Mountain' deputies to Barère's report was critical. Robespierre denounced it, contending that the suppression of the revolutionary committees would disturb the tranquillity of Paris. He stressed how necessary it was for the Committee of Public Safety to pursue the deputies who had fled, like Barbaroux, whose correspondence proved the existence of plots.[68] Robespierre was quite right to fear the writings of Barbaroux and the other refugees. In less than a month, they had sent out several pamphlets, and on 18 June, Barbaroux addressed a manifesto to the citizens of Marseilles in which he wrote: 'Men of France. Let us march on Paris not to fight the people of Paris but to deliver them.' He did not want the dissolution of the Convention, but its freedom which included the 'punishment of the assassins'.[69]

There were several demands from men like Marat for a change in the membership of the Committee of Public Safety. He attacked the committee several times in June and July for not having reported on the escaped deputies.[70] According to the more radical Jacobins and 'Mountain' deputies, the committee had been far too lenient and moderate. Desmoulins blamed the committee for its mismanagement of the war. Under this committee's leadership, France had suffered its 'most humiliating defeats'.[71] The editor of the new Jacobin journal wrote that the committee 'was asleep' and 'deserved the name of the committee of public destruction'.[72] Marat singled out Barère for special criticism, calling him the 'most dangerous of men' and blaming him for 'paralysing all vigorous measures'. On the day of Saint-Just's report, Marat urged the exclusion of Barère from the new committee.[73] When Bourdon stated at the Jacobin session of 8 July that the committee members would be renewed in three days, he complained that the current committee was often negligent in its duties, and that it had not 'made the most of our important denunciations and useful discoveries'. Chabot suggested retaining Couthon, Saint-Just and Saint-André, but replacing the rest.[74] Marat's opinion did not seem to hold much weight, for when the Convention did elect a new committee on 10 July, Barère received the highest number of votes along with Saint-André. Both received 192 votes.[75]

Saint-Just finally presented a report in the name of the Committee of Public Safety to the Convention on 8 July with which he had been assigned on 19 June. Why had it taken over three weeks since the 19th and over a month since 2 June for the committee to report on the expelled deputies? Presumably because at the time of their expulsion they had done nothing wrong, and, as stated above, the committee and the city could not find evidence against them. In addition, with most of the country opposed to the Convention's actions on 2 June, it would have been suicidal to take severe measures at the time. Many deputies had hoped for a reintegration of their expelled colleagues. It was only after the majority of the purged deputies fled that the Convention could act. The delay had provided the fugitives the time to create a great number of headaches for the Convention. Saint-Just designated the leaders as Brissot, Buzot, Vergniaud (even though Vergniaud had obeyed the law), Pétion, Barbaroux, Valazé, Louvet and Gorsas. He declared Buzot, Barbaroux, Louvet, Gorsas, Pétion and the others who had fled and assembled in Normandy to be traitors because they had conspired to bring about a civil war and thereby destroy the republic: 'The really guilty men are those who have fled. Proscribe those who have fled and taken up arms . . . Judge the rest and pardon the majority.' The salient theme of the report was clemency. Saint-Just said that 'all of those who have been detained are not guilty; most of them are merely confused and have been led astray'.[76] Brissot was not grouped with the men who were declared 'traitors to the nation'. Perhaps this was due to the fact that he had not joined the counter-revolutionary headquarters. The Convention had already issued a decree of accusation against him on 23 June, but he had not been declared a traitor. Saint-Just proposed a decree of accusation against the three Bordelais, even though only Guadet had escaped. He justified this decree by claiming that they were thought to have been accomplices to the conspirators. Presumably, Vergniaud's latest letter had not helped them either. He had written a very insolent letter to Barère and Lindet on 28 June. It indicated a change in his attitude towards the committee, which he denounced as a group of 'impostors and murderers for producing a report which did not dare to propose a decree of accusation'. Here he was referring to earlier reports, such as Barère's of 6 June and Lindet's address to Frenchmen of 26 June. Vergniaud added that the reason the departments were in a state of rebellion against the Convention was because they believed it had been violated.[77] Again, the Convention was in no hurry to close the affair of the detained and escaped deputies. Discussion at the Convention on Saint-Just's report did not take place until 28 July when a much more violent and radical committee presented another report.

The reaction from the more militant deputies was not positive. They felt that Saint-Just had not gone far enough. After Saint-Just presented his report, the Jacobin club devoted its entire meeting to the Committee of Public Safety and the proscribed deputies. Statements made by leading 'Mountain' deputies reveal their impatience with the weak measures taken by the committee and a new militancy at the club. As stated above, Desmoulins went so far as to blame the committee for all military disasters that had taken place over the past three months. The current committee's time had passed. 'Today', he stated, 'we need revolutionary men, men to whom we can entrust the fate of the Republic without fear, men who will answer to us for it, body and soul.'[78] Chabot, also calling for a change of personnel at the committee, recommended Saint-Just, Couthon and Saint-André, 'whose abilities are proven, whose patriotism and character are known throughout France'. Robespierre, who felt that Chabot was too 'hot-headed', was more circumspect in his comments about the committee, telling members that it would be unwise to encourage popular disfavour of a committee on which depended the safety of the state. Robespierre also praised Saint-Just's report, unlike many of the more radical members. After Robespierre spoke, no decision was made on the future of the committee. However, on 9 June, the 'Mountain' deputies seemed to have reached an agreement and the committee's personnel was changed the next day.[79]

THE DEATH OF MARAT

The event which determined the final fate of the leading 'Brissotins' regardless of whether or not they had fled and incited rebellion in the provinces, was the assassination of Marat on 13 July by Charlotte Corday, a young educated Norman woman of aristocratic origin. The very next day, Chabot, reporting in the name of the Committee of General Security, condemned the plotters at Caen for their criminal correspondence sent to their colleagues (pointing to the right side) still sitting in the Convention. He continued by implicating Barbaroux's colleague, Deperret, as Corday's co-conspirator. The first project of the 'faction' was Marat's assassination. Corday was nothing more than an instrument used by these men. 'What could be easier to influence', he asked, 'than the imagination of a woman?' According to Chabot, she had told Marat before stabbing him, of several plots which were being contemplated by the conspirators hiding out at Caen. Couthon argued that Corday was merely a tool used by the group:

> It is now mathematically demonstrated that this monster which nature has given the form of a woman, is a messenger of Buzot, Barbaroux, Salle and all those other conspirators who have escaped to Caen. It is well demonstrated that this messenger is in concert with Deperret; that the purpose of her mission is to assassinate Garat, Marat and perhaps many other patriots . . . It is mathematically proven that Buzot, Barbaroux, Salle and all the conspirators which you have expelled, are nothing more than assassins, that desperate to assassinate the freedom of their country, they have driven the dagger into the heart of its most intrepid defenders.

He closed by ordering that they be tried before the revolutionary tribunal. In addition, he demanded that all deputies from the department of Calvados, including Fauchet, be arrested.[80] On 15 July, the substitute deputies were called in to replace Gorsas, Guadet, Louvet, Barbaroux, Buzot, Brissot and Pétion. There was now no hope of them returning to their seats. On the same day, Couthon called for the act of accusation against Brissot to

Charlotte Corday, by Duplessis-Bertaux. (Bibliothèque nationale de France)

be heard immediately. Billaud, in his most violent speech to date, delivered on the same day, demanded the immediate appearance of the detained deputies before the revolutionary tribunal and a decree of accusation against the entire twenty-nine proscribed deputies. Thuriot argued that Buzot and Barbaroux were the prime suspects and accused them not only of Marat's murder, but also that of Lepelletier, who had been murdered by a royalist fanatic on 20 January 1793, immediately before Louis' execution. Delacroix demanded that Buzot's home be levelled.[81] Carra's newspaper pointed out that there was no concrete evidence to prove the complicity of Barbaroux and the others in Charlotte Corday's action. Barbaroux's letter and Deperret's recommendation did not prove direct complicity. It told its readers to wait for more tangible evidence before arriving at conclusions. This was the work of a party. This article was not written by Carra, who was away on mission at the time, but by another journalist, who signed his articles with the letter 'S'.[82] The *Annales* may well have been right in its judgement, but by this time, the tone of indulgence and humanity had clearly turned to one of vengeance and violence.

The Jacobin club seemed to follow the lead of the Convention, issuing a new circular on the subject of Marat's death, dated 26 July. It merely repeated the statements made by men like Chabot and Couthon at the Convention: Charlotte Corday was a messenger who was sent to Paris by the conspirators at Caen. She was carrying 'incendiary works', including a letter from Barbaroux to Deperret. Robespierre had already demanded that the murderers of Marat and Lepelletier be executed at the Place de la Révolution the day after Marat's death.[83] In dying, Marat became a martyr, while his one-time friends and now enemies, were brought closer to their own deaths.

FINAL FATE OF THE MEN OF 1792

A worsening military situation did not help the ex-deputies either. With Belgium lost to the Austrians, the Rhine front collapsed and the anti-Convention forces still strong in the south and the west, on 28 July a decree passed by the Convention made these men traitors for causing rebellion in the departments of Eure, Calvados, Rhône et Loire, for preventing the establishment of the republic and for attempting to restore the monarchy. This decree, presented by Barère, was based on Saint-Just's report of 8 July. On the same day, a decree of accusation was passed against Vergniaud and Gensonné.[84] The decree revealed a new Barère, who up to this point, had been conciliatory. When he told the Convention that the 'moment had come to assume the proud attitude befitting national justice and strike down all conspirators without distinction', he had at last turned against his former friends and colleagues. At the time, he believed, with a civil and foreign war engulfing the country, that there was no alternative. In the case of Barère, Saint-Just, and a good many others, the decision to denounce their former republican colleagues came partly as a pragmatic measure – it was a decision made out of the necessity to survive – and partly as a reaction to the irresponsible and vindictive behaviour of those who had fled and opposed the Convention. The Committee of Public Safety did not have the proof it needed to convict the purged deputies in June because there was none. It had behaved in a conciliatory and moderate fashion presumably because many deputies interpreted the expulsion as temporary. Now, almost two months later, it was clear that the Committee had more than enough reason to imprison their former colleagues. Barère, at the start of his report, stated clearly that 'at last, citizens, the proof has arrived; it is in "Barbaroux aux Marseillais" [an address written by Barbaroux to the municipality] where he depicts you as favouring the Vendean revolts and having prepared everything to deliver the northern frontier to our enemies'. This letter had been sent to the committee on 19 July. In addition, Barère quoted the *Rennes Bulletin* which stated that the 'central assembly [of the Commune] has decreed that it will write to General Custine and ask him to stay in his post while the seditious at the Convention dismiss him'.[85] The majority were declared to be traitors for having fled from Paris on 2 June and for inciting rebellion in the departments of Calvados, Eure and Rhône et Loire in an attempt to destroy the republic and restore the monarchy. Those who remained in Paris were accomplices of their friends in the provinces. This group included Vergniaud and Gensonné.[86]

The case of Carra, often mistakenly associated with Brissot, presumably because they were executed at the same time, is somewhat different. What happened to Carra illustrates the powerful impact that perceived or real friendships could have on one's personal fate in the French Revolution. Returning from a mission to Samur on 31 May, he went directly to the Convention. On 2 June, he addressed a letter to his constituents in which he warned them against rumours that the Convention had not been 'free' on this day and against those 'who say that they will march on Paris and crush the rebels'. Rather than taking the side of Brissot and his allies, Carra's newspaper, on 6 June, told its readers that the central revolutionary committee (which was disbanded that day on the orders of the Committee of Public Safety), was busy collecting evidence necessary for a decree of accusation against the 'gangrened members'.[87] In addition, he was one of the first to denounce the letters written by the deputies, 'full of resentment', and the escaped men, who were already in the departments.[88] On 22 June his newspaper reported that the *Annales* had been denounced at the Jacobins for having sold its pen to Bordeaux, and a few days later, he responded to a denunciation made by Marat at the Convention's meeting on 18 June and in his newspaper the previous day. Marat was critical that Carra was still sitting in the Convention.[89] Although Gaston demanded a decree of accusation against him on 28 July, this proposal was sent to the Committee of Public Safety on Robespierre's suggestion. Gaston had wanted to add Carra's name to the proscribed deputies precisely because of his previous friendship with Brissot.[90] Carra defended himself by insisting that he had not written to Brissot or any of the others, and that he had not spoken to Brissot or Pétion, the only two of the thirty-two deputies that he knew, more than three times since the previous September. He did concede that he regretted their flight.[91] Carra was arrested on the basis of Couthon's report of 2 August on the charge of restoring royalty. Couthon cited a passage from Carra's journal written in favour of the Duke of York, dated 26 July 1791. In addition, there were accusations of meetings with Buzot, Barbaroux and Gorsas when he was supposed to be on mission.[92] While on mission to Blois, Carra was accused of overstepping his mandate. There, he had overturned the local government and replaced it with a new one. But he had done this on 13 June and was denounced for his behaviour by Bentabole but nothing was done at the time.[93]

By 28 July with Barère's report, it was clear that not only were the parliamentary careers of the 'Brissotins' over, they were considered to be traitors to the French republic. However, at this time, most of them remained at large. A month later, a report from the Justice Minister on the state of the departments in the former province of Brittany told the Convention of the necessity to arrest the rebellious and conspiratorial deputies. Early in September, the Convention was once again invaded by the mob. Although the working people of Paris had many other grievances in addition to the imprisoned and escaped deputies, the forty-eight sections did petition the Convention to judge the conspirators. Barère, under pressure, declared that 'terror shall be the order of the day'. He later depicted himself as 'the forced executioner, the passive and unwilling instrument of the wishes emanating from the bosom of the Convention, and coming from its own movement'. At the Committee of Public Safety, the decision was taken to create a revolutionary army and to send former ministers Clavière and Lebrun to the revolutionary tribunal. Barère later wrote that the aim of the meeting of the Committee of Public Safety on 5 September, was 'to justify, to complete the execrable days of 31 May and 2 June, and to consolidate the dictatorship of Danton and Robespierre'.[94] The federalist revolt was not put down until the end of September. At last, the Convention was ready to condemn the imprisoned and escaped men to death. It took another decree, presented by Amar in the name of the Committee of General Security on 3 October, and show trials later that month to finally condemn them to death. In the report, Vergniaud and Gensonné were now grouped with the men who had escaped. All were accused and later convicted of 'conspiracy against the unity and indivisibility of the Republic, and conspiracy against the security of the French people'. Gensonné explained that the decree based on Amar's report had completely changed the nature of the problem. It was no longer simply that the deputies had fled and incited rebellion in various departments as in the first decree passed in July. It was now a much more 'vague and general accusation for which no evidence was produced'. It was a conspiracy against the republic. Gensonné who did not flee, as he stated in this manuscript, was nevertheless condemned to the same fate as those who did.[95] Robespierre opposed adding the seventy-five who had signed the protests. He felt that only the leaders should be executed.[96] The protesters, with some exception, such as Condorcet, were merely retained under arrest, but the majority of the leaders such as Brissot, Vergniaud, Gorsas, Barbaroux, Guadet and others were executed. Mercier and Louvet managed to hide out and re-emerge after the Terror. Both re-entered the Convention after Thermidor.[97]

On the other hand, their former friends and colleagues continued their revolutionary careers, with many assuming powerful positions. Robespierre replaced Gasparin on the Committee of Public Safety on 27 July, and on 6 September, Billaud and Collot were added to what has become known as the 'Great' Committee of Public Safety. Others such as Saint-Just, Fouché and Collot became important representatives on mission.

The uprising of 31 May to 2 June did successfully purge the leading 'Brissotins' from the Convention, but this event did not bring about their ultimate destruction. In many ways, they were responsible for that themselves. As demonstrated above, many deputies, particularly the more moderate, favoured their return to the Convention. A good number signed protests or stayed away. Even the Committee of Public Safety was conciliatory when it finally produced its reports. It was only after the majority of the expelled men had not only fled, but had tried to exact revenge by joining the counter-revolutionary forces in Normandy, that the Committee of Public Safety and then the Convention took extreme measures against them. By the time of Marat's assassination, the Assembly had proof that the expelled men were engaged in counter-revolutionary activities. Although there is no concrete evidence that connects Barbaroux, Buzot and others to Corday's intention of murder and the murder itself, they were still blamed for it. This is understandable given the precarious state of the revolution at the time. With most of the country against it, the Convention could not afford to be conciliatory. This is one interpretation. Another is that the revolutionaries were simply looking for a pretext to condemn the expelled men, and the death of Marat provided it. What is certain is that Marat's death was a decisive event. Only after his murder were serious measures taken against the group. Not long afterwards, Barère received the 'evidence' that the Committee of Public Safety required to condemn their former colleagues. With pressure coming from the sans-culottes in the form of a petition and an invasion of the Convention early in September, it was time that those in control acted.

At least three leading 'Mountain' deputies, Desmoulins, Danton and Barère were reported to have expressed regret at the deaths of the 'Brissotins'. Since their statements were made a number of years after the event, caution is advised. Barère, as stated above, portrayed himself in his *Memoirs* as a 'forced executioner' who was later sorry. If one can believe Villate, Desmoulins was reported to have said that he was responsible for the death of Brissot and the others because he had written a denunciatory pamphlet. While Danton was out of Paris from 13 September to 22 November, Desmoulins had thought of leaving politics. He had requested to be a representative on mission, but was denied a posting.[98] Danton left Paris for the countryside ostensibly for reasons of poor health, but presumably to avoid being in Paris when his former friends were executed. He was reported as having said he thought that he 'deserved death as much as they did and would soon suffer that fate'.[99] This was not the case for everyone, but it was for the majority, for a year later most of the former radicals had met their deaths.[100] Of the twenty-six, only Fouché, Barère, Garran Coulon, Robert, Mercier and Louvet survived the Terror. Fouché and Barère were the most astute politicians, Louvet hid out, while Garran Coulon and Mercier had kept quiet during the most explosive and decisive arguments. Robert was more involved in the grocery business than politics during the period of the High Terror. Accused of hoarding, his house was pillaged. In 1795, he was sent to Belgium as a representative on mission and never returned to Paris. The remainder were either executed or committed suicide. Such was the tragic nature of the French Revolution that many of its leading politicians never survived the event.

POSTSCRIPT

WHAT BECAME OF THE FRENCH REVOLUTIONARIES?

Death by Guillotine

Robespierre, Couthon, Saint-Just, Danton, Desmoulins, Brissot, Vergniaud, Guadet, Gensonné, Carra, Gorsas, Barbaroux, Fabre d'Eglantine, Manuel.

Suicide

Condorcet, Buzot, Pétion.

Murder

Marat

Survived the Revolution

Louvet died in 1797.
Fouché died in 1820.
Barère died in 1841.
Mercier died in 1814.
Billaud-Varenne died in Haiti in 1816.
Collot d'Herbois died in Guiana in 1796.
Garran Coulon died in 1826.
Robert returned to his native Belgium and died in 1826.

APPENDICES

1: PLACES AND DATES OF BIRTH

Places of Birth

Paris

Jean-Marie Collot d'Herbois
Jean-Baptiste Louvet de Couvray
Louis-Sébastien Mercier

The Provinces

Charles-Jean-Marie Barbaroux: Marseilles
Bertrand Barère: Tarbes
Jacques-Nicolas Billaud-Varenne: La Rochelle
Jacques-Pierre Brissot: Chartres
François-Nicolas-Léonard Buzot: Evreux
Marie Jean Antoine-Nicolas Caritat de Condorcet: Ribemont
Jean-Louis Carra: Pont-de-Veyle
Georges Danton: Arcis-sur-Aube
Camille Desmoulins: Guise
Philippe-François-Nazaire Fabre d'Eglantine: Carcassonne
Joseph Fouché: Le Pellerin
Jean-Philippe Garran Coulon: Saint-Maixent
Arnaud Gensonné: Bordeaux
Antoine-Joseph Gorsas: Limoges
Marguerite-Elie Guadet: Saint-Emilion
Pierre-Louis Manuel: Montargis
Jean-Paul Marat: Boudry, Switzerland
Jérôme Pétion: Chartres
Pierre-François-Joseph Robert: Gimnée, Belgium
Maximilien-Marie-Isidore Robespierre: Arras
Louis Antoine Saint-Just: Blérancourt
Pierre-Victurnien Vergniaud: Limoges

Dates of Birth

1740s

Mercier: 1740
Collot: 1749
Carra: 1745
Marat: 1743
Garran Coulon: 1748
Condorcet: 1743

1750s

Louvet: 1758
Barère: 1755
Danton: 1759
Robespierre: 1758
Brissot: 1754
Billaud: 1756
Gorsas: 1751
Guadet: 1755
Vergniaud: 1753
Gensonné: 1758
Manuel: 1751
Pétion: 1756
Fabre d'Eglantine: 1750

1760s

Saint-Just: 1767
Barbaroux: 1767
Desmoulins: 1760
Robert: 1763
Buzot: 1760
Fouché: 1760

2: PRE-REVOLUTIONARY CAREERS AND LOCATIONS

Paris from 1780s or Before

Lawyers

Danton
Desmoulins: part-time writer of satire
Billaud-Varenne: playwright; part-time pamphleteer
Garran Coulon: part-time aspiring man of letters

Aspiring Writers, Scientists, Booksellers

Brissot: legally trained; aspiring *philosophe*; hack writer; police spy
Carra: hack writer; aspiring scientist
Gorsas: legally trained; schoolmaster turned pamphleteer
Fabre d'Eglantine: actor and playwright
Marat: doctor and scientist; aspiring *philosophe*
Manuel: bookseller and hack writer; police spy
Mercier: established man of letters
Louvet: man of letters on the rise; bookseller

The Provinces and Outside France

Lawyers

Robespierre: part-time man of letters; academician; member of literary society
Barère: part-time man of letters; academician
Robert: Belgium
Barbaroux: part-time man of science; member of literary society
Guadet
Gensonné: member of literary society

Vergniaud: some-time man of letters in youth; member of literary society
Pétion: part-time pamphleteer
Buzot
Couthon: member of local literary society; freemason

Aspiring Writers

Saint-Just: legally trained
Collot d'Herbois: actor and playwright

Teachers

Fouché: member of Rosati society; amateur scientist

3: RADICALS AND THE WAR

Paris-based

Deputies

Pro	Anti	Opinion Not Known
Brissot		Garran Coulon
Vergniaud		
Guadet		
Gensonné		
Condorcet		
Couthon		

Non-deputies

Pro	Anti	Opinion Not Known
Carra	Robespierre	Pétion
Collot	Desmoulins	Gorsas
Manuel	Marat	Robert
Louvet	Billaud	Danton
Mercier		Fabre
		Barère
		Barbaroux
		Buzot
		Fouché
		Saint-Just

4: PRESIDENTS AND SECRETARIES OF THE NATIONAL CONVENTION, 20 SEPTEMBER–13 DECEMBER 1792

20 September

President: **Pétion**
Secretaries: **Condorcet**, **Brissot**, Rabaut Saint-Etienne, Lasource, **Vergniaud**, Camus. On 23 September, Charlier replaced **Condorcet** who became vice-president.

4 October

President: Delacroix
Secretaries: **Guadet**, Sieyès, **Buzot**

18 October

President: **Guadet**
Secretaries: **Danton**, **Gensonné**, Kersaint, **Barbaroux**

1 November

President: Hérault-de-Séchelles
Secretaries: **Barère**, Jean Debry, Grégoire

15 November

President: Grégoire
Secretaries: Mailhe, **Carra**, Lepelletier de Saint-Fargeau, Defermon

29 November

President: **Barère** (Constituent Assembly)
Secretaries: Treilhard, **Saint-Just**, Jeanbon Saint-André

13 December

President: Defermon (Constituent Assembly)
Secretaries: Creuzé-Latouche, **Louvet**, Osselin

The office of the president changed every fifteen days, while of the six secretaries, three were replaced fortnightly. There appears to have been only one vice-president, Condorcet. If the president was unable to attend a session, a former president took the chair. All presidents had sat in a previous revolutionary assembly.

5: COMMITTEE AND OFFICE COMPOSITION, 20 SEPTEMBER –13 DECEMBER 1792

Barbaroux: substitute member of Constitution; secretary
Barère: Constitution, Legislation, Public Instruction; secretary and president
Billaud: no committees or offices
Brissot: Constitution, Diplomatic; secretary
Buzot: secretary
Carra: secretary
Collot: substitute member of Diplomatic and Archives
Condorcet: Constitution, Public Instruction; secretary and vice-president
Couthon: Legislation
Danton: Constitution and substitute member of Diplomatic; secretary
Desmoulins: no committees or offices
Fabre: War committee
Fouché: Finances, substitute member of Public Instruction
Garran Coulon: Legislation and Colonial
Gensonné: Constitution and Diplomatic
Gorsas: General Security, Public Instruction

Guadet: Diplomatic, Legislation; secretary and president
Louvet: Agriculture; secretary
Manuel: substitute member of General Security and Public Instruction
Marat: no committees or offices
Mercier: Public Instruction
Pétion: Constitution; president
Robert: Legislation
Robespierre: Legislation
Saint-Just: secretary
Vergniaud: Legislation, Constitution

6: REFERENDUM VOTE

Should the Decision of the National Convention be Ratified by the People?

Yes

Barbaroux, Brissot, Buzot, Garran Coulon, Gorsas, Manuel, Pétion, Gensonné, Guadet, Vergniaud, Louvet.

No

Barère, Billaud-Varenne, Carra, Desmoulins, Fabre d'Eglantine, Fouché, Robert, Robespierre, Saint-Just, Marat, Couthon, Condorcet, Mercier.

Absent on Mission

Collot d'Herbois, Danton.

7: SECTIONS: APRIL–24 MAY 1793

Moderate

1. Champs-Elysées
2. Bonne-Nouvelle
3. 1792
4. Butte-des-Moulins (divided)
5. Mont Blanc
6. Fédérés
7. Muséum
8. Gardes-Françaises (divided)
9. Fraternité
10. Quinze-Vingts
11. Halle-aux-Blé (divided)
12. Molière-et-la-Fontaine
13. Tuileries
14. République Française
15. Poissonnière (divided)
16. Amis-de-la-Patrie
17. Pont Neuf
18. Droits-de-l'homme
19. Invalides

20. Beaurepaire
21. Croix-Rouge
22. Luxembourg
23. Finistère
24. Piques

Radical

 1. Montreuil
 2. Popincourt
 3. Temple
 4. Gravilliers
 5. Marchés
 6. Contrat-Social (divided)
 7. Lombards (divided)
 8. Bon-Conseil (divided)
 9. Arsenal
10. Réunion
11. Marais
12. Arcis
13. Cité
14. Unité (Quatre-Nations)
15. Marseilles (Théâtre-Français)
16. Sans-culottes
17. Panthéon-Français (divided)
18. *Faubourg* Montmartre
19. Bondy

Unknown

1. *Faubourg* du Nord
2. Maison Commune
3. Fontaine-la-Grenelle
4. Observatoire
5. Hôtel de Ville

8: Vote on Marat at Session of 13 April 1793

'Brissotins'

Brissot: absent
Vergniaud: absent
Guadet: declared himself incompetent to judge
Gensonné: declared himself incompetent to judge
Louvet: declared himself incompetent to judge
Mercier: for impeachment
Condorcet: abstained
Pétion: abstained
Buzot: abstained
Gorsas: for impeachment
Carra: on mission
Barbaroux: for impeachment

'Mountain'/Jacobins

Danton: absent
Desmoulins: against impeachment
Robespierre: against impeachment
Robert: absent
Marat: absent
Collot d'Herbois: on mission
Billaud-Varenne: on mission
Couthon: on mission

Independents

Fabre d'Eglantine: abstained
Saint-Just: on mission
Fouché: on mission
Barère: absent
Garran Coulon: for adjournment

9: THE PROSCRIBED DEPUTIES

Barbaroux: Hid with Pétion and Buzot in Saint-Emilion in the Gironde after the failure of the federalist revolt in Normandy. They eventually left their retreat and were recognized. Barbaroux unsuccessfully attempted to shoot himself, was arrested and executed in Bordeaux on 25 June 1794.
Brissot: Remained in prison until his execution on 31 October 1793.
Buzot: Committed suicide at Saint-Emilion, 18 June 1794.
Carra: Remained in prison until his execution on 31 October 1793.
Gensonné: Remained in prison until his execution on 31 October 1793.
Gorsas: Remained in prison until his execution on 31 October 1793.
Guadet: Discovered in Saint-Emilion on 19 June 1794 and executed one day later.
Louvet: Hid until after the Terror. Reintegrated into Convention with decree of 18 ventôse year III (8 March 1795). Died in 1797.
Pétion: Committed suicide with Buzot on 18 June 1794.
Vergniaud: Remained in prison until his execution on 31 October 1791.
The Protesters and Accomplices
Condorcet: Committed suicide on 9 April 1794.
Manuel: Arrested and executed as an accomplice of the proscribed deputies on 14 November 1793.
Mercier: Arrested on 3 October 1793. Remained in prison until after the Terror. Reintegrated into the Convention with decree of 18 frimaire year III (8 December 1794). Died in 1814.

NOTES

The place of publication for books in English is London and for books in French Paris, unless otherwise stated.

Preface

1. See Keith Baker, *Inventing the French Revolution* (Cambridge, 1990), particularly the section on the importance of ideology and the Constituent Assembly. François Furet, *Interpreting the French Revolution*, trans. Elborg Forster (Cambridge, 1981). Norman Hampson, *Will and Circumstance. Montesquieu, Rousseau and the French Revolution* (Duckworth, 1983).
2. See the classic studies by French historians Albert Mathiez, *La Révolution Française* (3 vols, Colin, 1922–4), vol. 19 and Albert Soboul, *La Révolution Française* (2 vols, Gallimard, 1962).
3. M.J. Sydenham, *The Girondins* (Athlone, 1961), pp. 19, 43.
4. Alison Patrick, *The Men of the First French Republic* (Baltimore, Johns Hopkins, 1972), pp. 6–8, 14–17.
5. See Appendix 1 for a list of the names and dates of birth of the politicians under consideration.

1. Future Radicals: An Introduction to the Men of 1792

1. J.M. Thompson, *Robespierre* (2 vols, Oxford, 1935), vol. 1, p. 33; Norman Hampson, *Will and Circumstance: Montesquieu, Rousseau and the French Revolution* (1983), p. 131.
2. For a summary of Robespierre's academic essays, see Norman Hampson, *Will and Circumstance*, pp. 131–3, and Thompson, *Robespierre*, vol. 1, pp. 22–32, 41–3.
3. Hampson, *Will and Circumstance*, p. 136.
4. Robespierre's speech defending Dupond, in ibid., pp. 139–40.

5. *Nouvelle Biographie Générale*, vol. 4, p. 419; J.F. Michaud and L.G. Michaud (eds), *Biographie Universelle Ancienne et Moderne*, reprint, 2nd edn (45 vols, Graz, 1966–70), vol. 8, p. 612.
6. Barbaroux to his mother, 5 July 1788, *Correspondance et Mémoires de Barbaroux*, C. Perroud (ed.) (1923), p. 28.
7. M. Dorigny, 'Barbaroux', in Albert Soboul (ed.), *Dictionnaire Historique de la Révolution Française* (1989), p. 73; Claude Manceron, *L'Album des Hommes de la Liberté* (1989), p. 291.
8. Barbaroux to Chavelot, 15 November 1787, *Correspondance*, p. 15.
9. M.L. Kennedy, *The Jacobin Club of Marseilles, 1790–1794* (Ithaca, NY, 1973), p. 18.
10. Albert Soboul, 'Georges Couthon' *AHRF* (avril–juin, 1983), pp. 204–7; Franco Piro, *La Festa della Sfortuna* (Milan, 1989), p. 54.
11. Jean-Paul Fanget, 'Georges Couthon et la disparition du régime féodal dans le Puy-du-Dôme (1789-an II)', *AHRF* (1983), p. 239.
12. A. Kuscinski, *Dictionnaire des Conventionnels* (1916), p. 598; J. Guadet, *Les Girondins, leur vie privée, leur vie publique, leur proscription et leur mort* (2 vols, 1861), vol. 1, p. 24; Louis Lussaud, *Eloge Historique de M.E. Guadet (1758–1794)* (Bordeaux, 1861); Bertrand Favreau, 'Gensonné ou la fatalité de la Gironde', in F. Furet and M. Ozouf (eds), *La Gironde et les Girondins* (1991), pp. 410–11.
13. Vergniaud to M. Alluaud, 3 March 1783, *Vergniaud, manuscrits, lettres et papiers*, C. Vatel (ed.) (1873), p. 77.
14. The membership list of 1787, the only existing one, includes the names of Vergniaud and Gensonné among its 155 members. See Johel

Coutura, 'Le Musée de Bordeaux', *DHS* 19 (1987), pp.149–63; Alan Forrest, *Society and Politics in Revolutionary Bordeaux* (Oxford, 1975), pp. 27–8; Roche is quoted in Paul Butel and Jean-Pierre Poussou, *La vie quotidienne à Bordeaux au XVIIIe siècle* (1980), p. 243.

15. Leo Gershoy, *Bertrand Barère, the Reluctant Terrorist* (Princeton, 1962), pp. 4–5; Kuscinski, *Dictionnaire*, p. 55.

16. J.J. Régnault-Warin, *Vie de Pétion, maire de Paris* (Bar-le-Duc, 1792), p. 16; 'Vie politique de Jérôme Pétion', in *Histoire de deux célébrés législateurs du dix-huitième siècle contenant plusieurs anecdotes curieuses et intéressantes* (1793), pp. 11–12; Kuscinski, *Dictionnaire*, p. 487.

17. Soboul, *Dictionnaire*, p. 167.

18. L. Atheunis, *Le conventionnel Belge François Robert (1763–1826) et sa femme Louise de Kéralio (1758–1822)* (Wetteren, 1955), pp. 5–8.

19. M. Fuchs, 'Collot d'Herbois comédien', *RF* 79 (1926), pp. 20, 23.

20. Kuscinski, *Dictionnaire*, p. 145.

21. Michaud, *Biographie*, vol. 8, p. 612; Barry Rothaus and Samuel F. Scott (eds), *Historical Dictionary of the French Revolution* (2 vols, 1985), vol. 1, p. 203. Henry Lyonnet, 'Collot d'Herbois, critique dramatique', *AR* 1 (1908), p. 665.

22. Robert Darnton, *The Literary Underground of the Old Regime* (Cambridge, Mass., 1982), p. 38.

23. Hubert Cole, *Fouché. The Unprincipled Patriot* (1971), pp. 16–19; André Castlelot, *Fouché, le double jeu* (1990), pp. 15–16, 29.

24. Saint-Just's biographers seem to be in disagreement over this: Geoffrey Bruun says he was awarded his licence ès lois in February 1788. Françoise Kermina agrees, stating he studied at Rheims for six months and then got his degree. The older biography by Hamel claims he never qualified, as does Saint-Just's most recent biographer, Norman Hampson. See Bruun, *Saint-Just, apostle of the terror* (Hampden, Conn., 1966), p. 12; Françoise Kermina, *Saint-Just, la Révolution aux mains d'un jeune homme* (1982), p. 27; E. Hamel, *Histoire de Saint-Just* (2 vols, Brussels, n.d.), vol. 1, p. 37; Hampson, *Saint-Just* (Oxford, 1991), p. 9.

25. Hampson, *Saint-Just*, p. 17.

26. L. Béclard, *Sébastien Mercier, sa vie, son oeuvre, son temps* (1903).

27. Robert Darnton, *The Corpus of Clandestine Literature in France 1769–1789* (New York, 1995), pp. 194, 199.

28. Hampson provides an insightful survey of Mercier's writings in Chapter 4 of *Will and Circumstance*. For a useful summary of *L'an 2440*, see Robert Darnton, *The Forbidden Best-sellers of Pre-revolutionary France* (New York, 1995), pp. 118–36.

29. Soboul, *Dictionnaire historique*, p. 687. See Claude Manceron, *The French Revolution: Blood of the Bastille 1787–1789*, tr. Nancy Amphoux (5 vols, New York, 1989), vol. 5, p. 61; F.A. Aulard, 'Figures oubliées de la Révolution française, le conventionnel Louvet' *NR* (novembre 1885), p. 346; F.A. Aulard, 'Préface', *Mémoires de Louvet de Couvray sur la Révolution française* (2 vols, 1889), vol. 1, p. 5.

30. Jacques Guilaine, *Billaud-Varenne l'ascète de la Révolution* (1969), pp. 13–15, and Arthur Conte, *Billaud-Varenne: géant de la Révolution* (1989), pp. 57–8.

31. R.R. Palmer, *The Year of the Terror: Twelve who Ruled; the Committee of Public Safety during the Terror (1793–1794)* (Princeton, 1941), p. 12.

32. Both works are summarized in Guilaine, *Billaud-Varenne*, pp. 20–8.

33. Norman Hampson, *Danton* (Oxford, 1988), pp. 19–25.

34. Violet Methley, *Camille Desmoulins* (1914), pp. 20–37; J.B. Morton, *Camille Desmoulins and other studies of the French Revolution* (1950), pp. 10–11; Jacques Janssens, *Camille Desmoulins, le premier républicain de France* (1973), pp. 88–95.

35. Janssens, *Camille Desmoulins*, pp. 88–90.

36. *La Grande Encyclopédie*, Berthelot, Hartwig et al. (eds) (31 vols, 1886–1902), vol. 18, p. 563; Gary Kates, *The Cercle Social, the Girondins and the French Revolution* (Princeton, NJ, 1985), p. 24; Barry M. Shapiro, *Revolutionary Justice in Paris, 1789–1790* (Cambridge, 1993), p. 20.

37. Louis Jacob, *Fabre d'Eglantine, Chef des 'Fripons'* (1946), p. 33.

38. Robert Darnton, 'The Facts of Literary Life in Eighteenth Century France', in Keith Baker (ed.), *The French Revolution and the Creation of Modern Political Culture: The Political Culture of the Old Regime* (4 vols, Oxford, 1987), vol. 1, pp. 280–2.

39. Bibliothèque municipale d'Orléans, Lenoir papers, MSS in Darnton, *The Literary Underground of the Old Regime* (Cambridge, Mass. 1982), p. 28.

40. Pierre Montarlot, 'Les Députés de Sâone-et-Loire au Tribunal révolutionnaire' in *Les Mémoires de la Société* 33 (1905), pp. 217–73; *APL*, 10 January, 22 February 1792.

1. Robinet to Carra, 2 January 1771, in Montarlot, p. 223. M.L. Kennedy, 'The Development of a Political Radical: Jean-Louis Carra, 1742–1787', *Proceedings of the Third Annual Meeting of the Western Society for French History*, December 4–6, 1975, B. Gooch (ed.) (Texas, 1976), pp. 142–50.

2. Simone Balayé, 'De la Bibliothèque du Roi à la Bibliothèque Nationale', in Jean Claude Bonnet (ed.), *La Carmagnole des Muses* (1988), n. 5, p. 46.

3. Parish Registers of St Pierre-du-Queyvoix, in Louis Guibert, *Un journaliste girondin* (Limoges, 1871), p. 5. Gorsas' widow wrote a biographical piece in *Précis rapide des événements qui ont eu lieu à Paris dans les journées des 30 et 31 mai; premier et 2 juin 1793, par A.J. Gorsas, député à la convention nationale, l'un des xxxiv proscrits* (n.d.).

4. Guibert, *Un journaliste*, p. 5. *Dictionnaire de biographie française*, M. Prévost, J. Balteau, M. Barroux (eds) (107 vols, 1933–93), vol. 62, pp. 632–3.

5. 'Vie secrète de Pierre Manuel' in *Histoire de deux célébrés législateurs*, p. 9; Kuscinski, *Dictionnaire*, p. 427.

6. Darnton, *Literary Underground*, pp. 38, 61.

7. Brissot, *Recherches sur la Propriété et le Vol* (Neuchâtel, 1780), p. 2.

8. J.P. Brissot, *Réponse à tous les libellistes* (1791), p. 40. There is a copy of the formal accusation among his papers. See 'Bastille Mémoire' Fragment, 21 August 1784, in AN Papiers Brissot, 446 Archives Privées (AP) Carton 2.

9. Leonore Loft, 'La Théorie des loix criminelles: Brissot and Legal Reform', *A J FS* 26 (1989), 247–8.

50. Louis Gottschalk, *Jean-Paul Marat: A Study in Radicalism* (Chicago, 1927), p. 7; Kuscinski, *Dictionnaire*, p. 42.

51. For summaries of Marat's ill-fated scientific career, see Hampson, *Will and Circumstance*, pp. 117–19 and Gottschalk, *Marat*, pp. 26–30.

52. J.P. Brissot, *De la Vérité* (Neuchâtel, 1782), p. 173. See Marat's letter of praise to Brissot (n.d.), in AN 446 AP 7.

53. Brissot, *De la Vérité*, pp. 30, 73.

54. Marat, *AmP*, 4 June 1792.

55. H.T. Dickinson, *Liberty and Property: Political Ideology in Eighteenth Century Britain* (1977), pp. 210–15.

56. F. Chevremont, *Jean Paul Marat* (2 vols, 1880), vol. 1, pp. 40, 63. Louis Gottschalk, 'The Radicalism of Jean Paul Marat', *SR* (1921), pp. 155–70; and Hampson, Ch. 6, 'Marat', *Will and Circumstance*.

57. Ian Germani, *Jean-Paul Marat, Hero and Anti-Hero of the French Revolution* (Lewiston, 1992), pp. 7–12.

58. Louis Peit Bachaumont, *Mémoires secrets pour servir à l'histoire de la république* (36 vols, 1777–89), vol. 22, 15 February, 27 May 1783.

59. Elisabeth and Robert Badinter, *Condorcet un intellectuel en politique (1743–1794)* (1988).

60. See Villar's letters to Brissot, 5 March and 24 September 1783 in Brissot, *Correspondance et Papiers*, C. Perroud (ed.) (1912), pp. 73–5.

61. Brissot to Condorcet, 19 May 1785, and Garat to Brissot, 1785, AN 446 AP 7; Badinter, *Condorcet*, p. 190.

62. Brissot, *Mémoires*, C. Perroud (ed.) (2 vols, 1912), vol. 1, pp. 284–6; T. Vincent Benn, 'Bibliographie critique des ouvrages de L.S. Mercier', unpublished Ph.D. (Leeds University, 1925), pp. 101–3.

63. For the only existing membership list, see C. Perroud, 'La société française des amis des noirs', *RF* 49, pp. 125–6. The rules are printed in Léon Cahen, 'La société des Amis des Noirs et Condorcet', *RF* 50 (1906), 484–511.

64. Mesmerism is the term to describe the theories of animal magnetism developed by Franz Anton Mesmer. Robert Darnton, *Mesmerism and the end of the Enlightenment in France* (Cambridge, Mass., 1968), p. 4.

65. Brissot frequently worked for Clavière. For Clavière see, Jean Bouchary, *Les manieurs d'argent à Paris à la fin du XVIIIe siècle* (2 vols, 1939), vol. 1, pp. 11–101. Brissot, *Mémoires*, vol. 2, p. 415. This claim was made some years later.

66. *Un mot à l'oreille des académiciens de Paris*, published anonymously (n.d., 1785?), pp. 8, 14; Badinter, *Condorcet*, p. 189.

67. *Déclaration du Sieur Gorsas, au sujet des lettres de Beaumarchais, citées dans la cause de M. Kornmann* (1789), p. 3 ; *CG*, 11 December 1792.

68. *Point de Banqueroute* (1787), Part 1, pp. 18–25, 32, 40–1; Part 2, pp. 6–27.

69. Pétion's relationship with Brissot dates from their childhood. *Mémoires de Madame Roland*, C. Perroud (ed.) (2 vols, 1905), vol. 2, p. 231; J. Pétion, 'Notice sur Brissot', in *Mémoires inédits de Pétion et Mémoires de Buzot et de Barbaroux*, C.A. Dauban (ed.) (1866), p. 524. His name is on the list of members who frequented Kornmann's salon by Etienne Lamy, in *Un défenseur des principes traditionnels sous la Révolution, Nicolas Bergasse (1750–1832)*, (1910), pp. viii, 40, and Léopold de Gaillard, in

182   *N o t e s*

Autres Temps: Nicolas Bergasse (1893), p. 22. and Lamy, pp. viii, 40.

70. Pétion referred to the Kornmann affair in several letters to Brissot. See those of 7, 24 June, 24 July and 4 August 1787, AN, 446 AP 8.

71. Leigh Whaley, 'Made to practice virtue in a republic: Jérôme Pétion: A pre-revolutionary radical advocate', in *Selected Proceedings. Consortium on Revolutionary Europe 1750–1850*, Donald Horward (ed.) (Tallahassee, 1995), pp. 167–76.

72. J. Pétion, *Les Lois civiles et l'administration de la justice ramenées à un ordre simple et uniforme* (1782), pp. 206–8, 215, 246.

73. Pétion, 'Preface', *Avis au français sur le salut de leur patrie*, in *Oeuvres* (4 vols, 1793), vol. 2, p. xxxvi.

74. Pétion, *Avis*, vol. 2, pp. 193, 66, 83, 199.

75. Ibid., pp. 108, 125–7, 178, 233, 254.

76. Ibid., pp. 277–8.

2. *Revolutionary Networking, 1789–91*

1. APL, 3 July 1790.

2. AP, 18 September 1789, vol. 9, p. 537.

3. Ibid., 21 September 1789, p. 56.

4. See Barry Shapiro's discussion of Pétion and the veto question in 'Opting for the Terror?: A Critique of Keith Baker's Analysis of the Suspensive Veto of 1789', Paper presented to the 26th annual conference of the Western Society for French History, 7 November 1998, Boston, pp. 5–7.

5. PF, 4, 5 September 1789.

6. Robert married Kéralio on 20 May 1790. *François Robert à ses frères de la société fraternelle et du Club des Cordeliers* (1792?), p. 2. MN, 6 June 1790.

7. Carra, *L'Orateur des Etats-Généraux pour 1789*, Seconde partie (1789), pp. 13, 20; MN, 25 April 1791.

8. APL, 25 April 1791; RFB, no. 1; 'Discours de la lanterne aux Parisiens', in Jules Claretie (ed.), *Oeuvres de Camille Desmoulins* (2 vols, 1874), vol. 1, p. 188. AmP, 12, 15 September 1789.

9. Lucy M. Gidney, *L'influence des Etats-Unis d'Amérique sur Brissot, Condorcet et Madame Roland* (1930), p. 85.

10. MN, 24 April 1791; APL, 25 April 1791; 11 February 1790.

11. PF, 9 April 1791, 5 September 1789.

12. APL, 26 February 1790, 8 April 1791.

13. RP, no. 8, 3–10 October 1789; *Hist Parl*, vol. 3, pp. 109–10.

14. CG, 8 October 1789.

15. F.A. Aulard, 'Danton au district des Cordeliers et à la Commune', *RF* 24 (1893), pp. 118–19.

16. PF, 6, 7 October 1789; Brissot, 'Adresse à l'Assemblée générale des Représentants de la Commune de Paris à toutes les municipalités du royaume de France', in Sigismund Lacroix (ed.), *Actes de la Commune de Paris pendant la Révolution* (16 vols, 1894–1909), vol. 2, pp. 245–6; *PF*, 2 December 1789; AmP, 7 October 1789.

17. APL, 6, 7 October 1789.

18. J.M. Thompson, *Leaders of the French Revolution* (Oxford, 1929), pp. 95–6.

19. M. Robespierre, *Oeuvres complètes* (10 vols, 1910–67), vol. 6, pp. 106–7; Gershoy, *Barère*, p. 75.

20. APL, 30 March 1790; RFB, no. 33, 12 July 1790.

21. Assembly, 8 April 1790, AP, vol. 12, p. 581; *Hist Parl*, vol. 5, pp. 185–7.

22. Pétion to Brissot, April 1789 in AN 446 AP 7; 'Liste des Amis du Peuple', AN AD 9, in C.L. Chassin (ed.), *Les Elections et les Cahiers de Paris en 1789* (4 vols, 1888–9), vol. 2, p. 12.

23. Isabelle Bourdin, *La société de la section de la Bibliothèque* (1937), p. 17. Collot d'Herbois, *Adresse de la section de la Bibliothèque à l'Assemblée nationale* (n.d.).

24. The Paris deputy Camus was one of the thirty-six commissioners charged with the publication of the *cahiers* of the Third Estate. The *Collection Officielle* was the title of the published *cahiers* from the Paris constituency.

25. Chassin, *Les Elections*, vol. 3, p. 403; Carra, 'Projet du Cahier', in ibid., pp. 214–15.

26. Chassin, *Les Elections*, vol. 2, p. 357; Lacroix, *Actes*, vol. 2, pp. 376–7.

27. Badinter, *Condorcet*, pp. 262–4, 274–5.

28. AmP, 30 September, 1 October 1789. See the report on the evening session of the assembly of the Commune in Lacroix, *Actes*, vol. 2, p. 202.

29. Kéralio-Robert to Brissot, 1789 in AN 446 AP 7.

30. RFB, no. 9, 25 January 1790.

31. APL, 17 October 1789.

32. CG, 19, 23 January 1790.

33. Brissot to Desmoulins, dated 'ce mercredi', in Jane Lohrer, 'A Letter of Brissot to Desmoulins', *JMH* 6 (March–December 1934), pp. 441–3. Delapoype was Fréron's brother-in-law and associate editor of Desmoulins' newspaper. *PF*, 8 November 1789.

34. *RFB*, no. 37, 9 August 1790; *AmP*, 19 August 1790; Garran Coulon to Brissot, 30 July 1790, *PF*, 3 August 1790.

35. Kates, *Cercle Social*, pp. 19–20.

36. Although not a member of the Commune's constitutional committee, Brissot wrote a plan which he hoped would be of some influence. See his 'Projet du plan de la municipalité de Paris', in AN 446 AP 12. Brissot published excerpts from this plan in the *PF*, 16, 17 August 1789. Leigh Whaley, 'The Emergence of the Brissotins during the French Revolution', D.Phil. (University of York, 1989), pp. 115–18.

37. *RP*, 14–21 November 1789.

38. *RFB*, nos 36, 38; 2, 16 August 1790.

39. Hampson, *Danton*, p. 39; *RFB*, nos 38, 63; 16 August 1790, 7 February 1791.

40. Robespierre to Desmoulins, 7 June 1790, Bibliothèque Historique de la Ville de Paris, Papiers de Desmoulins, MS 986, Rés. 25, vol. 2; *PF*, 9 June 1790; 28 February 1791.

41. *AmP*, 28, 20 December 1790.

42. Ibid., 16 January 1791. There is no list of proposed members. Isabelle Bourdin, *Les sociétés populaires à Paris, pendant la Révolution* (1937), p. 55.

43. *RFB*, no. 54, 6 December 1790.

44. F.A. Aulard, *La Société des Jacobins. Recueil de Documents* (6 vols, 1889–97), vol. 1, p. xxxvi; Lucile Desmoulins to her mother, 23 June 1791, BHVP, MS 986 (Rés 25, fol. 181).

45. Aulard, *Société*, vol. 1, p. 283.

46. *RFB*, no. 45; *AmP*, 31 August–10 September 1790.

47. Collot d'Herbois, *Rapport fait le . . . 26 juin 1791 . . . en réclamation de justice* (1791); *Rapport fait . . . le 6 juillet 1791* (n.d.).

48. See Robert's account of this session in *MU*, no. 41; Letter of Lanthenas, 15 May 1791, *Lettres autographes de Madame Roland adressées à Bancal* (1835), p. 218; *CG*, 10 September, 9 November 1790.

49. C. Perroud, 'A Propos de l'abolition du droit de l'aînesse', *RF*, 54 (1908), 193–202.

50. Lanthenas to Bancal, 10 January 1791, *Lettres de Madame Roland*, C. Perroud (ed.) (1900–2), vol. 2, p. 217.

51. *RFB*, no. 69, 7 March 1791.

52. Lanthenas to Brissot, 12 September 1790, AN 446 AP 7; *PF*, 17 January 1791; Pétion to Lanthenas, 20 September 1790, 446 AP 8; Pétion to the National Assembly, 23 February 1790, *AP*, vol. 11, p. 690.

53. *Mémoires de Madame Roland*, C. Dauban (ed.) (1864), pp. 231–2.

54. Lanthenas to Bancal, 10 January 1791, *Lettres*, vol. 2, p. 217; Craig Dotson, 'The Paris Jacobin Club and the French Revolution', Ph.D. (Queen's University, Kingston, 1974), p. 85; Roland to Lanthenas, 22 January 1790, Papiers Roland, Bibliothéque Nationale (BN), naf MS 9532, fol. 168.

55. Lanthenas to Bancal, 22 May 1791, *Lettres*, vol. 2, p. 280.

56. *PF*, 17 May 1791; Aulard, *Société*, vol. 2, pp. 396–411.

57. For an analysis of Fabre's plays, see Barbara Anne Walker, 'Collot d'Herbois: Revolutionary dramatist', M.A. (The University of Calgary, 1976).

58. Fabre d'Eglantine, *Le Philinte de Molière ou la suite du Misanthrope* (1791), p. 86.

59. Hampson, *Danton*, p. 31; Jacob, *Fabre*, pp. 72–3; Billaud-Varenne, *Mémoires inédites et correspondance*, A. Bégis (ed.) (1893), p. 20. *PF*, 25 February 1790; 28 July 1791.

60. Kates, *Cercle Social*, pp. 332–3.

61. For a list of members of the club, see Appendix A of Kates, *Cercle Social*, pp. 277–81. As Kates indicates, a contemporary list does not exist. His list can only be taken as a guide and is most likely incomplete. *RF*, no. 17, 22 March 1790.

62. *APL*, 5 September 1790.

63. *CG*, 11 August 1789, 28 October 1790.

64. *APL*, 19, 22 October 1790, 11 April 1791.

65. *RFB*, nos 49, 55, 61; 1 November, 13 December 1790, 24 January 1791.

66. Ibid., nos 63, 69; 7 February, 7 March 1791.

67. Paris Registers of Saint-Suplice, cited in Jules Claretie, *Camille Desmoulins* (1875), p. 151.

68. She asked if Robert could borrow another 200 *livres* from Brissot, and called herself his 'good sister' and 'fellow citizen'. Kéralio to Brissot, 29 August 1790, AN 446 AP 7. For further correspondence with Brissot, see AN, 446 AP, Cartons 4 and 7; *PF*, 21 August 1789; 2 February, 20 March, 16 June, 13 September, 19 December 1790.

69. *PF*, 29 May 1791.

70. *MN*, 21 March, 18 April, 1790; *APL*, no. 33, 4 November 1789.

71. David Andress, 'Economic Dislocation and Social Discontent in the French Revolution: Survival in Paris in the Era of the Flight to Varennes', *FH*, 10, no. 1 (March 1996), pp. 30–55.

72. *BdeF*, 11, 24 May, 1, 4 June 1791.

73. Ibid., 23 June 1791; *CG*, 26 June 1791; *RFB*, 27 June 1791. See Brissot's speech to the Jacobins, *RFB*, no. 84, 11 July 1791 and Desmoulins' comments in the same issue. For Carra's attitude, see his article advocating a republic, *APL*, 8 July 1791.
74. Bégis (ed.), *Billaud*, p. 21.
75. Roland to Bancal, 23 June 1791, *Lettres*, vol. 2, p. 306; *Le Républicain ou le Défenseur du Gouvernement représentatif*, 3 July 1791. See their speeches to the Jacobins in *MU*, 8, 10, 15 July 1791.
76. Assembly, 25, 26 June 1791, *LM*, vol. 8, pp. 746–7, 756.
77. Albert Mathiez, *Le Club des Cordeliers pendant la crise de Varennes et le massacre du Champ de Mars* (1913), did not include Laclos in his list; while F. Braesch in 'Les Pétitions du Champ de Mars, 15, 16, 17 juillet 1791', *RH*, pp. 142–3 (janvier–avril 1923), pp. 192–209 and (mai–août 1923), pp. 1–39, argued that Laclos was a member of the committee. For a detailed explanation of the petitioning, see Graham E. Rodmell, 'Laclos, Brissot and the petition of the Champ de Mars', *Studies on Voltaire and the Eighteenth Century*, 183 (1980), pp. 189–222.
78. Jacobins, 23 June 1791, André Fribourg (ed.), *Discours de Danton* (1910), p. 111; Carra, 'Discours sur la déchéance de Louis XVI, prononcé le 11 juillet à la tribune des Jacobins', *APL*, 13 July ; *Supplément*, 14 July 1791; Jacobins, 3 July 1791, *Débats*, 3 July 1791, *RP*, no. 109, 6–13 August 1791.
79. *Bde F*, no. 96, 20 July 1791; Procédure du Champ de Mars et procès Bailly au tribunal révolutionnaire cited in Mathiez, *Le club*, p. 168.
80. Dotson, 'Jacobin Club', pp. 124–5. Mathiez, *Le club*, p. 129; Georges Michon, *Essai sur l'histoire du parti feuillant: Adrien Duport* (1924), p. 262; Augustin Challamel, *Les clubs contre-révolutionnaires* (1895), has produced a list of Feuillant members, pp. 286–93.
81. Jacobins, 17 July 1791, *Société*, vol. 3, pp. 26–8; 'Lettre de J. Pétion, *Débats*, 3 August 1791.
82. Extract from *Journal de la Révolution*, after the session of 29 July 1791, in Aulard, *Société*, vol. 3, p. 61. Kennedy suggests that some deputies had ceased to go to Jacobin sessions before 16 July, implying that the Feuillants existed before this date, and that it was composed of men like Lafayette and former members of the conservative 1789 society. Kennedy, *The Jacobin clubs in the French Revolution: the Middle Years* (Princeton, 1988), p. 285.
83. Barbaroux, *Correspondance*, p. ix; M.L. Kennedy, *The Jacobin Club of Marseilles, 1790–1794* (Ithaca, NY, 1973), pp. 36, 62, 77, 94. Norman Hampson, *Saint-Just*, pp. 29–30.
84. Fanget, 'Georges Couthon', pp. 242–3; Robert Schnerb, 'Notes sur les débuts politiques de Couthon et de Monestier dans le département du Puy-de-Dôme', *AHRF* (1930), 323–7.
85. J.H. Bancal, 'Réflexions sur l'institution du pouvoir exécutif . . .', in *PF*, 3 July 1791.
86. E.B. Courtois, *Rapport fait au nom de la commission chargée de l'examen des papiers de Robespierre et ses complices* (1794), p. 122.
87. Archives Départmentales de la Gironde, 12 L 13, 19 May, 19 June 1790. A. Vermorel (ed.), *Oeuvres de Vergniaud, Gensonné, Guadet* (1867), pp. 2–3.
88. Louis Madelin, *Fouché* (1900), pp. 18–20; Hubert Cole, *Fouché: The Unprincipled Patriot* (1971), p. 14.

3. *Radicals during the Legislative Assembly*

1. Report by Gensonné and Gallois to the Legislative Assembly, 9 October 1791, *Hist Parl*, vol. 12, pp. 87–91.
2. Assembly, 7, 26 October 1791, ibid., pp. 76, 125.
3. Assembly, 14 November 1791, ibid., p. 375.
4. Condorcet, 'Sur la nécessité d'ôter au clergé l'état civil', in *Oeuvres de Condorcet*, F. Arago and A. Condorcet O'Connor (eds) (12 vols, 1847–9), vol. 12, p. 11.
5. Assembly, 20 October 1791, *LM*, vol. 10, p. 173.
6. *RFB*, no. 98, 26 October 1791.
7. *AmP*, 25 October 1791.
8. Jacobins, 24 November 1791, *Société*, vol. 3, p. 266.
9. Assembly, 8 November 1791, *LM*, vol. 10, p. 325.
10. Aulard, *Société*, vol. 3, pp. 21, 24, 158, 172, 195, 232, 298.
11. Jacobins, 21 October 1791, ibid., vol. 3, p. 199.
12. 'La société des amis de la constitution séante aux Jacobins à Paris, aux sociétés affiliées', 16 November 1791, ibid., Vol. 3, pp. 251–2.
13. *Débats*, no. 109.
14. Robespierre to Brissot, 11 November 1791, AN, 446 AP 8.

15. *PF*, 12 December 1791.
16. *Discours de J.P. Brissot sur la nécessité de déclarer la guerre aux princes allemands qui protégèrent les ennemis, prononcé le 16 décembre 1791 à la Société des Amis de la Constitution*, p. 2; Jacobins, 18 December 1791, in Robespierre, *Oeuvres*, vol. 8, p. 58.
17. Brissot, *Discours sur la nécessité*.
18. Ibid., p. 6.
19. Jacobins, 28 November 1791, *Débats*, no. 101.
20. Billaud-Varenne, 5 December 1791, Supplement, *Débats*, no. 107, 6 December 1791.
21. *Discours de M. Robespierre sur le parti que l'Assemblée Nationale doit prendre relativement à la proposition de guerre, annoncée par le pouvoir exécutif, prononcé à la Société des Amis de la Constitution, le 18 décembre 1791*; MU, 20 January 1792.
22. Jacobins, 12 December 1791, *Débats*, no. 101.
23. Jacobins, 18 January 1792, Ibid., no. 130.
24. See Appendix 3.
25. CG, 16 October, 13, 19 December 1791.
26. Ibid., 20 December 1791.
27. Ibid., 18, 20 January 1792.
28. Jacobins, 9 December 1791, *Débats*, no. 109.
29. APL, 14 January 1792.
30. Assembly, 25 December 1791, LM, vol. 10, pp. 727–9.
31. Couthon to his consituents, 17 December 1791, *Correspondance inédite de Georges Couthon, 1791–1794*, F. Mège (ed.) (1872), pp. 57–8.
32. Couthon, Letters, 20, 31 December 1791, 3 January 1792, ibid., pp. 59-63.
33. Geoffrey Bruun, 'The evolution of a terrorist: Georges Auguste Couthon', *JMH* 2, no. 3 (1930), p. 417. Couthon, 17 April 1792, *Correspondance*, p. 120.
34. Jacobins, 19 March 1792, *Société*, vol. 3, p. 439.
35. Billaud-Varenne, *Discours sur cette question: Comment doit on faire la guerre au cas qu'il faille la déclarer?*, 19 December 1791; Desmoulins, *Discours sur le parti que l'Assemblée nationale doit prendre relativement à la proposition de guerre annoncée par le pouvoir exécutif*, 25 December 1791.
36. AmP, 15 December 1791.
37. Danton beat Collot by 1,162 votes to 654 in the election in December 1791 to replace one of Manuel's deputies. Hampson, *Danton*, p. 53. APL, 18 December 1791.
38. Desmoulins to his father, 3 April 1792, *Correspondance inédite de Camille Desmoulins* (2 vols, 1836), vol. 2, p. 123.
39. Pétion to Robespierre, 15 June 1791, Robespierre, *Oeuvres*, vol. 3, p. 114.
40. E.D. Bradby, *The Life of Barnave* (2 vols, Oxford, 1915), vol. 2, pp. 272–3.
41. *Débats*, 3 February 1792; Aulard, *Société*, vol. 3, p. 331.
42. Aulard, *Société*, vol. 3, p. 381.
43. Jacobins, 26 February 1792, ibid.
44. *Débats*, nos 148, 150, 167.
45. Their letters are in the Archives municipales of Marseilles, D 4, arts. 13 and 46. Cited in *Correspondance*, p. 58.
46. See Barbaroux and Loys' letters to the municipality of Marseilles, dated 11, 21 February, 7, 13 March 1792, ibid., pp. 57–77.
47. *Chronique du Mois*, 30 January 1792. Brissot stated that: 'The organization of the executive power is the cause of all disorders which affect the nation.' *PF*, 14 November 1791.
48. AP, vol. 69, pp. 534–5, 549.
49. E. Dumont, *Souvenirs sur Mirabeau et sur les deux premières assemblées législatives* (Brussels, 1832), pp. 70, 203; Garran to Brissot, 6 March 1792, AN 446 AP 7.
50. *Tribune des Patriotes*, no. 1, 20 April 1792.
51. *Débats*, nos. 163, 164, 172.
52. AmP, 13 April 1792; CG, 30 March 1792; *PF*, 24 March 1792; *Tribune*, no. 4.
53. Couthon, 20 March 1792, *Correspondance*, p. 108.
54. *François Robert à ses frères de la société des amis de la constitution, de la société fraternelle et du club des Cordeliers* (1792), pp. 4–5.
55. Roland, *Mémoires*, vol. 1, pp. 165–7.
56. Madame Roland to Bosc, 23 March 1792, *Lettres*, vol. 2, p. 339.
57. *PF*, 22 March 1792
58. Barbaroux to the municipality of Marseilles, 20 March 1792. *Correspondance*, p. 94.
59. RP, no. cxlvi, in *Hist Parl*, vol. 14, pp. 171–2.
60. Jacobins, 20 April 1792, in Robespierre, *Oeuvres*, vol. 8, pp. 292–3.
61. *PF*, 22, 26 April; 3 June 1792.
62. Jacobins, 20, 23 April 1792, *Société*, vol. 3, pp. 517–18.
63. Jacobins, 25 April 1792, *Débats*, 27 April 1792.
64. CP, 26 April 1792.
65. *PF*, 28 April 1792.
66. Jacobins, 28 April 1792, *Défenseur de la Constitution*, no. 1.
67. CG, 20 April, 2 May 1792.
68. Barbaroux, 27 April 1792, *Correspondance*, pp. 139–40.

69. Pétion, *Discours . . . prononcé à la société le 29 avril 1792*. Pétion wrote to Robespierre about his proposed reconciliation speech, delivered that evening. Letters to Robespierre, 26, 29 April 1792, Robespierre, *Oeuvres*, vol. 3, pp. 147–8.
70. *APL*, 1, 2 May; 14, 24 April 1792.
71. Jacobins, 10 May 1792, Fribourg, *Danton*, p. 144; Desmoulins to his father, 3 April 1792, *Correspondance*, vol. 2, p. 123.
72. Aulard, *Société*, vol. 3, pp. 665–7.
73. Jacobins, 14 June 1792, *Débats*, no. 214.
74. This letter was signed by Chabot, president and Audouin, Fabre, and Collot, secretaries. Jacobin circular, 20 June 1792, Aulard, *Société*, vol. 4, p. 28.
75. Jacobins, 14 June 1792, *Débats*, no. 214.
76. *Tribune*, no. 4.
77. Jacobins, 14, 15 June 1792, *Débats*, nos 214, 215.
78. *PF*, 13, 14, June 1792.
79. Jacobins, 18 June 1792, *Débats*, no. 218.
80. Curtis, *Saint-Just* (New York, 1935), p. 30. For the fullest discussion of Saint-Just's ideas at this time, see Hampson, *Saint-Just*, ch. 3.
81. Robespierre, *Oeuvres*, vol. 6, p. 70.
82. Barère to Dumouriez, 30 March 1792, Collection Liesville, BHVP in Gershoy, *Barère*, p. 123.
83. Kennedy examined the clubs' opinions between December 1791 and April 1792. Kennedy, *Jacobin Clubs*, p. 130.
84. Cole, *Fouché*, p. 23.

4. Demise of the Monarchy

1. Albert Soboul, *Précis d'histoire de la Révolution* (1962), p. 201; Albert Mathiez, *La Révolution française* (3 vols, Paris, 1922–4), vol. 2, p. 191.
2. Sergent, 'Notice historique sur les événements du 10 août et des 20 et 21 juin précédents', *Revue Rétrospective*, seconde série III (1835), p. 342. Claude Perroud, when citing Sergent, maintained he was an 'insufficient source'. Perroud, 'Le Premier Ministre Roland', *RF*, 42 (1902), p. 525.
3. Chabot's statement to the Tribunal Criminel Révolutionnaire, *LM*, 27 October 1793, vol. 18, pp. 244–5.
4. *Débats*, no. 272.
5. Kennedy, *Jacobin Club of Marseilles*, p. 108.
6. 'Déclaration de Layrenie, garde nationale du bataillon de l'Ile Saint Louis, imprimée dans le recueil de 1792, sous le No. xxxviii bis; in *Hist Parl*, vol. 15, pp. 116–17.
7. Jean-Paul Bertaud, *Camille et Lucile Desmoulins* (1986), p. 170.
8. R.B. Rose, *The Making of the Sans-Culottes: democratic ideas and institutions in Paris, 1789–92* (Manchester, 1983), pp. 154–5.
9. Guilaine, *Billaud-Varenne*, pp. 62–3.
10. Abbé Ratel to d'Antraigues, 15 June 1792, Archivo Historico de Madrid, Fonds Estado: Lettres, mémoires, rapports concernant la contre-révolution, 1791–1795 (E 4999), Jacqueline Chaumié, *Le Réseau d'Antraigues et la Contre-Révolution, 1791–1793* (1965), p. 181.
11. Louis Mortimer-Ternaux, *L'Histoire de la Terreur: 1792–1794* (8 vols, 1863), vol. 1, pp. 132–3.
12. Frédéric Braesch, *La Commune du dix août* (1911), pp. 46–7.
13. *PD*, nos. 146, 128, 143.
14. *CG*, 22 June 1792.
15. *APL*, 25 June 1792.
16. 'Fragments des Mémoires de Charles-Alexis Alexandre sur les journées révolutionnaires de 1791 et 1792', *AHRF* 24 (1953), p. 170.
17. Pétion, *Conduite tenue par M. le maire sur l'occasion des événements du 20 Juin* (n.d.), p. 3.
18. Alexandre, 'Fragments des Mémoires', p. 170.
19. Pétion to the Department of Paris authorizing the march in his *Conduite*, pp. 3–4; and Alexandre, 'Fragments', p. 172.
20. P.L. Roederer, *Chronique de Cinquante Jours du 20 juin au 10 août* (1832), pp. 19–20.
21. Assembly, 20 June 1792, *LM*, pp. 714–16.
22. Jacobins, 18 June 1792, *Débats*, no. 217.
23. Jacobins, 19 June 1792, ibid, no. 218.
24. *Tribune*, no. 4.
25. Proceedings and petitions from the sections of Tuileries, Louvre and *faubourg* Montmartre in BN nouv. acq. franç., 2646; Petitions from Palais Royal, Quatre Nations, Luxembourg and Mauconseil in BN nouv. acq. franç., 2667.
26. *Pétition de plusieurs citoyens du faubourg Saint-Marcel en faveur de Pétion, Maire de Paris* (1792); P. Bardin, *Pétition à tous les départements du royaume* (1792).
27. Braesch, *Commune*, pp. 80–9.
28. Jacobins, 27 May, 1 June 1792, Aulard, *Société*, vol. 3, pp. 617, 639. The official *Journal des débats* does not provide a list of names either.
29. Ibid., pp. 32–3.
30. *Hist Parl*, vol. 17, pp. 243–9.
31. Assembly, 1, 3 July 1792 *LM*, vol. 13, pp. 3, 10–11.
32. *APL*, 1 July 1792.
33. *Tribune*, no. 4.
34. *Discours de M. Billaud-Varenne sur notre situation actuelle et quelques mesures à prendre pour assurer le salut public* (1792).

35. *Opinion de J.M. Collot d'Herbois sur les coupables démarches du Général Lafayette* (1792).

36. AN AD xl 14 1. 60, p. 37, in Alexandre Tuetey, *Répertoire général des sources manuscrites de l'histoire de Paris pendant la Révolution Française* (10 vols, 1890–1914), vol. 4, no. 1139.

37. *LM*, vol. 13, 3, 4 July 1792, pp. 32–6, 43–4.

38. Condorcet, 'Opinion sur les mesures générales propres à sauver la Patrie des dangers imminents dont elle est menacée, prononcée . . . le 6 juillet 1792' (Paris, Imprimerie nationale, 1792).

39. Guadet, Gensonné and Vergniaud to Boze, 17 July 1792, AN W 292, Interrogation of Gensonné. This letter was published by Gensonné after he was accused by Gasparin at the Convention, 3 January 1793, in A. Mathiez, 'Les Girondins et la Cour à la veille du 10 août', *AHRF* 8 (1931), p. 200.

40. Barbaroux to the municipality of Marseilles, 18 July 1792, *Mémoires*, p. 211.

41. Assembly, 9 July, *LM*, vol. 13, p. 87.

42. Brissot, 'Discours pour alonger la discussion et dans l'espérance de déterminer le ministère congédié', in *AP*, vol. 11, pp. 161–3.

43. Vergniaud to Louis XVI, 29 July 1792, in Mathiez, 'Les Girondins', pp. 207–8.

44. *PF*, 1 August 1792.

45. Mathiery, 'Les Girondins', p. 206.

46. Pierre René Choudieu, *Mémoires et Notes*, V. Barrucand (ed.) (1897), p. 221.

47. *Débats*, 20 July 1792; Jacobins, 29 July 1792, Robespierre, *Oeuvres*, vol. 8, pp. 413–14.

48. The Reunion club was composed of deputies from the Legislative Assembly, and may have come into being in late June, although Mitchell thought it began earlier. He maintained that those who prefer the later date believe the Reunion club arose out of serious divisions at the Jacobins and served as a kind of breakaway club made up entirely of 'Brissotins'. Mitchell argued that this was not true. See C.J. Mitchell, 'Political Divisions within the Legislative Assembly of 1791', *FHS*, no. 2 (Spring, 1984), pp. 381–3. There is no complete list of members of this rather obscure club; however, Mitchell had compiled a list based upon contemporary sources. Included in this list were: Brissot, Chabot, Fauchet, Ducos, Gensonné, Isnard, Lasource, Antonelle, Basire, Condorcet, Jean Debry, Guadet, Merlin, Cambon, Choudieu. Mitchell, *The French Legislative Assembly* (Leiden, 1991), pp. 241–2.

49. Jacobins, 1 August 1792, *Société*, vol. 4, pp. 165–6.

50. *Débats*, no. 232.

51. Ibid., 29 July 1792.

52. The *commission extraordinaire* was one of the more important committees of the Legislative Assembly. Until Mitchell's recent study, the work of this commission has been neglected by historians of the French Revolution. Aulard provides information in his *Recueil des Actes du Comité de Salut Public (10 août–21 janvier 1793)* (28 vols, 1889–1964), vol. 1, pp. xlix–lii; while Braesch cites it in a reference to Chaumette's proceedings of the Commune after 10 August. See Braesch, *Commune*, p. 399.

53. *Recueil*, vol. 1, p. xlix.

54. Assembly, 24, 25 July 1792, *LM*, vol. 13, pp. 228, 235.

55. *Recueil*, vol. 1, p. xlix; Assembly, 18 June 1792, cited in Vatel, *Vergniaud*, vol. 1, p. 129; Assembly, 3 August 1792, *LM*, vol. 13, p. 333; *CP*, 5 August 1792.

56. Mitchell, *French Legislative Assembly*, pp. 101, 304–19; *CP*, 9 August 1792.

57. *AmP*, 2 August, 8 July 1792.

58. 'Le Jugement dernier', in Braesch, *Commune*, p. 143.

59. Jacobins, 8 July 1792, *Débats*, no. 230, and 15 July 1792, *Hist Parl*, vol. 16, pp. 121–4.

60. Aulard, *Société*, vol. 4, pp. 81, 93, 95.

61. The text of the Cordelier club sessions of 15–16 July 1792 is found in MSS Barthélemy Saint-Hilaire, Bibliothèque Victor Cousin, BVC, Rég. 1.

65. *RP*, vol. 13, pp. 208–10.

62. *Débats*, 31 July 1792.

63. Jacobins, 29 July 1792, *Hist Parl*, vol. 16, pp. 218–30.

64. *CG*, 26 July 1792.

65. Petition, 17 July, AN C 154 no. 294, in *LM*, vol. 13, p. 170; Petition, 23 July 1792, AN DXL 17; Address, 2 August 1792, AN D XX 7, in Tuetey, *Répertoire*, vol. 4, nos 85, 1320, 12. *LM*, vol. 13, pp. 317–18.

66. *PD*, nos. 150, 164 bis.

67. Jacobins, 18, 20 July 1792, *Société*, vol. 4, pp. 111–12, 119.

68. Archives de le Préfecture de Police, C. 100. I. 22, printed in Braesch, *La Commune*, p. 152.

69. Braesch, *La Commune*, p. 156.

70. Louvet to Brissot, 3 August 1792, AN 446 AP Carton 7; *Sentinelle*, no. 45, 8 August 1792.

71. 'Lettre adressée à Messieurs le maire et administrateurs de la ville de Paris', in Mortimer-Ternaux, *Terreur*, vol. 2, p. 222.

72. Fournier l'Américain, *Mémoires Secrets* (1890), pp. 62–3. Carra, 'Précis historique et très exact

sur l'origine et les véritables auteurs de la
célèbre insurrection du 10 dernier, qui a sauvé
la république', *APL*, 30 November 1792;
Charles-Alexis Alexandre, 'Fragments des
Mémoires de Charles-Alexis Alexandre sur les
journées révolutionnaires de 1791 et 1792',
AHRF 24 (1952), p. 200.

73. Choudieu, *Mémoires*, p. 200, n. 11.
74. Fournier, *Mémoires*, pp. 62–3.
75. *Journal des hommes du 14 juillet*, no. 25,
    8 August 1792.
76. Carra, 'Précis historique'.
77. Choudieu, *Mémoires*, p. 128.
78. *APL*, 4 August 1792.
79. Barbaroux's signature was on a petition in
    favour of dethronement on 25 July. Tuetey,
    Répertoire, vol. 4, no. 1970.
80. Barbaroux, *Mémoires*, pp. 466–71. Vaugeois was
    president of the central committee of the *fédérés*.
    Albert Mathiez, 'Gabriel Vaugeois, l'organisation
    du 10 août', *AR* 3 (1910), p. 584.
81. Barbaroux, *Mémoires*, pp. 480–1.
82. Carra, 'Précis'.
83. Barbaroux, *Mémoires*, pp. 482–3.
84. *Les Députés des Bouches-du-Rhône à la Convention
    Nationale à Marat* (1792).
85. *Discours sur la nécessité d'un camp de citoyens dans
    les murs de Paris* (1792).
86. 'Notes de Topino LeBrun', juré au tribunal
    révolutionnaire, Procès de Danton, session of
    14 Germinal an II (13 April 1794), in J.F.E.
    Robinet, *Danton, Homme d'Etat* (1889), p. 451.
87. 'Fragment du journal de Lucile Duplessis', BHVP,
    Papiers Desmoulins, MSS 989, fols 181–4.
88. Braesch, *Commune*, p. 147–8.
89. Victor Fournel, 'Fabre d'Eglantine le comédien,
    l'auteur dramatique et le révolutionnaire', *RQH*
    54 (juillet 1893), p. 195.
90. Hampson, *Danton*, pp. 72–3; Frédéric Bluche,
    Danton (1984), pp. 176–7.
91. Choudieu, *Mémoires*, pp. 124–7.
92. Guadet to Berthoumieu Meynot, 14 August
    1792, Joseph Guadet, *Les Girondins, leur vie
    privée, leur vie publique, leur proscription et leur
    mort* (2 vols, 1861), vol. 1, p. 382. In a footnote
    concerning the source of this letter, Joseph
    Guadet, nephew of the deputy, wrote that the
    letter is in the 'archives de la commission
    militaire de Bordeaux, dossier Saint-Brice
    Guadet'. It was written to Berthoumieu Meynot,
    childhood friend of Guadet; p. 381, n.
93. Pétion, 'Pièces intéressantes pour l'histoire,
    servant à constater les principaux événements

qui se sont passés sous le Mairie de Paris' in
Mortimer-Ternaux, *Terreur*, vol. 2, p. 221.
94. *Pétion, maire, Pétition de la commune de Paris à
    l'assemblée nationale sur la déchéance du roi*
    (1792).
95. 'Réponse de Maximilien Robespierre à Jérôme
    Pétion', in *Oeuvres*, vol. 5, p. 104.
96. Jacobins, 8 August 1792, *Débats*, no. 246.
97. Gershoy, *Barère*, pp. 122–4.

5. New Conflicts

1. Braesch, *Commune*, pp. 245–63, 272.
2. *Sentinelle*, nos 46, 49: 12, 17 August 1792.
3. Aulard, *Receuil*, vol. 1, p. liii; *AP*, vol. 48, p. 76.
4. Assembly, 10 August 1792, *LM*, vol. 13, p. 382.
5. Brissot, *Projet de déclaration de l'Assemblée
   Nationale aux puissances étrangères* (1792), p. 5.
6. Assembly, 13 August 1792, *AP*, vol. 48,
   pp. 94–7.
7. Assembly, 11–13 August 1792, ibid., vol. 48,
   pp. 33, 69, 78, 93.
8. Jacobins, 10 August 1792, *Société*, vol. 4,
   p. 193.
9. Convention, 5 November 1792, *LM*, vol. 14,
   p. 394.
10. *AP*, vol. 48, pp. 24, 376; Assembly, 12 August
    1792, ibid., p. 79.
11. Brissot's statement at the session of 7 brumaire,
    'Procès des Girondins', *Hist Parl*, vol. 30, p. 84.
12. Danton to Brissot, 30 August 1792, AN 446 AP 7.
13. Condorcet, 'Fragment de Justification', *Oeuvres*,
    vol. 1, p. 602.
14. C. Perroud, 'Roland et la presse subventionée',
    RF 62 (1912), p. 318; *Hist Parl*, vol. 19,
    pp. 336–7.
15. Ibid., pp. 181–2.
16. Jacob, *Fabre*, p. 130.
17. See letters from Servan and Pache to Fabre,
    dated 15 September and 14 December 1792, in
    ibid., pp. 139–40.
18. Pierre Caron, *La Première Terreur* (1950), p. 8.
19. *Mémoires*, vol. 1, pp. 97–8.
20. Caron, *Première Terreur*, pp. 16–20.
21. Buzot, *Mémoires sur la Révolution française*
    (1828), p. 88.
22. *APL*, 18 September 1792.
23. Momoro's report to Danton from Bernay,
    8 September 1792, published in *RP*, no. 166,
    pp. 479–83.
24. Buzot, *Mémoires*, p. 88, n. 1.
25. AN C 179 doss. 54, fol. 25, in Caron, *Première
    Terreur*, pp. 71–2.

26. The commissioners in question were Dufourney and Sentex, appointed on 29 August, who arrived in Rouen on 5 September and spent four days there. AN F7 4394 1, in Caron, *Première Terreur*, pp. 16–17, 105.

27. *AP*, 14 September 1792, vol. 49, pp. 647–8.

28. *LM*, vol. 13, p. 797.

29. Roland's Circular, AN AD I, 89, in Caron, *Première Terreur*, p. 116.

30. *PF*, 28 August 1792.

31. Girey-Dupré's letter to the Provisional Commissioners of the Commune, *CP*, 2 September 1792.

32. 'Travaux de la commission des douze. Objet de ses rapports', in Vatel (ed.), *Vergniaud*, p. 137; Assembly, 30 August 1792, *LM*, vol. 13, pp. 585–6.

33. *FP*, 31 August 1792, in Braesch, pp. 448–9. Braesch, *Commune*, wrote that *Le jugement dernier* was not anonymous as Robespierre claimed, but was signed by 'Fr. August Becquevillier, citoyen actif', and both libels attacked only Robespierre and not the Commune, as they were written before 10 August and thus predate its existence.

34. *APL*, 2 September 1792.

35. Assembly, 30–1 August 1792, *Hist Parl*, vol. 17, pp. 166–8.

36. Couthon, 1 September 1792, *Correspondance*, pp. 187–8.

37. *Adresse des représentants de la Commune de Paris à leurs concitoyens* (Paris, J. Duplain, n.d.).

38. Procès-verbaux of the Commune in Barrière (ed.), *Mémoires sur les Journées de Septembre* (1858) pp. 249–50.

39. *Mémoires de Louvet*, Berville et Barrière (eds) (1825), p. 43.

40. Chèvremont, *Marat*, vol. 2, p. 96; Mortimer-Ternaux, *Terreur*, vol. 3, p. 205.

41. At Danton's trial, one of the charges brought against him was that he had opposed Robespierre's attempt to prevent Brissot from 'renewing his plots'. See Robespierre's notes for Saint-Just's report published by Mathiez, *Etudes sur Robespierre* (1951), pp. 137–8.

42. Robespierre, *Oeuvres*, vol. 8, p. 458, n. 8. 'Notes' by Robespierre for Saint-Just's report on Danton, published in Mathiez, *Etudes*, p. 137.

43. Assembly, 4 September 1792, *LM*, vol. 13, p. 617.

44. Fabre d'Eglantine, 'Tribunal Révolutionnaire, Procès de Girondins', *Hist Parl*, vol. 30, p. 84.

45. Pierre Caron, *Les Massacres de Septembre* (1935), pp. 233–4.

46. *Discours de Danton*, ed. A. Fribourg (1910), p. 173.

47. *FP*, 3 September 1792.

48. The section does not name Billaud, but simply provides a summary of the Commune's decision to ask the Assembly to name four commissioners to go to the Abbaye prison to seize its registers, save the debtor prisoners and massacre the rest. Cited in Mortimer-Ternaux, *Histoire de la Terreur*, vol. 3, p. 479.

49. Jacob, *Fabre*, p. 133.

50. *Hist Parl*, vol. 17, pp. 432–3. *Compte Rendu au peuple souverain*, no. 7, September 1792.

51. *JRF*, 6 October 1792.

52. *CG*, 18, 29 August 1792. M. Dorigny, 'Violence et révolution: Les Girondins et les massacres de septembre', in Albert Soboul (ed.), *Actes du Colloque Girondins et Montagnards* (1980), p. 115.

53. Madame Roland to Bancal, 2 September 1792, *Lettres*, vol. 2, p. 433.

54. Ibid., pp. 434, 436.

55. J.M. Roland, *Lettre . . . à l'Assemblée Nationale*, 3 September 1792 (1792), p. 8.

56. 'Le ministre de l'intérieur aux Parisiens', 13 September 1792, *LM*, vol. 13, pp. 673–4.

57. *CP*, 4 September 1792.

58. *PF*, 3, 4, 7 September 1792.

59. *CG*, 2, 5, 12 September 1792.

60. Ibid., 5, 12 September 1792.

61. *APL*, 4, 5 September 1792.

61. Couthon, 4, 8 September 1792, *Correspondance*, p. 189.

62. *Sentinelle*, 8 September, 6 November 1792.

63. *Procès-verbaux de la Commune*, pp. 286–7.

64. *Hist Parl*, vol. 17, p. 365.

65. *Sentinelle*, 21 August 1792; *Aux Electors. Supplément intéressant à liste de la Sentinelle*, E. Charavay, *L'Assemblée Electorale* (2 vols, 1905), vol. 2, pp. 597, 600–1.

66. 'Liste des sujets démérritants proposés par l'auteur de *La Sentinelle*; 'Extrait de l'affiche de Marat' in Chèvremont, *Marat*, vol. 2, pp. 100–3.

67. *CG*, 6, 7 September 1792.

68. *AP*, vol. 47, p. 582 provides the results of the vote. Brissot, Vergniaud and Guadet all voted yes to indict Lafayette, while Condorcet and Gensonné did not cast a vote.

69. *Débats*, 24, 29 August 1792; Charavay, *L'Assemblée*, vol. 2, p. 99.

70. Hampson, *Robespierre*, provides a summary of the Paris elections to the Convention, pp. 127–30.

71. *Débats*, 24 August 1792.

72. Michael Reisch, 'The Formation of the Paris Jacobins: Principles, Personalities and Politics' (2 vols, State University of New York, Binghampton, Ph.D., 1975), vol. 1, p. 525, n. 42; Robespierre, *Oeuvres*, vol. 8, p. 459.
73. Charavay, *L'Assemblée*, vol. 2, pp. 8, 10–11, 31, 62, 70–2.
74. *PF*, 4 September 1792.
75. Hampson, *Robespierre*, p. 129. Elected deputies from Paris were Danton, Desmoulins, Collot, Billaud, Fabre, Robespierre, Marat, Manuel and Robert.
76. *APL*, 17 September 1792.
77. Louvet, *Mémoires*, vol. 1, p. 56.
78. *PF*, 19 September 1792.
79. Ibid., 20 September 1792.
80. Patrick, *Men*, pp. 176–8.
81. Jean Bariller, *François Buzot, Un Girondin normand* (Evreux, 1993), p. 154.
82. Gershoy, *Barère*, p. 125.
83. Curtis, *Saint-Just*, p. 32.
84. Léon Kammacher, *Joseph Fouché* (1962), p. 28.

6. *The French Republic*

1. P. Paganel, *Essai historique et critique sur la Révolution française* (3 vols, 1815), vol. 2, p. 11.
2. Convention, 24 September 1792, *AP*, pp. 124–5.
3. Monestier to Jacobins of Clermont-Ferrand, 11 October 1792, BN nouv. acq. franç., 6902.
4. Condorcet, 'Sur la nécessité de l'union entre tous les citoyens', in *Oeuvres*, vol. 12, pp. 217–20; *CP*, 26 September 1792.
5. Couthon, *Correspondance*, p. 151; Jacobins, 12 October 1792, Aulard, *Société*, vol. 4, pp. 379, 381.
6. *CP*, 20 October 1792.
7. Jacobins, 24 September 1792, Robespierre, *Oeuvres*, vol. 9, pp. 32–9.
8. *Débats*, 24 October 1792; Hampson, *Saint-Just*, pp. 79–80.
9. Barbaroux to his constituents, 13 October 1792, *Correspondance*, p. 217.
10. *FP*, nos 38, 82; 25 September, 10 November 1792.
11. *PF*, 11 November 1792.
12. Convention, 6 November 1792, *AP*, vol. 53, p. 249; *APL*, 26 October.
13. Jacobins, 24 September 1792, Aulard, *Société*, vol. 4, p. 323.
14. Convention, 21 September 1792, *LM*, vol. 14, pp. 5, 13.
15. *JRF*, no. 1, 21 September 1792.
16. Desmoulins' 'Phlegmatics' included Pétion, Barère, Rabaud, Condorcet, Lacroix and Vergniaud. *Tribune*, no. 25, 8 November 1792.
17. *JRF*, nos 20, 22; 14, 16 October 1792.
18. A. Aulard, *Histoire politique de la Révolution française* (2 vols, 1905), vol. 2, ch. 5; A. Mathiez, *Girondins et Montagnards* (1930), ch. 4.; G. Lefebvre, *Les Cours de Sorbonne: La Révolution française; La Convention* (2 vols, 1944–5), vol. 1, p. 272.
19. M.J. Sydenham, *The Girondins* (1961), p. 149.
20. See Appendix 5.
21. *AP*, vol. 55, p. 44.
22. See Appendix 4.
23. Convention, 25 September 1792, *LM*, vol. 14, p. 131.
24. Convention, 26 September 1792, *Hist Parl*, vol. 29, p. 141.
25. *PF*, 30 September 1792.
26. *CG*, 2 October 1792.
27. Gadolle remains a mysterious figure whose name appears on the report submitted by Brival against the Rolands. See the copy of Gadolle's letter to Madame Roland, 19 October 1792, in *Convention Nationale: Rapport fait par Brival au nom du comité de sûreté générale relativement aux papiers trouvés chez le citoyen Roland et inventionés par les commissaires de la Convention* (1793), p. 23.
28. Garat, *Mémoires sur la Révolution* (1795), p. 193.
29. Dotson, 'Jacobins', pp. 280–2; Reisch, 'Formation', vol. 1, p. 210.
30. Mitchell posits that the 'remarkable lack of knowledge about this club must be due at least in part to the long-established belief that the disagreement between Brissotins and future Montagnards was already far advanced and more worthy of study than their cooperation.' *French Legislative Assembly*, pp. 241–2.
31. *Débats*, 19, 23 September 1792, Aulard, *Société*, vol. 4, pp. 320–8.
32. Jacobins, 1 October 1792, Aulard, *Société*, vol. 4, p. 354.
33. Jacobins, 30 September 1792, ibid., pp. 352–3.
34. Mathiez, *Girondins*, p. 78.
35. Jacobins 23, 24 September 1792, Aulard, *Société*, vol. 4, pp. 327–8, 332, 335; *FP*, no. 37, 24 September 1792.
36. Ibid., 11 October 1792.
37. *Débats*, no. 282.
38. *RFB*, no. 13.
39. Jacobins, 12 October 1792, Aulard, *Société*, vol. 4, p. 378.

40. The circular is printed in *Débats*, 22–3 October 1792, and in Aulard, *Société*, vol. 4, 15 October 1792 , pp. 394–9.
41. AN 446 AP carton 11.
42. *PF*, 2, 8 November, Kennedy, *Jacobin Clubs: Middle Years*, p. 305.
43. See Appendix E in ibid., p. 415.
44. Jacobins, 5 October 1792, Aulard, *Société*, vol. 4, p. 360.
45. Jacobins, 12 October 1792, ibid., p. 379.
46. Aulard, *Société*, vol. 4, p. 404; vol. 5, p. 33.
47. *RFB*, no. 12, 17 October 1792.
48. Brissot, 'A tous les Républicains de France sur la Société de Jacobins', in *Hist Parl*, vol. 20, pp. 123–44.
49. *CG*, 27, 30 October 1792.
50. *RFB*, no. 24, 8 November 1792.
51. Aulard, 'Figures oubliées', *NR*, p. 361. Aulard remarked that the speech was 'well-known, and famous before it was delivered'.
52. Jacobins, 29 October 1792, Aulard, *Société*, vol. 4, pp. 442–6.
53. Convention, 5 November 1792, *LM*, vol. 14, pp. 390–2.
54. *CP*, 20, 26, 31 October, 6 November 1792; Badinter, *Condorcet*, p. 446.
55. Jacobins, 14 October 1792, Aulard, *Société*, vol. 4, p. 393.
56. Cited in Bowers, *Vergniaud*, p. 273.
57. Convention, 5 November 1792, *LM*, vol. 14, p. 396.
58. Jacobins, 5 November 1792, *Hist Parl*, vol. 20, pp. 234–5; *FP*, no. 79, 10 November 1792.
59. Jacobins, 5 November 1792, *Débats*.
60. *FP*, no. 80, 8 November 1792.
61. Jacobins, 7 November 1792, Aulard, *Société*, vol. 4, pp. 465–7.
62. 'Discours de Jérôme Pétion sur l'accusation intentée contre M. Robespierre', *LM*, vol. 14, pp. 428–9.
63. *CP*, 29 November 1792.
64. Condorcet to electors, September 1792, MS 864, fol. 309, Bibliothèque de l'Institut, cited in Badinter, *Condorcet*, p. 502.

7. *New Challenges to the Republicans*

1. Patrick, *Men*, Part 2.
2. Convention, 13 November 1792, *AP*, vol. 53, pp. 385, 395–6.
3. *PF*, 4 December 1792.

4. Ibid., 6 December 1792.
5. *LM*, 14 January 1793.
6. *PF*, 14 November 1792.
7. Badinter, *Condorcet*, pp. 515, 529–30.
8. Desmoulins used the term 'Mountain' to designate those who sat in the higher seats of the Convention, in *RFB* no. 25, 8 November 1792
9. Sydenham, *Girondins*, p. 138. Patrick disagreed with Sydenham, arguing that the proposal would not have been introduced had there not already been a good deal of support for it. Patrick, *Men*, p. 56.
10. See Appendix 6.
11. *TJ* 3, 4 January 1793.
12. 'Lettre de Maximilien Robespierre à MM. Vergniaud, Gensonné, Brissot et Guadet sur la souveraineté du peuple et sur leur système de l'appel du jugement de Louis Capet', in *Lettres à ses Commettants*, Deuxième série, no. 1, in *Oeuvres*, vol. 5, pp. 1–44.
13. *PF*, 3 January 1793.
14. *Discours contre la défense de Louis Capet, dernier roi des Français . . . prononcé la séance du 3 janvier 1793*, p. 1.
15. Convention, 15 January 1793, *AP*, vol. 57, pp. 128; 179–80; 314–16.
16. Ibid., pp. 152–53.
17. Convention, 15 January 1793, 28 December 1792, *AP*, vol. 57, pp. 92–3; vol. 56, pp. 18–22.
18. *PF*, 6 January 1793.
19. Couthon, 5 January 1793, *Correspondance*, p. 212; Jacobins, 6 January 1793, *FP*, 7 January 1793.
20. Madelin, *Fouché*, vol. 1, pp. 52–4.
21. Alison Patrick, 'Regicides and Anti-Regicides in January 1793: the Significance of Fouché's vote', *HS*, vol. 14, no. 55 (1970), pp. 341–60.
22. Henry Buisson, *Fouché, duc d'Otrante* (1968), pp. 72–4.
23. *Réflexions de J. Fouché (de Nantes) sur le jugement de Louis XVI* (1793), pp. 5–6.
24. Aulard, *Société*, vol. 4, p. 518; *PF*, 28 November 1792.
25. *PF*, 25 December 1792; *CG*, 3 December 1792.
26. Jacobins, 31 December 1792, Aulard, *Société*, vol. 4, p. 630.
27. *RP*, no. 181, *Hist Parl*, vol. 22, p. 361; *FP*, 27 December 1792.
28. *Débats*, 13 January 1793.
29. Robert wrote three speeches on the king's trial. He preferred a trial rather than immediate execution in his first speech, dated 7 November.

His second speech, although it rejected the referendum, recognized the reasons in favour of it. Finally, his third speech, written after 4 January, was much more radical and factional. In it, he depicted the Bordelais as having been royalists since the previous July. *Opinion . . . concernant le jugement de Louis XVI; Suite de l'opinion . . . sur le jugement et les crimes du ci-devant roi; Troisième opinion . . . sur le jugement de Louis Capet.*

30. *JF*, no. 54, 7 January 1793.
31. Jacobins, 21 December 1792, Aulard, *Société*, vol. 4, pp. 603–6.
32. For a detailed examination of Roland's subsidized press throughout the autumn of 1792, see C. Perroud, 'Roland et la presse subventionnée, *RF* 62 (1912), pp. 315–22, 396–419.
33. For example, see club debates in Aulard, *Société*, vol. 4, pp. 501–2, 514.
34. Circular, 9 January 1793, ibid., pp. 655–6.
35. Jacobins, 7, 12 December 1792, ibid., vol. 4, pp. 556, 577–8.
36. Kennedy, 'L'oracle des Jacobins des Départements: Jean-Louis Carra et ses Annales Patriotiques', in A. Soboul (ed.), *Actes du Colloque. Girondins et Montagnards* (1980), pp. 247–68.
37. *Jacobin Correspondance*, 1, 4, 6, 29 October, 1 November 1792.
38. Jacobins, 1 Janaury 1793, Aulard, *Société*, vol. 4, p. 635. Examples of letters from individual clubs included those from Villefranche which complained about the Paris electoral assembly choosing Marat over Priestley, and Brissot's expulsion. Noiret and Bordeaux were also displeased. Bordeaux had cut off its affiliation with Paris at the end of December. *CG*, 1 November 1792, *PF*, 14 November 1792, *Jacobin Correspondance*, 24, 29 November, 15, 27 December 1792. Marseilles was angry about denunciations made against one of its deputies, namely Barbaroux. *Journal des débats* (Marseilles), 13–22 December 1792, in Kennedy, *Marseilles*, p. 116.
39. Gorsas named Arles and Condillac-sur-Garonne and added there were several more holding the same opinion. *CG*, 13 January 1793. Again on 27 January, he reported that he continued to receive complaints from many societies. They had written to the Jacobins of Paris to convince them to 'return to their true principles'. Ibid., 27 January 1793.

40. Jacobins, 7 December 1792, Aulard, *Société*, vol. 4, p. 556.
41. On 28 September, the journal's printer, Anne-Félicité Colomb, received 250 *livres*, on 28 October 300 and on 1 November 30. See Perroud, 'Roland et la prese subventionée', p. 328.
42. Ibid., pp. 606, 610; *Débats*, 23 December 1792.
43. AN F7 4430, minutes of 1 December 1792; *Débats*, 11 December 1792.
44. Jacobins, 1 January 1793, Aulard, *Société*, vol. 4, p. 633.
45. Circular of 9 January 1793. Ibid., pp. 655–66.
46. *PF*, 3 January 1793.
47. Patrick maintains that his resignation was a reaction to the anxiety of the previous thirty-six-hour session. Patrick, *Men*, pp. 86–7; *LM*, vol. 15, pp. 242–3.
48. Convention, 16 January 1793; Gershoy, *Barère*, p. 145.
49. *Sentinelle*, no. 73, 21 November 1792.
50. The club voted on 23 January to exclude anyone who had voted for the referendum. *Débats*, 2–26 January 1793, in Kennedy, *Jacobin clubs*, p. 117.
51. *CG*, 6 February 1793.
52. Vergniaud to his sister, Madame Alluaud, Letter no. 146, January 1793, in Vatel, *Manuscrits*, pp. 166–7.
53. *PF*, 22 January 1793.
54. *Hist Parl*, vol. 20, pp. 405–11.
55. *PF*, 28 November 1792.
56. Excerpt from his speech of 13 December 1792, *Correspondance*, p. 209.
57. *PF*, 30 November 1792.
58. See Hampson, *Saint-Just*, pp. 87–92, for an analysis of Saint-Just's speech.
59. *MU*, 1 December 1792.
60. Convention, 12 February 1793, *Hist Parl*, vol. 24, pp. 263–74.
61. *JF*, no. 101, 25 February 1793; Jacobin Circular, 1 March 1793, Aulard, *Société*, vol. 5, pp. 51–6.
62. *APL*, 11 January 1793; *Débats*, 23 December 1792, 28 February 1793.
63. *Lettres à ses commettants*, in *Oeuvres*, vol. 5, pp. 283–90.
64. *FP*, 12 February 1793.
65. Cited in Albert Mathiez, *La vie chère et le mouvement social sur la Terreur* (1927), p. 141.
66. Ibid., p. 143.
67. 'Adresse au peuple français, telle qu'elle a été, adoptée par la Convention dans la séance du 23 janvier', in *LM*, vol. 15, p. 295. This address

was signed by Vergniaud, president; Bancal, Gorsas, Salle, Lesage and Dufriche-Valazé, secretaries.

68. Couthon to his constituents, 26 January 1793, *Correspondance*, p. 213.
69. Cited in Badinter, *Condorcet*, p. 533.
70. Members who voted on 4 January included Brissot, Guadet, Dubois-Crancé, Cambon, Defermon, Gensonné, Barère, Sieyès, Fonfrède, among others. Aulard, *Recueil*, vol. 1, pp. 389–91.
71. See Patrick's article, 'Committee of Public Safety', in *Historical Dictionary*, vol. 1, p. 209.
72. Aulard, *Recueil*, vol. 1, p. 444.
73. 'Rapport fait par Brissot, sur les dispositions du gouvernement britannique', *Hist Parl*, vol. 23, p. 63.
74. *PF*, 4 February 1793.
75. Aulard, *Receuil*, vol. 2, pp. 5, 8; vol. 1, p. 498; vol. 2, pp. 25, 28, 209, 254.
76. Convention, 1 February 1793, *Hist Parl*, vol. 24, pp. 200–4.
77. Barère, *Mémoires* (4 vols, Brussels, 1842–4), vol. 2, pp. 297–8.
78. *LM*, vol. 15, p. 391.
79. Ibid., pp. 423–4.
80. *PF*, 8 February 1793.
81. The societies which accused him of partiality were located in the Paris region: Beauvais, Versailles and Seine-et-Oise. Seine-et-Oise demanded an account of his behaviour. *CG*, 5 February 1793.

8. *The Disasters of March*

1. *Chronique du Mois*, March 1793, pp. 24–39; *PF*, 7 March 1793.
2. Brissot printed letters from the clubs of Chartres on 2 March and Cette on 19 March, in his newspaper. He continued his contact with the Bordeaux club, writing that a 'class of perfidious men' threatened a third revolution. This letter is printed in Brissot's *Correspondance*, pp. 336–7 and the manuscript is found in Archives Départmentales de la Gironde, 12 L 4: 'Société des Amis de la Constitution devenue les Amis de la Liberté et de l'égalité. Procès-verbaux des séances, juin 1791–octobre 1793', Session of 28 March 1793.
3. The circular had been suggested at the meeting of 8 February. The circular was dated 6 March. *Débats*, 8 February 1793.
4. Lajouski, a former inspector of manufactures, had been involved in the insurrection of

10 August and was a member of the Finistère section.
5. *Débats*, 2 March 1793.
6. *JF*, no. 107, 3 March 1793.
7. Ibid., no. 114, 10 March 1793; Aulard, *Société*, vol. 5, p. 74.
8. *CG*, 8 March 1793.
9. Robespierre, *Oeuvres*, vol. 9, pp. 295–9; *FP*, no. 193.
10. Aulard, *Société*, vol. 5, pp. 69–72.
11. *PF*, 8, 10 March 1793.
12. *Hist Parl*, vol. 25, p. 24.
13. *MU*, 9 March 1793.
14. *Hist Parl*, vol. 25, p. 23.
15. A.M. Boursier, 'L'émeute parisienne du 10 mars 1793', *AHRF*, no. 208 (avril–juin 1972), pp. 204–30.
16. Ibid., 9 March 1793.
17. *Hist Parl*, vol. 25, pp. 26, 29.
18. *PF*, 9 March 1793.
19. *TJ*, 12 March 1793.
20. Boyer-Fonfrède to the Bordeaux Jacobins, 19 March 1793, Archives Départmentales de la Gironde, 12 L 19.
21. *PF*, 14 March 1793; Convention, 10 March, *AP*, vol. 60, p. 60.
22. Aulard, *Société*, vol. 5, p. 73.
23. *CP*, 6 March 1793.
24. *PF*, 12 March 1793.
25. Printed in Mortimer-Ternaux, *Terreur*, vol. 6, p. 194.
26. *CG*, 19 March 1793.
27. Desfieux was president of the correspondence committee at this time and the leader of the radical section of the club. Jacobins, 8 March 1793, *CG*, 9 March 1793; Aulard, *Société*, vol. 5, p. 79.
28. *LM*, vol. 15, p. 704; Albert Soboul, *Les sans-culottes en l'an II* (1962), p. 523.
29. *Hist Parl*, vol. 25, pp. 30–1.
30. Ibid., p. 58.
31. *TJ*, no. 442, 17 March 1793.
32. Convention, 13 March 1793, *AP*, pp. 700, 702–5.
33. *FP*, no. 200, 14 March 1793.
34. *Hist Parl*, vol. 25, p. 99.
35. *FP*, no. 204, 18 March 1793.
36. Jacobins, 12 March, Aulard, *Société*, vol. 5, p. 85.
37. Ibid., pp. 87–8.
38. *CG*, 24 March 1793.
39. *Débats*, 14 March 1793.
40. Ibid., 14, 15 March 1793.
41. Aulard, *Société*, vol. 5, pp. 69–72.

42. *Débats*, 19, 24 February 1793.
43. *PRF*, no. 145, 15 March 1793.
44. Aulard, *Société*, vol. 5, p. 71.
45. The six secretaries at the time were Julien de Toulouse, Mallarmé, Charlier, Isnard, Guyton-Morveau and Grangeneuve. *AP*, vol. 59, pp. 681, 689.
46. Convention, 9 March 1793, *Hist Parl*, vol. 25, p. 22.
47. *FP*, no. 204, 18 March 1793; *Débats*, 20 March 1793.
48. Jacobins, 17 March 1793, Aulard, *Société*, vol. 5, p. 93.
49. *PRF*, no. 147, 19 March 1793.
50. Convention, 17 March 1793, *AP*, vol. 60, p. 261.
51. *PF*, 23 March 1793; 27 October 1793.
52. Miranda, originally from Venezuela, had captured Antwerp and commanded the siege of Maastricht. At the battle of Neerwinden, he commanded the weak left wing of the army which led to its defeat. Miranda wrote an extensive letter on this defeat to Pétion. He put the blame squarely on Dumouriez's shoulders, stating that Dumouriez had not communicated to him in the usual fashion before the battle, but he received his 'order by writing'. Miranda to Pétion, 21 March 1793, AN F^7/4774.70 Dossier Pétion.
53. Kennedy, *Marseilles*, p. 120; *CG*, 24, 27 March 1793.
54. *MU*, 23 March 1793.
55. *PRF*, 21 March 1793; Robespierre, *Oeuvres*, vol. 9, pp. 329–30.
56. *Débats*, 24 March 1793.
57. *CP*, 24 March 1793. It was printed in the *PF* 26 March, and in *LM* 25 March 1793.
58. *LM*, vol. 16, p. 35.
59. Arthur Chuquet, *La Trahison de Dumouriez*, (1891), pp. 131–2; Mortimer-Ternaux, *Terreur*, vol. 6, pp. 304, 485–90.
60. At the Convention on 22 March, Isnard had demanded a Committee of Public Safety. The result was the reorganization of the existing Committee of General Defence on 25 March. The members of this committee were Dubois-Crancé, Pétion, Gensonné, Guyton-Morveau, Robespierre, Barbaroux, Rhul, Vergniaud, Fabre, Buzot, Delmas, Guadet, Condorcet, Bréard, Camus, Prieur de la Marne, Desmoulins, Barère, Quinette, Danton, Sieyès, Lasource, Isnard, Cambacérès and Jean Debry. *LM*, vol. 15, p. 774; Aulard, *Recueil*, vol. 2, pp. 491–2, 514–15.
61. C. Parra Perez, *Miranda et la Révolution Française* (Caracas, 1989), p. 223. Miranda gave a full account of this meeting in the speech he had prepared to deliver to the Convention on 29 March. See 'Discours que le général Miranda se proposait de prononcer à la Convention nationale, le 29 mars dernier, le lendemain de son arrivée à Paris', in Vincente Davilla (ed.), *Archivo del General Miranda* (14 vols, Caracas, Ven., 1932), vol. 12, pp. 24–36.
62. Pétion to Miranda, 23 February, 13 March 1793 in ibid., vol. 13, pp. 64, 67; Miranda to Pétion, 21 March 1793, in, AN F^7/4774.70 Dossier Pétion. Miranda's letter is printed in his archive in vol. 13, pp. 114–17.
63. *PF*, 2 April 1793.
64. Robespierre, *Oeuvres*, vol. 9, p. 342.
65. *Hist Parl*, vol. 25, pp. 148–9.
66. Convention, 30 March 1793, *LM*, vol. 16, p. 8.
67. Jacobins, 31 March 1793, *Société*, vol. 5, p. 116.
68. *CG*, 5 April 1793.
69. Convention, 1 April 1793, *LM*, vol. 16, pp. 23–30; Hampson, *Danton*, pp. 106–7.
70. *LM*, vol. 16, p. 14.
71. Aulard, *Société*, vol. 5, p. 118. The circular of 26 March was signed by many unfamiliar names: Lafaye, vice-president, Brival, Jary, deputies, Deguainé, Gaillard, Fouquier-Tinville, Renaudin, secretaries. Ibid., pp. 102–7.
72. Convention, 2 April 1793, *MU*, 3 April 1793; *LM*, vol. 16, p. 35.
73. *MU*, 4 April 1793.
74. Boyer-Fonfrède to the Jacobins of Bordeaux, 28 March 1793, in Archives Départmentales de la Gironde, 12 L 19.
75. *PF*, 2 April 1793.
76. Convention, 3 April 1793, *LM*, vol. 16, pp. 52–5; *PF*, 5 April 1793.
77. *PF*, 15 March 1793.
78. Convention, 12 March 1793, *LM*, vol. 15, pp. 693–4.
79. Aulard, *Société*, vol. 5, pp. 83–4.
80. Convention, 12 March 1793, *AP*, vol. 60, p. 125; *PRF*, 20 March 1793; *Débats*, 20 March 1793.
81. *MU*, 28 March 1793; *Débats*, 3 April 1793.
82. *APL*, 5 April 1793.

9. *The Crystallization of Factions*

1. *PF*, 13 April 1793.
2. *Débats*, 10 April 1793.
3. Ibid., 12 April 1793.

4. This is the petition of 4 May 1793, Tuetey, *Répertoire* vol. 8, no. 2438; *AP*, vol. 54, p. 153.
5. See Appendix 7.
6. *PF*, 10 April 1793.
7. Convention, 8 April 1793, *MU*, 10 April 1793.
8. Ibid., 11 April 1793.
9. A new Committee of Public Safety was formed on 6 April 1793. It was composed of nine members, and was to deliberate in private to be more efficient than the Committee of General Defence which it replaced. The members of the first Committee of Public Safety were Danton, Barère, Delmas, Bréard, Cambon, Guyton-Morveau, Treilhard, Delacroix and Robert Lindet.
10. Convention, 10 April 1793, *LM*, vol. 16, p. 104.
11. *CG*, 13 April 1793.
12. *Hist Parl*, vol. 25, pp. 428–9.
13. Convention, 10 April 1793, *LM*, vol. 16, pp. 113–16.
14. These letters are printed in Perroud (ed.), *Correspondance*, pp. 314–19. Dumouriez and Brissot quarrelled over this issue when Dumouriez refused to release Miranda.
15. *J.P. Brissot sur la dénonciation de Robespierre, et sur l'adresse prêtée aux 48 sections de Paris* (1793).
16. *Réponse très succincte de Jérôme Pétion au long libelle de Maximilien Robespierre* (1793).
17. Convention, 12 April 1793, *Hist Parl*, vol. 25, pp. 428–9.
18. Convention, 2 April 1793, *AP*, vol. 61, pp. 96–7.
19. According to Calvet, a sort of 'central committee' had been in existence since January, formed by men from the Gravilliers section. Gensonné made a reference to it at the Convention on 14 January. *LM*, vol. 15, p. 142. Henri Calvet, 'Les origines du comité de l'évêché, *AHRF* 7 (1930), pp. 12–23.
20. For example, the sections of Mail, Arcis and Marais did so on 6 April. See *AP*, vol. 61, pp. 92–3; *Débats*, 5, 7 April 1793.
21. Jacobin circular, 5 April 1793, Aulard, *Société*, vol. 5, pp. 126–8; Jacobins, 3 April 1793, in Robespierre, *Oeuvres*, vol. 9, p. 370.
22. *CG*, 8 April 1793.
23. Convention, evening, 11 April 1793, *LM*, vol. 16, p. 126.
24. Convention, 13 April, ibid., p. 136; Convention, 12, 13 April 1793, *Hist Parl*, vol. 25, pp. 429–30; *LM*, vol. 16, pp. 150–1.
25. *PF*, 14 April 1793.
26. See Appendix 8.
27. *PF*, 15 April 1793.
28. The article is printed in the edition of 17 April, in the section, 'Paris, 16 avril', under the heading of 'William Johnson'. 'Tribunal Révolutionnaire', 24 April 1793, in *Hist Parl*, vol. 26, pp. 114–20.
29. AN W 269, no. 16 in Tuetey, *Répertoire*, vol. 8, no. 2355.
30. *PF*, 15 April 1793.
31. Paganel, *Essai*, vol. 1, p. 456.
32. *LM*, vol. 16, pp. 179–81. A list of items found in the packages is on p. 180. Some of them included a letter from the deputy J.B. Lacoste to his constituents in Cantal, Collot's denunciation of Roland, a letter by Desfieux, a pamphlet by Clootz against the Gironde, an address from Marseilles to the Convention, a pamphlet by Marat, dated 30 March, and documents from the Convention on the subject of Dumouriez's desertion and treason in Jacobin circulars dated 26 March and 5 April and in the *Point du Jour*, 10 April 1793.
33. Aulard, *Société*, vol. 5, pp. 156–66.
34. *PF*, 20 April 1793.
35. Ibid., 30 April 1793.
36. *Débats*, 28, 30 April, 1 May 1793.
37. Aulard, *Société*, vol. 5, pp. 140–9.
38. Ibid., p.149. Desfieux was acting president in Marat's absence. Coindre, Prieur, Dupeiret and Champertois were secretaries.
39. *Débats*, 16, 21 April 1793.
40. *PF*, 17 April 1793.
41. Robespierre, *Oeuvres*, vol. 9, p. 348.
42. Convention, 20 April 1793, *LM*, vol. 16, pp. 190–7.
43. Fabre d'Eglantine, 'Discours sur l'acte de la commune de Paris tendante à demander la retraite des 22 membres', in Charles Vellay (ed.), *Oeuvres politiques de Fabre d'Eglantine* (1914), p. 107. This speech was delivered to the club on 1 May 1793.
44. *PF*, 7 May 1793.
45. *Hist Parl*, vol. 26, pp. 400–1.
46. *JF*, No. 156, 22 April 1793.
47. *LM*, vol. 16, p. 73; Aulard, *Recueil*, vol. 2, p. 533; vol. 3, p. 305.
48. R.B. Rose, *The Enragés: Socialists of the French Revolution* (Melbourne, 1965), pp. 11–13.
49. *LM*, vol. 16, pp. 175–6.
50. Convention, 20 April 1793, *Hist Parl*, vol. 26, pp. 66–86.
51. Convention, 27 April 1793, *AP*, vol. 63, pp. 427–33.
52. Hampson, *Danton*, p. 112.

53. *RP*, no. 199, 27 April–4 May 1793.
54. *PF*, 3 May, 1793.
55. Mathiez, *Vie chère*, pp. 186–7.
56. *JP*, no. 121, 1 May 1793.
57. At the session of 2 May, Buzot remarked that at the 'formerly celebrated society, one only finds debtors and criminals. Less than thirty of its founders are members.' *LM*, vol. 16, pp. 271–2.
58. Convention, 3 May 1793, *Hist Parl*, vol. 26, pp. 343–7.
59. Aulard, *Société*, vol. 5, p. 180, *Débats*, 15 May 1793.
60. *PF*, 10 May 1793. *AP*, vol. 64, p. 336, n. 1.
61. *PRF*, no. 188, 7 May 1793.
62. *PF*, 9, 7 May 1793.
63. *Ibid.*, 20 May 1793.
64. *Lettre de Jérôme Pétion aux Parisiens* (1793), pp. 15–16.
65. *PF*, 15, 20 May 1793.
66. Ibid., 21 May 1793.
67. *PD*, no. 234.
68. Jacobins, 20, 24 May 1793, Aulard, *Société*, vol. 5, pp. 201–20.
69. See Appendix 7.

10. The Destruction of the 'Brissotins'

1. Daniel Guérin, *La Lutte des Classes sous la Première République* (2 vols, 1968), vol. 1, pp. 132–42.
2. Morris Slavin, *The Making of an Insurrection: Paris Sections and the Gironde* (Cambridge, Mass., 1986), p. 144. Slavin stresses that the insurrection was started by Varlet and Fournier. Calvet also supports the belief that it was this committee which directed the insurrection of 31 May. 'Les origines du Comité . . .', *AHRF* 7 (1930), p. 12.
3. On Barère's proposal, a Committee of Twelve was created to deal with the suspected plots against the Convention. Boyer-Fonfrède, Rabaut Saint-Etienne, Kervélegan, Mollévault, Bergoeing, St Martin, Vigée, Gomaire, Boileau, Larivière, Gardien and Bertrand were its members.
4. *Précis tracé à la hâte par le citoyen Rabaut-Saint-Etienne et chargé du rapport, au nom de la commission des Douze dont il était membre* (n.p., n.d.)
5. *PF*, 30 May 1793.
6. Robespierre, *Oeuvres*, vol. 9, p. 527.
7. Aulard, *Société*, vol. 5, pp. 217–18.
8. Pierre Caron, *Paris pendant la Terreur* (7 vols, 1910–78), vol. 5, pp. 246–7.
9. *LM*, vol. 16, p. 509.
10. L.S. Mercier, *Le Nouveau Paris* (1862), ch. 21, 'Le comité central de l'Evêché; Garat, *Mémoires* (1795), pp. 102–4.
11. F. Braesch (ed.), *Papiers de Chaumette* (1918), p. 180.
12. Vatel, *Vergniaud*, vol. 2, pp. 158–62. Ducos, who recorded the session of 31 May, wrote that the Convention believed it to be 'just and prudent' to praise the sections for their 'firm and wise behaviour during this day'. He added that the decree was suggested by Vergniaud. *CP*, 31 May 1793.
13. Tuetey, *Répertoire*, vol. 9, p. 90.
14. P.C.F. Daunou, *Mémoires pour servir à l'histoire de la Convention nationale* (n.p., 1841), p. 317; *LM*, vol. 16, pp. 530–1.
15. Barère, *Mémoires*, vol. 2, p. 92.
16. A.J. Gorsas, *Précis rapide des événements qui ont lieu à Paris dans les journées des 30 et 31 mai, et premier juin 1793* (1793). Gorsas is confused about the dates. He provides an account of the events of 2 June as well as 31 May and 1 June. The deputy Saladin's *Compte Rendu et déclaration à ses commettants sur les journées des 27 et 31 mai, 1er et 2 juin 1793* (1793), published immediately after the events, supports Barère's memoirs and Gorsas' account.
17. *LM*, vol 16, p. 537.
18. Convention, 2 June 1793, *LM*, vol. 16, p. 531.
19. The deputies put under house arrest were Gensonné, Vergniaud, Brissot, Guadet, Gorsas, Pétion, Barbaroux, Louvet, Buzot, Salles, Chambon, Biroteau, Rabaut St Etienne, Lasource, Lanjuinais, Grangeneuve, Lesage (Eure et Loir), Valazé, Douclet, Lidon, Lehardy, the members of the Committee of Twelve and the two ministers, Clavière and Lebrun. *LM*, vol. 16, p. 554.
20. Danton, 2 June in the Convention, in *Discours*, p. 472.
21. Convention, 2 June 1793, *AP*, vol. 65, pp. 706–7.
22. Barère, *Memoirs of Barère*, V. Payen-Payne (tr.) (4 vols, 1896), vol. 1, p. 78.
23. *AP*, vol. 65, p. 706.
24. Vatel, *Vergniaud*, vol. 1, p. 174; J. Pétion, 'Mémoires de Pétion', in C. Vatel (ed.), *Charlotte Corday et les Girondins* (3 vols, 1864–72), vol. 3, p. 478.
25. 'Aux citoyens Français sur la nouvelle constitution', written a few days after 2 June, in Condorcet, *Oeuvres*, vol. 12, p. 654.

26. Durand-Maillane, *Mémoires*, pp. 127–8.
27. *AP*, vol. 66, p. 7. This was not always carried out to the letter of the law. Lanjuinais protested to the Convention that he was being guarded by two policemen rather than by one. Tuetey, *Répertoire*, vol. 8, no. 3038.
28. Jacobins, 3 June 1793, Robespierre, *Oeuvres*, vol. 9, p. 544.
29. *AP*, vol. 66, p. 23.
30. Ibid., pp. 514–15. The address is printed on pp. 530–1.
31. Léonce Pingaud, *Jean Debry 1760–1835* (1909), p. 32.
32. This pamphlet is printed in Condorcet, *Oeuvres*, vol. 12, pp. 653–75.
33. Convention, 8 July 1793, *AP*, vol. 68, pp. 438–9.
34. Convention, 30 June 1793, ibid., vol. 67, p. 681.
35. Mortimer-Ternaux, *Histoire*, vol. 7, p. 549.
36. Claude Perroud, *La Proscription des Girondins* (Toulouse, 1917), pp. 50–1.
37. AN F7 4443. The names of deputies who signed this protest are reproduced by Mortimer-Ternaux, *Histoire*, vol. 8, pp. 541, 549–52.
38. Aulard, *Société*, vol. 5, pp. 270–1.
39. Convention, 10 June 1793, *AP*, vol. 66, pp. 253–6; *APL*, 12 June 1793.
40. *AP*, vol. 66, pp. 280, 537, 595, 642–5.
41. Pétion, *Mémoires*, Dauban (ed.) (1866), p. 126; Meillan, *Mémoires de Meillan; Collection des Mémoires relatifs à la Révolution française* (65 vols, 1821), vol. 48, p. 85.
42. *AP*, vol. 68, p. 137.
43. Brissot to the Convention, 10 June 1793 in AN W 292B, no. 204, 'Affaire des Girondins', 1ère partie.
44. Convention, 12 June 1793, *AP*, vol. 66, pp. 449–50.
45. According to Barère, Danton was the first to offer himself as a hostage and he first suggested this at the Committee's meeting on 3 June. Barère, *Memoirs*, vol. 1, p. 79.
46. *AP*, vol. 66, pp. 480–3.
47. Robespierre's speech is dated 24 June, the date that Pétion's escape was revealed to the Convention. Ibid., vol. 67, pp. 136–7; Robespierre, *Oeuvres*, vol. 9, pp. 590–3.
48. *APL*, 25 June 1793; *AP*, vol. 67, p. 136.
49. *AP*, vol. 66, pp. 482, 484.
50. Aulard, *Société*, vol. 5, pp. 235–41.
51. Robespierre, *Oeuvres*, vol. 9, p. 559.
52. Jacobins, 16 June 1793, Aulard, *Société*, vol. 5, p. 263.
53. Jacobins, 17 June 1793, ibid., p. 265.
54. Garat, *Mémoires*, pp. 240–2. Garat claims that Saint-Just was involved in them.
55. Jacobins, 12 July 1793, Aulard, *Société*, p. 300; *AP*, vol. 66, p. 496.
56. Tuetey, *Répertoire*, vol. 8, no. 3475; Mortimer-Ternaux, *Terreur*, vol. 8, pp. 466–7.
57. Tuetey, *Répertoire*, vol. 8, no. 3207; Louvet, *Mémoires*, vol. 1, p. 101. See Pétion, *Mémoires*, pp. 128–40, for an account of his escape to Normandy.
58. Barbaroux to Lauze Deperret, 15 June 1793, from Caen, in Mortimer-Ternaux, *Terreur*, pp. 468–9.
59. Barbaroux's letters are printed in *Correspondance*, pp. 367–404. Some of the originals are held at the BN, nouv. acqu. franç., 6140. Pétion's manuscript draft for a federalist state has been published by R. Brouillard as 'Fragment inédit des Mémoires de Pétion' in *Revue historique de Bordeaux et du Département de la Gironde*, vol. 35, no. 3/4 (1942), pp. 78–84.
60. Mortimer-Ternaux, *Histoire de la Terreur*, vol. 7, p. 557.
61. Vatel, *Manuscrits*, vol. 2, pp. 182–3.
62. Vergniaud's second letter is printed in ibid., vol. 2, pp. 190–1. Apparently, Robespierre, who had some connection with the *Moniteur*'s editor, did not want this letter published at all. The only newspaper which published the letter in its entirety was the *Républicain Français* in its issue of 6 June. Bowers and Vatel believe that the *Moniteur* was under Robespierre's scrutiny. See Bowers, *Vergniaud*, p. 417. Letters from the *Moniteur*'s editor, addressed to Robespierre, were found among his papers and are reproduced by Vatel. These letters were written in response to Robespierre's complaints that the *Moniteur* sometimes gave both sides of the story. The editor, defending himself, wrote: 'However, you must have remarked that the Moniteur has always reported much more fully the speeches of the Mountain than the others. I gave only a short extract from the first accusation that was made against you by Louvet, while I inserted your answer entirely.' Vatel, *Manuscrits*, vol. 2, pp. 192–3.
63. Convention, 6 June 1793, *AP*, vol. 66, pp. 101–2.
64. This letter was dated 16 June 1793 and is printed in Vatel, *Manuscrits*, vol. 2, p. 194.
65. *Pétion to the president of the Convention*, BN Lb 41.3059. His letter is printed in *AP*, vol. 66, pp. 122–3.

66. Meeting of the Committee of Public Safety, 5 June 1793, Aulard, *Recueil*, vol. 4, p. 452. The members present included Cambon, Danton, Guyton, Barère, Treilhard, Delacroix, and Ingrand from the Committee of General Security.
67. Convention, 6 June 1793, *AP*, vol. 66, pp. 111–12.
68. Convention, 8 June, Robespierre, *Oeuvres*, vol. 9, pp. 544–7.
69. This 'manifesto' was written from Caen and is published in Barbaroux, *Correspondance*, pp. 380–6.
70. See nos 223, 224 and 237, 21, 23 June; 8 July 1793 *PFR*.
71. Convention, 10 July, *AP*, vol. 69, p. 513.
72. *Journal de la Montagne*, 21 June 1793.
73. *PRF*, nos 223, 237 and 242, 21 June; 1, 14 July 1793.
74. Aulard, *Société*, vol. 5, pp. 291–2.
75. The new Committee of Public Safety was also composed of Gasparin, 178 votes, Couthon, 176, Hérault-de-Séchelles, 175, Thuriot, 155, Prieur de la Marne, 142, Saint-Just, 126 and Robert Lindet, 100. *AP*, vol. 68, p. 520.
76. Convention, 8 July 1793, *AP*, vol. 68, pp. 426–36. Saint-Just's report is also reprinted in *Oeuvres complètes* (1984), pp. 457–78.
77. Vergniaud's letter is printed in H. Wallon, *Histoire du Tribunal Révolutionnaire de Paris* (6 vols, 1880), vol. 1, pp. 357–8.
78. *Débats*, 10 July 1793.
79. Aulard, *Société*, vol. 5, pp. 294–6; Robespierre, *Oeuvres*, vol. 9, pp. 614–15.
80. *AP*, vol. 68, pp. 722–3.
81. Convention, 17 July 1793, ibid., vol. 69, p. 75.
82. *APL*, 18 July 1793. Barbaroux's letter to Deperret dated 7 July, had nothing to do with Marat. It was a letter of introduction for Charlotte Corday, indicating that Barbaroux was willing to help her get a pension for a former nun, now an *émigré* in Switzerland. He asked Deperret if he would get some 'papers from the Minister of the Interior and send them to me'. The letter is printed in *AP*, vol. 68, p. 720. There is no indication that Corday ever discussed her intention to kill Marat with any of the escaped deputies.
83. Aulard, *Société*, vol. 5, pp. 315–16; Robespierre, *Oeuvres*, vol. 9, p. 624.
84. *AP*, vol. 69, pp. 630–1.
85. Ibid., p. 630.
86. Convention, 28 July 1793, ibid., p. 631. Buzot, Brissot, Pétion, Gorsas, Barbaroux, Louvet and Guadet were declared traitors along with Salle, Bergeoing, Chasset, Fermon, Kervélegan, Larivière, Chambon, Lidon, Valady, Rabaut Saint-Etienne and Lesage de l'Eure.
87. Carra, 'A mes commettants', 2 June 1793, in *APL*, 4 June 1793; article on Paris, dated 6 June, in *APL*, 7 June 1793.
88. Ibid., 8, 28 June 1793.
89. Ibid., 22 June 1793; *JRF*, no. 219, 17 June 1793.
90. *AP*, vol. 69, p. 631
91. *APL*, 31 July 1793.
92. Ibid., 3 August 1793; *AP*, vol. 70, p. 133.
93. Ibid., vol. 66, p. 464.
94. Barère, *Memoirs*, pp. 310, 315.
95. 'Mémoire inédit de Gensonné composé pendant sa détention à la Conciergerie et remis à Talma', in Henri Chauvot, *Le Barreau à Bordeaux de 1775 à 1815* (1865), pp. 604–6.
96. *AP*, vol. 75, pp. 520–1.
97. See Appendix 9.
98. Villate was an agent of the Committee of Public Safety and a friend of Robespierre. When he was arrested on 9 Thermidor, to save his own head he presented himself as an enemy of Robespierre and friend of Desmoulins wanting to save the 'Brissotins'. Bertaud, *Desmoulins*, pp. 222–3, 229.
99. Hampson, *Danton*, p. 137.
100. See Postcript.

BIBLIOGRAPHY

Place of publication for books in English is London and for books in French Paris, unless otherwise stated.

MANUSCRIPT SOURCES

Archives Nationales AN 446 Archives Privées, Papiers Brissot
AN BB³73 Affaires criminelles, Justice Révolutionnaire
AN BB³80 Journées du 31 mai au 2 juin 1793
AN C 233 à 352 Minutes et pièces diverses pour la rédaction de procès-verbaux des séances. 1792–93
AN F⁷ 4774.70 Dossier Pétion
AN F⁷ 4432 Police générale
AN W 1–75, 268–434 Jurisdictions extraordinaires, Fonds des Tribunaux Révolutionnaires
Bibliothèque Historique de la Ville de Paris
MSS 807, Collection Etienne Charavay
MSS 986, Papiers Desmoulins
MSS 743–45, Section Papers
Bibliothèque Nationale (BN)
Manuscrits Français
Nouvelles acquisitions françaises (naf), 3531–3534, Collection Charles Deslys: Pièces sur la Révolution et Correspondances diverses
Naf 2633–2720, Collection des pièces historiques sur la Révolution française, composée principalement des papiers de différentes muncipalités de Paris
Naf 6902–6904, Registres des lettres écrites par Jean-Baptiste-Benoît Monestier du Puy-de-Dôme, membre de la Convention Nationale, 1792–1810
Naf 6140, Correspondance de Barbaroux, député à la Convention nationale, avec la muncipalité de Marseille, 1792–1793
Naf 6238–6244; 9532–9534, Papiers du ministère Roland de la Platière et de Madame Roland, légués par M.P. Faugère
Bibliothèque Victor Cousin
MSS Barthélemy Saint-Hilaire, Rég. 1
Archives Départementales de la Gironde
AJ 705 Fonds Bigot
Série L, Epoque Révolutionnaire
12 L 13–14 Jacobins of Bordeaux, Registre des procès-verbaux des séances, 1790–1793
12 L 19 Jacobins of Bordeaux, Correspondance Générale, 1790–an II

PRINTED PRIMARY SOURCES

Personal Papers and Collected Speeches

Barbaroux, C. *Correspondance et Mémoires de Barbaroux*, C. Perroud (ed.), Société de l'histoire de France, 1923

Brissot, J.P. *Correspondance et Papiers de Brissot*, C. Perroud (ed.), Picard et fils, 1912

Brouillard, R. (ed.). 'Dumouriez et les Girondins, Correspondance inédite de Gensonné', *RHB* 36 (1943), 35–47

Chaumette, Pierre-Gaspard. *Papiers de Chaumette*, F. Braesch (ed.), Siège de la société, 1908

Condorcet, Marie Jean Caritat de. *Oeuvres de Condorcet*, F. Arago and A. Condorcet O'Connor (eds), 12 vols, Firmin Didot, 1847–9

Couthon, Georges. *Correspondance inédite de Georges Couthon, 1791–1794*, F. Mège (ed.), Aug. Aubry, 1872

Danton, Georges. *Discours de Danton*, A. Fribourg (ed.), Siège de la société, 1910

Desmoulins, Camille. *Correspondance inédite de Camille Desmoulins*, Matton aîné, 1836

——. *Oeuvres de Camille Desmoulins*, J. Claretie (ed.), 2 vols, Charpentier, 1874

——. *Oeuvres de Desmoulins*, Ebrard, 1838

——. *Oeuvres de Desmoulins*, 3 vols, Marpon, 1865

Krebs, A. (ed.). 'Deux lettres de Boyer-Fonfrède au Club de Bordeaux', *AHRF* 21 (1949), 172–5

Lohrer, Jane. 'A letter of Brissot to Desmoulins', *JMH* 6 March–December 1934, 441–3

Marat, Jean-Paul. *Oeuvres Politiques, 1789–1793*, Jacques DeCock and Charlotte Goëtz (eds), 10 vols, Brussels, Pole Nord, 1995

Mercier, L.S. *Paris pendant la Révolution ou le nouveau Paris*, 2 vols, Poulet-Malasus, 1862

Miranda Francesco de. *Archivo del General Miranda*, Vincente Davilla (ed.), 14 vols, Caracas, Ven., Su-America, 1929–33

Pétion, J. *Oeuvres complètes*, 4 vols, Garnery, 1792–3

Robespierre, M. *Oeuvres complètes*, 10 vols, E. Leroux, 1910–67

Roland, Marie-Jeanne Philipon. *Lettres autographes de Madame Roland adressées à Bancal-Des-Issarts, membre de la Convention Nationale*, E. Renduel, 1835

——. *Lettres de Madame Roland*, C. Perroud (ed.), 2 vols, Imprimerie Nationale, 1900–2

Saint-Just, Louis Antoine de. *Oeuvres complètes*, Michèle Duval (ed.), G. Lebovici, 1984

Vermorel, A. (ed.). *Oeuvres de Vergniaud, Gensonné et Guadet*, Faure, 1867

Vatel, Charles, (ed.). *Charlotte Corday et les Girondins*, 3 vols, H. Plon, 1864–72

——. *Dossiers du Procès criminel de Charlotte De Corday devant le Tribunal Révolutionnaire*, Poulet-Malassis, 1861

——. *Vergniaud, Manuscrits, Lettres et Papiers*, 2 vols, J.B. Dumoulin, 1873

Proceedings of Revolutionary Assemblies and Collections of Documents

Archives Parlementaires 1787 à 1860, 82 vols, 1787–94, Librairie administrative de Paul Dupont, 1879–

Aulard, F. (ed.). *La Société des Jacobins*, 6 vols, Jouaust, 1889–97

——. *Receuil des actes du Comité de Salut public (10 août 1792–21 janvier 1793)*, 28 vols, Imprimerie nationale, 1889–1964

Barrière, F. (ed.). *Mémoires sur les Journées de Septembre*, Firmin-Didot, 1858

Buchez, P.J. and Prosper, C. (eds). *Histoire Parlementaire*, 40 vols, Paulin, 1834–48

Caron, Pierre. *Paris pendant la Terreur*, 7 vols, Picard, 1910–78

Chassin, C.L. *Les Elections et les Cahiers de Paris en 1789: documents recueillis*, 4 vols, Jouaust, 1888–9

Charavay, E. *L'Assemblée Electorale de Paris, 18 novembre 1790–12 août 1792*, 2 vols, Jouast, 1890–1905

Lacroix, Sigismund. *Actes de la Commune de Paris pendant la Révolution*, 16 vols, Cerf, 1894–1909

Mortimer-Ternaux, Louis. *Histoire de la Terreur: 1792–1794*, 8 vols, Michel-Lévy, 1863

Schmidt, Adolf. *Tableaux de la Révolution*, Leipzig, Veit, 1867–71

Tourneux, Maurice. *Bibliographie de l'histoire de Paris pendant la Révolution française*, Imprimerie nouvelle, 1890–1

——. *Procès-verbaux de la Commune de Paris (11 août 1792–1er juin 1793)*, Siège de la société, 1894

Tuetey, Alexandre. *Répertoire générale des sources manuscrites de l'histoire de Paris pendant la Révolution française*, 11 vols, Imprimerie nouvelle, 1890–1914

Newspapers

Almanach du Père Gérard, 1792
Amis des Citoyens, 1791–3
Ami du Peuple, 1789–93 (also entitled *Journal de la République Française* and *Publiciste de la République Française*, 1793)
Annales Patriotiques et Littéraires, 1789–93 (*Supplément* in the footnotes refers to a supplement of this newspaper)
Année Littéraire, 1772
Bouche de Fer, 1790–1
Chronique de Paris, 1789–93
Chronique du Mois, 1791–3
Courrier de Gorsas, 1789–93
Feuille de Paris, 1793
Journal Français, 1792–3
Journal de la Montagne, 1793
Journal de Paris, 1789–93
Journal des débats de la Société des Amis de la Constitution, 1791–3 (abbreviated to *Débats* in the footnotes)
Journal des hommes du 14 juillet, 1792
Journal Français, 1792–3
Journal de la Revolution, 1790–1
Mercure de France, 1772
Mercure National, 1789–91
Mercure Universel, 1791–3
Patriote Français, 1789–93
Père Duchesne, 1792
Point du Jour, 1789–91
Premier Jour de la Convention Nationale, ou le Point du Jour, 1792–3
Républicain ou le Défenseur du Gouvernement représentif, 1791
Révolutions de France et de Brabant, 1789–92
Révolutions de Paris, 1789–93
Réimpression de l'ancien Moniteur, 32 vols, Plon, 1858–63
Sentinelle, 1792
Thermomètre du Jour, 1791–3
Tribune des Patriotes, 1792

Revolutionary Pamphlets

Adresse des représentants de la Commune de Paris à leurs concitoyens, J. Duplain, n.d.
Convention Nationale: Rapport fait par Brival au nom du comité de sûreté générale relativement aux papiers trouvés chez le citoyen Roland et inventionés par les commissaires de la Convention, Imprimerie nationale, 1793
Histoire de deux célébrés législateurs du dix-huitième siècle contenant plusieurs anecdotes curieuses et intéressantes, Franklin, 1793
Les Députés des Bouches-du-Rhône de la Convention Nationale à Marat, n.p., n.d.
Pétition de plusieurs citoyens du faubourg Saint-Marcel en faveur de Pétion, maire de Paris, n.p., 1792
Point de banqueroute, n.p., 1787
Bardin, P. *Pétition à tous les départements du royaume*, Féret, 1792
Bergeoing, F. *Bergeoing, député de la Gironde et membre de la commission des douze à ses commettants et à tous les citoyens de la République*, Caen, LeRoy, 1793
Billaud-Varenne, J. *Despotisme des Ministres de France ou Exposition des principes et moyens employés par l'aristocratie pour mettre la France dans les fers*, 3 vols, Amsterdam, n.p., 1789
——. *Discours de M Billaud-Varenne sur notre situation actuelle et quelques mesures à prendre pour assurer le salut public*, Patriote Français, 1792

——. *Discours sur la nécessité d'un camp de citoyens dans les murs de Paris, prononcé à la séance du 3 août 1792*, Patriote Français, 1792

——. *Discours sur cette question: Comment doit faire la guerre au cas qu'il faille la déclarer?*, Patriote Français, 1791

——. *Le dernier coup porté aux préjugés et à la superstition*, n.p., 1787

Brissot, J.P. *De la France et des Etats-Unis, ou de l'mportance de la Révolution d'Amérique pour la bonheur de la France*, n.p., 1787

——. *De la Vérité*, Neuchâtel, Société Typographique, 1782

——. *Discours de J.P. Brissot sur la nécessité de déclarer la guerre aux princes allemands qui protègerent les ennemis*, Patriote Français, 1791

——. *J.P. Brissot à tous les républicains de France, sur la société des Jacobins de Paris*, Cercle Social, 1792

——. *J.P. Brissot . . . à ses commettants sur la situation de la Convention nationale, sur l'influence des Anarchistes et les maux qu'elle a causé, sur la nécessité d'anéantir cette influence pour sauver la République*, Prévost, n.d.

——. *J.P. Brissot sur la dénunciation de Robespierre, et sur l'adresse prêtée aux 48 sections de Paris*, Patriote Français, 1793

——. *Projet de déclaration de l'Assemblée Nationale aux puissances étrangères*, Imprimerie nationale, 1792

——. *Recherches sur la propriété et le vol*, Neuchâtel, Société Typographique, 1780

——. *Réponse à tous les libellistes*, Courrier de Provence, 1791

——. *Un mot à l'oreille des académiciens de Paris*, n.p., 1786

Carra, J.L. *Discours contre la défense de Louis Capet, dernier roi des Français . . . prononcé la séance du 3 janvier 1793*, Imprimerie nationale, 1793

——. *Discours sur la déchéance de Louis XVI, prononcé le 11 juillet à la tribune des Jacobins*, Imprimerie nationale, 1791

——. *L'Orateur des Etats-Généraux pour 1789*, n.p., n.d.

——. *M. de Calonne tout entier*, Brussels, n.p., 1788

Collot d'Herbois, J.M. *Adresse de la section de la Bibliothèque à l'Assemblée nationale*, Imprimerie nationale, n.d.

——. *Opinion de J.M. Collot d'Herbois sur les coupables démarches du Général Lafayette*, Patriote Français, 1792

——. *Rapport fait à la société le 26 juin en réclamation de justice pour quarante-un soldats du régiment de Châteauvieux*, Imprimerie nationale, 1791

——. *Rapport fait à la société le 6 juillet 1791 pour trente carabiniers, victimes d'une grande justice ordonnée par le général Bouillé à la suite de l'affaire de Nancy*, Baudoin, 1791

Condorcet, Jean-Antoine-Nicolas de Caritat, Marquis de. 'Opinion . . . sur les mesures générales propres à sauver la Patrie des dangers imminents dont elle est menacée, prononcée . . . le 6 juillet 1792', Imprimerie nationale, 1792

Courtois, J.B. *Rapport fait au nom de la commission chargée de l'examen des papiers de Robespierre et ses complices*, Imprimerie nationale, 1794

Desmoulins, Camille. *Discours sur le parti que l'Assemblée nationale doit prendre relativement à la proposition de guerre annoncée par le pouvoir exécutif*, Patriote Français, 1791

Fabre, D'Eglantine. *Le Philinte de Molière ou la suite du Misanthrope*, Prault, 1791

——. *Oeuvres politiques de Fabre d'Eglantine*, Charles Vellay (ed.), Charpentier, 1914

Fouché, J. *Réflexions de J. Fouché (de Nantes) sur le jugement de Louis XVI*, Imprimerie nationale, 1793

Fournier, (l'Américain). *Mémoires secrets*, Siège de la société, 1890

Gorsas, A.J. *Déclaration du sieur Gorsas au sujet des lettres de Beaumarchais citées dans la cause de M. Kornmann*, n.p., 1789

——. *Précis rapide des événements qui ont eu lieu à Paris dans les journées des 30–31 mai et le premier juin 1793*, Gorsas veuve, n.d.

Isnard, M. *Maxim Isnard à ses collègues*, Imprimerie nationale, 1793

——. *Proscription d'Isnard*, Isnard, 1795

Manuel, L.P. *Discours sur la guerre prononcé aux amis de la constitution*, Momoro, 1792

Pétion, J. *Conduite tenue par M. le maire sur l'occasion des événements du 20 juin*, Luttin, n.d.

——. *Discours . . . prononcé à la société le 29 avril 1792*, Patriote Français, 1792

——. *Lettre de Jérôme Pétion aux Parisiens*, Gorsas, 1793

——. *Les Lois civiles et l'administration de la justice ramenées à un ordre simple et uniforme*, n.p., 1782

——. *Pétion, maire, Pétition de la Commune de Paris à l'Assemblée Nationale sur la déchéance du roi*, P. Provost, 1792

——. *Réponse très succincte de Jérôme Pétion au long libelle de Maximilien Robespierre*, Gorsas, 1793

Rabaut Saint-Etienne, J.P. *Précis tracé à la hâte par le citoyen et chargé du rapport, au nom de la commission des Douze dont il était membre*, n.p., n.d.

Régnault-Warin, J.J. *Vie de Pétion, maire de Paris*, Bar-le-Duc, Duval, 1792

Robert, P.F.J. *Discours sur l'état actuel de la république par François Robert, député de Paris*, L. Pottier de Lille, 1792

——. *François Robert à ses frères de la société fraternelle et du club des Cordeliers*, n.p., n.d.

——. *Opinion . . . concernant le jugement de Louis XVI*, Imprimerie nationale, n.d.

——. *Suite de l'opinion . . . sur le jugement et les crimes du ci-devant roi*, Imprimerie nationale, n.d.

——. *Troisième opinion . . . sur le jugement de Louis Capet*, Vatar 1793

Robespierre, M. *Discours de M. Robespierre sur le parti que l'Assemblée Nationale doit prendre relativement à la proposition de guerre, annoncée par le pouvoir exécutif, prononcé à la Société des Amis de la Constitution, le 18 décembre 1791*, Patriote Français, 1791

Roland, J.M. *Lettre . . . à l'Assemblée Nationale, 3 September 1792*, Imprimerie nationale, 1792

Saladin, J.B.M. *Compte Rendu et Déclaration par J.B.M. Saladin, député du département de la Somme, sur les journées des 27, 31 mai, 1er et 2 juin 1793*, Imprimerie de Robert, n.d.

Memoirs

Alexandre, Charles-Alexis. 'Fragments des Mémoires de Charles-Alexis Alexandre sur les journées révolutionnaires de 1791 et 1792', Jacques Godechot (ed.), *AHRF* 24 (1953), 113–251

Bachaumont, Louis Petit. *Mémoires secrets pour servir à l'histoire de la république*, 36 vols, J. Adamson, 1777–89

Barère, Bertrand. *Mémoires*, Hippolyte Carnot et David d'Angers (eds), 4 vols, Brussels, Meline, 1842–4

——. *Memoirs of Barère*, V. Payen-Payne (tr.), 4 vols, H.S. Nichols, 1896

Baudot, Marc-Antoine. *Notes historiques sur la Convention Nationale, le Directoire, l'Empire et l'Exil des Votants*, 1893, Geneva, Slatkine-Megariotis Reprints, 1974

Billaud-Varenne, J. *Mémoires inédites et correspondances accompagnées de notices biographiques sur Billaud-Varenne et Collot d'Herbois*, Bégis, A. (ed.), Librairie de la nouvelle revue, 1893

Brissot, J.P. *Mémoires*, C. Perroud (ed.), 2 vols, Picard, 1912

Brouillard, R. (ed.). 'Fragment inédite des Mémoires de Pétion', *RHB* 35 (1942), 78–84

Buzot, F. *Mémoires sur la Révolution française*, Pichon, 1828

Choudieu, René. *Mémoires et Notes*, V. Barrucand (ed.), Plon, 1897

Daunou, P.C.F. *Mémoires pour servir à l'histoire de la Convention nationale*, n.p., 1841

Dumont, E. *Souvenirs sur Mirabeau et sur les deux premières Assemblées législatives*, Brussels, Hauman, 1832

Fournier, C. (l'Américain). *Mémoires secrets*, Siège de la société, 1890

Garat, D.J. *Mémoires sur la Révolution*, J.J. Smits, 1795

Louvet de Couvray, J.B. *Mémoires de Louvet*, Berville et Barrière (eds), *Collection des Mémoires relatifs à la Révolution française*, vol. 47, Baudouin, 1821–39

——. *Mémoires*, F. Aulard (ed.), 2 vols, Librairie des bibliophiles, 1889

Meillan, Arnaud Jean. *Mémoires de Meillan. Collection des Mémoires relatifs à la Révolution française*, 65 vols, Baudouin, 1821–39

Paganel, Pierre. *Essai historique et critique sur la Révolution française*, 3 vols, 2nd edn, Panckouke, 1815

Pétion, J. *Mémoires inédites de Pétion et Mémoires de Buzot et de Barbaroux*, C. Dauban (ed.), Plon, 1866

Roederer, P.L. *Chronique de cinquante jours du 20 juin au 10 août*, Lachervardière, 1832

Roland, Marie-Jeanne Philipon. *Mémoires de Madame Roland*, C. Dauban (ed.), Plon, 1864

——. *Mémoires*, C. Perroud (ed.), 2 vols, Plon, 1905

Sergent, 'Notice historique sur les événements du 10 août et des 20 et 21 juin précédents', *Revue Rétrospective*, seconde série III, 1835

Thibaudeau, A.C. *Mémoires sur la Convention et le Directoire*, 2 vols, Baudouin, 1864

SECONDARY SOURCES
Unpublished Works
Theses

Benn, T. Vincent. 'Bibliographie critique des ouvrages de L.S. Mercier', Leeds University, Ph.D., 1925
Carrothers, Wendell Weir. 'An Examination of the Relationship between General Dumouriez and the 'Girondins', March 1792–April 1793', Carleton University, M.A., 1981
Darnton, Robert. 'Trends in radical propaganda on the eve of the French Revolution (1782–1788)', Oxford, D.Phil., 1964
Dotson, Craig. 'The Paris Jacobin Club and the French Revolution', Queen's University, Kingston, Ph.D., 1974
Reisch, Michael. 'The Formation of the Paris Jacobins: Principles, Personalities and Politics', State University of New York, Binghampton, 2 vols, Ph.D., 1975
Walker, Barbara Anne. 'Collot d'Herbois: Revolutionary Dramatist', University of Calgary, M.A., 1976
Whaley, Leigh Ann. 'The Emergence of the Brissotins during the French Revolution', University of York, D.Phil., 1989

Conference Paper

Shapiro, Barry. 'Opting for the Terror? A Critique of Keith Baker's Analysis of the Suspensive Veto of 1789', Paper presented to the 26th annual conference of the Western Society for French History, 7 November 1998, Boston

Biographical Collections

Berthelot, Hartwig et al. (eds). *La Grande Encyclopédie*, 31 vols, H. Lamirault, 1886–1902
Kuscinski, A. *Dictionnaire des Conventionnels*, Siège de la société, 1916
Lemay, Edna Hindie. *Dictionnaire des Constituants*, 2 vols, Oxford, Voltaire Foundation, 1991
Michaud, J.F. and Michand, L.G. *Biographie universelle, ancienne et moderne*, 45 vols, reprint, Graz, Austria, 1966–70
Prévost, M., Balteau, J., Barroux, M. (eds). *Dictionnaire de biographie française*, 107 vols, Letouzey et Ané, 1933–93
Rothaus, Barry and Scott, Samuel F. (eds). *Historical Dictionary of the French Revolution*, 2 vols, Aldwych, 1985
Soboul, A. (ed.). *Dictionnaire Historique de la Révolution française*, Presses universitaires de France, 1989

Books

Arnold, Eric Jr. *Fouché, Napoleon and the General Police*, Washington, University Press of America, 1979
Atheunis, L. *Le conventionnel Belge François Robert (1763–1826) et sa femme Louise de Kéralio (1758–1826)*, Wetteren, Editions Bracke, 1955
Aulard, F.A. *Etudes et leçons sur la Révolution française*, Félix Alcan, 1910
——. *Histoire politique de la Révolution française*, 3rd edn, 2 vols, Colin, 1905
Badinter, Elisabeth and Badinter, Robert. *Condorcet. Un intellectuel en politique*, Fayard, 1988
Baker, Keith (ed.). *The French Revolution and the creation of Modern Political Culture: The Political Culture of the Old Regime*, 4 vols, Oxford, Pergamon Press, 1987–94
Bariller, Jean. *François Buzot, Un Girondin normand, 1760–1794*, Evreux, Société libre de l'Eure, 1993
Béclard, L. *Sébastien Mercier, sa vie, son oeuvre, son temps*, H. Champion, 1903
Bertaud, Jean-Paul. *Camille et Lucile Desmoulins*, Presses de la Renaissance, 1986
Biard, Michel. *Collot d'Herbois*, Lyon, Presses Universitaires de Lyon, 1995
Biré, E. *La Légende des Girondins*, new edn. Perrin et cie, 1896
Bluche, Frédéric. *Danton*, Perrin, 1984
Bornarel, F. *Cambon et la Révolution française*, Alcan, 1905
Bouchary, Jean. *Les manieurs d'argent à Paris à la fin du XVIIIe siècle*, 2 vols, M. Rivière, 1939
Bourdin, Isabelle. *La société de la section de la Bibliothèque*, Receuil Sirey, 1937

——. *Les sociétés populaires à Paris, pendant la Révolution*, Recueil Sirey, 1937

Bowers, Claude G. *Pierre Vergniaud, voice of the French Revolution*, New York, Macmillan, 1950

Brace, Richard Munthe. *Bordeaux and the Gironde*, Ithaca, Cornell University Press, 1947

Bradby, E.D. *The Life of Barnave*, 2 vols, Oxford, Clarendon Press, 1915

Braesch, Frédéric. *La Commune du dix août*, Hachette, 1911

Brébisson, Jean de. *Fouché, duc d'Otrante*, Gabriel Beauchesne, 1906

Bruun, Geoffrey. *Saint-Just, apostle of the terror*, Hampden, Conn., Archon Books, 1966

Buisson, Henry. *Fouché, duc d'Otrante*, Bienne, Suisse, Panorama, 1968

Butel, Paul, Pousseau, Jean-Pierre. *La vie quotidienne à Bordeaux au XVIIIe siècle*, Hachette, 1980

Caron, Pierre. *La Première Terreur*, Presses universitaires de France, 1950

——. *Les Massacres de Septembre*, Maison du livre français, 1935

Castlelot, André. *Fouché, le double jeu*, Perrin, 1990

Chaumié, Jacqueline. *Le Réseau d'Antraigues et la contre-révolution, 1791–1793*, Plon, 1965

Challamel, A. *Les clubs contre-révolutionnaires: cercles, comités, sociétés, salons, réunions, cafés*, Cerf, 1895

Chauvot, Henri. *Le Barreau à Bordeaux de 1775 à 1815*, Durand, 1856

Chevremont, F. *Jean Paul Marat*, 2 vols, Chevremont, 1880

Claretie, Jules. *Camille Desmoulins. Lucile Desmoulins. Etude sur les Dantonistes*, Plon, 1875

Chuquet, Arthur. *La Trahison de Dumouriez*, Cerf, 1891

Cole, Herbert. *Fouché: The Unprincipled Patriot*, Eyre & Spottiswoode, 1971

Conner, Clifford, D. *Jean-Paul Marat. Scientist and Revolutionary*, Atlantic Highlands, N.J. Humanities Press, 1997

Conte, Arthur. *Billaud-Varenne: géant de la Révolution*, O. Orban, 1989

Coutura, Johell. *Les Francs-Maçons de Bordeaux au 18e siècle*, Marcillac, Reignac, Editions du Glorit, 1988

Crépel, Pierre. *Colloque International, Condorcet*, Minerve, 1989

Curtis, E.N. *Saint-Just*, New York, Columbia University Press, 1935

Darnton, Robert. *The Corpus of Clandestine Literature in France, 1769–1789*, New York, W.W. Norton, 1995

——. *The Forbidden Best-sellers of Pre-revolutionary France*, New York, W.W. Norton, 1995

——. *The Literary Underground of the Old Regime*, Cambridge, Mass., Harvard University Press, 1982

——. *Mesmerism and the end of the Enlightenment in France*, Cambridge, Mass., Harvard University Press, 1968

Dauban, C.A. *Etude sur Madame Roland et son temps*, Plon, 1864

Delsaux, Hélène. *Condorcet journaliste 1790–1794*, Honoré Champion, 1931

Deville, Paul Saint-Claire. *La Commune de l'an II*, Plon, 1946

Dickinson, H.T. *Liberty and Property: Political Ideology in Eighteenth-Century Britain*, Methuen, 1977

Ellery, Eloise. *Brissot de Warville*, Boston, Houghton, 1915

Forrest, Alan. *Society and Politics in Revolutionary Bordeaux*, Oxford University Press, 1975

Furet, François and Ozouf, Mona (eds). *La Gironde et les Girondins*, Payot, 1991

Gaillard, Léopold de. *Autre temps: Nicolas Bergasse*, Plon, 1893

Germani, Ian. *Jean-Paul Marat, Hero and Anti-hero of the French Revolution*, Lewiston, E. Mellen, 1992

Gershoy, Leo. *Bertrand Barère: a Reluctant Terrorist*, Princeton University Press, 1962

Gidney, Lucy M. *L'influence des Etats-Unis d'Amérique sur Brissot, Condorcet et Madame Roland*, Société de l'histoire de la Révolution française, 1930

Gottschalk, Louis. *Jean-Paul Marat: A Study in Radicalism*, University of Chicago Press, 1927

Guadet, J. *Les Girondins, leur vie privée, leur vie publique, leur proscription et leur mort*, 2 vols, Dibier, 1861

Guérin, Daniel. *La lutte des classes sous la première république, 1793–1797*, 2 vols, Gallimard, 1968

Guibert, Louis. *Un Journaliste girondin*, Limoges, Sourilas-Ardillier fils, 1871

Guilaine, Jacques. *Billaud-Varenne, l'ascète de la Révolution*, Fayard, 1969

Hamel, E. *Histoire de Robespierre*, 3 vols, Lacroix, 1865–7

——. *Histoire de Saint-Just*, 2 vols, Brussels, Meline, n.d.

Hampson, Norman. *Danton*, Duckworth, 1978

——. *Saint-Just*, Oxford, Blackwell, 1991

——. *Will and Circumstance: Montesquieu, Rousseau and the French Revolution*, Duckworth, 1983

——. *The Life and Opinions of Maximilien Robespierre*, Duckworth, 1974

Hemmings, F.W.J. *Theatre and State in France 1760–1905*, Cambridge University Press, 1994

Hesse, Carla. *Publishing and Cultural Politics in Revolutionary Paris, 1789–1810*, Berkeley, University of California Press, 1991

Jacob, Louis. *Fabre d'Eglantine, 'Chef des Fripons'*, Hachette, 1946

Janssens, Jacques. *Camille Desmoulins, le premier républicain de France*, Perrin, 1973

Jordan, David. *The Revolutionary Career of Maximilien Robespierre*, New York, Free Press, 1985

——. *The King's Trial*, Berkeley, University of California Press, 1979

Jullian, Camille. *Histoire de Bordeaux depuis les origines jusqu'en 1895*, Marseille, Laffitte, 1975

Kammacher, Léon. *Joseph Fouché*, Editions du Scorpion, 1962

Kates, Gary. *The Cercle Social, the Girondins and the French Revolution*, Princeton University Press, 1986

Kennedy, M.L. *The Jacobin Club of Marseilles, 1790–1794*, Ithaca, Cornell University Press, 1973

——. *The Jacobins Clubs of the French Revolution: the Middle Years*, Princeton University Press, 1988

Kermina, Françoise. *Saint-Just, la Révolution aux mains d'un jeune homme*, Perrin, 1982

Lamy, E. *Nicolas Bergasse, un défenseur des principes traditionnels sous la Révolution (1750–1832)*, Perrin, 1910

Lefebvre, Georges. *Les Cours de Sorbonne: La Révolution française; La Convention*, 2 vols, Sorbonne, 1944–5

Lemay, Edna Hindie and Patrick, Alison. *Revolutionaries at Work. The Constituent Assembly, 1789–1791*, Oxford, Voltaire Foundation, 1996

Lintilhac, Eugène. *Vergniaud*, Hachette, 1920

Lussaud, Louis. *Eloge historique de M.E. Guadet (1758–1794)*, Bordeaux, Picot et Matheron, 1861

Madelin, Louis. *Fouché de Nantes*, 2 vols, Plon, 1900

Manceron, Claude. *L'Album des Hommes de la Liberté*, R. Laffont, 1989

——. *The French Revolution: Blood of the Bastille 1787–1789*, Nancy Amphoux (tr.), 5 vols, New York, Simon & Schuster, 1989

Mathiez, Albert. *Le club des Cordeliers pendant la crise de Varennes et le massacre du Champ de Mars*, H. Champion, 1910

——. *Etudes Robespierristes*, 2 vols, Colin, 1917–18

——. *Girondins et Montagnards*, Firmin-Didot, 1930

——. *La Révolution française*, 3 vols, Colin, 1922–4

——. *La vie chère et le mouvement social sur la Terreur*, Payot, 1927

May, Gita. *Madame Roland and the Age of Revolution*, New York, Columbia University Press, 1970

Mellié, Ernest. *Les Sections de Paris pendant la Révolution française*, Siège de la société, 1898

Methley, Violet. *Camille Desmoulins*, Secker, 1914

Michel, Georges. *Pétion*, Librairie de la société bibliographique, 1876

Michon, Georges. *Essai sur l'histoire du parti feuillant: Adrien Duport; correspondance inédite de Barnave*, Payot, 1924

Mitchell, C.J. *The French Legislative Assembly of 1791*, Leiden, E.J. Brill, 1991

Morton, J.B. *Camille Desmoulins and Other Studies of the French Revolution*, W. Laurie, 1950

Palmer, R.R. *The Year of the Terror: Twelve who ruled; the Committee of Public Safety during the Terror, 1793–1794*, Princeton, University Press, 1941

Patrick, Alison. *The Men of the First French Republic*, Baltimore, Johns Hopkins University Press, 1972

Parra Perez, Caracciolo. *Miranda et la Révolution française*, 2nd edn, Caracas, Editions du Banco del Caribe, 1989

Perroud, C. *La Proscription des Girondins*, Toulouse, Privat, 1917

Pingaud, Léonce. *Jean Debry 1760–1835*, Plon, 1909

Piro, Franco. *La Festa della Sfortuna*, Milan, Rizzoli, 1989

Robinet, J.F.E. *Danton, Homme d'Etat*, n.p., 1889

Rodmell, Graham. *French Drama during the Revolutionary years*, Routledge, 1990

Rose, R.B. *The Enragés: Socialists of the French Revolution*, Melbourne, 1965

——. *The Making of the Sans-culottes: democratic institutions in Paris, 1789–92*, Manchester University Press, 1983

Sené, Clovis. *Cambon le financier de la Révolution*, J.C. Luttès, 1987

Schapiro, J. Salwyn. *Condorcet and the Rise of Liberalism*, New York, Octagon Press, 1963

Shapiro, Barry. *Revolutionary Justice*, Cambridge University Press, 1993

Slavin, Morris. *The Making of an Insurrection: Paris Sections and the Gironde*, Cambridge, Mass., Harvard University Press, 1986

Soboul, A. *La Révolution française*, 2 vols, Gallimard, 1964
——. *Les sans-culottes parisiens en l'an 2; mouvement populaire et gouvernement révolutionnaire, 2 juin*, 2nd edn, Librairie Clavreuil, 1962
——. *Précis d'histoire de la Révolution*, Editions sociales, 1962
——. (ed.) *Actes du Colloque. Girondins et Montagnards*, Société des Robespierristes, 1980
Sydenham, M.J. *The Girondins*, Athlone Press, 1961
Taillandier. A.H. (ed.). *Documents Biographiques sur P.C.F. Daunou*, F. Didot, 1841
Thompson, J.M. *Leaders of the French Revolution*, Oxford, Blackwell, 1929
——. *Robespierre*, 2 vols, Oxford, Blackwell, 1935
Wallon, H. *Histoire du Tribunal Révolutionnaire de Paris*, 6 vols, Hachette, 1880–2
Zweig, Stefan. *Joseph Fouché. The Portrait of a Politician*, New York, Viking, 1930

Articles, Chapters in Books

Andress, David. 'Economic Dislocation and Social Discontent in the French Revolution: Survival in Paris in the Era of the Flight to Varennes', *FH*, vol. 10, no. 1 (March 1996), 30–55
Aulard, A. 'Danton en 1791 et en 1791', *RF* 24 (1893), 304–44
——. 'Figures oubliées de la Révolution. Le conventionnel Louvet', *NR* (1885), 346–78
——. 'Danton au district des Cordeliers et à la Commune de Paris', *RF*, 24 (1893), 113–44
Balayé, Simone. 'De la Bibliothèque du Roi à la Bibliothèque Nationale' in *La Carmagnole des Muses*, Jean Claude Bonnet (ed.), A. Colin, 1988
Bourne, H. 'Municipal politics in Paris in 1789, *AHR*, 9, no. 2 (1906), 263–86
Boursier, M. 'L'émeute parisienne du 10 mars 1793', *AHRF*, no. 208 (avril–juin 1972), 204–30
Braesch, F. 'Les pétitions du Champ de Mars, 15, 16, 17 juillet 1791', *RH*, 142–3 (janvier–avril; mai–août 1923), 192–209; 1–39
Brouillard, Roger. 'Nouvelles recherches sur les Girondins proscrits 1793–1794', *RHB*, 6 (1913), 36–55
Bruun, Geoffrey. 'The evolution of a terrorist: Georges Auguste Couthon', *JMH*, 2, no. 3 (1930), 410–29
Cahen, Léon. 'La société des amis des noirs et Condorcet', *RF*, 50 (1906), 484–511
Calvet, Henri. 'Les origines du comité de l'évêché, *AHRF*, 7 (1930), 12–23
Claretie, Jules. 'Fabre d'Eglantine à la Comédie française', *RF*, 33 (1897), 385–404
Coquard, Olivier. 'La politique de Marat', *AHRF* (juillet–septembre 1992), 325–51
Coutura, Johel. 'Le Museé de Bordeaux', *DHS*, 19 (1987), 149–63
Darnton, Robert. 'The Grub Street Style of Revolution', *JMH*, 42 (3) (September 1968), 301–27
Fanget, Jean-Paul. 'Georges Couthon et la disparition du régime féodal dans le Puy-de-dôme (1789–an II)', *AHRF* (1983), 238–73
Fitch, Nancy. 'Speaking in the name of the people: Joseph Fouché and the Politics of the Terror in Central France', in Reinhardt, Steven G. and Cawthon, Elizabeth A. (eds), *Essays on the French Revolution: Paris and the provinces*, Texas, A&M Press, 1992
Fournel, V. 'Fabre d'Eglantine le comédien, l'auteur dramatique et le révolutionnaire', *RQH*, 54 (juillet 1893), 142–215
Fuchs, M. 'Collot d'Herbois comédien', *RF*, 79 (1926), 14–26
Gershoy, Leo. 'Barère in the Constituent Assembly', *AHR*, 36, no. 2 (1931), 295–312
Gottshchalk, Louis. 'The radicalism of Jean-Paul Marat', *SR* (1921), 155–70
Kennedy, M.L. ' The Development of a Political Radical: Jean-Louis Carra, 1742–1787', *Proceedings of the Third Annual Meeting of the Western Society for French History*, B. Gooch (ed.), Texas, A&M University, 1976, 142–50
Kuhlmann, C. 'The Relation of the Jacobins to the Army, the National Guards and Lafayette', *UNS*, VI 2 (April, 1906), 153–92
Kuscinski, A. 'Couthon et Roland', *RF*, 57 (1913), 412–16
Lhéritier, M. 'La Révolution à Bordeaux de 1789 à 1791', *RHB* (1915), 113–30; 186–201; (1916), 102–11
Loft, Leonore. 'La Théorie des loix criminelles: Brissot and legal reform', *AJFS*, 26 (1989), 242–59
Lyonnet, Henry. 'Collot d'Herbois, critique dramatique', *AR*, 1 (1908), 665–9
Maspero-Clerc, Hélène. 'Une gazette anglo-française pendant la guerre d'Amérique', *AHRF*, no. 227 (1976), 572–612

Mathiez, Albert. 'Gabriel Vaugeois, l'organisation du 10 août', *AR*, 3 (1910), 584–9

——. 'Les Girondins et la Cour à la veille du 10 août', *AHRF*, 8 (1931), 193–212

Mitchell, C.J. 'Political divisions within the Legislative Assembly of 1791', *FHS*, vol. XIII, no. 3 (Spring 1984), 356–89

Morineau, Michel. 'Mort d'un terroriste', *AHRF* (avril–juin 1983), 292–339

Montarlot, Pierre. 'Les Députés de Sâone-et-Loire au Tribunal révolutionnaire', in *Les Mémoires de la Société*, 33 (1905), 217–73

Patrick, Alison. 'Regicides and Anti-Regicides in January 1793: the Significance of Fouché's vote', *HS*, 14, no. 55 (1970), 341–60

Perroud, C. 'A propos de l'abolition du droit de l'aînesse', *RF*, 54 (1908), 193–202

——. 'Enfance, première jeunesse et débuts politiques de Barbaroux', *RF*, 71 (1919), 501–36

——. 'La société française des amis des noirs', *RF*, 66 (1916), 122–47

——. 'Le premier ministre Roland', *RF*, 42 (1902), 511–28

——. 'Roland et la presse subventionée', *RF*, 62 (1912), 206–13, 315–22, 396–419

Proschwitz, Gunnar von and Proschwitz, Mavis. 'Beaumarchais et le Courier de l'Europe', *Studies on Voltaire and the Eighteenth Century*, no. 273, Oxford, Voltaire Foundation, 1990

Roche, Daniel. 'Négoce et culture dans la France du XVIIIe siècle', *RHMC* (juillet–septembre 1978), 375–95

Rodmell, Graham. 'Laclos, Brissot and the Petition of the Champ de Mars', *Studies on Voltaire and the Eighteenth Century* 183, Oxford, Voltaire Foundation, 1980, 189–222

Rufas, Marcel. 'Les origines sociales de Fabre d'Eglantine', *AHRF*, 32 (1960), 294–300

Schnerb, Robert. 'Notes sur les débuts politiques de Couthon et des Monestier', *AHRF* (1930), 323–8

Soboul, Albert. 'Georges Couthon', *AHRF* (avril–juin 1983), 204–27

Trousson, Raymond. 'Un Socrate révolutionnaire: Collot d'Herbois', *Die Neuren Sprachen* (1970), 416–20

Vidier, A. 'Lenoir, Bibliothècaire du roi (1784–1790), ses démêlés avec Carra', *Bulletin de l'Histoire de Paris et de l'Ile de France*, 51 (1924), 1–13.

Whaley, Leigh. 'Made to Practice Virtue in a Republic: Jérôme Pétion: a Pre-revolutionary Radical Advocate', in *Selected Proceedings. Consortium on Revolutionary Europe, 1750–1850*, Donald Horward (ed.), Talahassee, Florida State University, 1995, 167–76

INDEX